Party Politics and the Struggle for Democracy in Mexico

U.S.–Mexico Contemporary Perspectives Series, 17
Center for U.S.–Mexican Studies
University of California, San Diego

CONTRIBUTORS

Alberto Aziz Nassif
Tonatiuh Guillén López
Alonso Lujambio
Carlos R. Menéndez Losa
Kevin J. Middlebrook
David A. Shirk
Guadalupe Valencia García
Steven T. Wuhs

This volume was published with the assistance of the William and Flora Hewlett Foundation.

Party Politics and the Struggle for Democracy in Mexico

National and State-Level Analyses of the Partido Acción Nacional

edited by

Kevin J. Middlebrook

CENTER FOR U.S.–MEXICAN STUDIES
UNIVERSITY OF CALIFORNIA, SAN DIEGO

Cover photograph courtesy of *Reforma* (Mexico City).
Cover design by Sirious Design.

Printed in the United States of America

ISBN 1-878367-44-7 (paper)

Contents

List of Tables and Figures

TABLES

FIGURES

Acknowledgments

This volume examines the Partido Acción Nacional (National Action Party, PAN) and its role in Mexico's lengthy process of political democratization. Five of the chapters were presented in draft form at an international conference, "Conservative Parties, Democratization, and Neoliberalism in Latin America: Mexico in Comparative Perspective," hosted by the Center for U.S.–Mexican Studies in May 1996; the chapters by David A. Shirk and Steven T. Wuhs were added to the collection of essays in 2000. The conference papers analyzing conservative parties and democracy in Argentina, Brazil, Chile, Colombia, El Salvador, Peru, and Venezuela during the 1980s and 1990s were published in Kevin J. Middlebrook, ed., *Conservative Parties, the Right, and Democracy in Latin America* (Johns Hopkins University Press, 2000).

International conferences are complex undertakings. Diana Platero and other Center for U.S.–Mexican Studies staff members made outstanding contributions to the organization of the 1996 meeting. Financial support for the Mexico portion of the conference came from the William and Flora Hewlett Foundation.

Collaborative books depend heavily upon the commitment and goodwill of the participating authors. The contributors were exemplary in their dedication to this collective effort, especially given the unanticipated delays in bringing this project to conclusion.

In the course of preparing this volume, the editor benefited from the talented research assistance of Mauricio Benítez and Eric Magar.

Sandra del Castillo supervised the editing and production processes with her customary skill, efficiency, and grace.

List of Acronyms

ACJM	Asociación Católica de la Juventud Mexicana / Catholic Association of Mexican Youth
CD	Convergencia por la Democracia / Convergence for Democracy
CDE	*comité directivo estatal* / state directive committee
CDM	*comité directivo municipal* / municipal directive committee
CEDEM	Centro Estatal para el Desarrollo Municipal / State Center for Municipal Development
CEE	Comisión Estatal Electoral / State Electoral Commission
CEM	Centro de Estudios Municipales / Center for Municipal Studies
CEN	Comité Ejecutivo Nacional / National Executive Committee
CNC	Confederación Nacional Campesina / National Peasants' Confederation
CNOP	Confederación Nacional de Organizaciones Populares / National Confederation of Popular Organizations
COPARMEX	Confederación Patronal de la República Mexicana / Mexican Employers' Confederation
CORETT	Comisión para la Regularización de la Tenencia de la Tierra / Commission to Normalize Landownership Titles
CORPEG	Comisión Coordinadora para la Reforma Política del Estado de Guanajuato / Coordinating Commission for Political Reform in the State of Guanajuato
CTM	Confederación de Trabajadores de México / Confederation of Mexican Workers
EZLN	Ejército Zapatista de Liberación Nacional / Zapatista Army of National Liberation
FDN	Frente Democrático Nacional / National Democratic Front
IEE	Instituto Estatal Electoral / State Electoral Institute

IFE	Instituto Federal Electoral / Federal Electoral Institute
IMSS	Instituto Mexicano del Seguro Social / Mexican Social Security Institute
ITESM	Instituto Tecnológico y de Estudios Superiores de Monterrey / Monterrey Institute of Technology and Advanced Studies
LOPPE	Ley Federal de Organizaciones Políticas y Procesos Electorales / Federal Law on Political Organizations and Electoral Processes
MIR	Movimiento de Izquierda Revolucionaria / Revolutionary Leftist Movement
NAFTA	North American Free Trade Agreement
PAN	Partido Acción Nacional / National Action Party
PARM	Partido Auténtico de la Revolución Mexicana / Authentic Party of the Mexican Revolution
PAS	Partido Alianza Social / Social Alliance Party
PC	Partido Cardenista / Cardenista Party
PCD	Partido del Centro Democrático / Party of the Democratic Center
PCDP	Partido del Comité de Defensa Popular / Party of the Committee for Popular Defense
PCM	Partido Comunista Mexicano / Mexican Communist Party
PDM	Partido Demócrata Mexicano / Mexican Democratic Party
PDS	Partido Democracia Social / Social Democracy Party
PFCRN	Partido del Frente Cardenista de Reconstrucción Nacional / Party of the Cardenista Front for National Reconstruction
PFP	Partido Fuerza Popular / Popular Force Party
PMS	Partido Mexicano Socialista / Mexican Socialist Party
PMT	Partido Mexicano de los Trabajadores / Mexican Workers' Party
PNR	Partido Nacional Revolucionario / Revolutionary National Party
PPS	Partido Popular Socialista / Socialist Popular Party

PRD	Partido de la Revolución Democrática / Party of the Democratic Revolution
PRI	Partido Revolucionario Institutional / Institutional Revolutionary Party
PRM	Partido de la Revolución Mexicana / Party of the Mexican Revolution
PRONASOL	Programa Nacional de Solidaridad / National Solidarity Program
PRS	Partido de la Revolución Socialista / Party of the Socialist Revolution
PRT	Partido Revolucionario de los Trabajadores / Revolutionary Workers' Party
PSN	Partido de la Sociedad Nacionalista / Party of Nationalist Society
PST	Partido Socialista de los Trabajadores / Socialist Workers' Party
PSUM	Partido Socialista Unificado de México / Mexican Unified Socialist Party
PT	Partido del Trabajo / Labor Party
PVEM	Partido Verde Ecologista de México / Mexican Ecological Green Party
SAGAR	Secretaría de Agricultura, Ganadería y Desarrollo Rural / Ministry of Agriculture, Livestock, and Rural Development
SNTE	Sindicato Nacional de Trabajadores de la Educación / National Education Workers' Union
STPRM	Sindicato de Trabajadores Petroleros de la República Mexicana / Mexican Petroleum Workers' Union
TFE	Tribunal Federal Electoral / Federal Electoral Tribunal
UCL	Unión Cívica Leonesa / León Civic Union
UNAM	Universidad Nacional Autónoma de México / National Autonomous University of Mexico
UNS	Unión Nacional Sinarquista / National Sinarquist Union

1

Party Politics and Democratization in Mexico: The National Action Party in Comparative Perspective

Kevin J. Middlebrook

The historic victory by Vicente Fox Quesada in Mexico's July 2000 presidential election had two immediate political consequences. First, Fox's election ended seventy-one years of uninterrupted national rule by the postrevolutionary "official" party and convincingly marked the consolidation of electoral democracy in the country. From the late 1970s through the mid–1990s, a series of political reforms gradually liberalized Mexico's electoral and party systems. Over this period, the number and strength of opposition parties grew considerably, opposition parties and nongovernmental organizations gradually made headway in their long struggle to establish more transparent electoral procedures, and the governing Institutional Revolutionary Party (PRI) slowly but continuously lost ground to rivals on the left and right. In the 1997 midterm elections, for example, the PRI lost its majority in the federal Chamber of Deputies for the first time.

In the lead-up to the year 2000 general elections, the Federal Electoral Institute (independent of government control since 1996) strove to build citizen confidence in the electoral process and limit government agencies' use of public resources to benefit particular parties and candidates. Opposition forces' more equitable access to the mass media also created a much more level playing field. As a consequence, the elections proved highly competitive. But until Fox won the presidency, there remained some doubt as to whether these transformations had been sufficient to permit an opposition party or coalition to end the long-ruling PRI's control over the federal executive, an event that many

The author thanks Helga Baitenmann for her valuable comments on a preliminary version of this chapter.

observers viewed as the litmus test of electoral democratization in Mexico.

Second, Fox's election focused national and international attention squarely on the Partido Acción Nacional (National Action Party, PAN). The PAN had long served as an important vehicle for articulating the anti–PRI protest vote in both local and federal elections, and during the presidency of Carlos Salinas de Gortari (1988–1994) the party had sufficient political leverage to make it an important partner in Salinas's program of market-oriented economic reforms. However, Fox's personal charisma, a decade-long history of policy and tactical differences between Fox and some PAN leaders, and the fact that Fox created his own organization ("Amigos de Fox") to compete first for the PAN's presidential nomination and then for the presidency all meant that Fox's candidacy somewhat overshadowed the party during the presidential campaign. Yet after the elections on July 2, 2000, more public attention naturally concentrated on the PAN (its historical evolution, ideological profile and programmatic platform, internal divisions, and so forth), the lessons that the PAN's extensive experience in governing at the state and municipal levels since the early 1980s might have now that its candidate had won the federal executive, and the implications that continuing tensions between Fox and the party apparatus could have for President Fox's capacity to implement his policy agenda.

The purpose of this book is to analyze the PAN and its role in Mexico's lengthy process of political opening. By examining the party and its evolution in recent decades, the contributors seek a better understanding of how the PAN's ideological positions and relations with core constituencies have changed over time, the interaction between shifting political and economic conditions and variations in the party's electoral strength, what advances the party has made organizationally, and the challenges facing the PAN as it moved from the opposition into national government. Their analyses make valuable contributions to scholarship on parties and electoral change in Latin America and especially to the growing literature on conservative political parties.

This introductory chapter sets the stage for the essays that follow by placing the PAN experience in a comparative Latin American context. In particular, it examines similarities and differences between Mexico's National Action Party and other Latin American parties on the center-right and right of the partisan spectrum. In addition, this essay addresses the ideological and constituency bases on which the PAN can be characterized as a "conservative" party, paying special attention to the party's complex historical relationship with the Catholic Church and changes over time in its links with economic elites. It also assesses the PAN's contributions to electoral democratization in Mexico and the institutional challenges the PAN has faced as its role changed from increasingly influential opposition force to governing party, first at the municipal and state levels and then at the national level.

The first part of this volume consists of three essays examining the origins and historical trajectory of the PAN (by Alonso Lujambio), the party's organizational development and expansion during the 1980s and 1990s (by David A. Shirk), and the principal factional divisions within the party (by Steven T. Wuhs). These chapters principally focus on the PAN at the national level; they are important for their insights into the origins of the party's municipal-federalist strategy, the elements shaping the party's development over time, and the challenges it faced after the early 1980s as its national influence grew. By situating their analyses in the context of national-level political change, the authors demonstrate how the PAN contributed to gradual political opening in Mexico and, in turn, how the PAN evolved organizationally in an increasingly competitive electoral context.

The second section comprises four chapters evaluating the PAN and local-level democratization processes in the states of Baja California, Chihuahua, Guanajuato, and Yucatán. These state-level studies provide an important complement to discussions of the PAN's development and political opening at the national level, offering more fine-grained assessments of such issues as the social bases of opposition politics, the multiple obstacles opposition forces faced in their struggle to win municipal and state-level offices, and the relationship between changes in electoral rules and the growth of party competition. Assessing the PAN at the state level is especially appropriate in view of the party's long emphasis on competing effectively in municipal and statewide elections as a strategy for ultimately winning national power. Moreover, because these essays place their discussion of the PAN in the broader context of party alternation in power, they illuminate the dilemmas that the party faced as it has moved from opposition force to governing party. In this regard, these chapters highlight some of the challenges that confronted the National Action Party in the wake of Fox's dramatic victory in the July 2000 presidential election.

These four states were selected in order to provide a reasonably representative portrayal of the PAN's development and its role in political democratization at the local level.[1] The state-level studies by Tonatiuh Guillén López (Baja California), Alberto Aziz Nassif (Chihuahua), Guadalupe Valencia García (Guanajuato), and Carlos R. Menéndez Losa

---

[1] Practical considerations were also involved. The predominant tendency in studies of Mexican politics is either to concentrate analysis at the national level (with local, state-level, or sectoral cases sometimes included for illustrative purposes) or to focus on local or state-level case studies and their potential national implications. State-level analyses by qualified authors are comparatively rare.

(Yucatán) examine these states' distinctive political histories; the interplay among citizen mobilizations, institutional reforms, and the emergence of the PAN as a leader of opposition to the dominant PRI; dilemmas of party-building; and changes over time in the PAN's role in state and municipal government. They are especially valuable for their analysis of the PAN's relations with key constituencies, including urban middle-class groups, the private sector, the Roman Catholic Church, regionally influential newspapers, and so forth.

Baja California, Chihuahua, Guanajuato, and Yucatán are not fully representative of Mexican electoral politics during the 1980s and 1990s in part because partisan competition in these states focused principally on the PAN and the PRI, reflecting the PAN's electoral strength in these states since the 1960s and 1970s. With some exceptions (particularly Cuauhtémoc Cárdenas's victory in statewide voting in Baja California during the 1988 presidential election), opposition parties other than the National Action Party played a much more limited role in these states than in other parts of the country. Nevertheless, these four states offer important insights into both the PAN's development and the more general phenomena of opposition politics and electoral democratization during these two crucial decades:

- *Baja California* was the site of the PAN's historic gubernatorial triumph in 1989, the first occasion during the PRI's long rule on which federal electoral authorities recognized a state-level victory by an opposition party. Despite some subsequent reverses in municipal and state legislative elections, the PAN retained control of the governorship in this key border state. Baja California provides an important example of the way in which the democracy agenda has shifted over time, from the initial struggle by opposition forces to win statewide office to the broader political and administrative reforms required to promote democratic representation and citizen participation in government.

- In *Chihuahua*, as in Baja California, the PAN began to play a significant political role in the 1950s and gradually emerged as the leader of a broad civic opposition to the dominant Institutional Revolutionary Party. However, it was widespread government/PRI electoral fraud in 1986 that placed the state at the center of the national democratic struggle. The PAN won statewide political control in 1992, yet the PRI subsequently regained both the legislature (1995) and the governorship (1998). Chihuahua thus became the first Mexican state to experience PRI–PAN–PRI alternation in power. For this reason, the state offers important examples of the challenges involved in consolidating democratizing political reforms.

- *Guanajuato*, like the other states highlighted in this volume, has a long history of opposition to postrevolutionary political centralism. The strength of local conservative forces, and the ideological and programmatic congruity between these social and religious groups and the National Action Party, gradually made the PAN the principal leader of the state's political opposition. Ties between the local private sector and the PAN, as well as private-sector leaders' expanding role in party affairs and as PAN candidates, exemplify several important trends underlying the party's growing national prominence during the 1980s and 1990s. Moreover, the PAN's experience in Guanajuato is of special interest because Vicente Fox's term as governor (1995–1999) constituted a principal base for his successful bid for the presidency.

- Although *Yucatán* did not experience a statewide PAN victory during the 1980s or 1990s, the party did become the focal point of a broad civic movement in favor of free and fair elections in the state. The PAN won control of the capital city, Mérida, in 1990 and subsequently used the municipal presidency to consolidate its position as the main partisan rival to the PRI. As in Baja California, Chihuahua, and Guanajuato, local opposition to federal government/PRI impositions has been a central dynamic in state politics. Yucatán illustrates the many dilemmas that opposition parties faced in their efforts to erode the sociopolitical alliances that the PRI wove from Mexico City during its decades-long control of the federal government.[2]

THE NATIONAL ACTION PARTY IN COMPARATIVE LATIN AMERICAN PERSPECTIVE

There are both significant parallels and major differences between Mexico's National Action Party and other Latin American parties occupying the center-right or right of the partisan spectrum. Perhaps most obvious, the PAN, like center-right and rightist parties elsewhere in the region, has long had strong links with conservative sociopolitical forces

---

[2] In May 2001 the PAN—in coalition with the Party of the Democratic Revolution (PRD), the Mexican Ecological Green Party (PVEM), and the Labor Party (PT)—finally won the governorship of Yucatán. Its candidate, Patricio Patrón, defeated the PRI's Orlando Paredes by a margin of 53.5 percent to 45.4 percent of the valid vote. The Convergence for Democracy (CD) and the Social Alliance Party (PAS) received, respectively, 0.6 percent and 0.1 percent of the vote. For an overview of the race, see *New York Times*, May 27, 2001, A3; for electoral results, see www.ieey.org.mx.

and, especially in the late 1930s and again after the early 1980s, economic elites. From its founding in September 1939, the party has drawn
support from social conservatives and entrepreneurs (particularly the
owners of small and midsize businesses) who were viscerally opposed
to the postrevolutionary regime's strong support of public secular education, extensive state intervention in the economy, and policies advocating collective social rights (for instance, the *ejido* system, a collective
land tenure arrangement that figured prominently in Mexico's postrevolutionary agrarian reform) that conflicted with private property
interests. Manuel Gómez Morin's idea of founding an opposition party
can be traced to José Vasconcelos's 1929 opposition presidential campaign (in which Gómez Morin served as unofficial treasurer), but the
immediate context for the PAN's creation was the intense conservative
mobilization against President Lázaro Cárdenas's (1934–1940) radical
economic and social policies. In fact, the National Action Party was
founded soon after Cárdenas organized the "official" Party of the Mexican Revolution (PRM) around worker, peasant, military, and popular
sectors in April 1938.[3]

However, it is important to emphasize from the outset that there
have been notable differences in the PAN's sociopolitical profile across
Mexico's states and regions. For example, ties between the PAN and
conservative social and religious groups have been much stronger historically in west-central states such as Guanajuato (one of the states in
which there was sustained violent conflict over church-state issues in
the 1920s, and the birthplace of several nationally important conservative sociopolitical movements) than in states such as Baja California or
Chihuahua.[4] Moreover, sustained support for the PAN from Mexico's
most important entrepreneurs dates only from the 1980s, following the
nationalization of private banks in 1982 and the severe strains that
prolonged economic crisis placed on business-state relations.

Second, the PAN shares with several other center-right parties in
Latin America its historical links to church-state conflict. Disputes over
the Roman Catholic Church's social and political influence, accumulated wealth, and inherited privileges erupted throughout Spanish-
speaking Latin America and Brazil during the nineteenth and early
twentieth centuries.[5] However, not all these conflicts between state-

---

[3] See Loaeza 1999: 105–106, 109, 138, 146, 151–52, 168, 182; Mabry 1973: 23. In advocating a selective party of "excellent minorities," Gómez Morin sharply contrasted
the PAN with the mass PRM, in which party membership was established indirectly through affiliation with labor, peasant, or other organizations.

[4] Wuhs (this volume) comments briefly on the heterogeneity of the PAN at the state
and regional level.

[5] This discussion draws on Middlebrook 2000: 7–11.

building, secularizing elites and the church gave rise to political parties.[6] Whether struggles over church-state issues redrew existing lines
of partisan conflict and promoted durable party organization depended
upon a combination of three factors: (1) the church's organizational
strength (its physical assets, number of personnel, and relative institutional autonomy from political forces in the period before efforts at
secularization began); (2) the intensity and scope of issues involved,
with the status of church property and educational policy being especially sensitive matters; and (3) whether the broader sociopolitical context favored religious-based competitive mobilization. What was particularly significant in this last regard was whether political conditions
were sufficiently open to permit the emergence of issue-based partisan
organizations. Moreover, much depended upon whether the church
and landowners were together capable of (or prepared to risk) mobilizing peasants or rural laborers for electoral or military action in support
of the conservative cause.

In Chile, Colombia, and Venezuela, church-state conflicts and partisan
mobilization over religious issues in the nineteenth and mid-twentieth
centuries gave rise to strong conservative political parties. In nineteenth-century Chile (the Partido Radical [Radical Party]) and Colombia (the Partido Conservador [Conservative Party]), especially, these
parties were initially elite-centered groupings that competed for power
under conditions of restricted suffrage. The religious content of these
parties' programs and partisan identities often diminished over time,
particularly after the resolution of major policy disputes concerning the
legal status and social role of the Catholic Church. In all three cases,
however, religious cleavage contributed decisively to the formation of
nationally organized center-right parties with enduring electoral appeal—the Partido Demócrata Cristiano (Christian Democratic Party) in
Chile, the Conservative Party in Colombia, and the social-Christian
Comité de Organización Política Electoral Independiente (Committee
for Independent Electoral Political Organization, COPEI) in Venezuela.
Moreover, it laid the bases for the longer-term development of com-

---

[6] Conversely, neither can one trace the origins of all conservative parties in the region to church-state cleavages.

For an overview discussion of the reasons why religious conflict did not produce strong conservative parties in Argentina, Brazil, El Salvador, and Peru, see
Middlebrook 2000, especially pp. 17–26. In brief, sociopolitical conditions—
including the absence of a significant peasantry or a settled rural labor force in
Argentina, sharp regional divisions and elite concerns about the political behavior
of freed slaves in Brazil, and economic and social elites' intense resistance to extensive political mobilization in ethnically divided El Salvador and Peru—were
major impediments to conservative party development. On the rural-urban conflict origins of the Partido Colorado in Uruguay, see González 1995: 140–41.

petitive party systems in these countries. In Chile, a long history of conservative party activity and strong partisan identifications on the right contributed greatly to the electoral success of conservative forces following the restoration of democratic governance in 1989.[7]

The PAN was not founded as a confessional or clerical party, and it did not originate directly in the violent religious conflict that shook Mexico in the late 1920s. Although party founder Manuel Gómez Morin (1897–1972) was himself a Catholic, he was strongly secular in his political orientations, and he opposed formal ties between the party and either the Mexican Catholic Church or the international Christian Democrat movement. Over time, the National Action Party's principal basis for attracting electoral support was its position as the most viable opposition party contesting political centralism and the rule of the hegemonic PRI. Nevertheless, its ideology has consistently reflected social Christian principles, and, at least until the PAN's electoral appeal began to expand significantly in the 1980s, Catholics represented the party's most loyal bases of support—the original impulse for which was the PAN's opposition to postrevolutionary anticlericalism and political controls on church activities, especially church involvement in education. In this regard the PAN historically shared with several other Latin American conservative parties its reliance on a Catholic identity to help mobilize a multiclass political constituency. Indeed, during the 1950s in particular, the party's Catholic identity and its close links with Catholic lay organizations substantially democratized its membership by drawing in peasants, artisans, and lower-middle-class elements to what had been a "party of notables" (Loaeza 1999: 236).

Third, like center-right and rightist parties in several Central and South American countries, the PAN benefited significantly from overlapping processes of political and economic opening during the 1980s and 1990s. Throughout Latin America in the 1980s, the revival of elections as a forum for articulating alternative policy proposals and choosing governments, business groups' disenchantment with clientelist ties to the state apparatus as a means of protecting their interests, and the discrediting of the armed forces as a potential political ally in the wake of what were often particularly brutal military dictatorships all bolstered the Right's commitment to developing party alternatives. The Unión del Centro Democrático (Union of the Democratic Center) in Argentina; the Partido da Frente Liberal (Party of the Liberal Front), the Partido Progressista Brasileiro (Brazilian Progressive Party), the Partido Trabalhista Brasileiro (Brazilian Labor Party), the Partido Liberal (Liberal Party), and other parties in Brazil; Renovación Nacional (National Renovation) and the Unión Demócrata Independiente (Independent

---

[7] For further discussion of these three cases, see Middlebrook 2000: 11–17.

Democratic Union) in Chile; the Alianza Republicana Nacionalista (Nationalist Republican Alliance) in El Salvador; and Acción Popular (Popular Action), the Partido Popular Cristiano (Christian Popular Party), and the Movimiento Libertad (Liberty Movement) in Peru were all examples, among others, of conservative parties that emerged during this period to compete for power by electoral means. Although support for the privatization of state-owned enterprises, market opening, and other liberalizing economic reforms linked these parties programmatically, they varied enormously in terms of their specific historical origins, their sociopolitical profiles and the main constituencies they represented, their links to the military and the degree to which they defended the institutional and policy legacies of authoritarian rule, and, especially, the degree of electoral success they achieved.

Mexico's National Action Party shared with these other parties its criticism of excessive state economic intervention and its vigorous advocacy of private-sector initiative, and like these other parties the PAN benefited greatly from an international *zeitgeist* in the 1980s and early 1990s that favored state "shrinking." However, despite entrepreneurs' increasingly significant involvement in party affairs, the PAN retained a more heterogeneous social and electoral base than pro-business parties like the Partido Liberal in Brazil. The importance of Catholic social thought in *panista* ideology also gave the party a more explicit commitment to socially equitable economic development than some neoliberal-inspired conservative parties in Latin America, and unlike some of its regional counterparts, the PAN carried no political baggage from a past association with military dictatorship. And not least, the PAN's involvement in electoral competition since the 1940s and its established position in the Mexican party system permitted it to maximize new political opportunities in the 1980s and 1990s, rapidly expanding its electoral presence and gradually strengthening its organizational structures.[8] As a consequence, the PAN was competing seriously for national power even as conservative parties in Argentina and Peru faded from political relevance.

However, the most important differences between the National Action Party and its center-right and rightist counterparts in Latin America concern the historical environment in which it developed. Rather than emerging in a competitive party context in which it might appeal, on the basis of established or emerging sociopolitical cleavages, to landowners, Catholics, or other potential constituencies, the PAN formed

---

[8] The experience of center-right and rightist parties in Latin America during this period demonstrated that, with the exception of Brazil, conservative forces' electoral performance following democratic transitions varied closely with their prior strength or weakness. See Middlebrook 2000.

in the aftermath of a successful social revolution. At least three major consequences flowed from this fact. First, the party's issue agenda was to some extent also the agenda of the 1910–1920 Mexican Revolution. The revolution effectively severed intellectual and organizational links to nineteenth-century conservative movements, and from the outset the PAN's founders viewed the party as a conservative modernizing project for the postrevolutionary era (von Sauer 1974: 14; Loaeza 1999: 106, 180). Early *panistas* were bitterly opposed to the Cárdenas government's efforts to establish "socialist" education, and they criticized the collective distribution of lands via the *ejido* system for both its productive inefficiency and the network of political controls the postrevolutionary agrarian reform established over peasants. However, they shared the broad postrevolutionary commitment to promoting economic development and social justice, some seeing themselves as the legitimate heirs of President Francisco I. Madero (1911–1913).[9]

Second, *panistas* faced the immense task of building a party organization and establishing an electoral presence in a political context almost completely dominated by the quasi-official "party of the revolution"—the Revolutionary National Party (PNR) after 1929, the PRM after 1938, and the PRI after 1946. In its early years, the PAN had only limited prospects for gaining elective office even at the municipal level, and its first statewide victory (the 1989 gubernatorial election in Baja California) came five decades after its founding. This crushing political reality focused the party's long-term goals on public education and the gradual development of an electoral following. In fact, most support for the PAN came from voters who wished to register their protest with the governing party and the established political order. This, however, meant that the party's base was vulnerable to erosion as the government mobilized material incentives or threatened recriminations in its efforts to undercut opposition to the PRI.[10] Few center-right or rightist parties in Latin America faced such daunting odds, making all the more impressive in comparative terms the PAN's long-term success in establishing itself as a partisan option.[11]

Third, the postrevolutionary setting shaped the role of key political actors in particular ways and thereby defined the PAN's available strategic options. In many Latin American countries during the twentieth century, upper-class economic and social groups unable to defend their core interests through electoral means forged alliances with the

---

[9] See Mabry 1973: 55–56, 186; von Sauer 1974: 44–59; Loaeza 1999: 219.

[10] Ames (1970) was among the first analysts to demonstrate that the government channeled additional spending to areas where electoral opposition was strongest.

[11] Argentine conservatives' efforts to organize party alternatives to the dominant Peronist movement are a partial parallel.

armed forces in order to pursue their goals through military intervention. In Mexico, however, the political landscape was reconfigured by the slow, uneven process of establishing reliable civilian control over the postrevolutionary armed forces that unfolded between the 1920s and the early 1940s. There is nothing in the political biographies of either Manuel Gómez Morin or Efraín González Luna (1898–1964), the two most visible founders of the PAN, to indicate an inclination toward extra-constitutional political options. Nor, it is important to note, was the PAN part of the proto-fascist Mexican Right of the late 1930s or one of the groups advocating the violent overthrow of the established regime.[12] But beyond the question of founders' political convictions, the military's status in Mexican politics—including institutional representation of the armed forces through the governing party—had already been defined by the time the PAN was formed in 1939. Indeed, the last military revolt of the postrevolutionary era occurred in May 1938; Saturnino Cedillo, the remaining revolutionary general with an independent political and military power base, mobilized extremely little support from within military ranks, and his rebellion was rapidly and thoroughly suppressed (and Cedillo killed).

Given these significant points of congruence and difference between the National Action Party and other center-right or rightist parties in Latin America, are there more systematic bases for characterizing the PAN as a "conservative" party?

IS THE PAN A CONSERVATIVE PARTY?

Recent scholarship on Latin American political parties suggests two possible approaches to identifying a party as conservative. One way, following the line of analysis established by Edward L. Gibson's *Class and Conservative Parties* (1996), emphasizes a party's core constituencies—that is, those elements that have a particularly important impact on a party's ideological orientation, policy positions, financial base, and so forth. In particular, scholars adopting this perspective highlight the relationship between conservative parties and their supporters among economic and social elites. They argue that, although parties' ideological orientations and programmatic agendas are important considerations in determining their position on the partisan spectrum at any given time, defining conservative parties in terms of their core constitu-

---

[12] The PAN notably differed in this regard from some rightist groups, including elements of the National Sinarquist Union (UNS). See von Sauer 1974: 41. The PAN eventually absorbed into its different state-level organizations the remnants of some of these ultraconservative groups. On developments in Guanajuato, see Valencia García, this volume.

encies avoids the analytic confusion created by changes over time in what constitute conservative ideological or programmatic positions.[13] In contrast, other researchers maintain that it is often difficult in practice to identify conservative parties on the basis of their allegedly privileged links with upper-class groups (Mainwaring, Meneguello, and Power 2000). They therefore devote more emphasis to what is distinctive in these parties' ideological profiles and programmatic agendas, as well as to the characteristics of conservative party voters and those individuals who identify closely with individual conservative parties. Analysts adopting this perspective seek, for example, to determine whether there are substantial differences between conservative parties and other partisan groupings in terms of their electoral constituencies' demographic and socioeconomic traits and self-placement in left-right terms.

Ultimately, however, these two approaches represent complementary lines of inquiry. In assessing Mexico's Partido Acción Nacional, the following discussion combines elements of both positions in order to identify the intellectual origins of the party's ideological and programmatic positions, shifts over time in its main constituencies, and the principal reasons for the PAN's electoral success in the 1980s and 1990s. The analysis particularly focuses on the philosophical-political bases of *panismo* (especially the party's complex links to Catholicism and the Catholic Church) and change and continuity in the PAN's major constituencies.

Ideology and Programmatic Positions

Throughout its history, two major philosophical-political currents have informed the National Action Party's doctrines and its programmatic positions: Catholic social thought, and a commitment to active citizen engagement in public affairs, especially at the municipal level. These currents were personified by, respectively, party ideologue Efraín González Luna and PAN founder Manuel Gómez Morin. Together these elements defined both the party's identity and the municipal-federalist strategy that the PAN chose as its path to power. At the same time, these orientations determined the party's policy agenda as it gradually gained influence in the 1980s and 1990s, and they significantly influenced its specific contributions to the broader process of political democratization in Mexico.

---

[13] See Gibson 1996: 2–9, for a discussion of alternative approaches to the conceptualization of conservatism and the difficulties encountered in employing conservatism as an ideological tradition in electoral contexts.

Catholic Social Thought Gómez Morin's vision of political action was essentially secular. However, he himself was influenced by early-twentieth-century European Catholic thinkers such as Jacques Maritain and Charles Maurras, and Catholic activists were among his most important allies in the formation of the National Action Party (Loaeza 1999: 126, 163–65). González Luna, as well as PAN presidents Adolfo Christlieb Ibarrola (1962–1968) and Efraín González Morfín (1975),[14] made especially important contributions to the development of a coherent, Catholic-inspired party ideology. Although the PAN's doctrinal tone varied significantly over time (strongly conservative and anti-communist in the 1940s and 1950s, much more socially progressive in the 1960s and 1970s), Donald J. Mabry argues that the party originated as a "Catholic alternative to revolution" within the broader twentieth-century Catholic reform movement in Latin America.[15]

Specifically, the National Action Party has drawn on the major social encyclicals (*Rerum Novarum*, 1891; *Quadragessimo Anno*, 1931; *Mater et Magistra*, 1961; *Pacem in Terris*, 1963; *Populorum Progressio*, 1967) as principal sources of inspiration. The party labels its doctrine "political humanism" to emphasize that the person has both material and spiritual qualities.[16] Party ideology stresses that the right to acquire and use property is crucial to permitting the human person to control her or his own affairs, and that the private sector is the key motor of economic development. Nevertheless, property rights are not absolute; instead, they are limited by their social function. *Panista* doctrine thus expresses a preference for labor over property as the appropriate ordering principle of political economy (Mabry 1973: 101–102), leading the party to adopt social protectionist positions regarding workers' rights, minimum wages, labor conditions, and so forth. The PAN was, for instance, the first party in Mexico to advocate workers' participation in enterprise profit-sharing (Mabry 1973: 74–75, 164), a proposal that became law in 1963.

The PAN's evolving views on the appropriate role of the state in economic and social affairs usefully illustrate the ways in which its positions have been influenced by Catholic thought. Although the party has consistently criticized excessive state intervention, it has long rec-

[14] González Morfín was the son of PAN founder Efraín González Luna.

[15] See Mabry 1973: xii, 158–59, 183, and Martínez-Valle 1999. On the PAN's anti-communist orientation, see also Loaeza 1999: 190 n. 12, 239.

[16] The title of González Luna's overview of the PAN's political philosophy was *Humanismo político* (Mexico City: Editorial Jus, 1955). For summaries of PAN doctrines, see Mabry 1973: 99–112, and Estrada Sámano n.d. The latter work, written circa 1995, draws extensively on party documents and works of *panista* ideologues in its discussion of party positions on political economy issues.

ognized a legitimate role for governmental authorities in promoting social justice in a market economy. For example, even though the PAN's 1940 "minimum political action program" offered a strong defense of private enterprise, it advocated state involvement in labor-capital relations and in general economic matters in order to promote social justice (Loaeza 1999: 167–69, 193–94). By the 1960s and 1970s, under the leadership of Christlieb Ibarrola and González Morfín, the PAN embraced Christian Democratic policies on such matters as the social market economy and the importance of "solidarity" as a core principle governing complex societal interactions. This was part of its continuing effort to forge an alternative to both liberalism and socialism. The PAN's 1970 platform, for instance, strongly advocated state-led economic development as a means of achieving social justice.[17] The party's public identification with neoliberal positions after the 1980s reflected Catholic ideologues' lessening influence in party affairs and the rising prominence of entrepreneurs radically opposed to state economic intervention.[18]

Despite the marked influence of Catholic social thought on party ideology, it is important to underscore that the PAN has never been formally aligned with the Catholic Church.[19] Conservative Catholic activists led the party from 1949 through 1962 and assumed as one of their principal missions the defense of church positions;[20] the PAN formed electoral alliances with the Catholic-origin, ultraconservative National Sinarquist Union (UNS) in state and federal elections from the mid–1940s through the mid–1950s;[21] since the early 1960s, the PAN has

---

[17] Loaeza 1999: 302, 532–33. Also see Loaeza, pp. 525–26, on the influence of German Christian Democrats and Catholic thinkers such as Osvald von Nell-Bruening on the PAN's programmatic positions after the late 1970s.

[18] By the late 1990s, the PAN was substantially more market oriented than Christian Democratic parties in Chile, Costa Rica, Ecuador, or Venezuela. See Mainwaring and Scully n.d.: tables 1.4, 1.5.

[19] It is significant in this regard that the PAN never challenged the constitutional separation of church and state. See Mabry 1973: 111–12.

[20] For example, in the mid–1940s the PAN opposed the expansion of Protestantism in Mexico; von Sauer 1974: 53.

Party presidents Juan Gutiérrez Lascuráin (1949–1956), Alfonso Ituarte Servín (1956–1959), and José González Torres (1959–1962) had all been leaders of such groups as the Catholic Association of Mexican Youth (ACJM) and Acción Católica (Catholic Action). Indeed, Catholic influence over the party leadership was very strong until at least 1972, when José Ángel Conchello began his three-year term as party president. See Mabry 1973: 50–51, and Loaeza 1999: 17, 182–83, 224, 232, 234.

[21] In 1946 this alliance permitted the PAN to win representation in the federal Chamber of Deputies for the first time. These ties were, however, an exceptional

had fraternal ties with Christian Democratic or social Christian parties in countries such as Chile and Venezuela, and in 1998 it formally joined the Christian Democrat International;[22] and, at different moments, both local priests and senior Roman Catholic officials have addressed social and political topics—including the electoral choices facing voters—in ways that mainly benefited the National Action Party. Nonetheless, throughout its history the PAN has avoided formal identification with the Catholic Church or Catholic lay organizations.

This orientation in part reflects the lasting influence of Gómez Morin, who dominated the party during the first ten years of its existence (and played an influential role in PAN affairs through at least the early 1960s) and who, for both philosophical and practical political reasons, resolutely opposed formal ties between the party and religious organizations.[23] His experience as rector of the National Autonomous University of Mexico (UNAM) during 1933–1934—a period of abrasive tensions between leftist groups and Catholic students as a national debate raged over proposals to promote socialist education in Mexico—convinced him that religious and political spheres were properly separate (Loaeza 1999: 135). Even more important, Gómez Morin rightly feared that an overt identification with the Catholic Church would cripple the PAN by making it the object of substantial anticlerical sentiment.

The Catholic Church's alliance with dictator Porfirio Díaz during his long rule (the Porfiriato, 1876–1911) and its backing of Victoriano Huerta (whose counterrevolutionary coup d'état overthrew Francisco I. Madero's democratic government in 1913) fueled strong opposition to the church and its allies during the 1910–1920 revolution. Indeed, the 1917 Constitution's articles 3, 5, 24, 27, and especially 130 contained some of Latin America's most stringent restrictions on the church. They prohib-

---

arrangement reflecting complementarities between the two organizations' regional and class bases of support, at a time when the PAN's own electoral appeal was limited and the UNS was in decline. Although they shared some doctrinal common ground, the PAN and the UNS generally had distant relations, in part because the PAN's urban, middle-class constituency differed so greatly from the UNS's peasant base. See Mabry 1973: 26, 43–44, 52–53, and Loaeza 1999: 142, 160, 209–11, 231, 235.

[22] See Mabry 1973: 66–70, 72, 74, and Mainwaring and Scully n.d.: 2. This organization is formally known as the Christian Democrat and People's Party International.

[23] For instance, Gómez Morin helped block PAN president José González Torres's efforts to link the PAN formally with the international Christian Democrat movement in the early 1960s. See von Sauer 1974: 123; Loaeza 1999: 164–65, 270–71; Lujambio, this volume. For other examples of Gómez Morin's long-term influence in the PAN, see Loaeza 1999: 265, 270, 273, 299, 434.

ited church involvement in elementary and secondary education or its ownership of real property, granted federal government agencies and state legislatures the authority to regulate important aspects of church life, banned church involvement in political affairs and prevented political parties from using religious names or symbols, and denied religious personnel the right to vote or even to appear in public in clerical garb. The decision by President Plutarco Elías Calles (1924–1928) to enforce these provisions sparked the 1926–1929 Cristero war, a violent conflict centered in the rural areas of west-central Mexico in which tens of thousands of Catholics took up arms against the federal government.[24] These divisions were still fresh in the late 1930s and amply explain Gómez Morin's reserve.

Thus, even though Gómez Morin drew extensively on Catholic support to build a durable party organization and the PAN has long counted Catholics as among its most important constituencies, the party has not encapsulated a religious-secular cleavage in the same way that conservative parties in some Latin American countries have done.[25] In any event, given the considerable evolution that occurred in Catholic social thought in Latin America over the course of the twentieth century—especially following the Second Vatican Council (1962–1965) and the Second Latin American Bishops' General Conference in Medellín, Colombia, in 1968—even a more explicit religious identification would not necessarily have defined the PAN as rightist.[26] In char-

---

[24] Mabry 1973: 2, 4, 6, 18–21. See Mecham 1966 [1934]: 340–415, for an in-depth analysis of church-state relations in Mexico during the nineteenth and early twentieth centuries. Meyer (1973–1976) provides the most complete study of the Cristero conflict. Von Sauer (1974: 26, 38–40) notes similarities in the programmatic positions advocated by the Cristeros, the National Sinarquist Union formed in May 1937, and the National Action Party. For parallels between the Partido Católico Nacional (National Catholic Party, formed in 1911) and the PAN, see von Sauer 1974: 18–21.

[25] In part, the character of the PAN's relationship with the Catholic Church has reflected the Catholic hierarchy's own preference for avoiding the political controversies that would inevitably have accompanied formal ties with a partisan organization (Loaeza 1999: 229–30). However, Loaeza (p. 230) notes that, because Catholic lay organizations like the Catholic Association of Mexican Youth and Catholic Action have been directly dependent upon the church hierarchy, their support for the PAN represents de facto church backing.

Viewed comparatively, Mainwaring and Scully (n.d.: 13–15) observe that formal church-party separation has been the norm for Latin American Christian Democratic parties, at least since the 1930s.

[26] PAN president Adolfo Christlieb Ibarrola was particularly influenced by European Christian Democratic parties and progressive movements within the Latin American Catholic Church during the 1960s; Mabry 1973: 74–75, 186–87. Indeed, Mabry (pp. 186–87) concludes that by the early 1970s the PAN was essentially

acterizing the party, it is also important to note in this context that the PAN's steadfast commitment to democratic governance and its opposition to the use of violence distinguished it from more radical conservative groups active in the 1930s. Nevertheless, in a postrevolutionary setting in which extensive state intervention in socioeconomic matters was widely accepted as the legitimate axis of public affairs, the PAN's advocacy of private property rights, its strong defense of the right to private education, and its opposition to the *ejido* system placed it on the center-right of the Mexican political and ideological spectrum.

Local-level Civic Engagement The second major philosophical-political orientation shaping the PAN was founder Gómez Morin's commitment to citizen engagement in public affairs, particularly at the local level. Soledad Loaeza's careful analysis of the National Action Party stresses Gómez Morin's dedication to active political involvement (1999: 171–72). It was this outlook that largely accounted for the PAN's commitment to electoral participation at a time when the party's prospects for winning—and, sometimes even more to the point, having its victories recognized by government officials—were close to nil.[27]

Mabry maintains that the PAN's Catholic reform and municipal-level good government impulses were linked via the social Christian principle of democratic subsidiarity. In this view, the fulfillment of the person depends upon complementarities among different social structures: "Between the individual who determines his own destiny and the State which insures the existence of the common good exists a multitude of natural intermediate societies to serve the needs and desires of the persons composing them" (Mabry 1973: 100). The closest governmental unit to the family is the *municipio*, and it is at that level that civic participation and pursuit of the public good are most meaningful.

In contrast, Alonso Lujambio (this volume) argues that the PAN's municipal-federalist mission reflected Gómez Morin's liberal convictions, which predated the party's organization in 1938–1939 and the involvement of Catholic intellectual Efraín González Luna. Specifically, Lujambio traces the PAN's municipal-federalist strategy for gradually gaining adherents and influence to Gómez Morin's formative experi-

---

center-left in its programmatic positions. See also Loaeza 1999: 273, 275–76, 300–302.

[27] From the very beginning, Gómez Morin's advocacy of this position met opposition from González Luna and other party leaders who argued that participating in elections without adequate procedural safeguards only served to legitimate the ruling party's victories and the established political order. See, for example, Loaeza 1999: 171 n. 136.

ences while working as a ministry of finance representative in New York in 1920–1922. There he was exposed to the ideas and practices of the U.S. Progressive Movement, and he henceforth advocated municipal reform as a practical response to Mexico's political and social problems. Indeed, Gómez Morin viewed the municipality as the most meaningful sphere for citizen participation and the exercise of responsible government, as well as a bulwark against the excessive political centralism and abuses of authority that he felt had placed the Mexican Revolution on the wrong course.[28]

Lujambio clearly identifies non-Catholic influences on Gómez Morin's thinking about public institutions.[29] Yet Loaeza demonstrates that Gómez Morin's more proximate model may have been the modernizing dictatorship of General Miguel Primo de Rivera in Spain between 1923 and 1930. In particular, Loaeza suggests that Gómez Morin highlighted the importance of the *municipio* not as an institution of representative government, but as part of a system of organic democracy in which municipal affairs were a natural extension of the family.[30] Somewhat ironically, then, the PAN may have arrived at its commitment to municipal autonomy and local good government—perhaps the most compelling basis for the party's expanded electoral appeal in the 1980s and 1990s—via a path other than the traditional tenets of political liberalism. Indeed, it was only in the 1960s that the PAN, particularly through its increasingly formal acceptance of the policy positions advocated by European Christian Democracy, embraced political pluralism and the support for representative government with which the party's political ascendance is often associated (Loaeza 1999: 274).

These issues of intellectual history are significant for determining the PAN's place within the Mexican political tradition. However, it is equally important to note that, where the conceptualization of the PAN's municipal-federalist strategy was concerned, political realities greatly reinforced the founders' convictions. Given the "official" party's electoral dominance, a strategy of gradually building support at the municipal level and promoting citizen awareness through a long-term

---

[28] His advocacy of citizen participation contrasted sharply with the party-led mass mobilization of the Cárdenas era. See Prud'homme 1997: 4.

[29] Indeed, referring to Gómez Morin's law school thesis, Lujambio (this volume) states that "Gómez Morin was an admirer of Mexican liberal thought." With regard to the social Christian principle of subsidiarity, Lujambio notes that this was the means through which González Luna arrived at his support for a municipal-federalist strategy to reform Mexican public life.

[30] Loaeza 1999: 116, 119–24, 167–68, 217. See also Marván Laborde 1988.

Loaeza observes (p. 123 n. 35) that the social Christian party formed in April 1931 following the collapse of the Primo de Rivera regime was named Partido Acción Nacional.

program of public education were the only viable strategies available to a minority party concerned about its survival in postrevolutionary Mexico. In fact, the PAN's commitment to municipal-level involvement intensified as the relative importance of its original opposition to *cardenista* radicalism declined (Loaeza 1999: 198, 216). Over time, a focus on municipal-level affairs also greatly facilitated the PAN's efforts to build a multiclass constituency, permitting the party to capitalize effectively on regionalist opposition to political centralism exercised from Mexico City.

Core Constituencies

There have been both important shifts and notable continuities in the PAN's principal sources of political, financial, and electoral support since its founding in 1939. For the purposes of establishing the party's profile in comparative Latin American terms, its ties to entrepreneurs and the private sector are of special interest. The character of this relationship has changed substantially in the six decades since the party's formation.

In the first years after its founding, the PAN received significant political and financial backing from business interests. In part this reflected founder Manuel Gómez Morin's contacts and credibility with major Mexican entrepreneurs; earlier in his career, he had worked both as a senior official in the Ministry of the Treasury (actively engaged in creating the Banco de México and drafting Mexico's first income tax law) and as a corporate attorney (Mabry 1973: 32–33). More important, however, the PAN appealed to private-sector interests on both general ideological grounds and as a potential alternative to a regime seemingly committed—at least during the Cárdenas administration—to implementing socialism in Mexico. It was noteworthy, then, that the PAN's founding leadership included prominent industrialists and financiers, and during the 1940s the party regularly received private-sector financial support.[31]

However, the hegemony of Mexico's postrevolutionary governing coalition proved a powerful disincentive to leading entrepreneurs' involvement with the PAN. The more conservative policies of Cárdenas's successors—particularly the pro-business orientation of President Miguel Alemán (1946–1952)—reassured the private sector, and by the late 1940s the business presence within the PAN's leadership had declined sharply (Mabry 1973: 42, 52, 162–64). Under Mexico's import-

---

[31] See Mabry 1973: 34–36, 135, for profiles of the party's founding leaders and the PAN's early support from the private sector.

substituting model of industrialization, the state held significant lever-age over private firms through its control of tariffs and import quotas, tax policy, labor legislation, and so forth. As a result, major entrepre-neurs found it politically risky to support the PAN, however compati-ble they may have found the party's positions in ideological or pro-grammatic terms.[32] Many small and midsize businesses were less dependent upon government contracts or subsidies (and therefore less vulnerable to political sanctions), and the PAN continued to enjoy con-siderable support from this sector. Yet, as Carlos R. Menéndez Losa observes in his chapter on Yucatán in this volume, at the state level the PRI's political dominance and the private sector's multiple forms of dependence on the goodwill of government officials made it potentially costly for even some smaller firms to support the PAN openly. Indi-vidual entrepreneurs might do so discreetly, but chambers of industry or commerce generally sought to avoid such ties.[33]

This situation began to change significantly in the 1980s. The depth of the country's post–1982 economic crisis undermined the "alliance for profits" that had long bound together state elites and the national busi-ness community.[34] However, it was President José López Portillo's (1982–1988) nationalization of private banks in 1982 that marked a water-shed in state–private sector relations and conspicuously increased en-trepreneurs' support for, and direct involvement with, the National Action Party. They sought to end "economic populism" and promote democratic accountability by creating a check on the discretionary power of the federal government.[35] Especially in northern states, indi-vidual business owners joined the PAN, channeled financial resources to the party, and frequently ran as its candidates for state and munici-pal offices. Several of the PAN's most important figures of the 1980s and 1990s came from private-sector backgrounds, including Francisco Barrio Terrazas in Chihuahua, Alberto Cárdenas in Jalisco, Fernando

---

[32] The withdrawal of leading entrepreneurs and financiers from open party in-volvement de facto increased the importance of Catholic activists in the PAN's leadership during the 1950s and 1960s, which in turn made the party even less at-tractive to entrepreneurs who sought to avoid unnecessary sources of tension with government officials. See Mabry 1973: 52, and Loaeza 1999: 225.

[33] For examples from Jalisco, see Alonso Sánchez 1996: 90.

[34] See Haggard and Kaufman 1995: chaps. 1 and 2, for a comparative analysis of the impact of economic crisis on the erosion of authoritarian regimes.

[35] On the impact of the bank nationalization on entrepreneurs' changing political views, see Camp 1989: 136–38; Mizrahi 1995: 83–85; Loaeza 1999: 12, 17, 23.

The 1982 bank nationalization had a catalytic effect on the expansion of PAN support parallel to the impact of the 1968 Tlatelolco massacre on the formation of leftist parties in the early 1970s. On the 1968 crisis and the creation of new leftist parties, see Middlebrook 1986.

Canales Clariond in Nuevo León, Manuel J. Clouthier in Sinaloa, Vicente Fox Quesada in Guanajuato, Felipe González in Aguascalientes, Ignacio Loyola in Querétaro, and Ernesto Ruffo Appel in Baja California (Mizrahi n.d.1: 130 n. 16).[36] Thus, by the 1990s, the PAN had recovered extensive ties to the private sector; indeed, entrepreneurs' organizational skills and financial support were key elements in the PAN's growing electoral success.[37]

The continuities in the PAN's support bases are equally noteworthy. As previously noted, Catholic activists were among the most important elements at the PAN's founding convention in September 1939,[38] and a regional network of Catholic supporters proved crucial to the party's early organizational development (Mabry 1973: 34; Loaeza 1999: 154–55, 157). In the wake of protracted, violent church-state conflict during the late 1920s, many Catholics embraced the new party as the most viable opposition to the postrevolutionary political order. The PAN's opposition to Article 3 of the 1917 Constitution (guaranteeing public, secular education and expressly banning religious groups' involvement

---

[36] This change produced important tensions within the party as the "barbarians from the North" (the label apparently coined by Fidel Velázquez, the longtime leader of the PRI–affiliated Confederation of Mexican Workers [CTM] to describe these hard-charging *panista* entrepreneurs) displaced from candidate and leadership positions more traditional elements with a much longer history of involvement in party affairs. See Mizrahi n.d.1: 149–50.

Loaeza (1999: 330, 367) notes that one consequence of the rise of so-called *neopanismo* was a decline in Mexico City's relative importance as a source of leadership recruitment and a base of electoral support; see also Lujambio, this volume, table 2.2, for data on the Federal District share of the PAN's electoral support in federal Chamber of Deputies elections between 1943 and 2000. There was also a shift in the PAN's tone and tactics, as *neopanistas* advocated more aggressive direct-action means (collective protests, building occupations, and so forth) of opposing electoral fraud and defending *panista* gains.

[37] Mizrahi (1995: 83) observes that owners of small and midsize businesses were most actively engaged in party affairs. On PAN–private sector relations more generally, see Mizrahi 1996a and n.d.1: 119–54.

Social Christian ideas linked the PAN, the Mexican Employers' Confederation (COPARMEX, the organizational base for many entrepreneurs who later joined the PAN), and the private universities (particularly the Monterrey Institute of Technology and Advanced Studies [ITESM] and the Universidad Iberoamericana) where many of these entrepreneurs were educated. See Mizrahi n.d.1: 138 n. 28, 139. For examples of COPARMEX–PAN ties at the state level in Baja California and Guanajuato, see, respectively, Hernández Vicencio 2001: 60, and Valencia García, this volume.

[38] Catholic activists constituted a majority of the party's nineteen-member organizing committee; Loaeza 1999: 153 n. 104. Many of them had been involved in the Unión Nacional de Estudiantes Católicos (National Union of Catholic Students), formed in 1931.

in elementary and secondary education and in schools for workers and peasants), and especially its reform in December 1934 to promote socialist education, won it widespread Catholic support.[39] Catholic lay organizations like Catholic Action long remained a major source of leadership recruitment and community-level support for the PAN, even though heavy reliance on the party's Catholic base from the 1940s through the 1970s may also have been an obstacle to its autonomous organizational development. Moreover, the Catholic identity of many *panistas* was a vital source of internal organizational coherence during the long decades when the party appeared to have little or no chance of electoral success. Indeed, the lack of electoral prospects and the scarcity of material incentives reinforced Catholic dominance at a time when party membership was mainly meaningful in expressive terms.[40]

From the beginning, the PAN also won strong backing among middle-class and professional groups. Its original leadership was comprised mainly of professionals and university-based intellectuals, many of whom had personal ties to former UNAM rector Manuel Gómez Morin (Mabry 1973: 34). In the late 1960s, Mabry (1973: 139) estimated that about 70 percent of the PAN's members were professionals and businesspeople, drawn from both the urban and rural middle classes. Middle-class elements have been an especially important source of party activists, presumably drawn to the party because of the PAN's practical commitment to promoting good government at the local level, its support for the private sector, its strong condemnation of public-sector corruption, and its long-term position as the principal opposition to the popular-based PRI.[41]

---

[39] Mabry 1973: 16, 25, 27. On the revolutionary and anticlerical origins of Article 3, see Loaeza 1988: 73–78.

[40] Mabry 1973: 150–51, 165–66; Loaeza 1999: 24, 182, 208, 225, 241. The PAN continues to advocate traditional Catholic positions on some issues, including its call for freedom of religious education and its opposition to abortion. By the end of the twentieth century, however, the political relevance of religiosity had declined substantially in Mexico. Magaloni and Moreno (n.d.: 16, 18) found that PAN and PRI voters could not be distinguished on the basis of religious beliefs, though PAN voters were significantly more religious than supporters of the center-left Party of the Democratic Revolution. PAN elites were more conservative than the party's mass supporters.

[41] See Mabry 1973: 136–39, 149, for the occupational profile of the party's leadership in the late 1960s. Camp (1995: 67–69, 77–78) similarly found that the party's leadership came predominantly from middle- and upper-middle-class strata, and that a high proportion of party leaders had attended private, often religious-affiliated primary and secondary schools. See Tarrés 1990 for a case study of linkages between urban middle-class protests and the PAN.

With comparatively few (and relatively recent) exceptions, the PAN has been much less successful at winning support among industrial workers and peasants. For many years even the protest votes that it drew from these groups were modest in number (Mabry 1973: 166; Loaeza 1999: 428–29). The principal reason was that organized labor and the peasantry were for several decades the most fully consolidated mass bases of the PRI; they were, at once, the constituencies that benefited most directly from postrevolutionary social reforms, and the groups that could be most reliably mobilized—via a combination of material incentives and the threat of political sanctions—to vote for PRI candidates. There is some indication that, in major urban areas and occasionally elsewhere, the PAN began in the 1980s and 1990s to make some inroads into what had historically been solid *priísta* terrain.[42] Certainly the breadth of some of the party's electoral victories since the early 1990s (including Fox's presidential victory in July 2000) would not have been possible without support from across the socioeconomic spectrum. However, for the reasons indicated above, industrial workers, peasants, and lower-class urban residents have never figured prominently in the party's formal membership and organizational life. This is one important reason why, compared to the PRI and its system of indirect (via affiliated unions and peasant organizations) mass membership, the National Action Party's membership has remained comparatively small: some 9,000 members in 1941, only 61,000 in 1990, and approximately 158,000 in 2000.[43]

The case of Guanajuato usefully illustrates the heterogeneity of the PAN's main constituencies at the state level. Even as Catholic influences on the national party became more socially progressive in the 1960s and 1970s, the state's intensely held Catholic tradition remained quite conservative in nature. The PAN enjoyed an important advantage in Guanajuato because of its early defense of religious liberty in a highly polarized regional and national context, and there were real affinities between local conservative forces and the PAN's Catholic-inspired

---

[42] For example, even though workers continued to favor the PRI over the PAN by very substantial margins in the early 1980s, Basáñez's analysis of public opinion polls (1991: 225, 249, 264, 301–302) found that the post–1982 economic crisis significantly eroded workers' support for the PRI. Workers in northern states were apparently more sympathetic to the PAN than to the PRI. Also see Menéndez Losa, this volume, for references to working-class and peasant support for the PAN in Yucatán.

[43] The 1941 membership total is from Mabry 1973: 142; the data for 1990 and 2000 are from Shirk, this volume, and include only active party members. If one adds the looser category of "party affiliates," the year 2000 total was 596,000. The PAN has not changed its formal rules for recruiting new members since 1939; see Mizrahi n.d.1: 109.

principles. Yet as a practical matter, the PAN was able to expand its electoral base in the state only as the Mexican Democratic Party (PDM, a political successor to the UNS, which had been founded in León, Guanajuato) lost its appeal as a vehicle for defending local interests against political centralism.[44] At the same time, the entrance of entrepreneurs into the state-level PAN and municipal and state politics during the 1980s mirrored the rise of *neopanista* elements within the party nationally; indeed, one of the most prominent representatives of this larger phenomenon was Vicente Fox, a native of Guanajuato. The presence (and continued strength) of both traditional Catholic elements and entrepreneurs-turned-politicians in Guanajuato encapsulates the diversity and complexity of the broader *panista* experience.

The PAN as Protest Party More generally, the PAN long benefited from its role as the most readily available vehicle for registering electoral dissent from the established regime. Especially in the first years after the PAN's founding, the PRI/PAN rivalry embodied in public perceptions the fundamental split between those elements favoring and opposing core elements of the Mexican Revolution's political and social agenda. From the mid–1940s through the late 1970s, the PAN was the only significant opposition party in Mexico.[45] It served as a catch-all opposition party in the 1958, 1964, and 1970 presidential elections and in all federal Chamber of Deputies elections between 1949 and 1976 (Loaeza 1999: 30–32). Of course, the nearly permanent presence of armed guerrilla movements in different parts of Mexico since at least the 1940s attests to the fact that not all sociopolitical discontent expressed itself via the ballot box. Nevertheless, the National Action Party regularly served as the principal vehicle for protest votes.

---

[44] Valencia García, this volume, and Loaeza 1999: 237, 502. In its first decades, the PAN's best performance in presidential voting in Guanajuato came in 1952 and 1970 when its candidates were prominent Catholic activists (Efraín González Luna and Efraín González Morfín, respectively).

[45] The Mexican Communist Party (PCM, founded in 1919) lost its official registry in 1946, at the beginning of the Cold War; the leftist parties that formed in the early 1970s did not receive official recognition until after the passage of the Federal Law on Political Organizations and Electoral Processes (LOPPE) in 1977. From the 1950s through the mid–1970s, then, the only continuously organized opposition parties other than the PAN were the Socialist Popular Party (PPS) and the Authentic Party of the Mexican Revolution (PARM). In practice, however, they operated as allies of the PRI, accepting government financial subsidies for their operations and regularly backing the PRI's presidential nominee. Loaeza (1999: 256) notes that, even in the mid–1960s, electoral returns showed that voters clearly identified the PAN as the only independent party opposition.

As a consequence, the PAN often benefited from splits in, defections from, or general disaffection with the PRI at the state or local levels. Among the most hotly contested state-level electoral contests in the 1950s and 1960s were gubernatorial races in Baja California in 1959, Sonora in 1967, and Yucatán in 1969; in all these instances, the PAN succeeded in mobilizing broad support (including PRI dissidents) against those elements controlling the PRI apparatus (Mabry 1973: 78–79, 83–84, 181). At the same time, the PAN capitalized on regional resentment of political centrism to build its support, especially in Baja California, Chihuahua, Nuevo León, and Yucatán, but also in Coahuila, Durango, Guanajuato, Jalisco, Michoacán, Sinaloa, and Sonora.[46] Although it no longer monopolized the role of independent opposition party after the formation of the National Democratic Front (FDN) and the Party of the Democratic Revolution (PRD) in 1988–1989, Vicente Fox again sought (successfully) to capitalize on the pro/con PRI division by defining the terms of the year 2000 presidential election as "Change Now!" ("*¡Cambio Ya!*").

The electoral support the PAN received as a protest party was quite substantial. In the Federal District, for example, the party effectively monopolized opposition to the PRI well into the 1980s, receiving an average of 26.4 percent of the vote in federal Chamber of Deputies elections held between 1946 and 1994 in Mexico's most important urban center.[47] In Chamber of Deputies elections nationally, the PAN's share of the total vote rose from 5 percent in 1943 and 2 percent in 1946 to 38 percent in 2000, averaging 14.2 percent over the entire 1943–2000 period and 21.8 percent in the eight elections held after the 1977 electoral reform (the 1979–2000 period).[48] In presidential elections, the PAN averaged 10.1 percent of the total vote during the 1952–1970 period and 25.8 percent during its 1982–2000 period of political expansion, receiving 15.6 percent in 1982, 17.1 percent in 1988, 26.7 percent in 1994, and 43.8 percent in 2000 (Mizrahi n.d.1: table 1).[49]

---

[46] See, for example, Mabry 1973: 178, and the essays by Guillén López, Aziz Nassif, Valencia García, and Menéndez Losa in this volume.

[47] Loaeza 1999: 34; see also pp. 99–100, 496–98. The rise of the center-left National Democratic Front—the coalition of parties backing Cuauhtémoc Cárdenas's 1988 presidential candidacy—and the subsequent consolidation of the PRD's base in the Federal District ended this monopoly.

[48] See Lujambio, this volume, table 2.2.

[49] Internal factional conflicts prevented the PAN from nominating a candidate for the 1976 presidential election. Loaeza (1999: table VII.6) provides data for the 1982–1994 period on the PAN's share of the presidential vote in the eleven states in which it performed best. See Mizrahi n.d.1: table 2 and Mizrahi n.d.2: table 3, for information on all elected positions won by the PAN in races for municipal

In its role as the most firmly established opposition to the PRI, the National Action Party was a principal beneficiary of business and middle-class discontent with the 1982 bank nationalization and the economic crisis of the 1980s. The flagrant fraud that the PAN suffered at the hands of government/PRI officials in the 1986 Chihuahua gubernatorial race was a decisive moment in this regard. In particular, the Chihuahua experience galvanized the Catholic Church to more active political involvement in favor of clean elections (a position which, given the PAN's Catholic identity, was of particular value to it),[50] and it led the PAN leadership to advocate more aggressive "direct action" tactics to defend its electoral gains. More generally, however, the PAN succeeded in capitalizing on societal discontent and attracting an expanding protest vote because of its long-term opposition to statism and presidentialism, its advocacy of private enterprise and municipal and state rights, and, especially, its established party organization.[51] That organization was still comparatively weak in some regards, but the decentralized character of the party made it more responsive to changes in regional society. Mizrahi (1995: 86), for example, argues that the PAN's organizational flexibility was what permitted entrepreneurs to lead electoral protests after 1982.

In the 1980s and 1990s, two other factors also contributed to the PAN's growing electoral appeal, permitting the party to maximize its position as a protest vehicle and emerge as a serious alternative to the long-ruling PRI.[52] First, the PAN acquired substantial administrative

---

president, governor, and the federal Chamber of Deputies and Senate between 1946 and 2000.

In geographical terms, Magaloni and Moreno (n.d.: map 1) show that in 1961 the PAN's strongest backing came from the Federal District, Baja California, and Chihuahua; it had more limited support in areas where the Cristero conflict of the 1920s had been most intense (Aguascalientes, Colima, Jalisco, Michoacán) and in Campeche, Morelos, and San Luis Potosí. By the 1980s, the party's support was increasingly concentrated in northern and central-western states (map 3). As late as 1997, the PAN's electoral presence was quite weak in the South and Southeast, except for the states of Quintana Roo and Yucatán (map 4).

[50] Chand (2001: chap. 4) discusses the impact of the Chihuahua experience on the Catholic Church's increasingly strong advocacy of electoral democracy; see also Loaeza 1999: 352, 391. Government officials were sufficiently concerned about the church's political involvement that the 1987 federal electoral law raised the sanctions on open church involvement in political matters; Chand 2001: 194.

[51] Lujambio (this volume) particularly develops this line of argument.

[52] See Magaloni and Moreno n.d. for evidence that, at the mass level, the PAN is a catch-all party with very heterogeneous bases of support on both economic policy (left-right) and moral (liberal-conservative) dimensions.

The PAN has long enjoyed disproportionate support from women voters, reflecting both the party's Catholic ties (and Mexican women's greater religiosity) and political experience after the early 1980s. In the decade following its first officially recognized gubernatorial victory in Baja California in 1989, the party also won statewide office in Aguascalientes, Chihuahua, Guanajuato, Jalisco, Nuevo León, and Querétaro.[53] By 1999, approximately one-third of the country's population lived under a *panista* municipal administration (Lujambio, this volume, table 2.1), and the PAN had at one time or another governed most of the largest urban areas in Mexico (including Guadalajara and Monterrey). By winning office in a growing number of states and municipalities, the PAN had an opportunity to demonstrate its stated commitment to honesty, efficiency, and rational planning in government by attempting to streamline administrative procedures, combat corruption, revise state election laws to promote electoral transparency, encourage citizen involvement in governmental processes, and so forth.[54] Of course, not all *panista* administrations were successful in such efforts, and as Tonatiuh Guillén López notes in his essay on Baja California in this volume, the PAN's commitment to deepening democracy by reforming representational arrangements sometimes flagged when such changes threatened to erode the party's own political advantage and newly acquired patronage resources. On the whole, however, the PAN managed to refute in practice an argument that the PRI had long used against its partisan opponents—namely, that no other party had the experience required to govern effectively.[55] Indeed, as the PAN demonstrated its increasing vi-

---

and the PAN's own policies. For example, the party advocated women's suffrage before the PRI; it had the first woman federal deputy; and significant numbers of PAN candidates and party officials have been women. See Mabry 1973: 180.

Several analysts have observed the strong positive association over time between urbanization and the PAN's expanding electoral support; see, for example, Mabry 1973: 142, and Camp 1995: 73–74.

[53] In the 2000 elections, the PAN also won the governorship of Morelos, and in 2001 it captured the governorship of Yucatán.

[54] In Chihuahua, for instance, the Barrio administration sought to end corruption by enhancing civilian oversight over police forces. It also attempted to regulate urban land use and promote affordable housing (Aziz Nassif, this volume). In Guanajuato, the PAN was particularly concerned with demonstrating transparent management of public funds (Valencia García, this volume). For an example of the PAN's specific proposals to promote good government (*buen gobierno*) in a complex urban environment, see Partido Acción Nacional 1997.

At the same time, greater governing experience contributed to the career development of individuals who would become national party leaders. For example, Ernesto Ruffo served as mayor of Ensenada before running for governor of Baja California, and Francisco Barrio was mayor of Ciudad Juárez before becoming governor of Chihuahua.

[55] There is now an extensive literature evaluating the PAN's experience in municipal and state government. See, for example, Alonso Sánchez 1996; Espinoza Valle

ability as an alternative to the PRI, it became more and more favored as a vehicle for opposing the governing party. A significant proportion of the electorate backed Vicente Fox and the PAN in the 2000 elections on the grounds that this was the most rational strategic choice (*voto útil*) for those opposing the PRI.[56]

Second, Vicente Fox's 1999–2000 presidential campaign mobilized support for the PAN from across the political spectrum. Campaigning under the slogan "Change Now!", the forceful and charismatic Fox succeeded in defining the presidential election as a referendum on the long-reigning PRI. Voters responded strongly to this appeal regardless of their normal partisan identifications, seizing the opportunity to punish the PRI for Mexico's devastating 1994–1995 financial crisis and long-standing problems of governmental corruption and the impunity of the wealthy and powerful. For example, on the basis of a *Reforma* exit poll, Magaloni and Moreno (n.d.: table 6) found that Fox received strong backing from across the socioeconomic, regional, and religious spectrums.[57]

This overview of the PAN's ideological and programmatic positions and its core constituencies indicates why one might appropriately characterize it as a conservative party located on the center-right of Mexico's partisan spectrum.[58] Yet this exercise also demonstrates that left-right characterizations are sometimes difficult. There have, for instance, been significant changes over time in some of the PAN's bases of support, particularly where backing from the business community is con-

---

1998; Mizrahi 1996b, 1998a; Rodríguez 1995; Rodríguez and Ward 1992; Vanderbush 1999; and Ward 1995.

[56] Some 10 percent of those voters who identified prinicipally with the center-left Party of the Democratic Revolution cast their presidential ballot for Fox in the July 2000 presidential election; *Reforma*, July 3, 2000, cited in Lujambio, this volume. Magaloni and Moreno (n.d.: table 6) found that Fox won the support of 29 percent of voters who had backed PRD founder Cuauhtémoc Cárdenas's presidential candidacy in 1994.

See Domínguez and McCann 1996 and Stansfield 1996 for an analysis of the *panista* vote in the 1988, 1991, and 1994 federal elections.

[57] Fox won significantly more support than other candidates from urban dwellers, younger voters (those under 39 years of age), better-educated voters (those with middle school, high school, or college education), and Catholics. Fox dominated in all the left-right self-placement categories (left, center-left, center, and center-right) *except* "right," where PRI presidential candidate Francisco Labastida Ochoa won. Fox outpolled Cárdenas among voters who identified themselves as "left" or "center-left."

[58] This partisan placement is one that is broadly accepted by PAN leaders themselves. See Lujambio, this volume, figure 2.2; Magaloni and Moreno n.d.: figure 4; and Mainwaring and Scully n.d.: table 1.6.

cerned. Nor does the label "conservative" always mean the same thing in all issue arenas. For example, in the mid–1970s the PAN's center-left Catholic wing (led by Efraín González Morfín) strongly advocated abstaining from electoral competition, while the more conservative, antistatist wing of the party (led by José Ángel Conchello) favored electoral participation (Loaeza 1999: 308; Lujambio, this volume). Most important, however, the PAN experience shows that there is no necessary inconsistency between advocacy of conservative policy positions or the defense of the private sector and opposition to political authoritarianism.[59]

THE PAN AND DEMOCRATIZATION IN MEXICO

In the wake of Vicente Fox's watershed electoral victory in July 2000, some observers were rather facilely inclined to attribute electoral democratization in Mexico to the force of Fox's personality, the National Action Party, or even the "inevitable" effects of market opening and the North American Free Trade Agreement. It is certainly not correct to give the PAN overall credit for pushing forward this long, highly complex process of political change. After all, the National Action Party was not a central actor in some of the most crucial episodes of democratic opening from the 1960s through the 1980s, including the student-popular mobilization that preceded the Tlatelolco massacre in 1968, the elaboration of reform legislation in 1977 that significantly expanded opposition political representation and channeled newly formed parties into the electoral arena, and the grassroots urban organization that followed devastating earthquakes in Mexico City in 1985. Nonetheless, over the years the PAN did make several significant contributions to electoral democratization in Mexico.

Most specifically, from the mid–1940s through the mid–1990s the National Action Party actively promoted the reform of electoral institutions and procedures.[60] For most of this period, it lacked the power to win legislative approval of particular initiatives, but the PAN did help

---

[59] Opinion survey data presented by Lujambio (this volume) show that even some *priístas* recognize that the PAN has been consistently committed to the principles of electoral democracy. It is certainly important in this regard that, unlike center-right or rightist parties in many Latin American countries, the PAN has never been associated with military rule.

[60] The PAN, probably anticipating that it would gain more than its competitors from women's electoral participation, was the first major party to sponsor women's suffrage legislation. In 1946–1948 it introduced initiatives that would have granted women the right to vote in municipal and federal elections. See Mabry 1973: 109–10.

define the agenda for electoral reform. For example, in the debates preceding the adoption of new federal electoral legislation in 1946 (the first adopted since 1918), the party advocated the creation of a national voter registry, the formation of a federal election commission, and proportional representation in the federal Chamber of Deputies.[61] The PAN's continuing demands for proportional representation were among the factors leading to the adoption of a limited proportional representation ("party deputy") system in 1963, and the party was an early advocate of the popular election of the Federal District government (Mabry 1973: 76, 110; von Sauer 1974: 90–91).

However, the PAN had its most significant impact in this area from the late 1980s through the mid–1990s. After the tumultuous, fraud-riddled 1988 elections and the PRI's loss of its two-thirds majority in the federal Chamber of Deputies, President Carlos Salinas de Gortari needed the PAN's support both to consolidate his immediate political position and to undertake the constitutional reforms necessary to pursue his far-reaching plans for economic liberalization and the privatization of state-owned enterprises. Although the PAN was acutely aware that collaborating with the Salinas government might undercut its credibility as an opposition party, its congressional representatives ratified Salinas's election as president and the party helped enact his market-oriented reforms—policies, including the privatization of banks and collectively held *ejido* lands, that in many cases coincided with the PAN's own long-standing proposals. In exchange, the PAN won Salinas's pledge that its municipal and statewide electoral victories would receive official recognition, as well as his commitment to further electoral reform.[62] The PAN particularly sought to end the federal government's control over elections by giving key electoral bodies full institutional autonomy, expanding citizen oversight of elections, and curtailing the PRI's ability to draw on government personnel and financial resources to support its campaigns. Progress toward these goals was slow and uneven, and the available evidence suggests that the PAN had only limited influence over the specific content of electoral reforms enacted in 1990, 1993, and 1994. Nevertheless, the PAN was a crucial force in promoting these initiatives to open further the political process, a prin-

---

[61] See Loaeza 1999: 213, and von Sauer 1974: 87, 89. In its subsequent demands for proportional representation, the PAN was joined by the leftist Partido Popular (Popular Party) led by Vicente Lombardo Toledano.

[62] Because Salinas sought approval of a North American free trade agreement, the need for international approval also encouraged him to promote continuing political liberalization.

cipal consequence of which was the party's enhanced capacity to compete successfully in municipal, state, and federal elections.[63]

More generally, during the 1980s and 1990s the PAN played an important role in institutionalizing opposition to the dominant Institutional Revolutionary Party. Because of its long tradition as an independent opposition, the PAN became a principal vehicle for directing through electoral channels the widespread popular discontent that accompanied repeated financial crises, persistent economic stagnation and perceptions of government policy failure, and evidence of corruption and the impunity of government officials.[64] Lujambio (this volume) persuasively argues that the PAN's building political success depended crucially upon its long electoral experience and the development of a party infrastructure capable of running candidates for local, state, and federal offices and competing with the PRI on a national basis. The interaction between a series of liberalizing electoral reforms and the PAN's growing strength was particularly important in this regard; the greater transparency of—and increasing public confidence in—electoral procedures, on the one hand, and the emergence of viable partisan alternatives, on the other, were essential to transforming the nature of the vote—and thus the nature of elections—in Mexico. Rather than a symbolic action or a form of protest (when ballots were damaged or not cast), voting became a political act with real meaning and practical consequences.

The state-level analyses in this volume illuminate two additional aspects of the National Action Party's role in Mexican democratization in the 1980s and 1990s. First, the PAN's efforts intersected with—and further accelerated—civic mobilization and growing public support for electoral transparency. One common element in the experiences of Baja California, Chihuahua, Guanajuato, and Yucatán during this period was that the PAN, regardless of its own conservative identity, gradually emerged as the leader of socially and politically heterogeneous pro-democracy, anti–PRI/regime coalitions. The party's roots in these four states date to the 1940s and 1950s, and, with the exception of Guanajuato (where the Mexican Democratic Party led the political opposition from its founding in 1971 until the early 1980s), during most of the subsequent period the PAN was the principal opposition to the PRI. This trajectory gave the PAN credibility as the focal point of local movements demanding electoral democracy and party alternation in power. In particular, it enabled the PAN to associate itself with local or regional traditions of civic resistance to federal government authority

---

[63] For an overview of the PAN's role in promoting electoral reform during this period, see Loaeza 1999: 408, 413–25, 477.

[64] See Loaeza 1999: 26, 334, for one assessment of the PAN's role in this area.

exercised from Mexico City.[65] In its historic gubernatorial victory in Baja California in 1989, for example, the party did not win by advocating a conservative policy platform; rather, the PAN's Ernesto Ruffo Appel received support from many voters who had cast their presidential ballots for FDN/PRD leader Cuauhtémoc Cárdenas in 1988 because his candidacy represented the possibility of meaningful change within the state. In Baja California and in these other states, then, the PAN came to power by heading a broad coalition whose central demand was democracy.

In some instances, the PAN's Catholic identity was an important part of its local political success. For example, in Baja California in the 1980s, the PAN's links with Catholic lay organizations facilitated its organizational development, and the party was the principal beneficiary of church efforts to promote expanded electoral participation (Hernández Vicencio 2001: 44–45, 47, 66–67). In Guanajuato, there was significant overlap between the party's postulates and the main tenets of the state's strongly Catholic political culture. Even more, in the León diocese, church officials played an active role in elections in the 1990s and explicitly endorsed the activities of *panista* municipal officials (Valencia García, this volume). Ties between the Catholic hierarchy and the PAN were more indirect in Yucatán. Nevertheless, Menéndez Losa (this volume) notes that church support for clean elections benefited the party in its drive to gain municipal and statewide offices. A common Catholic ethos and a shared advocacy of Christian values were, for instance, a key connection between the local PAN and the state's most important newspaper, the *Diario de Yucatán*. The paper's efforts to develop a civic consciousness in the state, as well as its campaign for good government and the public accountability of elected officials, dovetailed with the party's demands for electoral transparency.[66]

Second, events in Baja California, Chihuahua, Guanajuato, and Yucatán during the 1990s demonstrated the important interaction between institutional change and the consolidation of an opposition political presence in these states. Most scholarly discussions of electoral reform and its consequences in Mexico have focused on federal electoral law,

---

[65] Guadalupe Valencia García's essay on Guanajuato (this volume) is especially effective at showing the links between oppositionist traditions dating from the 1920s and 1930s and the PAN's electoral success in the state in the 1980s and 1990s. On the PAN's long-term development in Baja California, see Hernández Vicencio 2001. Hernández Vicencio notes (pp. 35–37) that some early *panista* activists had previously been involved in the UNS in central Mexico.

[66] The chapters by Aziz Nassif and Valencia García in this volume also document the key role of the media in struggles between the PAN and the PRI. See also Mizrahi 1998a: 167.

and the reform legislation of the 1970s, 1980s, and 1990s contributed significantly to the PAN's capacity to expand its electoral position.[67] However, the state-level studies in this volume amply demonstrate how important constitutional and statutory reforms were to democratization at the local level. Electoral fraud in its many forms—including not just voter intimidation, the stuffing of ballot boxes on election day, or the illegal disposal of opposition votes, but also purposeful error in the compilation of voter registries, election authorities' failure to circulate identification cards to voters or voter registries to political parties prior to elections, and so forth—had long been a major obstacle to the PAN. For this reason, one of the highest priorities for newly elected *panista* governors in Baja California, Chihuahua, and Guanajuato was to win passage of a new electoral code.[68]

Baja California was a pioneer in this process, and some of the reform measures adopted there (a fraud-proof photo identification card for each voter, for example) were later adopted at the federal level. By compiling a new state-level voter registry, establishing a politically independent State Electoral Institute and a new Electoral Justice Tribunal, and enacting stricter rules concerning voter registration, campaign financing, and balloting, the administration of Governor Ernesto Ruffo Appel (1989–1995) created conditions that permitted subsequent elections to proceed without major public controversy. Similarly in Chihuahua, the administration of Governor Francisco Barrio Terrazas (1992–1998) enacted reform legislation that increased citizen control over electoral institutions and enhanced the transparency of balloting and vote-counting procedures.[69] In Guanajuato in the early 1990s, the initially somewhat precarious balance of power between the PAN and the PRI slowed the electoral reform process, but the state eventually enacted a new electoral code that was in several ways more advanced than the federal legislation then in effect. Institutional reforms such as these were vital to ensuring greater electoral transparency, a chief consequence of which was citizens' increased confidence in elections and their willingness to invest time and resources in the political process in

---

[67] For a discussion of the impact of earlier electoral reforms (especially those adopted in 1946 and 1963) on the PAN, see Loaeza 1999: 214, 263–64.

[68] Yucatán's electoral code was also reformed in 1995, but the changes were not as significant in scope as in those states where party alternation in power occurred. See Menéndez Losa, this volume.

[69] The Barrio administration also pushed through an extensive constitutional reform that strengthened the rights of municipal governments; provided for greater legislative oversight over the executive branch; enhanced the legal and budgetary independence of the judiciary; provided for referenda, plebiscites, and popular initiatives; and established special protection for the rights of indigenous peoples.

the expectation that their partisan involvement might produce the outcome they desired at the polls. The PAN was a major beneficiary of these transformations in the local institutional landscape.

In retrospect, gradual political opening at the state and federal levels may appear to have been an uncomplicated process. It is important to recall, however, that the struggle to ensure clean, fair elections was long and hard. In Baja California, Chihuahua, Guanajuato, Jalisco, San Luis Potosí, Yucatán, and elsewhere, there were extensive citizen mobilizations to defend the integrity of the vote. In Guanajuato in 1985, for example, the PAN, PDM, UNS, and local Catholic-inspired groups banded together in the Guanajuato Union of Civic and Political Groups to safeguard the vote and challenge some official results (Valencia García, this volume). The Chihuahua experience was even more dramatic. The PAN's protests against fraud in the 1986 gubernatorial election included acts of civil disobedience (including the blocking of international bridges at the border with the United States) and a 41–day hunger strike by Luis H. Álvarez (a Chihuahua native who served as the PAN's presidential candidate in 1958 and mayor of Chihuahua in 1983–1986) and other party and civic leaders (Chand 2001: 117–21). The PAN's prominent involvement in these pro-democracy mobilizations contributed greatly to its electoral appeal.

Over the course of the 1980s and 1990s, the PAN itself experienced major transformations. Unlike some other Latin American conservative parties that demonstrated initial electoral strength during democratic openings in the 1980s but then rapidly lost political relevance, the PAN successfully negotiated the transition from more narrowly based protest vehicle to nationally competitive party. In the process, it made significant progress at party-building and institutionalization. As David A. Shirk observes in his chapter in this volume, for decades the PAN had been a very informal organization. Because of serious resource constraints, *panista* candidates for municipal and state offices frequently were forced to fund their own campaigns, and the party had only a skeletal administrative structure at the state and national levels. However, after much internal debate, the PAN decided in 1989 to accept public financing for campaigns and other party activities. As a consequence, it was able to expand significantly its organizational presence at the state and municipal levels, and for the first time the party could hire full-time administrative employees and offer salaries to key party leaders.[70]

---

[70] Shirk also overviews the PAN's formal decision-making and candidate selection structures. For additional discussions of the PAN's organizational responses to growing electoral opportunities, see Reveles Vázquez 1994; Mizrahi 1998b; and Wuhs 2000.

The principal incentives for these party-building initiatives were the challenges of running candidates for an increasing proportion of the public offices in contention, supervising the electoral process, and defending the party's gains against electoral fraud.[71] It was not until 1979 that the party was able to run candidates in all districts in federal Chamber of Deputies elections, and, despite the PAN's long-standing emphasis on electoral competition at the local level, it was not until the 1990s that the party could regularly run candidates for municipal president in the majority of races occurring in any given year.[72] In these efforts, the PAN linked its own future to the struggle for gradual political opening via a municipal-federalist electoral strategy, an approach that fit well with Mexico's institutional structure—and, somewhat ironically, with the PRI's own liberalization strategy of opening the regime by recognizing municipal and state-level opposition victories, in the hope that it could retain control of the federal Congress and the presidency.

Nevertheless, the PAN inevitably suffered growing pains, including significant internal factionalism. From its founding in 1939 through the 1970s, the principal division within the party was between those more pragmatic elements who favored electoral participation and those who advocated abstention from electoral processes. However, as Steven T. Wuhs shows in his essay in this volume, the bases of factional division became more complex after the early 1980s as the PAN's electoral fortunes rose and new groups joined the party. Wuhs argues that the PAN's greatly expanded resources—especially candidate nominations, given the much greater chances of actually being elected to public office, and the availability of paid positions for senior party leaders— stimulated the formation of identifiable party factions.[73] Indeed, the very pace of party growth became a point of dispute as some PAN leaders sought to limit the rate of membership expansion so as not to lose control over membership selection processes and risk diluting the party's distinctive identity (Shirk, this volume).

The four state-level analyses included in this book offer valuable insights into other challenges associated with the PAN's growing electoral success.[74] In all four of these cases, the PAN reaped important

---

[71] In states such as Chihuahua, the imperative of defending PAN electoral gains against government/PRI fraud was a significant incentive to the development of precinct-level party committees. See Chand 2001: 122–23.

[72] See Lujambio, this volume, tables 2.2 and 2.1, respectively.

[73] Also see Reveles Vázquez 1998 and Loaeza 1999: 510–19, on the internal tensions generated by the PAN's growing electoral success.

[74] Unfortunately, none of these chapters examines the phenomenon of PAN factions at the state level.

dividends from its municipal-federalist strategy by gradually building electoral support and organizational strength. Nevertheless, it experienced a difficult transition from minority party to its new status as a permanent political force capable of governing statewide. In Baja California, the very fact that the PAN initially gained statewide office at the head of a heterogeneous pro-democracy movement complicated the party's subsequent development; lacking strong ties to a stable electoral base, for some years the party faced a nearly permanent threat of defeat by the PRI in the next election (Guillén López, this volume). In Chihuahua, the inexperienced Barrio administration initially devoted considerably more time to reforming public administration and demonstrating its commitment to good government than to constructing an organized political base. Only after it lost the 1995 midterm elections to the PRI did the PAN develop a strategy for promoting voter awareness of its accomplishments in office (Aziz Nassif, this volume). The PAN's initial electoral successes in Guanajuato in the early 1980s renewed its commitment to an electoral strategy, leading the party to reorganize itself by forming municipal-level party committees, training mid-level personnel in political and administrative topics, and focusing more attention on the quality of its candidates' campaigns. An expanded territorial base and a capacity to run more candidates contributed directly to the PAN's accelerating electoral success (Valencia García, this volume). In Yucatán, however, the PAN's organizational presence outside of the capital city of Mérida remained somewhat thin, despite major electoral gains during the 1980s and 1990s and its growing experience in local government (Menéndez Losa, this volume).

THE PAN AND MEXICO'S POLITICAL FUTURE

Vicente Fox's presidential victory in July 2000 brought the Partido Acción Nacional to national power, presenting the party with both unprecedented opportunities and a series of new challenges. The purpose of this concluding section is to identify, based on the national- and state-level analyses included in this volume, some of the principal issues confronting the PAN as a key political actor in Mexico's democratic transition.[75]

---

[75] This discussion does not focus on specific public policy initiatives that might be promoted by the Fox administration over the 2000–2006 period. However, Valencia García's chapter in this book assesses Fox's record as governor of Guanajuato (1995–1999) and the lessons that experience might hold for his performance as president. In particular, she notes that Fox as governor extensively incorporated into state government individuals with private-sector backgrounds, sought to develop a new relationship between the state government and municipalities, ac-

Three of the numerous dilemmas facing the PAN at this political juncture hold particularly significant implications for the future character of Mexican democracy. The first concerns the obvious complications involved in the PAN's shift from opposition force to governing party. No longer a leading participant in a movement whose chief goal is to promote alternation in power, the PAN as a party may encounter unanticipated challenges to its own identity and to relations with its supporters. The characteristics that contributed to its success as a political opposition may not be the same as those required to demonstrate that it is best qualified to define efficacious solutions to urgent policy problems, even though political rivalry among major parties may now focus on which of them has the capacities and resources to best serve the common good. Intra-party factional disputes may also take on new significance, potentially with important policy implications. Moreover, as noted in the essays on Baja California and Chihuahua in this book, the PAN's gubernatorial victories have necessitated a substantial adjustment in the mind-set and conduct of party leaders. Indeed, a culture of opposition has often persisted well after the party assumes power. One consequence is that serious tensions sometimes arise between the PAN as party organization and the government it has helped elect. In Chihuahua, for example, the local PAN for some time retained such a strong opposition culture that it effectively abandoned the Barrio administration during its first three years in office (Aziz Nassif, this volume; Mizrahi 1998b: 110–11).

The national parallel here involves the PAN's relationship with President Fox. Shirk (this volume) documents some *panista* leaders' tenacious efforts to block Fox's presidential candidacy, leading Fox to bypass established party structures and create a parallel organization ("Friends of Fox") which so successfully demonstrated his broad public appeal that, in the event, he faced no serious rival for the PAN's presidential nomination.[76] In the weeks following his presidential victory, Fox and key party leaders like Diego Fernández de Cevallos (the PAN's 1994 presidential nominee and, beginning in 2000, leader of the *panista* delegation in the federal Senate) publicly reaffirmed their commitment

---

tively promoted economic liberalization, and emphasized education as an engine of socioeconomic development.

[76] By July 2000, the organization had as many as three million members; Mizrahi n.d.1: 181. There were precedents for this parallel electoral structure in entrepreneur-led campaigns in Chihuahua in the early and mid–1980s and in Manuel J. Clouthier's 1988 presidential campaign; see Mizrahi 1995: 87 and Loaeza 1999: 445–48. Arriola (1998), focusing especially on Carlos Castillo Peraza's term as PAN president (1993–1996), also notes many examples of tension between Fox and the PAN's leadership.

to work together effectively.[77] Nevertheless, the PAN's congressional delegation offered only tepid support for the Fox administration's first important legislative initiative, a constitutional reform to promote the rights of indigenous peoples (Hernández Navarro 2001). Some of the underlying difficulty in the PAN–Fox relationship may involve unresolved tensions within the PAN itself, especially political differences between a more ideologically coherent party leadership (in part a product of the party's tightly controlled internal selection procedures) and a much more heterogeneous voter base that in 2000 was mobilized in some measure by Fox's charisma and pragmatism.[78]

Second, the PAN will be challenged to define a longer-term agenda to promote democratic deepening in Mexico. Party alternation in power is a crucial step toward political democracy. It builds pluralism by increasing the number of politically relevant actors; encourages institutionality in interactions among different branches of government (between the legislature and the executive, for example, or between the federal and state governments) by giving renewed life to formal constitutional arrangements; invites the redefinition of relations between parties and societal actors; foments freedom of expression in the mass media; and, especially, transforms citizens' expectations about elections and the meaning of the vote. Yet, as the chapters in this volume on Chihuahua and Guanajuato amply demonstrate, partisan alternation in power is often conflictive. The character of this process depends upon both the policies that a new government pursues (and the errors it commits) and the attitudes and actions adopted by the party (in this case, the PRI) now in opposition. Because alternation in public office necessarily affects numerous interests, it is a process that produces multiple winners and losers.

Facing a new and sometimes highly uncertain environment, parties themselves may confuse elections with democracy. One risk is "partyarchy," a situation in which parties overwhelmingly dominate the political game and block initiatives from nongovernmental organizations or other groups in civil society.[79] For example, the Baja California PAN, once in power, had less incentive to undertake democratizing reforms in the broader structure of government, especially measures that would enhance the representativeness of political institutions and expand citizen participation in governmental processes (Guillén López, this volume). Promoting such changes—including the development of innovative arrangements to mediate state-society relations—may prove

---

[77] See *La Jornada*, July 4, 2000, p. 6; August 3, 2000, p. 6; August 6, 2000, p. 3.

[78] On this point, see Magaloni and Moreno n.d.

[79] See Coppedge 1994: 2, 18–20, for a definition of partyarchy and a discussion of the ills it produces.

to be a particularly difficult challenge for the PAN precisely because it has historically lacked strong ties to groups such as organized labor, peasants, and the lower-class urban population. The situation is particularly complicated because it is the PAN's principal electoral opponent, the PRI, that has traditionally monopolized the partisan representation of such groups.[80]

The PAN has not always passed these tests at the municipal and state levels. Constrained by both limited experience in public administration and a shortage of material resources, at times it has proved incapable of managing the citizenry's high expectations that party alternation in power will quickly translate into an immediate end to corruption in government and public security forces, the resolution of urgent social problems, and rapid improvements in the overall quality of life. The party has also often encountered difficulties in developing organizational arrangements to institutionalize relations between *panista* elected officials and major sociopolitical constituencies. As a consequence, the PAN has sometimes fared poorly in subsequent elections. For instance, although the PAN won 542 elections for municipal president between 1989 and 1998, it secured consecutive victories in only 123 cases (22.7 percent).[81]

Finally, the PAN will be challenged to design and implement public policies that reduce Mexico's immense socioeconomic inequalities, drawing on its Catholic social reform heritage to ensure that political democratization also delivers real improvements in the quality of life for average citizens. Perhaps the principal paradox of Fox's election was that the full realization of the Mexican Revolution's call for "effective suffrage, no reelection" brought to national power the party that PRI partisans long disparaged as the party of counterrevolution. In the revolutionary struggle that erupted in 1910, cries for liberal political freedoms were closely linked with insistent demands for improved economic and social opportunities for peasants and workers and constitutional guarantees of collective social rights. In marked contrast, during the 1980s and 1990s the PAN's advocacy of political opening was joined with its support for neoliberal economic measures that frontally challenged some of the principal social legacies of the Mexican Revolution. Even though the PAN historically has represented different forces

---

[80] For examples of the difficulties the PAN has encountered in building such linkages at the state level, see Mizrahi 1998a: 168–74.

[81] Mizrahi n.d.1: 40 n. 7, 123, 163 n. 12. Mizrahi (pp. 118–19, 167, 185–86) argues that the party's difficulties in consolidating its bases of support once in office may be related to its restrictive internal rules and organizational structure.

For examples of successful party-building efforts by *panista* gubernatorial administrations in Baja California and Guanajuato, see Mizrahi n.d.1: 189–92.

than those incorporated in the PRI–led coalition that ruled during the "century of the Mexican Revolution," its new responsibilities as national governing party will compel it to reassess how best to reconcile agendas of political *and* socioeconomic democratization.

REFERENCES

Alonso Sánchez, Jorge. 1996. "Jalisco: los problemas de una alternancia," *Frontera Norte* 16 (July–December).
Ames, Barry. 1970. "Bases of Support for Mexico's Dominant Party," *American Political Science Review* 64 (1).
Arriola, Carlos. 1998. "La lucha por el poder en el PAN." In *Homenaje a Rafael Segovia*, edited by Fernando Serrano Magallón. Mexico City: El Colegio de México/Fondo de Cultura Económica/Consejo Nacional de Ciencia y Tecnología.
Basáñez, Miguel. 1991. *El pulso de los sexenios: 20 años de crisis en México*. Rev. ed. Mexico City: Siglo Veintiuno.
Camp, Roderic A. 1989. *Entrepreneurs and Politics in Twentieth-Century Mexico*. New York: Oxford University Press.
———. 1995. "The PAN's Social Bases: Implications for Leadership." In *Opposition Government in Mexico*, edited by Victoria E. Rodríguez and Peter M. Ward. Albuquerque: University of New Mexico Press.
Chand, Vikram K. 2001. *Mexico's Political Awakening*. Notre Dame, Ind.: University of Notre Dame Press.
Coppedge, Michael. 1994. *Strong Parties and Lame Ducks: Presidential Partyarchy and Factionalism in Venezuela*. Stanford, Calif.: Stanford University Press.
Domínguez, Jorge I., and James A. McCann. 1996. *Democratizing Mexico: Public Opinion and Electoral Choices*. Baltimore, Md.: Johns Hopkins University Press.
Espinoza Valle, Víctor Alejandro. 1998. *Alternancia política y gestión pública: el Partido Acción Nacional en el gobierno de Baja California*. Tijuana, Mexico: El Colegio de la Frontera Norte.
Estrada Sámano, Fernando. n.d. "Economía y posición de Acción Nacional." Manuscript.
Gibson, Edward L. 1996. *Class and Conservative Parties: Argentina in Comparative Perspective*. Baltimore, Md.: Johns Hopkins University Press.
González, Luis E. 1995. "Continuity and Change in the Uruguayan Party System." In *Building Democratic Institutions: Party Systems in Latin America*, edited by Scott Mainwaring and Timothy R. Scully. Stanford, Calif.: Stanford University Press.
Haggard, Stephan, and Robert R. Kaufman. 1995. *The Political Economy of Democratic Transitions*. Princeton, N.J.: Princeton University Press.
Hernández Navarro, Luis. 2001. "PAN: cenit y nadir." *La Jornada*, January 30.
Hernández Vicencio, Tania. 2001. "De la oposición al poder: el PAN en Baja California, 1986–2001." Manuscript.
Loaeza, Soledad. 1988. *Clases medias y política en México: la querella escolar, 1959–1963*. Mexico City: El Colegio de México.

————. 1999. *El Partido Acción Nacional: la larga marcha, 1939–1994; oposición leal y partido de protesta.* Mexico City: Fondo de Cultura Económica.

Mabry, Donald J. 1973. *Mexico's Acción Nacional: A Catholic Alternative to Revolution.* Syracuse, N.Y.: Syracuse University Press.

Magaloni, Beatriz, and Alejandro Moreno. n.d. "Catching All Souls: The Partido Acción Nacional and Christian Democracy in Mexico." In *Christian Democracy in Latin America,* edited by Scott Mainwaring and Timothy R. Scully. Forthcoming.

Mainwaring, Scott, Rachel Meneguello, and Timothy J. Power. 2000. "Conservative Parties, Democracy, and Economic Reform in Contemporary Brazil." In *Conservative Parties, the Right, and Democracy in Latin America,* edited by Kevin J. Middlebrook. Baltimore, Md.: Johns Hopkins University Press.

Mainwaring, Scott, and Timothy R. Scully. n.d. "Christian Democracy in Latin America: An Overview." In *Christian Democracy in Latin America,* edited by Scott Mainwaring and Timothy R. Scully. Forthcoming.

Martínez-Valle, Adolfo. 1999. "Los militantes católicos y el PAN: una historia política, 1939–1962," *Este País* 102 (September).

Marván Laborde, María. 1988. "La concepción del municipio en el Partido Acción Nacional," *Revista Mexicana de Sociología,* April–June.

Mecham, J. Lloyd. 1966 [1934]. *Church and State in Latin America: A History of Politico-Ecclesiastical Relations.* Rev. ed. Chapel Hill: University of North Carolina Press.

Meyer, Jean. 1973–1976. *La cristiada.* 3 vols. Mexico City: Siglo Veintiuno.

Middlebrook, Kevin J. 1986. "Political Liberalization in an Authoritarian Regime: The Case of Mexico." In *Latin America.* Vol. 2 of *Transitions from Authoritarian Rule: Prospects for Democracy,* edited by Guillermo O'Donnell, Philippe C. Schmitter, and Laurence Whitehead. Baltimore, Md.: Johns Hopkins University Press.

————. 2000. "Conservative Parties, Elite Representation, and Democracy in Latin America." In *Conservative Parties, the Right, and Democracy in Latin America,* edited by Kevin J. Middlebrook. Baltimore, Md.: Johns Hopkins University Press.

Mizrahi, Yemile. 1995. "Entrepreneurs in the Opposition: Modes of Political Participation in Chihuahua." In *Opposition Government in Mexico,* edited by Victoria E. Rodríguez and Peter M. Ward. Albuquerque: University of New Mexico Press.

————. 1996a. "La nueva relación entre los empresarios y el gobierno: el surgimiento de los empresarios panistas," *Estudios Sociológicos* 41 (May–August).

————. 1996b. "¿Administrar o gobernar? El reto del gobierno panista en Chihuahua," *Frontera Norte* 16 (July–December).

————. 1998a. "Dilemmas of the Opposition in Government: Chihuahua and Baja California," *Mexican Studies/Estudios Mexicanos* 14 (1).

————. 1998b. "The Costs of Electoral Success: The Partido Acción Nacional in Mexico." In *Governing Mexico: Political Parties and Elections,* edited by Mónica Serrano. London: Institute of Latin American Studies, University of London.

————. n.d.1. "From Martyrdom to Power: The Partido Acción Nacional in Mexico." Manuscript.

————. n.d.2. "El Partido Acción Nacional: de la oposición al gobierno." Manuscript.

Partido Acción Nacional. 1997. *Plataforma política del Distrito Federal, 1997–2000: democracia para un buen gobierno.* Mexico City: Comité Directivo Regional/ Distrito Federal, Partido Acción Nacional.

Prud'homme, Jean-François. 1997. "The National Action Party's (PAN) Organization Life and Strategic Decisions." Documentos de Trabajo, no. 59. Mexico City: División de Estudios Políticos, Centro de Investigación y Docencia Económicas.

Reveles Vázquez, Francisco. 1994. "El desarrollo organizativo del Partido Acción Nacional," *Revista Mexicana de Ciencias Políticas y Sociales* 156 (April–June).

————. 1998. "Las fracciones del Partido Acción Nacional: una interpretación," *Revista Mexicana de Sociología* 60 (3).

Rodríguez, Victoria E. 1995. "Municipal Autonomy and the Politics of Intergovernmental Finance: Is It Different for the Opposition?" In *Opposition Government in Mexico,* edited by Victoria E. Rodríguez and Peter M. Ward. Albuquerque: University of New Mexico Press.

Rodríguez, Victoria E., and Peter M. Ward. 1992. *Policymaking, Politics, and Urban Governance in Chihuahua: The Experience of Recent Panista Governments.* U.S.–Mexican Policy Report No. 3. Austin: Lyndon B. Johnson School of Public Affairs, University of Texas at Austin.

Stansfield, David E. 1996. "The PAN: The Search for Ideological and Electoral Space." In *Dismantling the Mexican State?* edited by Rob Aitken et al. London: Macmillan/St. Martin's Press.

Tarrés, María Luisa. 1990. "Middle-Class Associations and Electoral Opposition." In *Popular Movements and Political Change in Mexico,* edited by Joe Foweraker and Ann L. Craig. Boulder, Colo.: Lynne Rienner.

Vanderbush, Walt. 1999. "Assessing Democracy in Puebla: The Opposition Takes Charge of Municipal Government," *Journal of Interamerican Studies and World Affairs* 41 (2).

von Sauer, Franz A. 1974. *The Alienated "Loyal" Opposition: Mexico's Partido Acción Nacional.* Albuquerque: University of New Mexico Press.

Ward, Peter M. 1995. "Policy Making and Policy Implementation among Non–PRI Governments: The PAN in Ciudad Juárez and in Chihuahua." In *Opposition Government in Mexico,* edited by Victoria E. Rodríguez and Peter M. Ward. Albuquerque: University of New Mexico Press.

Wuhs, Steven T. 2000. "Frequent Freedoms and Intermittent Interventions: Centralization in Mexico's Partido Acción Nacional." Manuscript.

PART 2

THE CHANGING CONTOURS OF THE PARTIDO ACCIÓN NACIONAL

2

Democratization through Federalism? The National Action Party Strategy, 1939–2000

Alonso Lujambio

In comparative perspective, what distinguishes Mexico's transition toward democracy is its timing. To some extent, the gradualist character of the Mexican transition was determined by the absence of inclusive opposition coalitions and the presence of a federal institutional framework that made such a gradual transitional route possible.[1] Without doubt, the key protagonist in the Mexican transition through federalism has been the National Action Party (PAN), founded in 1939.

This chapter analyzes the evolution of the PAN's electoral apparatus within Mexico's federal institutional framework and the dilemmas the party faced in the postrevolutionary era's noncompetitive party system. The first part of the essay examines the origin of the PAN's gradualist conception of political change. The second considers the way in which, over the course of six decades, the party has constructed its presence in Mexico. The third section discusses how the constitutional framework (especially federalism and presidentialism) shaped the character of the Mexican transition to democracy (1988–2000) and what role the PAN played in this twelve-year democratization process.

TWO FOUNDING FATHERS, ONE IDEA

This section has two fundamental objectives, one tied to the political debate in contemporary Mexico and the other to academic discussions.

The author thanks Felipe Calderón Hinojosa, Wayne Cornelius, Fernando Estrada Sámano, and especially Federico Estévez and Kevin J. Middlebrook for their comments on an earlier version of this essay. Translated by Robyn Gutteridge and Kevin J. Middlebrook.

[1] For the author's discussion of the tensions among exclusionary, majoritarian, presidentialist, and consensual-inclusive federalism in the Mexican transition to democracy, see Lujambio 1994a.

The first objective is to refute the widely held view that the PAN moved away from its oppositional stance following the highly contested 1988 presidential election and entered into a pact with the government of President Carlos Salinas de Gortari (1988–1994). Under this pact, the PAN supposedly altered its oppositionist character and promised its congressional support for certain constitutional reforms proposed by the Salinas administration, in exchange for recognition of PAN electoral victories at the municipal and state levels and for electoral reforms at the federal level. To the contrary, the evidence suggests that the PAN's strategy during the late 1980s and early 1990s was consistent with ideas that date from the 1930s.

The second objective is to offer a rejoinder to Donald Mabry, author of one of the best and most ambitious book-length studies of the National Action Party (Mabry 1974a). Mabry subsumes the municipal-federalist mission of the PAN within the thinking on subsidiarity (with a social Christian stamp) of Catholic intellectual Efraín González Luna (1898–1964), one of two principal *panista* ideologues. It will be demonstrated here that the PAN's municipal-federalist vocation has roots in the liberal thought of the party's founder, Manuel Gómez Morin (1897–1972), and that these roots predate the actual establishment of the PAN in September 1939. Influenced by several political and intellectual traditions (Gómez Morin's liberalism, Progressivism, and the subsidiarity of González Luna), the two founders/ideologues of the National Action Party concurred on a core political strategy for the PAN—that political change in Mexico ought to begin not with alternation in the presidency, but at the most basic organizational level of Mexican federalism, the municipality.[2]

Gómez Morin belonged to a generation of university faculty who, in the first years of reconstruction following the 1910–1920 revolution, wanted to bring "order out of chaos." In 1920, following the assassination of President Venustiano Carranza (1917–1920), Gómez Morin abandoned academia to become private secretary to General Salvador Alvarado, secretary of finance in the interim government of Adolfo de la Huerta (1920).[3]

In October 1920, Alvarado sent Gómez Morin to New York to serve as the Ministry's representative in that capital of world finance. Shortly after his return in 1921, Gómez Morin was named under-secretary of finance. In September 1921, he wrote a short essay on the role that mu-

---

[2] María Marván Laborde (1988) detected this duality, but she gave greater importance to social Christian thought in defining the PAN's municipal-federalist vocation. Based on new evidence, this essay offers a different argument.

[3] For more on the life of Gómez Morin until the early 1930s, see Krauze 1976; Garciadiego 1996.

nicipal government should play in postrevolutionary political change, and it is this author's belief that in this short piece the PAN found its municipalist and federalist vocation.[4]

In his essay—which appeared as a prologue to *El desastre municipal en la República Mexicana,* by Gómez Morin's friend, Modesto Rolland— Gómez Morin developed a central idea of liberal thought that he had sketched out earlier in his law school thesis (Gómez Morin 1919). Although this earlier writing reveals that Gómez Morin was an admirer of Mexican liberal thought, he felt it provided only rhetorical solutions and did not address in practical terms the problems that Mexico faced at the time. From 1920 onward, he was preoccupied with finding practical remedies for Mexico's political and social problems.

In his prologue to the Rolland book, Gómez Morin at last identified a concrete answer to his critique of classic nineteenth-century liberalism. To make liberalism's precepts more than "unattainable popular yearnings," Gómez Morin advocated the need to "make contact with reality" and discuss "the grave problems affecting the organization of Mexican cities." Gómez Morin was undoubtedly influenced by the Progressive Movement in the United States, with which he came into contact through intellectuals he met while working in New York for the Ministry of Finance. He conceived of the municipality as the perfect sphere for citizen participation, for the solution of social problems, and for the exercise of *responsible* government. This conceptualization shaped his vision of needed political changes in municipal institutionality. In line with the Progressives, who demanded open primaries and the direct election of senators and state and municipal officials in order to control local political bosses and their electoral machines, Gómez Morin insisted that municipal autonomy should not be understood as a shield for "underhanded politicians"—that is, the caciques who dominated local politics in Mexico.[5]

From 1921 forward, Gómez Morin became increasingly disenchanted with the Mexican Revolution. He thought of the municipality, "far from congressionalism, far from presidentialism, far from parliamentarism," as the sphere in which citizens could experience "a direct

---

[4] Surprisingly, this essay has largely been overlooked by Gómez Morin's biographers.

[5] The Biblioteca Gómez Morin contains several works from the 1920s and 1930s on municipal administration in the United States. Particularly noteworthy is *The Modern City and Its Government,* by William Parr Capes (1922). Capes was especially influenced by the Progressives' ideas. Gómez Morin underlined various sections in this publication, several of which are translated in the margins of the book. The author thanks Federico Estévez for suggesting the influence of the Progressives on Gómez Morin.

and immediate exercise of true liberty and democracy." Gómez Morin thought of the municipality as the institution from which citizens could control abuses of power.

Three months after writing the prologue to the Rolland book, Gómez Morin returned to New York on behalf of the Ministry of Finance. When he returned once more to Mexico City in 1922, he was made director of the school of law at the National Autonomous University of Mexico (UNAM). Along with other changes in the curriculum, Gómez Morin added a course on municipal administration (Garciadiego 1996: 33).

One of the candidates in the special presidential election held in 1929 was José Vasconcelos, former rector of the UNAM and secretary of education under President Álvaro Obregón (1920–1924). Vasconcelos embodied the interests of young academics, professionals, and the urban middle classes. He was also a teacher and friend of Gómez Morin. Gómez Morin, tired of "petty revolutions with little generals," enthusiastically supported his friend's candidacy. Nevertheless, he criticized Vasconcelos's messianic idealism and declared himself in favor of "gradual improvement," advocating a permanent political party that did not view the triumph of a single individual as its principal goal and the measure of its success. Gómez Morin was not an advocate of presidential campaigns; even the triumph of "the best man," he felt, would result in "a terrible state of affairs because of the lack of organizational discipline." He proposed instead to "sacrifice immediate triumph in favor of building a base of power, a foundation that could only come from an organization with a clear and correct orientation and the capacity for sustaining itself over the long term." Vasconcelos, however, scorned the idea of forming a permanent party (Krauze 1976: 242, 273, 279). The opportunity to create a political party for the long term—Gómez Morin's "gradualism"—lost out to messianic idealism in 1929.

The final chapter in the public life of Gómez Morin prior to the founding of the National Action Party involved his appointment as rector of the UNAM in 1933–1934,[6] at a moment when socialism was spreading throughout the educational system. As rector, Gómez Morin traveled across Mexico to present his ideas on academic freedom to university faculties. These tours proved important in the formation, five years later, of the National Action Party because the contacts Gómez Morin had made were useful in the early territorial organization of the party. By April 1940, the PAN had militants in seventeen of Mexico's (then) twenty-nine states (*Boletín de Acción Nacional*, April 1, 1940).

The PAN's other great ideologue, Efraín González Luna, concurred with Gómez Morin regarding the need to plot a municipal-federalist

---

[6] For more on this period in Gómez Morin's life, see Meyer et al. 1995.

route to political change in Mexico. Nevertheless, he appealed to a different doctrine and rationale.[7] Born in Jalisco in 1898 into a family with strong Catholic roots, in 1921 González Luna became president of the Jalisco chapter of the Catholic Association of Mexican Youth (ACJM), an organization founded to promote the church's social doctrine. Despite being a militant Catholic and certainly opposed to the religious intolerance of Mexico's postrevolutionary governments, González Luna—in contrast to many members of the ACJM—refused to participate in the Cristero movement in the 1920s and the National Sinarquist Union (UNS) in the 1930s (Meyer 1974, 1979), rejecting the violence of the former and the predominantly clandestine character of the latter. The National Action Party attracted González Luna precisely because it rejected violence and strove toward openness.

González Luna's extensive writings do not reveal his theoretical and doctrinal sources or his preferred authors in the municipal-federal literature (see González Luna 1974–1977). He was, however, clearly influenced by the experience of Christian Democratic parties in Europe, where federalist arrangements did much to encourage Catholic political involvement during the period of party system formation in the late nineteenth and early twentieth centuries.[8] In a report presented at the PAN's second regional convention in Jalisco in 1940, González Luna adhered closely to the subsidiarity argument in social Christian doctrine, concluding that the PAN's political struggle had to begin at the municipal level.[9] According to González Luna, the ideal institution to satisfy an individual's need for material and spiritual well-being was the family. But because family resources did not always suffice, the municipality was constructed as a sphere in which families could resolve "problems that overflow the confines of the home." For González Luna, the municipality would provide what the family could not. To this end, Mexican politics needed to be reconstituted "from the bottom up." In order to break the control of local caciques, communities had to confront electoral fraud, "a grotesque travesty that serves only to perpetuate *caciquismo* and corrupt government.... It is the municipalities

---

[7] There have been two attempts at a biography of González Luna: Bravo Ugarte 1968 and Alonso 1998, 1999.

[8] According to Carl Hodge (1987): "In Switzerland, Austria and Germany, federalism integrated the body of Social Christian thought in defense of solidarity, benefits, mutualism, pluralism and the value of local and regional autonomy within the framework of the unified State."

[9] This interpretation is also based on a 1942 essay entitled "El municipio mexicano," which extends the arguments in González Luna 1974–1977, vol. 2, pp. 29–57, and on the transcript of González Luna's speech to one of the commissions of the Jalisco regional convention.

that will save Mexico," González Luna concluded; "it is in the municipalities that the struggle must be waged that will decide the nation's destiny."

FROM CONCEPT TO STRATEGY

Preliminary Steps: Manuel Gómez Morin, 1939–1949

Popular reactions to the policies of President Lázaro Cárdenas (1934–1940) spurred forward Gómez Morin's project to establish a political party. At its inception, the PAN gathered together liberal followers of revolutionary leader Francisco Madero and Vasconcelos, Catholics averse to socialist education, entrepreneurs opposed to the economic and labor policies of the Cárdenas administration, and Catholic university students, including both progressive students belonging to the Unión Nacional de Estudiantes Católicos (National Union of Catholic Students) and conservative student members of the ACJM.[10] Their task was monumental: to push forward political change from the municipal level while enmeshed in a hegemonic system of local party organizations established after 1929 precisely to protect the "official" party's grip on political power.

Fifteen months after its formation, the National Action Party began participating in municipal elections.[11] As a first step, the party established its National Commission for Municipal Action, which included such prominent founding members as Carlos Ramírez Zetina, Enrique M. Loaeza, and Rafael Preciado Hernández. Then in the municipal elections of December 1, 1940, the PAN ran candidates in Guadalajara and Monterrey, displaying from the outset the party's predominantly urban character. The PAN also competed for municipal office in the port of Tampico, Tamaulipas.

The PAN lost to the ruling party's candidates in all three elections. Yet party members saw the losses as only one battle in a longer war. When asked what the PAN proposed to do, Gómez Morin responded, "We will carry on" (*Boletín de Acción Nacional*, December 15, 1940). His words became a refrain for *panistas* following subsequent electoral defeats.

---

[10] On the political attitude of the middle classes in the 1940 presidential succession, see Loaeza 1988: 78–118.

[11] After 1939, the PAN decided at its conventions whether to participate in elections. In 1939, 69 percent of convention delegates voted in favor of participation, and 31 percent voted for abstaining. However, the party was still so young that the decision had little practical impact (*Boletín de Acción Nacional*, September 2, 1942).

The party participated in only two municipal elections in 1941—in Morelia, Michoacán, and Chihuahua, Chihuahua (*Boletín de Acción Nacional*, January 1942; Calderón Vega 1967: 81). It ran no candidates in municipal-level elections in 1942 and 1943 (see table 2.1). Part of the explanation for this lack of electoral engagement may be Mexico's declaration of war on the Axis countries in May 1942. Indeed, on the very day that Mexico declared war, Gómez Morin and Roberto Cosío y Cosío (president and secretary general of the PAN, respectively) visited President Manuel Ávila Camacho (1940–1946). Ten days later, the PAN's National Executive Committee (CEN) issued a press release stating, "All Mexicans have a duty to contribute to the immense common effort ... to strengthen national unity.... [This] is an unconditional obligation ... of all Mexicans.... There is no room for partisan interests.... National Action subordinates all its activities [to this essential purpose of unity]" (Calderón Vega 1967: 86–87). The question, of course, is whether "all activities" was meant to include electoral activities. No official party explanation was ever offered for the PAN's absence from the municipal electoral arena during these years.

Nevertheless, the PAN did participate in 1943 (for the first time) in elections for the federal Chamber of Deputies (see table 2.2). At the party's convention in 1943, there were forty-nine votes in favor of competing in these elections and thirty-one against. The PAN ran candidates in ten out of twenty-nine states (Aguascalientes, Chihuahua, Coahuila, Guerrero, Jalisco, Michoacán, Nuevo León, Oaxaca, Querétaro, San Luis Potosí) and the Federal District, areas where the party reportedly had some organizational presence in 1940. In other areas (Colima, Hidalgo, Nayarit, Puebla, Tamaulipas, and Yucatán), the party apparatus was so weak that the PAN was unable to run any candidates (*La Nación*, July 10, 1943). The party won 5 percent of the total vote (Calderón Vega 1980: 80), claiming victory for four candidates (two in Guerrero and one each in Oaxaca and Querétaro). It also demanded that the Electoral College annul results in eight electoral districts because of vote fraud (Medina 1987: 207). This outcome suggests that the ruling party was not rewarding the PAN for supporting its policy of "national unity" by staging clean elections.

Thus the hypothesis that the PAN did not run candidates in order to avoid generating conflict during World War II does not stand. It is more likely that the PAN did not present candidates at the municipal level in 1942 and 1943 because of organizational weaknesses, because the party's electoral committees decided not to participate, because local authorities refused to allow the party to register candidates (as frequently happened in later years), or because of some combination of these factors. It may even be the case that the party *did* participate, but historical sources have failed to report these instances. It suffices to

Table 2.1. **PAN Participation in Municipal Elections, 1943–1999**

Year	Recognized Electoral Victories	Percentage of Population with PAN Government	Unrecognized Wins	PAN Vote as Percentage of Total Vote	Ratio of Municipalities with PAN Candidates to Total Municipalities Holding Elections, and Percent	Percentage of Voters Living in Municipalities with PAN Candidates
1943	0	0.00	0	NA	NA	NA
1944	0	0.00	0	NA	NA	NA
1945	0	0.00	0	NA	NA	NA
1946	1	0.00	0	NA	26/NA	NA
1947	0	0.04	0	NA	38/NA	NA
1948	1	0.04	0	NA	80/NA	NA
1949	0	0.06	0	NA	22/NA	NA
1950	2	0.02	1	NA	12/NA	NA
1951	0	0.08	0	NA	8/NA	NA
1952	6	0.08	1	NA	80/NA	NA
1953	0	0.1	0	NA	8/NA	NA
1954	0	0.02	0	NA	8/NA	NA
1955	1	0.12	0	NA	3/NA	NA
1956	3	0.17	1	NA	58/NA	NA
1957	0	0.17	0	NA	NA	NA
1958	0	0.05	0	NA	14/NA	NA
1959	1	0.01	4	NA	NA	NA
1960	0	0.02	0	NA	NA	NA
1961	0	0.02	0	NA	NA	NA
1962	1	0.02	0	NA	NA	NA
1963	1	0.09	0	NA	NA	NA
1964	0	0.09	0	NA	NA	NA

1965	3	0.09	0	NA	NA	NA
1966	2	0.08	0	NA	39/370 (11%)	NA
1967	10	0.19	0	NA	77/851 (9%)	NA
1968	2	1.42	5	NA	85/1,148 (7%)	NA
1969	1	1.62	0	NA	NA	NA
1970	0	1.51	0	NA	NA	NA
1971	2	0.29	1	NA	16/1,087 (1%)[1]	NA
1972	2	0.03	2	NA	53/377 (14%)	NA
1973	5	0.10	1	NA	67/807 (8%)[2]	NA
1974	7	0.63	7	NA	93/1,153 (8%)	NA
1975	1	0.97	1	NA	25/378 (7%)	NA
1976	3	0.71	0	NA	94/793 (12%)[3]	NA
1977	5	0.82	0	4	149/1,174 (13%)	35
1978	1	0.78	1	NA	34/378 (9%)	30
1979	7	0.91	0	NA	130/867 (15%)	32
1980	8	1.08	3	7	225/1,174 (19%)	62
1981	3	1.04	0	7	65/378 (17%)	55
1982	10	1.11	2	12	295/869 (34%)	61
1983	17	2.91	4	18	297/1,174 (25%)	69
1984	3	5.69	5	11	119/378 (31%)	70
1985	3	5.57	2	12	388/868 (45%)	72
1986	12	2.61	0	16	367/1,167 (31%)	74
1987	1	1.12	0	9	167/381 (44%)	81
1988	13	1.03	0	15	348/852 (41%)	68
1989	21	3.46	0	17	393/1,159 (34%)	81
1990	10	5.33	0	16	220/380 (58%)	84
1991	32	6.93	0	19	312/671 (46%)	75

Table 2.1 continued

Year	Recognized Electoral Victories	Percentage of Population with PAN Government	Unrecognized Wins	PAN Vote as Percentage of Total Vote	Ratio of Municipalities with PAN Candidates to Total Municipalities Holding Elections, and Percent	Percentage of Voters Living in Municipalities with PAN Candidates
1992	54	10.85	0	26	486/1,260 (39%)	83
1993	17	12.64	0	17	405/458 (88%)	96
1994	41	12.34	0	23	460/561 (82%)	93
1995	160	20.30	0	37	806/1,477 (55%)	90
1996	88	28.26	NA	28	318/353 (90%)	97
1997	36	33.38	NA	31	621/649 (96%)	99
1998	168	37.72	NA	29	833/1,416 (59%)	94
1999	80	33.10	NA	19	151/231 (65%)	86

Sources: For recognized electoral victories, Secretaría de Estudios, Partido Acción Nacional. For the proportion of Mexico's population living under PAN municipal governments, Lujambio 2000: 84. For unrecognized wins, Álvarez de Vicencio 1995: 107–53. For the PAN vote as a proportion of the total vote and for the proportion of voters living in municipalities in which a PAN candidate ran for the municipal presidency, electoral data from the Universidad Autónoma Metropolitana, the Instituto Tecnológico Autónomo de México, *Reforma*, Presidencia de la República, and de Remes 2000. For municipalities with PAN candidates for the municipal presidency, various issues of *La Nación*, Calderón Vega 1975, and de Remes 2000.

Note: Election timetables were altered in Chiapas (1994), Yucatán (1995), Tlaxcala and Jalisco (1997), and the State of México (1999).

[1] Data are unavailable for the state of Guerrero.

[2] Data are unavailable for the state of Tlaxcala.

[3] Data are unavailable for the states of Querétaro and Tlaxcala.

NA = Not available.

Table 2.2. **PAN Participation in Elections for the Federal Chamber of Deputies, 1943–2000**

Year	Percentage of Districts with a PAN Candidate	PAN Percentage of Total Vote	Percentage of PAN Vote Coming from the Federal District	PAN Percentage of Congressional Seats	PRI Percentage of Congressional Seats	Bills Presented by PAN in Congress
1943	14	5	NA	0	NA	—[3]
1946	39	2	60	3	91	—[3]
1947–1949	47	6	56	3	96	21
1950–1952	89	8	21	3	94	3
1953–1955	55	9	42	4	94	4
1956–1958	86	10	36	—[2]	94	9
1959–1961	53	8	50	3	96	0
1962–1964	98	12	37	10	83	4
1965–1967	99	11	37	9	83	36
1968–1970	95	14	38	9	84	18
1971–1973	88	16	41	11	82	12
1974–1976	67	9	45	8	82	23
1977–1979	100	12	30	11	74	8
1980–1982	100	18	25	13	75	55
1983–1985	100	16	22	10	72	23
1986–1988	100	18	21	20	52	86
1989–1991	100	18	16	18	64	102
1992–1994	100	27	13	24	60	39
1995–1997	100	27	9	25	48	71
1998–2000	100	38	11[1]	41	42	159

Sources: For the percentage of districts with PAN candidates, various issues of *La Nación*. For the PAN's percentage of the total vote, Calderón Vega 1980: 80; Comisión Federal Electoral; Instituto Federal Electoral. For the percentage of the PAN vote coming from the Federal District, Peschard 1989 and the author's analysis of data from the Instituto Federal Electoral. For percentages of congressional seats held by the PAN and the PRI, Molinar Horcasitas 1991: 51; Lujambio 1987: 43, 52, 55, 106–108; 1995: 115, 145, 149; 2000: 38. For the number of bills presented by the PAN in Congress, Martorelli 2000: 29.

Note: Beginning with the 1947–1949 period, data on various aspects of the PAN's electoral performance and on the PAN's and PRI's congressional representation refer to the last year indicated (for example, data given for 1947–1949 are from 1949). Information on PAN's legislative activity (the column at the far right) refers to the entire three-year period indicated.

[1] In the 2000 elections, the PAN allied with the Mexican Ecological Green Party (PVEM).

[2] The PAN withdrew i:s six representatives from the 1958–1961 session of the federal Chamber of Deputies.

[3] The PAN had no federal deputies in this legislative session.

NA = Not available.

note that the PAN's electoral apparatus was still weak and that many local electoral committees may have opted to abstain, especially in light of the 38.8 percent of delegates who took this position at the party's 1943 convention. Other factors that could have accounted for nonparticipation are the high financial cost of electoral competition and the expectation that, in any case, the ruling party would resort to fraud to deny the PAN its victories (as reportedly occurred in municipal elections in 1940 and 1941).

In 1944, the PAN ran candidates in municipal elections in the city of Aguascalientes and in La Piedad, Michoacán. And in Zamora, Michoacán, the party supported the candidate of another local party, the Club Cívico Zamorano (Zamoran Civic Club). In the Zamora case, the local PAN leader was jailed and then released following the election, and the election was marred by vote fraud—two tendencies that would surface with frequency in subsequent years (Calderón Vega 1967: 142). But the PAN's most important electoral action in 1944 was the presentation of its first gubernatorial candidate—Aquiles Elorduy, in the state of Aguascalientes (see table 2.3). According to Calderón Vega, "the election was one more consummate fraud" (1967: 132). What was new was that the PAN petitioned the Supreme Court to investigate this violation of the public trust, basing its case on provisions in constitutional article 97, paragraph 3. The Supreme Court, arguing that it was "not competent" to interpret the provisions in the article, rejected the petition,[12] and the PAN was left with no judicial recourse for demanding clean elections.

The PAN did not participate in any municipal elections in 1945, but it did support other parties' candidates in two elections for municipal president. One of these was Manuel Barragán, joint candidate of the Laborista Regiomontano (Monterrey Labor) and the Constitucionalista Democrático (Democratic Constitutionalist) parties for the municipal presidency of Monterrey, the capital of Nuevo León. Once again, fraud was widespread (Calderón Vega 1967: 175). The PAN unsuccessfully petitioned the Supreme Court to investigate the case.

In the second case, the PAN supported Carlos Obregón, the candidate of the Unión Cívica Leonesa (León Civic Union), for municipal president of León, Guanajuato. Fraud was rampant, and the December

---

[12] The "lack of competence" position, which dates from the second half of the nineteenth century, aims to avoid politicizing the Supreme Court by denying it the faculty to judge matters related to electoral irregularities. Yet Article 97 of Mexico's 1917 Constitution established that the Supreme Court could investigate—either on its own account or by petition from the president, one of the chambers of Congress, or a governor—matters that constitute a "violation of the ballot." Nevertheless, the Court systematically rejected such petitions in order to avoid becoming embroiled in political struggles.

16, 1945, elections were followed on January 2, 1946, by huge demonstrations. The army fired on the crowd, killing twenty-six protesters and seriously wounding at least thirty others. President Ávila Camacho then asked the Permanent Congressional Commission for a "declaration of the removal of powers" from the state of Guanajuato. On January 8, the state's governor, Ernesto Hidalgo, was removed from office, and in February 1946 Carlos Obregón assumed the municipal presidency of León.

The year 1946 ended the first stage of electoral competition by the PAN. Since its founding in 1939, the party had fielded its own candidates in only seven municipalities, and it had never won.[13] Nor had the PAN's congressional candidates met with success in 1943. Yet at the 1946 party convention there were 155 votes in favor of (and 13 against) participating in the upcoming July general elections.

In 1946 the PAN hoped to nominate Luis Cabrera, secretary of finance under President Carranza, as its first presidential candidate. Cabrera, however, declined to run under the PAN banner. Nevertheless, for the first time the PAN participated in senatorial elections, fielding twenty-four candidates, and the party increased the number of its candidates for the federal Chamber of Deputies, reaching 58 (39.4 percent) of the country's 147 electoral districts (table 2.2). (In 1943 the party had competed in only 14 percent of all electoral districts.)

And in 1946, for the first time in the PAN's history, its victories were recognized. Four PAN candidates won seats in the federal Chamber of Deputies. All of them represented predominantly urban areas: Aquiles Elorduy in Aguascalientes; Juan Gutiérrez Lascuráin in the Federal District; Miguel Ramírez in Tacámbaro, Michoacán; and Antonio L. Rodríguez in Monterrey. In the latter half of 1946, the PAN ran twenty-six candidates for municipal presidencies (table 2.1),[14] and in a four-month period, the PAN more than tripled the number of candidates who had represented the party in the first seven years of its history.

In part, this development reflected the party's municipalist strategy for building up to national elections, which joined the national party apparatus and all local party organizations in a common objective. It also reflected changes in 1946 in Mexico's election law that significantly reduced the number of parties in the system. When the Mexican Communist Party (PCM) lost its official registration at the beginning of the

---

[13] As a point of reference, there were 2,336 municipal governments in Mexico in 1950.

[14] Another member of the PAN competed for a municipal presidency in Durango under the banner of the Partido Electoral Gomezpalatino (Gómez Palacio Electoral Party) when he was denied registration as a PAN candidate.

Table 2.3. **PAN Participation in Gubernatorial Elections by State, 1946–1999 (election year and rounded percentage of total vote)[1]**

States[2]	1946–52	1952–58	1958–64	1964–70	1970–76	1976–82	1982–88	1988–94	1994–99
NORTH									
Baja California[3]	—	1953	1959	1965	1971 (35%)	1977 (29%)	1983 (30%)	1989 (52%)	1995 (50%)
Baja California Sur[4]	—	—	—	—	0	1981 (4%)	1987 (13%)	1993 (47%)	1999 (6%)
Chihuahua	1950	1956 (27%)	1962	1968	0	1980 (16%)	1986 (35%)	1992 (51%)	1998 (41%)
Coahuila	0	1957	0	0	0	1981 (16%)	1987 (14%)	1993 (26%)	1999 (34%)[10]
Durango	0	0	0	0	0	1980 (7%)	1986 (34%)	1992 (33%)[6]	1998 (30%)
Nuevo León	1949	0	0	0	1973 (16%)	1979 (22%)	1985 (23%)	1991 (33%)	1997 (49%)
San Luis Potosí	0	0	0	0	0	0	1985	1991 (33%)[7]	1997 (39%)
Sinaloa	0	0	0	0	0	1980 (8%)	1986 (29%)	1992 (36%)	1998 (32%)
Sonora	0	0	0	1967	0	1979 (16%)	1985 (28%)	1991 (24%)	1997 (32 %)
Tamaulipas	0	0	0	0	0	1980 (1%)	1986 (7%)	1992 (26%)[6]	1998 (26%)
Zacatecas	0	0	0	0	0	1980 (4%)	1986 (3%)	1992 (13%)	1998 (13%)
WEST CENTRAL									
Aguascalientes	1944	0	1962	0	1974 (17%)	1980 (10%)	1986 (17%)	1992 (20%)	1998 (52%)
Colima	0	0	1961	1967	1973 (2%)	1979 (8%)	1985 (9%)	1991 (14%)	1997 (38%)
Guanajuato	0	0	0	0	0	1979	1985 (18%)	1991 (35%)[8]	1995 (56%)
Jalisco	1952	0	1964	0	0	1982 (22%)	1988 (27%)	—[9]	1995 (53%)
Michoacán	0	1956	1962	1968	0	1980 (3%)	1986 (9%)	1992 (7%)	1995 (25%)
Nayarit	0	0	0	0	0	0	1987 (2%)	1993 (4%)	1999 (51%)[11]
Querétaro	0	0	0	0	0	0	1985 (13%)	1991 (19%)	1997 (45%)
CENTER									
Federal District	—	—	—	—	—	—	—	—	1997 (16%)[12]
Hidalgo	0	0	0	0	0	1981 (1%)	0	1993 (6%)	1999 (32%)[13]
México	0	0	0	0	1975 (12%)	1981 (8%)	1987 (11%)	1993 (18%)	1999 (35%)[13]
Morelos	0	0	0	0	0	0	1988 (8%)	1994 (10%)	—[14]
Puebla	0	0	0	0	1974 (16%)	1980 (9%)	1986 (12%)	1992 (17%)	1998 (29%)
Tlaxcala	0	0	0	0	0	1980 (3%)	1986 (2%)	1992 (3%)	1998 (8%)

SOUTH									
Campeche	0	0	0	0	0	0	1985 (2%)	0	1997 (3%)
Chiapas	0	0	0	0	0	1982 (3%)	1988 (5%)	1994 (9%)	—[14]
Guerrero	0	0	0	0	0	0	1986 (3%)	1993 (3%)	1999 (2%)
Oaxaca	0	0	0	1968	1974	1980 (4%)	1986 (4%)	1992 (5%)	1998 (10%)
Quintana Roo[5]	—	—	—	—	0	1981 (1%)	0	0	1999 (17%)
Tabasco	0	0	0	0	0	0	0	1994 (3%)	—[14]
Veracruz	0	0	0	0	0	1980 (1%)	1986 (4%)	1992 (3%)	1998 (26%)
Yucatán	0	0	0	1969	0	1981 (16%)	1987 (10%)	1993 (37%)	1995 (44%)
TOTAL	4/28	4/29	6/29	7/29	7/31	24/31	28/31	29/31	32/32
Percent	14%	14%	21%	24%	23%	77%	90%	94%	100%

Sources: Secretaría de Estudios of the Partido Acción Nacional; various issues of *La Nación*; electoral data compiled by Juan Molinar Horcasitas; and data banks of election results at the Universidad Autónoma Metropolitana, the Instituto Tecnológico Autónomo de México, the Instituto Federal Electoral, and Presidencia de la República. The 1956 results for Chihuahua come from Vicencio 1991, vol. 1: 306.

1 In some instances (for example, Baja California in 1953, 1959, and 1965) the available sources indicate that the PAN ran a gubernatorial candidate, but information concerning the PAN's share of the vote is unavailable. In these cases, the table includes only the date of the gubernatorial election. In cases in which the PAN did not run a candidate, the table reports "0."

2 The regional distribution of states was provided by Federico Estévez.

3 Gubernatorial elections were first held in Baja California in 1953.

4 Gubernatorial elections were first held in Baja California Sur in 1974.

5 Gubernatorial elections were first held in Quintana Roo in 1975.

6 In coalition with the Party of the Democratic Revolution (PRD).

7 In coalition with the Party of the Democratic Revolution (PRD) and the Mexican Democratic Party (PDM).

8 Post-election conflict resulted in the appointment of a *panista* as interim governor. Special gubernatorial elections were called for 1995, and the PAN won that election with 56 percent of the vote.

9 The election calendar was altered.

10 In coalition with the Party of the Democratic Revolution (PRD), Labor Party (PT), and Mexican Ecological Green Party (PVEM).

11 In coalition with the Party of the Democratic Revolution (PRD) and the Labor Party (PT).

12 In 1997, for the first time since the 1920s, the head of government for the Federal District was chosen through a popular election.

13 In coalition with the Mexican Ecological Green Party (PVEM).

14 Gubernatorial elections were held in 2000.

Cold War, the PAN consolidated its position as the principal opposition party to Mexico's postrevolutionary regime. From this point forward, the regime was forced to recognize some PAN victories in congressional elections in order to legitimate itself. In so doing, it walked a tightrope between recognizing a sufficient number of PAN victories to assure that the PAN would continue to play a role within the system, thereby legitimating the regime, but not so many as to allow the PAN to build strength.

Winning recognition of the four congressional election victories in 1946 encouraged the PAN to present more candidates at the municipal level. In elections held on December 1, 1946 (the day that President Miguel Alemán [1946–1952] took office), the PAN won its first municipal-level victory in Quiroga, a small, semi-rural municipality of 10,000 inhabitants in the state of Michoacán. Recognition of that victory produced extraordinary enthusiasm within the party, whose members saw the event as a turning point. On February 5, 1947, during the PAN's fifth national convention, Gómez Morin dedicated his speech to the municipal question:

> We have always focused on the municipality. And whenever possible, we have participated in municipal campaigns to overturn electoral "victories" won by fraud. This demonstrates the urgent need for citizen action to free the municipality—and along with it, the whole of Mexico—from the degradation of a system of lies, incompetence, and thievery.... Civic action that challenges persistent electoral fraud will not be subverted or stopped. It is the fruit of a mature recognition that *the process of social renovation must be gradual, advancing by increments, but ultimately successful and complete* (emphasis added).[15]

Of course, the "gradual and incremental" political change sought by the PAN did not satisfy all of its members all of the time. Although those who preferred to abstain from electoral competition remained a minority in 1947 (prior to the federal elections in 1946, only 8 percent of party convention delegates voted against participation), Gómez Morin had to convince them of the need to continue in the "eternal struggle."

---

[15] Gómez Morin 1950: 201. It must be remembered that, until 1977, national parties had to obtain permission from municipal authorities to compete in local elections. Opposition parties long argued that these authorities obstructed competition by demanding that opposition parties satisfy a plethora of requirements.

According to Gómez Morin, "To intervene in the municipalities' struggle is the road to power."[16]

However, the plan to pursue a municipal-federalist route to power required institutional changes to make it effective, and this encouraged the incorporation of new cadres into the PAN's ranks. In February 1947, the PAN—now with representatives in Congress—presented a bill to reform Article 115 of the Constitution. The initiative proposed a revised division of fiscal responsibilities among federal, state, and municipal governments; referenda to revoke the power of municipal authorities (paralleling the achievements of the Progressives); enabling district judges to hear complaints regarding violations of voters' rights in local elections; and, of special importance for a minority party, proportional representation in municipal councils. The PAN also proposed the creation of a federal electoral tribunal to administer Article 97 of the Constitution and to define the conditions under which the Supreme Court would investigate electoral fraud. The PAN's bill also included provisions for a national citizens' registry and permanent voter registration cards with photographs (PAN 1990: vol. 1). Yet in the end, all of these proposals were defeated.

During the 1947–1949 period, the PAN participated actively in races for municipal presidencies and for seats in Congress.[17] In 1948 the party put forward candidates in eighty municipalities, half of them in the states of Nuevo León and Jalisco. No doubt encouraged by the election of Antonio L. Rodríguez as a federal deputy representing Monterrey, the PAN launched a vigorous campaign in that city. When its municipal candidate lost, the party organized large demonstrations protesting fraud, but to no avail. Meanwhile, the PAN won the small municipality

---

[16] In various reports over his ten years as party president, Gómez Morin insisted on the inevitable, gradual character of political change in Mexico. In 1944, he said, "Complete political reform demands time; the creation of institutions must be measured; it has to be slow, tutelary, and educational work; it will also be the fruit of repeated and not always successful efforts. One does not overturn in a single day a state of affairs created over the course of a century." In 1946 he spoke of the need to take steps "on the long and difficult road to make democratic life flourish in Mexico.... We must not forget that our duty is unending; do not struggle for a day only, but for eternity and for the inheritance of our children." In 1948 he stressed the need to "fight responsibly to provide a gradual perfecting of our institutions." And in February 1949, he spoke of "the need to proceed gradually in the slow process of renovation" (Gómez Morin 1950).

[17] The PAN was denied registration in Puebla in 1947, but a party member competed for the municipal presidency of the state capital under the banner of the Unión Cívica Pro Puebla (Pro-Puebla Civic Union).

Notably, Calderón Vega's memoirs contain no mention of fraud in the 1947 elections.

of El Grullo in Jalisco, though Calderón Vega's memoirs mention "indisputable triumphs" in three other municipalities (Calderón Vega 1975: 133, 137).

Gómez Morin concluded his term as party president in 1949, a year in which the PAN participated in twenty-two municipal campaigns. With the exception of Santa Clara, Durango, party officials made no mention of fraud in these elections (Calderón Vega 1975: 226). Also in 1949, the PAN nominated its second gubernatorial candidate, Antonio L. Rodríguez of Nuevo León (table 2.3). However, the party's experience in Monterrey had disheartened party followers, and Rodríguez lost the election.

In the 1949 federal legislative elections, the PAN again increased its participation by running sixty-nine candidates (47 percent of all electoral districts). The party won four congressional seats, three in states where the PAN had stepped up its involvement in municipal elections (Jalisco, Michoacán, and Nuevo León) and the fourth in Mexico City. The PAN vigorously protested incidences of electoral fraud (allegedly, voters were transported to the polls in government trucks, some voters cast multiple ballots, ballot boxes were stolen, and so on), and it requested that the Supreme Court initiate an investigation. However, by a vote of fifteen to five, the Supreme Court declined to intervene (Calderón Vega 1975: 199). Once more, the institutional road for contesting electoral fraud was blocked, and this time the PAN was unable to mount a successful political protest.

During its first ten years, then, the PAN fielded 173 candidates for municipal president, 2 for governor, 79 for the federal Chamber of Deputies, and 24 for the federal Senate. In his farewell speech as party president, Gómez Morin called on the PAN to continue its struggle to "rescue the municipality." According to Gómez Morin, this could only be achieved through "strong organization, expanded cadres, and a flexible division of labor among them in order to make individual actions more effective and to lighten … the heavy burden of work" (Gómez Morin 1950: 277–98). Who in 1949 was willing to take on the "heavy burden of work" within the PAN? The answer was Catholic factions of the party. However, the evidence suggests that they did not follow Gómez Morin's injunction to strengthen the party's organization.

The "Catholic Era": Weak Organization and Anti-System Behavior, 1950–1961

In September 1949, Juan Gutiérrez Lascuráin was the unanimous choice for president of the PAN's National Executive Committee. His presidency marked the beginning of the "Catholic era" in the history of the National Action Party, the least studied and the most inscrutable stage in the PAN's development. Gutiérrez Lascuráin, born in Mexico City in 1911, was an engineer by profession. He had been a member of the ACJM before joining the PAN in 1943, and he later became leader of the party in the Federal District. He served in the federal Chamber of Deputies from 1946 to 1949, when, as coordinator of the party's parliamentary group, he worked closely with Gómez Morin. During his leadership of the CEN until 1956, the PAN presented 177 candidates for municipal presidencies. The efforts of the next two CEN presidents— Alfonso Ituarte Servín (1956–1959) and José González Torres (1959–1962), both former leaders of Catholic organizations—were similar.

In 1950, the PAN fielded twelve candidates for municipal president, nine in Michoacán and three in Morelos (table 2.1). Of these, two electoral victories were recognized (in Tzintzuntzan and Quiroga, both in Michoacán). Also that year, the PAN presented its third gubernatorial candidate—Juan Miramontes, in Chihuahua. Miramontes lost, and the PAN alleged that the PRI had stuffed ballot boxes prior to the opening of the polls (Calderón Vega 1975: 254). Although nothing suggests that support for the PAN was overwhelming, it is highly probable that Miramontes had some backing simply because Chihuahua was (and continues to be) a state where the PAN electoral apparatus is strong.[18]

In 1951, PAN candidates ran for municipal presidencies only in Nuevo León, competing in eight of the state's municipalities (down from twenty-one in 1948). The drop may have been due to the discour-

---

[18] The information on electoral fraud since 1950 is taken from the book by PAN sympathizer María Elena Álvarez de Vicencio (1995). Of course, it is by definition very difficult to know what impact fraud had on the PAN. Up to this point, this chapter has reproduced the observations made by Calderón Vega in his *Memorias*; even though his comments might be influenced by partisan interest, they probably contain some element of truth with regard to the phenomenon of electoral fraud. In her book, Álvarez de Vicencio presents a list not of municipalities in which there was fraud against the PAN (which would surely number in the hundreds), but of those municipalities in which "proof of victory was offered, but the decision was against [the PAN]" (p. 110).

Certainly some observers might think that some instances of fraud have not been included, or that the inclusion of other cases does not do justice to what in fact occurred there. However that may be, for the purposes of this essay it is certainly useful to have an account offered by the PAN itself, based on its own criteria and not those of this author. Moreover, there is no reason to believe that there is any exaggeration in a list of forty-one municipalities (stretching over a period of forty-five years) where the PAN won but where its victory was not recognized.

Álvarez de Vicencio does not indicate why her list begins in 1950 and not before, nor why it ends in 1985.

aging outcomes in the 1948 municipal elections and the 1949 gubernatorial election. The PAN did not win a single contest in 1951.

The most important electoral event for the PAN during the 1950–
1952 period was the nomination in 1952 of Catholic intellectual Efraín
González Luna as the party's first presidential candidate. On various
campaign tours he was accompanied by leaders of the National Sinarquist Union, an ultraconservative, Catholic-oriented organization
with fascist tendencies. Even though González Luna took pains to voice
his opposition to violence in politics, the growing relationship between
the PAN and the UNS (first fostered by Gutiérrez Lascuráin) reinforced
public perceptions of the PAN's Catholic identity, something Gómez
Morin had tried to avoid (Martínez Valle 1995: 60).

González Luna's presidential candidacy sparked broad interest in
the electoral process and stimulated the participation of PAN candidates in federal Chamber of Deputies and Senate races. The PAN
fielded 143 candidates for the Chamber of Deputies (89 percent of all
electoral districts) and 47 for the Senate (out of the 58 seats being contested). González Luna's intense presidential campaign greatly expanded the PAN's electoral constituency in geographic terms, although
the party was unable to capitalize fully on this achievement in subsequent local elections. In 1952, national election authorities recognized
five PAN victories in races for the federal Chamber of Deputies—two
seats from the Federal District, and one each from Jalisco, Michoacán,
and Oaxaca.

Eighty PAN candidates ran for municipal presidencies in 1952,
sixty-four of them in Jalisco (the home state of Efraín González Luna).
For governor of Jalisco, the PAN nominated Jaime Robles, one of four
PAN deputies in the 1949–1952 federal legislature. It is clear that the
PAN took advantage in Jalisco's municipal races of the organizational
energy derived from the presidential campaign. However, the PAN
failed to attend to other arenas of municipal competition, perhaps in-
hibited by a lack of resources. It is possible that the party was concen-
trating its scarce resources on those races in which it had the best
chances of success, but the narrowly focused PAN effort may also have
been due to a lack of political vision on the part of Gutiérrez Lascuráin.[19]

The 1953–1955 period was not a successful one for the PAN. In 1953
the party presented only eight candidates for municipal presidencies
(seven in Michoacán, one in Sinaloa). The PAN lost these contests, but
not because of fraud. One important event in 1953 was the nomination

---

[19] Six PAN municipal victories were recognized in 1952, one in Jalisco and five in
Oaxaca (four of these in municipalities with fewer than a thousand inhabitants).
See table 2.1.

of the PAN's first gubernatorial candidate in Baja California, a state that would become a bastion of PAN support. The PAN lost this election as well, even though the leader of the state PAN, Salvador Rosas Magallón, had been a preeminent advocate of statehood for Baja California, a status which it finally received in 1952.

The PAN had a very low electoral profile in 1954. Only four candidates ran for municipal presidencies in Nuevo León (compared with twenty-one in 1948 and eight in 1951), two in the State of México, and two in Guerrero. The PAN lost in all of these races, but no fraud was reported. In 1955, the PAN in Jalisco initially fielded candidates in eighty-four municipalities but subsequently withdrew them when it became clear that the elections would not be conducted honestly. The same thing happened in municipal elections in Baja California and Tamaulipas. These events led the PAN's leaders to stress the need for electoral reform at the party's national assembly in October 1955.

In 1955 the PAN's participation in municipal elections was restricted to Chiapas, where it ran three candidates. The candidate in Simojovel, a municipality with 14,000 inhabitants, won, and his victory was recognized. In the federal midterm elections held that year, the PAN reentered the competition for seats in the Chamber of Deputies, though it did not reach the level of activity it had achieved in 1952. The party only presented candidates in 55 percent of all electoral districts. It attracted 9 percent of the officially recorded vote and won in six districts, three in the Federal District and one each in Chiapas, Morelos, and Oaxaca.

In 1956, the PAN put forward candidates in fifty-eight municipalities, including thirty in Oaxaca, where it was no doubt motivated by its triumphs in 1952.[20] The party also presented its second candidate for governor of Chihuahua, Luis H. Álvarez, in 1956 (table 2.3). According to Calderón Vega, electoral fraud was scandalous in this race. Demonstrators strongly protested the fraud, and a caravan traveled from Chihuahua to Mexico City to petition the Supreme Court to launch an investigation. By a vote of sixteen to two, the justices declined.[21]

Alfonso Ituarte Servín became president of the PAN in 1956 and served in that capacity until 1959.[22] His Catholic credentials were strong;

---

[20] Victories were reported in three small municipalities.

[21] In table 2.1, the "unrecognized victory" in 1956 corresponds to the northern border city of Ciudad Juárez (hometown of Luis H. Álvarez), where the PAN claimed it had documented its victory.

[22] Data on the PAN's participation in elections are sketchy for these years, in part because Ituarte Servín focused on municipal elections in only one of his annual addresses, and in part because the publication *La Nación* stopped reporting de-

he had been a member of the Liga Nacional Defensora de la Libertad Religiosa (National League for the Defense of Religious Freedom), a member of the Asociación Pro-Libertad Religiosa (Association for Religious Liberty), and president of the ACJM from 1953 to 1955. In 1958, the PAN only participated in fourteen municipal elections, six of which were in Chiapas, where the party's rate of participation rose after its triumph in Simojovel.

Without doubt, the 1958 presidential election was a crucial point in the PAN's history. Luis H. Álvarez, a gubernatorial candidate in Chihuahua in 1956, was nominated as the party's presidential candidate. In federal Chamber of Deputies races, the PAN put forward candidates in 86 percent of the country's electoral districts (table 2.2), and its candidates contested fifty of the sixty Senate seats being filled. The PAN officially received 10 percent of the national vote, but the party detected fraud in several areas. Six PAN candidates won seats in the Chamber of Deputies, but the party withdrew them from the Congress to protest the extensive electoral irregularities. Tensions between the PAN and the PRI–led national government had reached a critical point.

This situation was exacerbated in 1959. José González Torres became president of the PAN in March of that year. He had previously been general secretary of the conservative Unión Nacional de Padres de Familia (National Union of Parents), president of Pax Romana (an international organization of Catholic students), president of the ACJM, and president of Acción Católica (Catholic Action). González Torres had joined the PAN in 1953 "searching for religious and educational liberty" (Vives Segl 2001), and he hoped to link the party with the World Union of Christian Democrats.[23] González Torres, whose discourse was vehemently anticommunist, was a Catholic militant whose actions were motivated by ideology; he aggressively repudiated anything to do with the established regime. Under his leadership, there was no possibility of negotiated political change.

But the government ratcheted up the conflict even further. In the 1959 gubernatorial election in Baja California, the PAN nominated Salvador Rosas Magallón as its candidate. The administration of Governor Braulio Maldonado, the first constitutional governor of Baja California, was widely viewed as a high-water mark of corruption in postrevolutionary Mexico, and in the election to choose Maldonado's successor, the PAN's Rosas Magallón demonstrated widespread popularity. He was, however,

---

tailed information on municipal elections. As a result, this author was unable to unearth all instances of PAN electoral participation at the municipal level.

[23] There was a blossoming of Christian Democracy in Latin America during the 1950s. Between 1950 and 1963, Christian Democratic parties were formed in fifteen Latin American countries. See Díaz 1996.

denied victory through fraud. In the ensuing protests, eight hundred PAN activists were arrested and sent to state prisons.

By the end of González Torres's period as PAN president in 1962, the percentage of Mexico's population governed by the PAN at the municipal level had not changed; it was still almost zero (see table 2.1). There is no evidence that the PAN grew as an organization or as an electoral apparatus at the municipal level from 1956 to 1962, and no data are available regarding the PAN's participation in municipal elections during the earlier years of the Catholic era. However, one can deduce that construction of the PAN's electoral machinery was neglected throughout the "Catholic era" (1950–1962). During this period, the party's discourse became increasingly combative (and anticommunist), but tangible actions such as the presentation of legislative initiatives in Congress were very weak. Although PAN candidates were elected to three national legislatures during this period, they presented only sixteen initiatives (compared to twenty-two bills submitted in the first legislature to which a PAN candidate was elected). It had become painfully clear that, under the direction of presidents representing the party's strongly pro–Catholic Church factions, the PAN was not advancing on any front. The party needed to redefine its ideology and strategy; the "Catholic era" had come to an end.

From Christlieb to Crisis, 1962–1976

In the debate over a successor to González Torres, González Luna—a Catholic, but more moderate in his views than González Torres—openly criticized the outgoing president: "Our road is not the road of a demagogue who wants to destroy everything in order to rebuild.... We need someone who will offer solutions." In 1962, the PAN convention selected Adolfo Christlieb, a young politician who in his first speech openly criticized González Torres and assured party members that he viewed politics as an opportunity for dialogue. However, he noted, "dialogue does not exist in Mexico's political reality.... Our politics has always been a series of monologues from the regime, with the regime, for the regime.... As long as there is no political reform ... the possibility for dialogue will remain closed" (*La Nación*, November 25, 1962).

Christlieb had represented the PAN on the Federal Electoral Commission in the 1961 midterm elections, and in this post he became well acquainted with Gustavo Díaz Ordaz, then secretary of the interior. After Díaz Ordaz became president of Mexico (1964–1970), he and Christlieb negotiated an important electoral reform that included semiproportional representation of minority parties in the federal Chamber of Deputies (Mabry 1974b). Díaz Ordaz also promised to respect the PAN's local electoral victories (Lujambio 1994b).

In the 1964 presidential election, Christlieb publicly recognized the triumph of Díaz Ordaz over the PAN's candidate, José González Torres (*La Nación*, July 12, 1964). This move further strained his relationship with González Torres, but public recognition was a first step in an exchange of gestures of goodwill between Christlieb and Díaz Ordaz. From 1962 to 1967, the PAN did not allege any electoral fraud at the local level, and it won official recognition of seventeen municipal victories—more than in the party's whole previous history (see table 2.1). The seventeen victories included two state capitals: Hermosillo, Sonora, and Mérida, Yucatán. Christlieb also managed to break through the one percent ceiling in terms of the share of the national population governed by the PAN.

Of course, recognition of a PAN victory was not always immediate. On occasion, Christlieb had to take proof of victory to Díaz Ordaz; the president would then pressure the local PRI apparatus to recognize the actual election outcome (Lujambio 1994b). Indeed, until the mid–1990s—given Mexico's inadequate legal framework (flawed local election laws and the absence of judicial bodies capable of ruling on electoral matters) and the regime's refusal to undertake reforms—the PAN had to rely on its relationship with the president in order to win recognition of its electoral victories at the local level.

Data on the number of PAN candidates competing at the municipal level during Christlieb's term as PAN president (1962–1968) are incomplete. Nevertheless, it is clear that Christlieb reenergized the party's electoral machinery because the PAN fielded 201 municipal presidential candidates from 1966 to 1968. During Christlieb's tenure, the PAN also ran ten gubernatorial candidates (compared to eleven in the previous twenty-three years) (see table 2.3). Moreover, thanks to Mexico's new semi-proportional electoral formula, Christlieb managed to run Chamber of Deputies candidates in nearly all of the country's electoral districts (98 percent in 1964, 99 percent in 1967; see table 2.2). In 1964, Christlieb placed candidates in races for 90 percent of the Senate seats being contested. Finally, encouraged by the spirit of dialogue with President Díaz Ordaz, the PAN submitted forty-three bills in Congress between 1964 and 1967.

In 1968, however, it became apparent that Christlieb's strategy had reached its maximum potential. In June of that year, the PAN claimed two municipal victories in Baja California, and in July it logged another three in Chihuahua. Not one was recognized (Christlieb 1968; Álvarez de Vicencio 1995). Witnessing the failure of the political direction he had provided to his party, Christlieb resigned as president in September, thereby severing the link between Díaz Ordaz and the rightist opposition. Five days later, on October 2, 1968, the Mexican army brutally repressed university students protesting in Mexico City's Tlatelolco plaza. This tragedy cost Díaz Ordaz all connection with his opponents on the left, and it marked the darkest week in the history of Mexico's postrevolutionary authoritarian regime.

The PAN's frustration with the electoral process escalated to the point that much of the party's membership favored abstaining from electoral participation, arguing that the conditions for free and fair competition did not exist. For example, there was widespread fraud in Yucatán's November 1969 gubernatorial election (in which the PAN had competed aggressively), and army troops took to the streets of Mérida, the capital city, to quell post-election protests. As a result of such developments, a right-leaning faction within the party, led by José Ángel Conchello (president of the PAN from 1972 to 1974), advocated supplementing electoral participation with even more aggressive actions.[24] Another faction, led by Efraín González Morfín (presidential candidate in 1970 and PAN president in 1975), favored abstaining from elections, but its motivations were linked with a more progressive position derived from social Christian thought.

By 1971, the PAN's participation in municipal elections was very low (tables 2.1, 2.4). Manuel González Hinojosa (president of the PAN from 1969 to 1971) reported that for 1971, local party organizations decided to abstain from participating in municipal elections in six states. His successor, José Ángel Conchello, attempted to increase the PAN's electoral participation, but it barely reached the levels attained by Christlieb between 1966 and 1968. At the 1973 party convention, those in favor of abstaining (44 percent of convention delegates) were stronger than ever before. Even so, in the midterm congressional elections Conchello managed to bring the PAN back to its historic participation level. The incumbent regime, perhaps hoping to quell the rising demand within the PAN for electoral abstention (which would have undermined the party's contribution to legitimating the regime) again began recognizing PAN victories. But it was too late.

In 1975, under the new leadership of González Morfín, the PAN once more scaled back its participation in municipal elections.[25] Over the course of the 1971–1976 period, twenty PAN victories were officially recognized, but twelve municipal elections were riddled with fraud, providing grist for both those party elements in favor of participating in elections and those in favor of abstaining. Internal tensions continued to rise.

---

[24] This group strengthened its anticommunist stance in reaction to the leftist discourse of President Luis Echeverría (1970–1976).

[25] In December 1975, González Morfín resigned as president of the PAN, accusing Conchello of maintaining a parallel presidency.

Table 2.4. **PAN Participation in Municipal Elections by Region, 1971–1999 (election year and rounded percentage of total vote)[1]**

States[2]	1971–73	1974–76	1977–79	1980–82	1983–85	1986–88	1989–91	1992–94	1995–97	1998–99
NORTH										
Baja California	1971 (31%)	1974 (21%)	1977 (30%)	1980 (27%)	1983 (31%)	1986 (35%)	1989 (47%)	1992 (47%)	1995 (49%)	1998 (44%)
Baja California Sur	1971 (1%)	1974[3]	1977[3]	1980[3]	1983 (10%)	1987 (14%)	1990 (32%)	1993 (54%)	1996 (39%)	1999 (16%)
Chihuahua	1971[3]	1974 (3%)	1977 (5%)	1980 (15%)	1983 (46%)	1986 (36%)	1989 (32%)	1992 (47%)	1995 (41%)	1998 (43%)
Coahuila	1972[3]	1975[3]	1978 (10%)	1981 (16%)	1984 (23%)	1987 (15%)	1990 (23%)	1993 (29%)	1996 (38%)	1999[6] (33%)
Durango	1971[3]	1974 (3%)	1977 (1%)	1980 (6%)	1983 (29%)	1986 (34%)	1989 (21%)	1992 (28%)	1995 (32%)	1998 (23%)
Nuevo León	1973 (16%)	1976 (24%)	1979 (13%)	1982 (10%)	1985 (18%)	1988 (21%)	1991 (34%)	1994 (45%)	1997 (49%)	—[7]
San Luis Potosí	1973[3]	1976[3]	1979 (1%)	1982 (16%)	1985 (18%)	1988 (21%)	1991 (36%)	1994 (31%)	1997 (39%)	—[7]
Sinaloa	1971 (2%)	1974 (0%)	1977 (1%)	1980 (13%)	1983 (24%)	1986 (26%)	1989 (27%)	1992 (33%)	1995 (41%)	1998 (33%)
Sonora	1973	1976 (15%)	1979 (16%)	1982 (34%)	1985 (24%)	1988 (20%)	1991 (25%)	1994 (30%)	1997 (31%)	—[7]
Tamaulipas	1971[3]	1974 (0%)	1977 (0%)	1980 (1%)	1983 (20%)	1986 (6%)	1989 (6%)	1992 (26%)	1995 (37%)	1998 (27%)
Zacatecas	1973 (1%)	1976[3]	1979 (1%)	1982 (5%)	1985 (3%)	1988 (7%)	—[5]	1992 (13%)	1995 (31%)	1998 (20%)

WEST CENTRAL

Aguascalientes	1971[3]	1974 (16%)	1977 (0%)	1980 (8%)	1983 (27%)	1986 (18%)	1989 (23%)	1992 (22%)	1995 (50%)	1998 (51%)
Colima	1973 (2%)	1976 (0%)	1979 (3%)	1982 (13%)	1985 (5%)	1988 (12%)	1991 (14%)	1994 (26%)	1997 (35%)	—[7]
Guanajuato	1973[3]	1976[3]	1979 (7%)	1982 (14%)	1985 (19%)	1988 (29%)	1991 (45%)	1994 (35%)	1997 (44%)	—[7]
Jalisco	1973	1976[3]	1979	1982 (21%)	1985 (20%)	1988 (29%)	—[5]	1992 (31%)	1995 (52%), 1997 (41%)	—[7]
Michoacán	1971[3]	1974	1977 (2%)	1980 (0%)	1983 (12%)	1986 (9%)	1989 (11%)	1992 (10%)	1995 (25%)	1998 (21%)
Nayarit	1972 (1%)	1975 (1%)	1978[3]	1981[3]	1984 (1%)	1987 (2%)	1990 (2%)	1993 (4%)	1996 (28%)	1999[8] (46%)
Querétaro	1973[3]	1976	1979[3]	1982 (18%)	1985 (15%)	1988 (20%)	1991 (23%)	1994 (30%)	1997 (45%)	—[7]

CENTER[4]

Hidalgo	1972 (1%)	1975[3]	1978[3]	1981 (0%)	1984 (5%)	1987 (1%)	1990 (4%)	1993 (6%)	1996 (16%)	1999 (22%)
México	1972	1975	1978 (6%)	1981 (7%)	1984 (13%)	1987 (13%)	1990 (16%)	1993 (16%)	1996 (30%)	—[5]
Morelos	1973 (2%)	1976 (2%)	1979 (2%)	1982 (6%)	1985 (9%)	1988 (8%)	1991 (4%)	1994 (9%)	1997 (18%)	—[7]
Puebla	1971 (9%)	1974	1977 (10%)	1980 (9%)	1983 (15%)	1986 (9%)	1989 (16%)	1992 (19%)	1995 (36%)	1998 (26%)
Tlaxcala	1973	1976	1979 (4%)	1982 (4%)	1985 (4%)	1988 (2%)	1991 (6%)	1994 (13%)	1996 (19%)	1998 (11%)

Table 2.4 continued

States	1971–73	1974–76	1977–79	1980–82	1983–85	1986–88	1989–91	1992–94	1995–97	1998–99
SOUTH										
Campeche	1973[3]	1976[3]	1979 (1%)	1982 (3%)	1985 (1%)	1988 (3%)	1991 (4%)	1994 (16%)	1997 (14%)	—[7]
Chiapas	1973[3]	1976 (1%)	1979 (2%)	1982 (7%)	1985 (4%)	1988 (4%)	1991 (6%)	—[5]	1995 (15%)	1998 (15%)
Guerrero	1971	1974	1977 (0%)	1980 (2%)	1983 (5%)	1986 (4%)	1989 (4%)	1993 (3%)	1996 (7%)	1999 (3%)
Oaxaca	1971[3]	1974 (2%)	1977 (1%)	1980 (1%)	1983 (4%)	1986 (3%)	1989 (4%)	1992 (4%)	1995 (18%)	1998 (17%)
Quintana Roo	1972	1975[3]	1978[3]	1981[3]	1984 (1%)	1987 (1%)	1990 (6%)	1993 (4%)	1996 (32%)	1999 (19%)
Tabasco	1973[3]	1976[3]	1979 (3%)	1982 (0%)	1985 (0%)	1988 (1%)	1991 (2%)	1994 (4%)	1997 (3%)	—[7]
Veracruz	1973	1976 (1%)	1979 (1%)	1982 (2%)	1985 (4%)	1988 (3%)	1991 (8%)	1994 (17%)	1997 (21%)	—[7]
Yucatán	1972 (8%)	1975[3]	1978	1981 (14%)	1984 (16%)	1987 (11%)	1990 (30%)	1993 (38%)	1995 (45%)	1998 (36%)

Sources: Various issues of *La Nación*, as well as data banks of election results at the Universidad Autónoma Metropolitana, the Instituto Tecnológico Autónomo de México, *Reforma*, the Instituto Federal Electoral, and Presidencia de la República.

[1] In some instances (for example, Jalisco and Sonora in 1973 and Michoacán in 1974) the available sources indicate that the PAN ran candidates for municipal president, but information concerning the PAN's share of the vote is unavailable. In these cases, the table includes only the date of the election.

[2] The regional distribution of states was provided by Federico Estévez.

[3] The PAN did not run candidates for municipal president in these elections.

[4] There are no elections for municipal president in the Federal District. The first popular elections for *delegados* were held in 2000.

[5] The election calendar was altered.

[6] The PAN ran coalition candidates (with the PRD, PT, and PVEM) in eight municipal contests: Francisco I. Madero, Frontera, Monclova, Muzquiz, Piedras Negras, Ramos Arizpe, Saltillo, and Torreón. See the List of Acronyms for individual party names.

[7] Municipal elections were held in 2000.

[8] The PAN ran in coalition with the PRD, PT, and the Partido de la Revolución Socialista (PRS), a local party.

NA = Not available.

At the next party convention, delegates decided in favor of continued participation, but they barely averted an acute crisis. Party rules demanded that 80 percent of convention delegates support a candidate in order for that candidate to become the official nominee. The centrist minority put forward their candidate, and on the first ballot this individual received 42 percent of the votes. By the seventh round, however, his support had slipped to 26 percent. Yet in open rejection of PAN tradition, the candidate did not withdraw. From this point forward, the convention became increasingly polarized and lacking in consensus regarding strategy. The ideologically moderate minority (inclined toward abstentionism) vetoed the decision of the right-wing majority faction (which strongly favored electoral participation). The result was institutional deadlock, and the delegates came to blows. As a consequence, the PAN did not nominate a presidential candidate in 1976, ran federal Chamber of Deputies candidates in only 67 percent of the electoral districts, and named federal Senate candidates in only half of the states in the country.[26]

From Crisis to Growth, 1977–1987

The 1976 presidential election was crucial for the regime. The PRI—along with its satellite parties, the Socialist Popular Party (PPS) and the Authentic Party of the Mexican Revolution (PARM)—nominated José López Portillo. However, the PAN, whose participation gave legitimacy to the system, did not nominate a candidate, and the ruling party had no one to campaign against. The result was a severe legitimacy crisis for the postrevolutionary regime. In 1977, the Congress approved a political reform that gave official registry to more opposition parties: the Mexican Democratic Party (PDM) on the right, and the Mexican Communist Party (PCM) and the Socialist Workers' Party (PST) on the left. The reform represented the regime's attempt to distance the political Left from the struggles of organized labor and guerrilla movements and to bring it into the institutional political sphere. At the same time that it increased the presence of opposition parties, the 1977 reform also undermined the PAN's monopoly over legitimation of the regime's political-electoral performance.

The reform created incentives for all opposition parties to increase their participation in electoral politics (Klesner 1988; Gómez 1991; Se-

---

[26] Loaeza 1987 is an excellent essay on this conflict.

Because of the PAN's internal crisis and minor parties' decisions to support the PRI's presidential candidate, the hegemonic PRI faced no registered opposition candidate in the 1976 presidential election. This was the first (and only) time this circumstance arose.

govia 1983). Three changes were especially important in encouraging the PAN to put forward more candidates on the municipal front. First, a constitutional reform made it possible for any nationally registered party to compete in state and municipal elections without hindrance from local-level election authorities. Second, officially registered parties were eligible for public funding, which meant that potential candidates were not so easily dissuaded by economic considerations. Third, the 1977 political reform established proportional representation for city councils in municipalities with more than 300,000 inhabitants—that is, the midsize and large urban areas that were important arenas of competition for the PAN. Thus, even when the PAN lost an election for municipal president, the party could still win representation in the city council.[27]

Yet institutional factors such as these, while important, ignore the internal variable that best explains the increase in PAN participation in municipal and state elections after 1977. In 1978, the PAN suffered a second internal split. The faction led by Efraín González Morfín abandoned the party, leaving the way clear for the party to pursue electoral participation. The PAN subsequently ran candidates in all electoral districts in federal Chamber of Deputies races (after 1979) and in all federal Senate elections (after 1982). The party also experienced a boom in terms of its participation in gubernatorial races. The PAN nominated gubernatorial candidates in twenty-four states in 1976–1982, twenty-eight states in 1982–1988, and twenty-nine states in 1988–1994 (table 2.3). Moreover, the PAN's presence increased rapidly at the municipal level, particularly after 1982 (see tables 2.1, 2.4). During the López Portillo administration (1976–1982), thirty-one PAN victories were recognized, and the party lost only four municipal elections because of fraud.

The sudden onset of severe economic crisis at the end of the López Portillo government and the 1982 bank nationalization drove businessmen into the PAN fold, including many from the middle classes and from Mexico's central and northern regions. All were eager to provide financial and other support to a party with which they felt an ideological affinity. In retrospect, it is clear that the economic debacle of 1982 initiated a realignment of voters that favored the PAN.[28]

The beginning of the administration of President Miguel de la Madrid (1982–1988) was a period of mixed relations between the PRI–led regime and the political opposition. In December 1982, the regime accepted four PAN victories but denied another through fraud. In 1983,

---

[27] The 1977 reform also established semi-proportional electoral systems for all state legislatures, thereby opening more avenues for advancing local opposition forces.

[28] For more on this period, see Loaeza 1990.

the government recognized seventeen additional PAN victories, although the PAN claimed that it lost four other races because of fraud. With these municipal victories (including Chihuahua, Ciudad Juárez, Durango, Uruapan, and Zamora), the PAN surpassed for the first time the 2 percent mark in terms of total population governed (table 2.1).

The first phase of the de la Madrid government ended in 1984, when electoral authorities recognized three PAN victories but denied the party five additional triumphs in races in which it claimed to have won (Álvarez de Vicencio 1995). The critical moment came in 1986. That year, extensive fraud in Chihuahua's gubernatorial election prompted national and international outrage (Molinar Horcasitas 1987), and the PAN demonstrated remarkable electoral strength in Baja California (winning the municipal presidency in Ensenada), in Sinaloa (garnering 29 percent of the vote in the gubernatorial race), and in Durango (obtaining 32 percent of the gubernatorial vote) (see tables 2.3, 2.4). These events strongly influenced the strategy that the PAN would follow in the 1988 presidential election, the most critical in twentieth-century Mexico.

THE PAN IN MEXICO'S TRANSITION TO DEMOCRACY, 1988–2000

In the months following the fraud-riddled 1988 presidential election, the PAN took decisions that would shape the evolution of Mexican politics in subsequent years. Cuauhtémoc Cárdenas's split from the PRI and the ensuing competition among opposition parties to list him as their 1988 presidential candidate had sparked confusion within the PAN leadership. In early 1988, some 85 percent of the members of the PAN's National Executive Committee believed that Cárdenas's candidacy was a smoke screen generated by the PRI to thwart the PAN's growing power (Lujambio n.d.). The fact that Cárdenas was standing as a candidate for three parties (the PPS, PARM, and the Socialist Workers' Party–Party of the Cardenista Front for National Reconstruction [PST–PFCRN]) that the PAN viewed as PRI satellites increased suspicion among the PAN membership. Furthermore, this manifestation of new *cardenismo* represented everything that the PAN rejected: corporatism, excessive state intervention in the economy, and postrevolutionary orthodoxy.

Following the official declaration of victory for the PRI's Carlos Salinas de Gortari in the 1988 presidential race, the PAN and Cárdenas initially agreed to form a political pact and demand a special election. Cárdenas later hardened his position and demanded that his victory in the presidential election be recognized. According to an official in the Salinas administration:

The PAN had nothing to gain in a special election. The election would go to the PRI or to Cárdenas. We had to convince the PAN that they would not gain anything. We pledged to reform the federal election law, and we promised that Chihuahua would not be repeated—that all future electoral victories by the PAN would be recognized. That was our offer (Lujambio n.d.).

The PAN accepted the offer: federal electoral reform and full recognition of PAN victories at the municipal and state levels.[29] The agreement between the PAN and Salinas in 1988 was somewhat reminiscent of the one with Díaz Ordaz in 1964. In both cases, the PAN accepted a PRI president in exchange for recognition of local electoral victories. But there was a difference. This time the PAN's cooperation came at a higher price, and now the PAN had the wherewithal to guarantee that the PRI kept its promises.

For the first time in postrevolutionary history, the PRI, with 52 percent of the seats in the federal Chamber of Deputies, could not reform the Constitution alone; it needed a coalition partner that would give it the needed two-thirds majority. And Salinas needed constitutional reform—first, to reprivatize the banks and implement an aggressive structural economic reform project, and second, to reform property rights in the countryside.[30] Salinas's economic project depended on the PAN's cooperation in the legislature. Moreover, the PAN's cooperation gave international credibility to Mexico's incipient process of economic and political change. Salinas recognized that a failure to fulfill promises made to the PAN would carry unacceptably high costs.

In December 1988, when the electoral authorities recognized PAN victories in eight municipalities (including the important cities of León and San Luis Potosí), a complex democratic transition began in which the president sometimes had to intervene to ensure that local PRI leaders—naturally ill-disposed to being the sacrificial victim—would accept defeat. Such actions underscored the urgent need for reform of federal and state-level election laws and the creation of trustworthy judicial authorities capable of ensuring free and fair local elections, obviating the need for presidential intervention in post-election conflicts.[31] In re-

---

[29] This decision brought about the third split in the PAN, when a minority, including José González Torres, helped form the Foro Democrático y Doctrinario (Democratic and Doctrinaire Forum). See Arreola 1994: chaps. 6 and 7; Reynoso 1993.

[30] The PAN, a democratic center-rightist party, had long demanded these constitutional reforms.

[31] Based on the federal electoral reforms of 1989–1990, 1993, 1994, and 1996, state-level election laws have undergone a parallel process of reform. See Crespo 1996; Becerra et al. 1996.

turn for its cooperation during the Salinas administration, the PAN won 185 municipalities, two governorships (Baja California in 1989 and Chihuahua in 1992), and one interim governorship (Guanajuato in 1991),[32] thus bringing some 20 percent of Mexico's population under a PAN government by 1994.

The new *cardenista* Party of the Democratic Revolution (PRD), which emerged out of a fusion in 1989 of the old Mexican Left and the fraction that had seceded from the PRI with Cárdenas, did not receive the same treatment. To the contrary, the Salinas administration systematically attacked it. When combined with the extreme weakness of the PRD's electoral apparatus and the party's more presidentialist orientation, its disadvantaged status impeded its advancement within the federal institutional framework (Lujambio n.d.).

The respective leaderships of the PRD and the PAN held markedly contrasting opinions regarding the relevance of the presidential versus the municipal-federalist route for Mexico's democratic transition (see table 2.5). The PRD bet everything on the 1994 presidential election, a very risky strategy.[33] The PAN, however, followed the federalist route, hoping to nibble away at the PRI bit by bit instead of devouring it in a single bite.

The PRD's problem in the 1994 elections was that Cuauhtémoc Cárdenas could only win the presidency if he had the backing of a broad opposition coalition. The PAN and the PRD, however, had become increasingly divided over the course of Salinas's term in office.

---

[32] The Guanajuato case was especially noteworthy. The PAN candidate, the very popular Vicente Fox Quesada, had been highly critical of Salinas. Fraud was rampant in the gubernatorial election, and postelectoral tensions ran high when Salinas allowed the PRI candidate, Ramón Aguirre, to be declared governor-elect. The PAN urged Aguirre to resign and demanded a new local election law and the holding of new elections. The PRI–dominated state legislature was being pressured to accept Aguirre's resignation and to name PAN member Carlos Medina Plascencia as interim governor (note that Fox was not included in the proposed solution) so that the state legislature and governor could negotiate a new election law. Later, Salinas made sure that a new gubernatorial election would be delayed until after he had left office. Medina's appointment to the governorship was seen in many circles as President Salinas's "gift" to the PAN. In the follow-up election in 1995, Fox won with 58.1 percent of the vote.

[33] However, at the end of Salinas's term in office, the PRD governed 4.7 percent of the country's population through the party's control of municipal presidencies. The party had 219 recognized municipal victories, 85 of them in Michoacán, the cradle of *cardenismo*. This figure far exceeded the PAN's performance over the first forty-four years of its history.

Table 2.5. **Party Leaders' Evaluation of Alternate Opposition Strategies: Federalism versus Presidentialism**

	PAN	PRD	PRI
	Percent N = 21	Percent N = 25	Percent N = 28
"The most important arena for the opposition is electoral competition for the presidency. The system will not change significantly unless change comes from the top. Once alternation in the presidency is achieved, democratization will follow in other areas of electoral competition (municipalities, governorships, state legislatures, and so on)."	0	80	4
"The most important arena for the opposition is electoral competition for local governments and especially for governorships. Winning elections at the local and state levels allows the opposition to gain experience and to prove itself as a viable political option. The likelihood of winning the presidency grows with each local- and state-level opposition electoral victory."	100	20	96

Sources: Author's interviews with PRI federal deputies and senators, members of the party's National Executive Committee, *priísta* cabinet officials, and three former presidents of Mexico; PRD federal deputies, senators, and members of the party's National Executive Committee; and PAN federal deputies, governors, and members of the party's National Executive Committee. The interviews were conducted between July 1993 and July 1994.

The PRD persistently criticized the PAN's federalist strategy because it presumed the legitimacy of the prevailing system and, hence, of the incumbent president.[34]

Between July 1993 and July 1994, eighty-six leaders of Mexico's three principal political parties were asked to rate all three parties in terms of their loyalty to the rules of the democratic game and to position the three parties on an ideological spectrum ranging from left to center to right (Lujambio n.d.). The leaders were also asked to consider how these variables had evolved over the span of the three elections in which all had participated (1979, 1985, and 1991), including the Left in its evolution from the PCM to the Mexican Unified Socialist Party (PSUM), the Mexican Socialist Party (PMS), and finally the Party of the Democratic Revolution (PRD). Figures 2.1, 2.2, and 2.3 present the responses.

PRI leaders perceived themselves as increasingly committed to democracy, although they acknowledged that much remained to be done (figure 2.1). They perceived the PAN as always and increasingly committed to democracy, and they recognized that the PRI came in second behind the PAN with regard to loyalty to the rules of the democratic game. However, PRI leaders viewed the Left as less democratic beginning at the time that dissenters exited the PRI with Cárdenas and united the Left. In ideological terms, PRI leaders perceived their party as center-right (having shifted from the center-left), and they increasingly perceived the opposition as centrists coming from the Left and the Right. That is, they viewed the PRI in the middle on both axes—situated between the democratic loyalty of the PAN and the disloyalty of the PRD, and between the *panista* Right and the *perredista* Left.

PAN leaders, for their part, considered their party the only democratic party in Mexico (figure 2.2). They recognized in their two rivals a growing commitment to democracy, but one still very far from their own degree of loyalty to the rules of the democratic game. In ideological terms, the *panistas* viewed themselves as having moved from center-right to center, and they did not see a great ideological distance between themselves and their rivals on the center-left (the PRD) and center-right (the PRI). Thus the obstacle to launching a PAN–PRD coalition candidate was not necessarily ideological; instead, it reflected deep distrust. PAN leaders did not perceive in the PRD a strong commitment to democracy.

---

[34] According to Porfirio Muñoz Ledo, then president of the PRD, "There are two strategies available, the gradualist and the democratic. The idea of gradual change supposes recognition of the illegitimate power of 'King Salinas'" (author interview, August 1993).

Figure 2.1. **PRI Perceptions of Parties' Ideological Positions and Commitment to Democracy, 1979–1993**

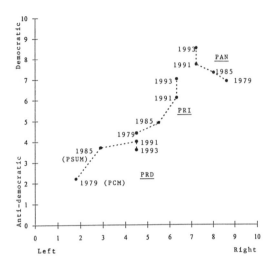

Sources: Same as in table 2.5.
Note: See List of Acronyms for individual party names.

Figure 2.2. **PAN Perceptions of Parties' Ideological Positions and Commitment to Democracy, 1979–1993**

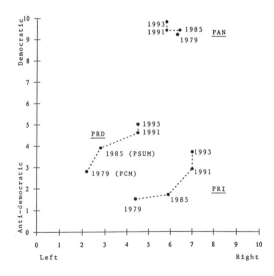

Sources: Same as in table 2.5.

Figure 2.3. **PRD Perceptions of Parties' Ideological Positions and Commitment to Democracy, 1979–1993**

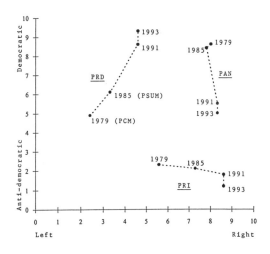

Sources: Same as in table 2.5.

According to PRD elites, their party was the only one occupying the democratic pole (figure 2.3). In the view of the PRD leadership, the PAN was committed to democracy in the late 1970s and early 1980s but then forgot its democratic mission and moved toward the anti-democratic pole, while the PRI, which already was authoritarian, became increasingly so. In ideological terms, the Mexican Left perceived itself as evolving from the left to the center-left. According to PRD leaders, the PRI shifted from a centrist position to the extreme right, a position it shared with the PAN. The obstacle that PRD leaders saw to organizing a broad opposition coalition in 1994 was two-fold—ideological, because they placed the PAN on the extreme right, and political, because they did not trust the PAN's commitment to democratic principles. Only the PRD saw polarization. Its leaders viewed their party as increasingly moderate and democratic, while they perceived the other parties as increasingly rightist and anti-democratic.[35]

---

[35] This section forms part of the author's dissertation research at the Department of Political Science at Yale University. The author gratefully acknowledges conceptual and methodological guidance from Juan J. Linz.

Why did the PAN not pursue a presidentialist transition route in 1994? In 1993, leaders of the PAN and the PRD met to discuss the possibility of a coalition candidate, someone who could unite the opposition vote and defeat the PRI once and for all. But the PAN was skeptical about fielding a unity candidate, especially because coalition candidates had lost in San Luis Potosí in 1991 and in Durango and Tamaulipas in 1992 (see table 2.3). And when the PRD stated that it would only accept Cuauhtémoc Cárdenas as the coalition candidate, the PAN rejected the proposal outright. Moreover, the PAN's federalist transition route was already yielding results and held the promise of more victories in the future. The PRD, by betting everything on a single card, stood to lose big if that card was trumped in the presidential election. Was the PAN's strategy of noncooperation in the presidential race well calculated? Everything indicates that it was, especially if one considers the attitudes not just of the PAN elite but of the entire electorate.

A study by Beatriz Magaloni, based on a survey carried out in Mexico's Federal District,[36] found that 33 percent of PAN voters refused to consider voting for anyone but a PAN candidate, 43 percent gave the PRI as their second choice, and 24 percent named the PRD as their second preference (Magaloni 1996). Therefore, if the PAN had supported Cárdenas in his presidential campaign, it is very likely that only a quarter of PAN votes would have gone to the PRD and the presidency would not have been won. Preferences among PRD voters were as follows: 49 percent would consider no option but their own party, 38 percent named the PAN as their second choice, and only 13 percent gave the PRI as a second option. One can surmise, then, that a coalition candidate from the PAN stood a much better chance of winning the presidency than did Cárdenas as head of the coalition.[37]

The 1994 presidential election demonstrated the extent to which Mexico's democratic transition could not be understood as alternation in the presidency, but as a process in which power is shared among the country's other constitutional arenas: the two chambers of Congress, state governorships, state legislatures, municipal presidencies, and city councils. In the presidential election, the PRI's Ernesto Zedillo Ponce de León won 50.4 percent of the valid votes cast. In other words, Zedillo won the same share of the vote in clean but unequal elections (there was no significant fraud, but the PRI accounted for some 78 percent of total campaign spending)[38] that Salinas de Gortari had won in 1988 in what were the most controversial elections in the history of postrevolu-

---

[36] Unfortunately, there are no national-level surveys of this type.

[37] For the PRI electorate, 34 percent were firm in their support of their party only, 14 percent listed the PRD as second preference, and 52 percent, the PAN.

[38] Instituto Federal Electoral sources.

tionary Mexico. Thus the first major difference between these two elections is that the 1988 process was dirty and inequitable (because parties filed no financial reports concerning such matters as the cost of radio and television advertising, it is impossible to know just how inequitable they were), while the 1994 elections were clean and inequitable.[39]

The second major difference between the 1988 and 1994 presidential elections was the sharp reversal in the distribution of the opposition vote. In 1988, the PAN's Manuel J. Clouthier received 16.8 percent of the valid vote, whereas in 1994 the PAN's candidate, Diego Fernández de Cevallos, won 26.8 percent of the vote. The PAN's ten-point gain came at the expense of the Left's candidate, Cuauhtémoc Cárdenas, who as the candidate of the National Democratic Front (FDN) "officially" obtained 31.0 percent of the vote in 1988 but received only 17.2 percent in 1994 as the candidate of the PRD, the largest and most important party on the center-left. Thus in 1994 the PAN once again became the principal opposition to the ruling PRI.

The third difference between these two presidential contests involved the political circumstances in which they took place. The 1994 elections did not occur in the context of a national economic crisis, as was the case in 1988, but political conditions were unstable. On January 1, 1994, some eight months before the election (August 21), the revolt of the Zapatista Army of National Liberation (EZLN) erupted in Chiapas. And on March 23, the PRI's presidential candidate, Luis Donaldo Colosio, was assassinated in Tijuana, Baja California. In these obvious conditions of instability, the "fear vote" (*voto de miedo*) favored the PRI's Ernesto Zedillo.

Without doubt, the 1994 elections marked the beginning of the second phase of the democratic transition initiated in 1988. All indicators of political pluralism exploded thereafter. For example, in 1988 only about 2 percent of the country's inhabitants had been governed by an opposition municipal government, whereas by the year 2000 approximately 46.5 million Mexicans (some 63 percent of the country's total population) had experienced opposition municipal government for at least three years. The PAN went from governing 12.3 percent of Mexico's population at the municipal level in 1994 to 33.1 percent in 1999, while the proportion of the population governed by the PRD at the municipal level jumped from 3.0 percent in 1994 to 12.3 percent in 1999.

The principal difference between the PAN and the PRD in this regard was in the size of the cities under their control. Between 1988 and 1999, the PAN governed for at least three years twenty-five of the thirty

---

[39] Thus the main challenges in the year 2000 presidential election were to make electoral procedures even more transparent and to establish conditions permitting parties to compete on more equal terms.

largest municipalities in the country.[40] The *panista* municipal governments included those in Aguascalientes, Aguascalientes; Guadalajara,
Jalisco (two different administrations, in Mexico's largest municipality);
Guadalupe, Nuevo León; Hermosillo, Sonora (three different governments); León, Guanajuato (four different administrations); Mérida, Yucatán; Mexicali, Baja California; Monterrey, Nuevo León; Saltillo, Coahuila; San Luis Potosí, San Luis Potosí; San Nicolás de los Garza,
Nuevo León; Tijuana, Baja California; Tlaquepaque, Jalisco; and
Zapopan, Jalisco. The PRD, in contrast, governed only two of Mexico's
thirty largest municipalities during this period—Nezahualcóyotl in
the State of México (the country's second largest municipality) and Morelia, Michoacán—and, in both cases, for only one three-year period.

At the level of state governorships, Mexico also experienced significantly greater pluralism between 1994 and 1999. Until 1989, the
"official" PRI and its predecessor organizations had never lost a gubernatorial election. In the 1988–1994 period, only three of Mexico's thirty-
one states were governed by the opposition—by the PAN, in Baja California, Chihuahua, and Guanajuato. However, in the 1994–2000 period
the opposition succeeded in defeating the PRI in seven states. These
victories went to the PAN (in Baja California, Guanajuato, and Jalisco in
1995; in Nuevo León and Querétaro in 1997; and in Aguascalientes in
1998), the PRD (in Zacatecas in 1998), and coalitions linking the PRD
and the Labor Party ([PT], in Baja California Sur in 1999) and the PRD,
the PT, and the Mexican Ecological Green Party ([PVEM], in Tlaxcala in
1999).

One unequivocal result of the PAN's municipal-federalist strategy is
the fact that the first non–PRI governors of the postrevolutionary period had previously been *panista* municipal presidents. Ernesto Ruffo
Appel, governor of Baja California between 1989 and 1995, had been
municipal president of Ensenada (1986–1989); Carlos Medina Plascencia, interim governor of Guanajuato in 1991–1995, had been municipal
president of León (1989–1991); Francisco Barrio, the PAN's governor of
Chihuahua between 1992 and 1998, had been municipal president of
Ciudad Juárez (1983–1986) and the party's gubernatorial candidate in
the 1986 elections; and Alberto Cárdenas, governor of Jalisco in 1995–
2001, was previously municipal president of Ciudad Guzmán (1992–
1995). The PRD's first governor was Cuauhtémoc Cárdenas, who in
1997 won the first popular election since the 1920s to choose the head of
the Federal District government.

Similarly in the legislative arena, the balance of power shifted significantly and the opposition acquired unprecedented influence. In-

---

[40] Of these twenty-five cases, the PAN governed fourteen municipalities for more
than one three-year period.

deed, the results of the 1997 midterm elections substantially transformed the political situation by creating the first divided national government in the country's postrevolutionary history. For the first time, a
priísta president did not have majority control of the Congress. During
the 1997–2000 period the PRI held only 47.6 percent of the seats in the
federal Chamber of Deputies and 59.4 percent of the seats in the federal
Senate. In single-chamber state legislatures as well, the opposition
gained more and more ground. From the beginning of the postrevolutionary era until 1989, there was no experience of divided government at the state level. In the 1988–1994 period, only four such cases
occurred. But between 1994 and 1999, fourteen of Mexico's thirty-one
states experienced divided government.

The 1994–2000 period not only produced more pluralism than did
the 1988–1994 phase of the transition, but it also was more densely institutionalized, more orderly, and much less conflictive. The explanation for these differences lies in two factors linked to the role that President Ernesto Zedillo played over the course of his administration (1994–
2000). First, Zedillo abandoned the policy of extreme hostility toward
the PRD that President Carlos Salinas de Gortari adopted. Second,
Zedillo advanced important changes that had been initiated during
Salinas's presidency. For example, he supported the 1996 constitutional
reform (unanimously approved by all the parties then represented in
Congress: the PRI, PAN, PRD, and PT) that gave full autonomy to the
agency responsible for organizing the electoral process (the Federal
Electoral Institute [IFE], created in 1990) and broad jurisdiction to the
Federal Electoral Tribunal (TFE, also established in 1990) to resolve
both federal and local electoral conflicts. The 1996 reform also significantly expanded public financing for parties (the amount rose from
US$65 million in 1994 to US$316 in 2000) and established a formula that
ensured an equitable distribution of both public resources and expo-
sure in mass communications media.

By the year 2000, all was ready for federal (presidential and legislative) elections that would mark the end of Mexico's democratic transition. Conditions existed for elections that were clean and equitable, organized by an autonomous electoral institution and with any disputes
judged by an electoral court with full authority to resolve conflicts. This
institutional environment was one of the key aspects of the general
elections held in the year 2000.

However, the other central institutional element at work in 2000 was
the power that had been distributed by an increasingly pluralist electorate over the course of twelve years of political transition. The two-
party structure of competition (PRI–PAN or PRI–PRD) in most parts of
Mexico had made possible party alternation in power at the municipal
and state levels. But in the country as a whole, the sum of these local

two-party competitions was a three-way competition (PRI–PAN–PRD) for power. The principal question posed regarding federal elections in the year 2000 was whether the end of Mexico's democratic transition would be marked by another PRI victory, or whether the transition would conclude with alternation not just at the municipal and state levels but also in the presidency.

With public opinion polls indicating that the PRI would win 40 to 45 percent of the vote, the first option explored by the PAN and PRD was the possibility of running a common presidential candidate. There were negotiations toward this end in September and October 1999, but they failed; once again, it proved impossible to construct an all-opposition coalition to defeat the PRI. Cuauhtémoc Cárdenas, head of the Federal District government (1997–2000) and making his third consecutive presidential bid, was unwilling to support a center-right party. But neither was Vicente Fox Quesada, the PAN's candidate and governor of Guanajuato between 1995 and 1999, willing to renounce his candidacy in order to join forces with Cárdenas. The disagreement no doubt reflected not only the ideological distance between the parties and the candidates, but also a certain lack of trust between them as well.

The principal consequence of these factors, however, was to increase the likelihood of a new PRI victory given the fact that the opposition vote would presumably remain divided between the PAN and the PRD. Moreover, the PRI would conserve veto power in the Congress to brake any opposition effort to reform election laws so as to force the electorate to redefine its oppositionist preferences in a run-off election pitting the PRI against the PAN, or the PAN or PRI against the PRD. Mexico's first-past-the-post electoral system enormously favored the PRI. In addition, the PRI's chances had been increased by the success of its first-ever presidential primary in November 1999, which was won by former secretary of the interior Francisco Labastida Ochoa. Indeed, in late November the most reliable opinion poll gave Labastida an impressive advantage that appeared difficult to overcome: Labastida, 53 percent; Fox, 32 percent; and Cárdenas, 10 percent.[41]

Nevertheless, Fox had the political ability to lead an intense (and successful) campaign focused primarily on two themes: his accomplishments as governor of Guanajuato and—much more important— the plebiscitary character of an election whose focus, he argued, was to "get the PRI out of Los Pinos"[42] after "seventy years of bad govern-

---

[41] The remaining 5 percent of preferences were divided among other, minor candidates. These percentages do not include "don't know" or "did not answer" responses. See *Reforma*, November 29, 1999.

[42] The presidential residence and office complex are commonly known as Los Pinos, a reference to their location in the heavily wooded Chapultepec park.

ment." He positioned himself at the center of the ideological spectrum in order to appeal to leftist voters to concentrate their support on only one of the two opposition options. Indeed, by June 2000 polls revealed a bipolar and highly competitive situation: Labastida, 42 percent; Fox, 39 percent; and Cárdenas, 16 percent.[43]

Fox was able to project his charisma successfully via an intelligent advertising campaign in mass communications media, and on July 2, 2000, Mexico's postrevolutionary era ended with Fox's presidential victory. He obtained 42.5 percent of the valid vote, followed by the PRI's Labastida with 36.1 percent and the PRD's Cárdenas with 16.6 percent. According to a *Reforma* poll taken on election day, 95 percent of voters who considered themselves *panistas* backed Fox; 88 percent of voters who considered themselves *priístas* opted for Labastida; and 84 percent of voters who considered themselves *perredistas* chose Cárdenas. On the other hand, 9 percent of self-identified *priístas* and 10 percent of self-identified *perredistas* voted for Fox (*Reforma*, July 3, 2000). This indicates very clearly that Fox was successful in promoting the plebiscitary nature of the election.

Nevertheless, two structural variables established the context for the election's outcome. The first was the PAN's construction of an organized electoral apparatus that culminated a sixty-year process of organizational development, and the second was the citizenry's experience (especially in urban areas) with what it was to be governed by an opposition party, especially the PAN. This latter factor reduced voters' fears and the uncertainty that naturally accompanied the end of seventy years of "revolutionary" governments.

The PAN's long-term strategy and organizational development played a crucial role in bringing about this scenario. This is what Vicente Fox told the author six years before his historic victory:

> The PAN and the PRD have taken different routes. The PAN prefers to advance gradually. Going for the brass ring requires resources and organization that have taken years to develop, which is why the PAN has engaged in a "guerrilla war" against the PRI. The PRD, in contrast, has no other option than to go directly for the presidency because it has no apparatus or long-term plans. They're looking for the main prize [the presidency] because they are led by a caudillo. The PAN's strategy has been more persistent.... Compared to the PAN, the PRD is still in its infancy. It doesn't really have electoral machinery, and it has not been especially concerned

---

[43] The remaining 3 percent of preferences were distributed among other, minor candidates. These percentages do not include "don't know" and "did not answer" responses. See *Reforma*, July 22, 2000.

to build an organization with a territorial presence. The PAN, despite everything, is ideologically rigid, and its campaign style requires modifications.... But the PAN has come a much longer way. Climb up on the PAN's electoral machinery, and you fly.[44]

CONCLUSION

Early studies of Mexican elections found a strong correlation between indicators of socioeconomic development (especially urbanization) and votes for the National Action Party.[45] It was clear from the early 1970s onward that the process of social change (particularly the growth of the urban middle class) promoted by postrevolutionary governments tended to undermine the PRI's political support base and strengthen opposition on the right. This process worked in favor of the PAN.

On the other hand, some analysts have correctly noted that substantial political realignment occurred as a result of the post–1982 economic crisis, especially among economic elites in center-west states and northern Mexico. This, too, fed the growing political strength of the center-right PAN, even if the party's subsequent electoral expansion was more gradual than abrupt or spectacular (see Loaeza 1990, 1999; Mizrahi n.d.).

This chapter does not question this interpretation of the PAN's growth, but it has presented evidence that this view is clearly incomplete. The existence of electoral machinery is not a sufficient condition for success at the polls, but it certainly is a *necessary* condition— especially if a party wishes to avoid volatility in its electoral support and consolidate new patterns of electoral preferences that modify existing balances in the party system. The data presented in the course of this essay indicate that the PAN had built a significant electoral apparatus well *before* Mexico's 1982 debt crisis, in the general absence of electoral competitiveness. It was, for example, capable of running candidates for municipal president in 24 percent of the country's municipalities (representing some 60 percent of the total population). And by the 1990s, the PAN could run candidates for municipal president in some 70 percent of all municipalities (accounting for more than 90 percent of the coun-

---

[44] Author interview, Mexico City, July 1994.

[45] See Ames 1970; Segovia 1974. Recent studies have found that, despite the fact that the size of the PAN vote has traditionally been positively correlated with higher levels of income and education, the party also attracted working-class voters in the 1994 national elections. The PAN has also received increasing support from younger voters. See, for example, Domínguez and McCann 1996.

try's population).[46] In population terms, one could argue that two-thirds of the electoral apparatus with which the PAN won the presidency in the year 2000 was constructed before the 1982 economic crisis, a surprising achievement in a noncompetitive electoral regime.

The crisis resulting from the 1976 conflict between forces favoring electoral participation and those advocating abstention had a negative impact on the PAN; indeed, the party apparatus (measured in terms of its capacity to run candidates) barely grew in the 1977–1979 period. There was, however, significant growth in party capacity in the years between 1980 and 1982. In these three years, the PAN presented candidates for municipal president in municipalities that represented, respectively, 62 percent, 55 percent, and 61 percent of Mexico's total population. These developments preceded the outbreak of economic crisis and the nationalization of the banks in 1982.

Over the period between 1939 and 1976, in a process full of vicissitudes and plagued by obstacles, the PAN constructed (particularly under Christlieb's leadership) a significant electoral apparatus. It did so even though there was an intense ongoing debate within the party over whether the best strategy was to participate in noncompetitive elections or to abstain from doing so. Once the PAN definitively inclined toward participation, its machinery grew apace. For instance, the 1976–1982 period witnessed a significant increase in the number of *panista* gubernatorial candidates, rising from seven candidates (in thirty-one states) in 1970–1976 to twenty-four candidates in 1976–1982. However, it was not until 1982 that the party's level of electoral support (slowly) began to expand.

This chapter has also demonstrated that the institutional density of an authoritarian regime has an enormous influence on its character and the rhythm of democratic transition. The longest-lasting authoritarian regime of the twentieth century experienced one of the slowest and most complex democratic transitions. The 1917 Constitution, republican and essentially liberal in content, combined with a long Mexican tradition of elections to define an institutional framework that marked both the nature of postrevolutionary authoritarianism and the Mexican transition process. Nonetheless, it is the actors themselves who, in the last analysis, define the character of constitutionally established institutions. In that sense, it is clear that the PAN's decades-long strategy of promoting gradual change greatly influenced the pace of political opening in Mexico. It should not be surprising that a party that is fundamentally urban, middle-class, and center-right should behave as an anti-rupture, institutionalist, and gradualist political opposition.

---

[46] See the data presented in table 2.1.

It is impressive how much political pluralism the 1988–2000 transition process produced in the Mexican constitutional system. Divided governments appeared; governors and municipal presidents were elected from all of the country's major parties. In the year 2000, for instance, about half of the population was governed by the PRI at the municipal level, while the other half was governed by other parties. In this highly pluralistic context, the PAN at the federal level moved from opposition to government. It was an opposition party (and, in historical perspective, a successful one) during seventy-one years. Time will tell how well it adjusts to the always serious and difficult task of governing.

REFERENCES

Alonso, Jorge. 1998. *Tras la emergencia ciudadana: un acercamiento a la personalidad política de Efraín González Luna*. Vol. 1. Guadalajara: Instituto Tecnológico de Estudios Superiores de Occidente.

———. 1999. *Tras la emergencia ciudadana: un acercamiento a la personalidad política de Efraín González Luna*. Vol. 2. Guadalajara: Instituto Tecnológico de Estudios Superiores de Occidente.

Álvarez de Vicencio, María Elena. 1995. *Municipio y democracia: tesis y prácticas de gobierno del Partido Acción Nacional*. Mexico City: Estudios y Publicaciones Económicas y Sociales, S.A.

Ames, Barry. 1970. "Bases of Support for Mexico's Dominant Party," *American Political Science Review* 64 (1).

Arreola, Carlos. 1994. *Ensayos sobre el PAN*. Mexico City: Miguel Ángel Porrúa.

Becerra, Ricardo, et al. 1996. *Así se vota en la república: las legislaciones electorales en los estados*. Mexico City: Instituto de Estudios para la Transición Democrática.

Bravo Ugarte, José. 1968. *Efraín González Luna: abogado, humanista, político, católico*. Mexico City: Ediciones de Acción Nacional.

Calderón Vega, Luis. 1967. *Memorias del PAN*. Vol. 1, 1939–1946. Mexico City: Jus.

———. 1975. *Memorias del PAN*. Vol. 2, 1946–1956. Mexico City: Jus.

———. 1980. *Reportaje sobre el PAN: 40 años de lucha política*. Mexico City: n.p.

Capes, William Parr. 1922. *The Modern City and Its Government*. New York: E. P. Dutton.

Christlieb, Adolfo. 1968. *Baja California: avanzada de la democracia*. Mexico City: Partido Acción Nacional.

Crespo, José Antonio. 1996. *Votar en los estados: análisis comparado de las legislaciones electorales estatales en México*. Mexico City: Miguel Ángel Porrúa/ Naumann/Centro de Investigación y Docencia Económicas.

de Remes, Alain. 2000. *Banco de datos electorales a nivel municipal, 1980–1999*. Mexico City: Centro de Investigación y Docencia Económicas.

Díaz, Alejandro. 1996. "La Democracia Cristiana: la paradoja ético-política." Mexico City: Instituto Tecnológico Autónomo de México. Mimeo.

Domínguez, Jorge I., and James A. McCann. 1996. *Democratizing Mexico: Public Opinion and Electoral Choices.* Baltimore, Md.: Johns Hopkins University Press.

Garciadiego, Javier. 1996. "Manuel Gómez Morin en los 'veintes': del abanico de oportunidades al fin de las alternativas." In *El Banco de México en la reconstrucción económica de México,* edited by Héctor Aguilar Camín. Mexico City: Jus.

Gómez, Leopoldo. 1991. "Elections, Legitimacy, and Political Change in Mexico, 1977–1988." Ph.D. dissertation, Georgetown University.

Gómez Morin, Manuel. 1919. "La Escuela Liberal en el derecho y en la política: ensayo crítico." Thesis, School of Law, Universidad Nacional Autónoma de México.

————. 1950. *Diez años de México: Informes del Jefe de Acción Nacional.* Mexico City: Jus.

González Luna, Efraín. 1974–1977. *Obras completas de Efraín González Luna.* 8 vols. Mexico City: Jus.

Hodge, Carl C. 1987. "The Supremacy of Politics: Federalism and Parties in Western Europe," *West European Politics* 10 (2).

Klesner, Joseph L. 1988. "Electoral Reform in an Authoritarian Regime. The Case of Mexico." Ph.D. dissertation, Massachusetts Institute of Technology.

Krauze, Enrique. 1976. *Caudillos culturales en la Revolución Mexicana.* Mexico City: Siglo Veintiuno.

Loaeza, Soledad. 1987. "El Partido Acción Nacional: de la oposición leal a la impaciencia electoral." In *La vida política mexicana en la crisis,* edited by Soledad Loaeza and Rafael Segovia. Mexico City: El Colegio de México.

————. 1988. *Clases medias y política en México: la querella escolar, 1959–1963.* Mexico City: El Colegio de México.

————. 1990. "Derecha y democracia en el cambio político mexicano, 1982–1988," *Foro Internacional* 30 (4).

————. 1999. *El Partido Acción Nacional, la larga marcha, 1939–1944: oposición leal y partido de protesta.* Mexico City: Fondo de Cultura Económica.

Lujambio, Alonso. 1987. "La proporcionalidad política del sistema electoral mexicano, 1964–1985." Bachelor's thesis, Instituto Tecnológico Autónomo de México.

————. 1994a. "Presidencialismo, federalismo y los dilemas de la transición a la democracia en México." In *Presidencialismo y sistema político: México y Estados Unidos,* edited by Alicia Hernández Chávez. Mexico City: El Colegio de México/Fondo de Cultura Económica.

————. 1994b. "El dilema de Christlieb Ibarrola: cuatro cartas a Gustavo Díaz Ordaz," *Estudios* 38 (Fall).

————. 1995. *Federalismo y congreso en el cambio político de México.* Mexico City: Universidad Nacional Autónoma de México.

————. 2000. *El poder compartido: un ensayo sobre la democratización mexicana,* with the assistance of Horacio Vives. Mexico City: Océano.

————. n.d. "Political Elites and Institutional Arrangements in the Mexican Transition to Democracy." Ph.D. dissertation, Yale University, in preparation.

Mabry, Donald J. 1974a. *Mexico's Accion Nacional: A Catholic Alternative to Revolution.* Syracuse, N.Y.: Syracuse University Press.

──────. 1974b. "Mexico's Party Deputy System: The First Decade," *Journal of Interamerican Studies and World Affairs* 16 (2).

Magaloni, Beatriz. 1996. "Dominancia de partido y dilemas duvergerianos en las elecciones nacionales de 1994," *Política y Gobierno* 3 (2).

Martínez Valle, Adolfo. 1995. "El Partido Acción Nacional: una historia política, 1939–1976." Bachelor's thesis, Instituto Tecnológico Autónomo de México.

Martorelli, Paola. 2000. "El lado azul de la Cámara: el activismo legislativo del Partido Acción Nacional, 1946–2000." Bachelor's thesis, Instituto Tecnológico Autónomo de México.

Marván Laborde, María. 1988. "La concepción del municipio en el Partido Acción Nacional," *Revista Mexicana de Sociología* 50 (2).

Medina, Luis. 1987. *Historia de la Revolución Mexicana, 1940–1952.* Vol. 20 of *Historia de la Revolución Mexicana.* Mexico City: El Colegio de México.

Meyer, Jean. 1974. *La cristiada.* 3 vols. Mexico City: Siglo Veintiuno.

──────. 1979. *El sinarquismo, ¿un fascismo mexicano?* Mexico City: Joaquín Mortiz.

Meyer, Jean, et al. 1995. *Cuando por la raza habla el espíritu: Manuel Gómez Morin, rector de la UNAM, 1933–1934.* Mexico City: Jus.

Mizrahi, Yemile. n.d. "From Mysticism to Power: The Partido Acción Nacional in Mexico." Manuscript.

Molinar Horcasitas, Juan. 1987. "Regreso a Chihuahua," *Nexos* 10 (March).

──────. 1991. *El tiempo de la legitimidad.* Mexico City: Cal y Arena.

PAN (Partido Acción Nacional). 1990. *Iniciativas de ley presentadas por el Partido Acción Nacional.* Mexico City: Estudios y Publicaciones Económicas y Sociales, S.A.

Peschard, Jacqueline. 1989. "50 años de participación electoral en el DF," *Estudios Políticos* 8 (July).

Reynoso, Víctor Manuel. 1993. "El PAN: ¿la oposición hará gobierno?" *Revista Mexicana de Sociología* 55 (2).

Rolland, Modesto C. 1921. *El desastre municipal en la República Mexicana.* Mexico City: Librería Cultura.

Segovia, Rafael. 1974. "La reforma política: el ejecutivo federal, el PRI y las elecciones de 1973," *Foro Internacional* 14 (3).

──────. 1983. "Elecciones y electores," *Diálogos,* September–October.

Vicencio Acevedo, Gustavo. 1991. *Memorias del PAN.* Vol. 4, 1952–1956. Mexico City: Estudios y Publicaciones Económicas y Sociales, S.A.

Vives Segl, Horacio. 2001. *Entre la fe y el poder: una biografía de José González Torres, 1919–1998.* Mexico City: Estudios y Publicaciones Económicas y Sociales, S.A.

3

Mexico's Democratization and the Organizational Development of the National Action Party

David A. Shirk

Official figures have deliberately obscured the true electoral strength of Mexico's National Action Party (PAN) for decades. The official numbers are belied by a stream of PAN electoral victories over the course of the 1980s and a swelling tide of wins in the 1990s. In 1987, the PAN controlled just 18 of the nation's roughly 2,400 local governments, and it governed less than one percent of the Mexican population. Ten years later, there were over two hundred PAN mayors and six PAN governors, with authority over roughly a third of the country's population. Indeed, since the early 1980s a great blue tsunami of *panismo* has swept over Mexico.

The PAN's electoral success has made a real difference in transforming the nature of politics and everyday life in Mexico. The party's municipal and state-level "opposition governments" brought new and innovative approaches to public administration, fierce advocacy of subnational governmental autonomy, and long overdue public works and services. With their slogans of transparency and efficiency in public administration, PAN governments began to foster new expectations with regard to the conduct of both government officials and average citizens.

The PAN's electoral victories brought with them unprecedented growth and development as a party, an urgent demand to fill and effectively administer previously inaccessible government posts, and the challenge of cultivating (rather than criticizing) relations between party and government. Over the course of the 1990s, the PAN's most daunting challenges went from winning elections and defending party victories to learning to govern and managing the party's organizational development.

Yet despite the PAN's fundamental influence on Mexico's democratic transition, there has been little scholarly analysis of the party as a political organization. Despite the election of the PAN's Vicente Fox Quesada to the Mexican presidency in July 2000, an enormous gap remains in empirical and historical understanding of the party that has presented the strongest, most consistently organized challenges against Mexico's long-ruling Institutional Revolutionary Party (PRI).

Numerous authors have evaluated the PAN's experiences with the electorate and in government since the party began racking up its electoral successes.[1] However, the vast majority of these authors give only limited insight into the party's workings or the fundamental organizational challenges it confronts in an increasingly democratic context. Indeed, the last major studies of the PAN by U.S. scholars were written nearly three decades ago (Mabry 1973; von Sauer 1974). Even Mexican scholars have produced relatively little to fill the gap.[2] And neither of the most significant Mexican analyses of the PAN published in the last decade (Arriola 1994; Loaeza 1999) covers the party's experience beyond 1994, the years during which the PAN underwent tremendous development and achieved important electoral advances.

This chapter examines the factors that have affected the PAN's organizational development since the party's founding in 1939. It explores the PAN's emergence and its original goals, statutes, ideology, and traditional bases of support as they relate to its future course of development. The analysis devotes particular attention to the way in which Mexico's democratization process altered the party's external opportunity structure and brought new possibilities for its organizational development; to the role of party leaders and competing coalitions; and to the development of cleavages within the party. The chapter ends with an exploration of the general implications of the PAN's experience, both for its own political future and for Mexico.

PARTY ORIGINS AND EARLY DEVELOPMENT

The formation of the PAN in Mexico City in September 1939 followed a wrenching period of national political consolidation that effectively fortified the Mexican political system's institutional arrangements and the hegemony of the postrevolutionary ruling coalition. The chief archi-

---

[1] Writings on this topic include, among others, Alemán Alemán 1993; Aziz Nassif 1994, 1996; Campuzano Montoya 1995; Espinoza Valle 1998; Guillén López 1992; Loaeza 1989; Montalvo Ortega 1996; and Rodríguez and Ward 1994.

[2] The important exceptions include Hernández Vicencio 1998; Mizrahi 1994, 1998; and Reveles Vásquez 1993, 1996.

tect of the new opposition party was Manuel Gómez Morin, a lawyer, financial guru, educator, and intellectual who personified Mexico's professional and entrepreneurial traditions. Gómez Morin had long been convinced that Mexico needed an alternative to the "official" party founded in 1929, and that an opposition force must rely on institutions rather than on individuals. Hence, although the PAN's birth and early development were heavily dependent upon Gómez Morin's leadership, connections, and charisma, he himself did not take advantage of this influence and worked instead to institutionalize his vision of an opposition party.

As Gómez Morin began to put his plan into action in 1938, he expended tremendous energy making contact with friends and colleagues throughout Mexico. By 1939, he felt sufficiently confident to initiate—with help from other party founders—formal procedures for constituting a new political party. An organizing committee was created in early 1939 to handle basic logistical and organizational matters and to define the party's general principles and objectives. In September 1939, the organizing committee called the party's constitutive assembly. Hundreds attended that first assembly, though fewer than three hundred individuals signed the PAN's founding document.

The following paragraphs focus on two aspects of the PAN in its early years. The first is the party's doctrine and early leadership. The second is its organizational structure, resources, and membership bases.

PAN Founders and Doctrine: A Political and Social Agenda

The PAN's doctrinal principles arose from concerns that had developed in the aftermath of the Mexican Revolution of 1910–1920. Many of these concerns paralleled those of postrevolutionary militant Catholic groups angered by secular reforms. Others reflected the anti-despotism of the late 1920s. However, one primary factor distinguishes the PAN from other opposition forces, and it is also one of the fundamental principles of the party's founder—the conviction that legality and institutionalization are the keys to achieving opposition political objectives.

The PAN's own doctrinal agenda holds none of the radically conservative elements often attributed to it. In fact, contrary to portrayals of the PAN as a reactionary party, its advocacy of free and fair elections, a competitive multiparty system, effective federalism (with due respect for state and local autonomy), and the separation of powers (especially a genuinely independent legislature) closely coincide with the Mexican Revolution's original goals (see, for example, von Sauer 1974). Indeed, there is considerable convergence between PAN doctrine and the primary goals of key Mexican revolutionaries, including Francisco I. Madero, who advocated effective suffrage and an end to the political monopoly of the Porfirio Díaz regime (1876–1911). In many ways, this convergence established the PAN as a legitimate member—albeit a distant cousin—in Mexico's revolutionary family.[3]

Gómez Morin also recognized that "anti-system" tactics were ineffective. To produce political change required a lasting opposition party capable of surviving individual personalities and occasional displays of social discontent. Gómez Morin had learned this lesson from his work on the unsuccessful independent presidential campaign of José Vasconcelos in 1929. Vasconcelos, who had been secretary of education under President Álvaro Obregón (1920–1924), in 1929 launched an "anti-reelection" campaign against the corruption and continued influence of President Plutarco Elías Calles (1924–1928). According to Gómez Morin, who served as campaign treasurer, this spontaneous, personalistic movement harked back to the revolution:

> Above all the movement was political and [Vasconcelos] didn't want to think about the possibility of the organization of a permanent party.... [He] wanted to put an end to the military dictators, to the "barbarous" dictators.... He wanted to establish a civilian government of political, not military, leaders, and subject to the norms of the Constitution (Wilkie and Monzón de Wilkie 1978: 27–28).

Vasconcelismo faded shortly after the election. Yet its example helped make organizational institutionalization an important priority for Gómez Morin. Thus the PAN quickly evolved an elaborate philosophy and doctrine, as well as a developed, participatory organizational hierarchy.

The basic tenants of PAN philosophy comprise two broad areas of emphasis. The first stems directly from Gómez Morin's political motives and philosophies; it advocates the practical application of liberal democratic principles to political organization, participation, and governance. The second area of emphasis speaks to a less precisely defined set of normative, spiritual, and social welfare concerns most closely associated with another of the party's prominent founders, Efraín González Luna. This aspect of PAN doctrine is typically described as a philosophy of "political humanism."

The PAN's advocacy of such principles placed it distinctly outside the nefariously illiberal brand of "right-wing" conservatism that many

---

[3] Loaeza (1989: 229–30) tends to agree with this assessment. She also notes a tendency to lump "the Right" together without distinction, defining it only in terms of opposition to the "positive qualities of the regime." As a result, by portraying the PAN solely as a party of the Roman Catholic Church and business, "values are attributed to it that go against its parliamentary and liberal tradition."

of its contemporaries adopted in Argentina, Bolivia, Chile, Ecuador, Uruguay, and elsewhere in Latin America. Hence, rather than a classic conservatism oriented toward preserving the traditional social order and hierarchy, the PAN's doctrine is better characterized as conservative in the sense that it promotes values of special importance to elites, such as the preservation of private property, low taxation, reduced government intervention in the economy and in labor relations, and the protection of beliefs and institutions traditionally associated with elites (such as the Roman Catholic Church and private education).

However, because of Efraín González Luna's commitment to "political humanism," one cannot categorize PAN conservatism as purely elitist.[4] González Luna, who achieved distinction as the party's first registered presidential candidate (1952), laid out a vision of the PAN that was far more numinous than Gómez Morin's practical, largely secular approach.[5] González Luna focused heavily on the notion of perfecting man as a spiritual entity.[6]

Yet González Luna also grounded his philosophy in Mexican political reality, using it to focus PAN doctrine around the combination of man's material and spiritual needs and toward realization of the common good. Accordingly, González Luna spoke to the problems of property, the rights of the family, liberty in education, free practice of religion, and the economic elevation of the worker in both the fields and the factories. His doctrine emerged as a kind of Mexican "compassionate conservatism," bringing a softer side to the technically oriented and legalistic PAN of Manuel Gómez Morin. This provided an antithesis to the PRI regime's paternalism, emphasizing the importance of encouraging individual development, rather than merely catering to the needs of

---

[4] González Luna's political philosophy can be found in a compendium of his works edited by the PAN's editorial staff; see González Luna 1991.

[5] Admittedly, even the practical Gómez Morin was not totally averse to spiritual rhetoric. One of his comments in particular became the *panistas'* battle cry for political change in Mexico: *"hay que mover las almas"* ("we must move people's souls").

[6] According to González Luna, "Man requires the emphatic accentuation of spiritual values as the essence of his ontological affirmation. He is not made a man by his greater capacity or intensity for material gain, by his greater, purely biological perfection. All of this does not transcend the zoological level. The satisfaction of the beast is not enough for the fulfillment of man.... We need that which makes us, that which, joined to the organic fact, transforms us into something infinitely higher than just an organism, that which makes us men: the spirit, the soul and its essence, its faculties and operation" (González Luna 1991: 36–37).

the flesh—in other words, reducing dependence on government hand-outs in favor of helping citizens to help themselves.[7]

Gómez Morin and González Luna also formulated coherent strategies for achieving their collective vision through government institutions and political action. In particular, the PAN developed clear doctrines on the state's role in the economy, the role of the municipality, the value of knowledge and learning, the importance of free expression, the need for community responsibility and collaboration, and the urgency of free individual (rather than corporatist) political participation. These doctrines have underpinned the party's political positions on a variety of issues, including Mexico's economic development, federalism and the role of the municipality, education, public-private partnerships in community development, and democracy and political organization.

Early PAN Organizational Structure and Membership Bases

The PAN's early leadership was concentrated in Mexico's geographic and figurative center and extended irregularly into the periphery. Gómez Morin's targeted recruitment strategy had produced a "party of notables" based primarily in Mexico City but with links to dedicated subnational actors throughout the country. Mexico's "carrot and stick" authoritarian regime provided institutional incentives and opportunities for the PAN to persist as an organization and occasionally to extend its strength in the periphery, but it prevented such development from exceeding the acceptable limits established by PRI hegemony. The PAN nevertheless survived decades of political exclusion thanks in part to its relatively developed institutional structure.

The PAN organization was initially divided between the national and regional levels. The party's national leadership was—and remains—centered in the National Executive Committee (CEN), which has considerable decision-making power and internal discretion. The concentration of authority in the CEN throughout the party's first decades was largely due to the PAN's early weakness at the subnational

---

[7] Contemporary critics of the PAN (Moctezuma Barragán 1997; Montalvo Ortega and Vallardo Fajardo 1997) view this "humanistic" philosophy as a precariously thin veil for what they see as the fundamentally religious core of *panismo*. This view is not completely inconsistent with reality, given that González Luna made no secret of his religious tendencies. Indeed, for many within the party, humanism becomes a surrogate for purely religious justifications for positions on such issues as the "right to life" (abortion and the death penalty). In this sense, "humanism" reveals the complicity of Catholic ideals with the PAN's political mission.

level. Decentralization of authority and responsibility to the subnational level was neither practical nor pursued as a goal.

The PAN was limited in its subnational organizational strength for several reasons. First, because the party expanded its presence from the center to the periphery largely through Gómez Morin's informal contacts, the party's links to the state and local levels depended at first on his personal connections with colleagues, business associates, and former students. These appear to have been strongest in Mexico's urban centers, especially in the North (Monterrey) and Center (Guadalajara, León, Puebla), but also in the South (Mérida). Second, in several notable cases where the PAN was able to develop its organizational and electoral strength subnationally—typically capitalizing on sudden citizen outrage over local instances of governmental corruption—its local leaders and supporters fell victim to violent repression.[8] Finally, the PAN's selective membership recruitment formula and its ideological aversion to aggregated interest representation limited the party's impetus to develop a mass base at the subnational level. The result was a party that more closely resembled a social club with political tendencies than a mass-oriented party organization.

Weak and sporadic subnational organization constrained the party's candidates for national office because their success depended on the capacity of the PAN's regional organizations to mobilize and protect the vote from possible fraud by the ruling party. A lack of resources also meant minimal or haphazard capacity to develop the party's internal functions. For example, early procedures for affiliating members—though relatively well defined in party statutes—were mainly a matter of informal participation. In most instances, the party lacked a permanent paid staff, basic supplies and equipment, and even the physical space in which to conduct its business. The problem of finding candidates willing to run for elected office—a difficult task given the party's dim prospects for victory—was exacerbated by the party's lack of resources. In fact, the candidates themselves typically had to shoulder most campaign expenses. One of the most noticeable effects of the party's resource limitations at the state and local levels was the lack of full-time, "professional" leadership capable of conducting party business on a regular basis. Local party leaders, who had to tend to their own private careers and businesses, could only devote their spare time to the party.[9]

---

[8] For specific examples of repression at the state and local levels, see Cicero MacKinney 1987; Ortega 1961; Shirk 1999, 2000.

[9] From a research standpoint, a frustrating aspect of the PAN's early resource limitations is the fact that record keeping was generally erratic, making it very difficult to gather precise information on many aspects of the party's internal organi-

Above all, the lack of organizational resources and the extent to which participation in the PAN meant both material and personal investments from its militants say a great deal about those who did participate. The resource-poor PAN lacked the kind of selective benefits that might serve to motivate collective action. Moreover, prospects for gaining public office through the PAN were slim, so supporting the PAN would have been of little use to voters who cared about achieving actual policy objectives. Thus, what motivated participation was often a dedication to the party's doctrinal principles and ideals; today party activists often describe themselves as they were in the party's earlier years as quixotic *ilusos*.[10]

Gómez Morin's experience as a leader in the financial community drew in businessmen and industrialists, many of whom had been alienated by the statist policies promoted by the left-of-center presidency of Lázaro Cárdenas (1934–1940). His brief but eventful stint as rector and defender of the National Autonomous University of Mexico (UNAM) won him the support of his colleagues and students. His university battles also won Gómez Morin the sympathies of Catholic activists who saw postrevolutionary government intervention as a tool of anticlericism and, under the Cárdenas administration, as an instrument of creeping, godless communism.[11]

Despite descriptions of the PAN as the "party of the rich," the organization itself was quite poor throughout most of its existence, and its active members were not people of great material wealth. Even at the national level, the party lacked the resources to develop as a truly professional organization, a problem that was compounded by its organizational limits at the subnational level. Baja California PAN leader Salvador Rosas Magallón responded to stereotypical portrayals of his party by asking why a party of bankers would choose to run journalists, workers, and carpenters as its candidates (Medina Valdés 1959). Senator Norberto Corella (Baja California) later noted, "Before, people in the party were very good people, good citizens, but not prominent or successful in their businesses or professions. So their image in the community was not the best. They may have been the best people, but they were not seen that way by the citizens."[12]

---

zation at the subnational level. The only real alternative is to rely on longtime militants' personal accounts or archives.

[10] Author interview with Roger Cicero MacKinney, Mérida, August 1997.

[11] The PAN's links to religious organizations are discussed in Moctezuma Barragán 1997; Mabry 1973.

[12] Author interview, Mexico City, June 1998.

In short, for most of its early life the PAN was not an effective mechanism for placing candidates in office. This situation changed as the pillars of Mexican authoritarianism began to weaken. Indeed, the PAN's opportunity structure improved dramatically in the course of democratization, bringing increasingly significant electoral victories, long-sought political reforms, and new possibilities for party building. New resources and a larger pool of supporters interested in participating in the party dramatically enhanced professionalization within the organization, but they also increased the number and intensity of intra-party conflicts.[13]

DEMOCRATIZATION AND PARTY BUILDING IN MEXICO

The PAN's early external environment—the economic foundations of the postrevolutionary regime, prevailing institutional arrangements, the cultural matrix, and competitive conditions—raised significant barriers to its development as a political opposition. The Mexican system had long been controlled by a dominant coalition that used both state resources for co-optation and electoral fraud and force to maintain the political monopoly exercised by the "revolutionary family." Indeed, the incremental creation of political spaces for opposition, contestation, and participation within that system contributed to the appearance of a gradual "perfection" of democracy.

Despite appearances, however, conditions in Mexico actually sustained a long period of postrevolutionary authoritarianism. Political pluralism was constrained by the nature of the institutional mechanisms regulating contestation and decision making. At the same time, the norms, attitudes, and beliefs encouraged by postrevolutionary leaders and embedded in the structures that empowered them created disincentives to genuine political participation and open contestation. Moreover, the performance legitimacy achieved via some fulfillment of revolutionary-era promises of land redistribution, economic nationalism under President Cárdenas, and a long period of economic prosperity from the 1940s through much of the 1970s helped cement these political arrangements. Finally, the ruling PRI's remarkable capacity to incorporate diverse groups and interests, and its intimate connection with the government, made genuine electoral competition a foreign concept in Mexico.

---

[13] Editor's note: The relationship between democratization and party growth, on the one hand, and party factionalism, on the other, is examined by Steven T. Wuhs in the following chapter.

The undoing of this system—and the possibilities this process opened for the PAN—hinged on cracks that developed in the pillars of Mexican authoritarianism. Beginning in the late 1960s, Mexico's political landscape began to change in ways that dramatically altered the PAN's opportunity structure. First, Mexico's socioeconomic troubles surfaced as early as the late 1960s, with the exhaustion of the import-substitution development model and the regime's decreased ability to satisfy rising expectations and to address corresponding demands. The political turmoil that erupted as a result of the violent repression of the 1968 student movement in Mexico City marked an important turning point in Mexican politics and led to President Luis Echeverría's (1970–1976) efforts to co-opt political support through increased state intervention in the economy. An abounding supply of credit—made possible by premium prices for petroleum exports and low international interest rates—encouraged continued co-optive strategies for maintaining the regime's performance legitimacy.

Even reversals in both petroleum prices and interest rates, which plunged Mexico into economic crisis beginning in 1981–1982, brought only half-hearted efforts to restructure the economy, and staggering inflation prevailed until the late 1980s. Failed economic policies reduced the state resources that could be used as patronage to generate support; the result was strained relations and increased divisions among key regime actors. Widespread citizen dissatisfaction with the ruling party produced increased opportunities for the opposition—on both the left and the right—to mobilize support against the regime.

The second change in the political landscape involved Mexico's institutional arrangements. Although the concentration of power in the federal executive and restrictions on electoral competition had underpinned PRI hegemony for decades, important changes beginning in the 1960s helped expand political spaces for the opposition. Reforms to provide limited legislative representation increased PAN candidates' political experience and gave them opportunities to monitor and criticize the regime, laying the groundwork for gains at the municipal and state levels. By the 1990s, an emphasis on election monitoring and multiparty participation in negotiating the terms of electoral competition spelled real improvements in the credibility of Mexican federal elections and served as a model for electoral reforms at the subnational level.[14]

Third, changing patterns of behavior, political beliefs, and attitudes in the 1980s and 1990s were very significant for the PAN. The political

---

[14] At the same time, the development and design of Mexico's Federal Electoral Institute (IFE) was heavily influenced by the autonomous state electoral entity set up by PAN governor Ernesto Ruffo Appel in Baja California.

culture of postrevolutionary Mexico had long contributed to the stability of PRI authoritarianism because it distorted people's perception of the opposition, presented disincentives for civic participation, and established a complex network of entrenched interests based on traditional practices of patron-clientage and interest aggregation. The norms, attitudes, and beliefs that facilitated the practice of PRI authoritarianism (including the symbolic nationalism that imparted "revolutionary" legitimacy to the ruling party) presented significant obstacles to PAN party building. Clearly, Mexicans do not prefer, nor are they inherently predisposed to, authoritarianism. Rather, political culture in Mexico has undergone important shifts correlated with the process of democratization that are relevant to both the PRI regime's decline and the opposition's ability to mobilize support.

In particular, when the pie that fed the PRI's patron-client networks shrank in the 1980s, the state's relationship with its corporatist labor organizations and client groups suffered—with significant cultural repercussions.[15] The regime's failure to respond to the multiple crises of the 1980s altered civic perceptions of the state by revealing the limitations of "the man behind the curtain"[16] An important illustration of this change came in the 1980s with the rise of new grassroots and urban popular movements. Bennett (1992) argues that such movements helped construct new channels for poor urban residents to express their needs, and they demonstrated the inability of corporatist organizations—such as the Confederation of Mexican Workers (CTM) and the National Confederation of Popular Organizations (CNOP)—to represent effectively the urban poor. To the extent that these movements emphasized civic awareness, local autonomy, and responsibility to the community, they also represented an important shift away from traditional norms of political behavior in Mexico.

Although the proliferation of urban popular movements in Mexico in the 1980s is typically linked to the improved electoral performance of the political Left, the new civic attitudes that were generated by outrage over recurring economic crises and inadequate government services were not limited to a particular ideology or class. Indeed, many of the concerns raised by PAN militants and supporters reflected de-

---

[15] For a discussion of how the economic crises of the 1980s and the state's responses to them affected the regime's relationship with its traditional supporters, see Dresser 1994.

[16] For example, at the national level, the state's limited capacity was made painfully clear in 1985 by the Mexico City earthquakes, which immobilized the city for days. The government's slow response prompted citizens to pool their own resources to deal with the damage, while some of the disaster relief that international sources sent to the Mexican government mysteriously disappeared.

mands for basic urban services (trash collection, piped water, housing, public safety), and they were expressed through strategies of popular mobilization, including public demonstrations, marches, occupations of public buildings, and the like.

In short, behavioral patterns that once obstructed political participation gave way, circumscribing the PRI's capacity to maintain control and providing new opportunities for opposition parties to mobilize support against the regime.[17] In their study of public opinion and democratization in Mexico, Domínguez and McCann argue that attitudes changed dramatically after the late 1950s in ways that have been favorable for the prospects of Mexican democracy.

> As time has passed, Mexicans have ... become less likely to prefer reliance on strong leaders over reliance on the rule of law; they do not favor the participation of nondemocratic institutions in political life; and they strongly favor the internal democratization of the ruling party's presidential nomination practices.... The point is that Mexico has changed, and its citizens are ready for a more democratic polity (1996: 47–48).[18]

One important element of this attitudinal adjustment is that the opposition became a real alternative. In this sense, attitudes about what *could be* in Mexican politics have changed dramatically. For the PAN, optimism about the opposition's prospects came with slogans like Baja California's "*¡Sí se puede!*" ("Yes, it can be done!"), now a national credo. The overt message is that anything is possible; the underlying implications are that Mexicans can work toward their goals collectively. The notion that political action can positively affect people's lives was a revelation for many Mexicans in the 1980s and 1990s, and it helped mobilize support for the opposition.

Finally, beginning in the late 1980s Mexico's changing competitive circumstances increased the PAN's political opportunities. Internal divisions within the PRI weakened the ruling party and even contributed to the emergence of a major new opposition force in the 1988 elections. During the late 1980s, divisions within the PRI over how to deal with Mexico's economic crisis sparked the formation of the Democratic Cur-

---

[17] Indeed, some activists from urban popular movements later became involved with the PAN. Author interview with Cuauhtémoc Cárdenas, Mexico City, March 1999.

[18] For Domínguez and McCann, these attitudinal changes resulted primarily from a more educated population, the limited impact and/or reform of the Catholic Church since the 1960s, "international influences," and the very increases in political competitiveness experienced in the institutional arena.

rent, which advocated reform of the PRI and a return to state-led growth. The PRI's selection of technocrat Carlos Salinas de Gortari as its presidential candidate for 1988 finally motivated members of the Democratic Current to bolt the party, and these renegade *priístas* formed an electoral alliance with leftist parties to support the candidacy of Cuauhtémoc Cárdenas.[19] Official election results gave the election to Salinas, over Cárdenas and PAN candidate Manuel J. Clouthier. However, electoral fraud had been widespread, and many observers hold that Cárdenas was, indeed, the winner. Thereafter, Cárdenas pressed continually for a new leftist alternative to the PRI and helped found the Party of the Democratic Revolution (PRD), which joined PRI dissidents with elements of Mexico's long-fragmented Left.

The emergence of the PRD contributed significantly to the regime's acceptance of PAN victories, something many scholars view as a necessary concession by the Salinas administration.[20] Indeed, many believe that the PAN "sold out" by negotiating a pact (*concertación*) with the PRI in exchange for political favors, including recognition of PAN electoral victories and the passage of political reforms.[21] What is clear is that—*concertación* or not—the PRI gained short-term benefits from PAN support. Its de facto recognition of Salinas's questionable election victory lent the PAN's good name to the legitimacy-starved government. Moreover, the PAN's acceptance of measures designed to protect PRI

---

[19] Cuauhtémoc Cárdenas is the son of General Lázaro Cárdenas (president of Mexico from 1934 to 1940), beloved in Mexico for having met formerly unrealized promises of the Revolution, such as the nationalization of foreign-owned properties and land redistribution.

[20] President Salinas (1988–1994) faced a severe legitimacy crisis at the beginning of his term, and the PAN provided crucial political and legislative support. In particular, the PAN supported Salinas's neoliberal economic package and helped pass constitutional amendments, which required a two-thirds majority vote in Congress. For the most comprehensive analyses of the political circumstances following Salinas's election, see Cornelius, Gentleman, and Smith 1989.

[21] Alcocer V. (1995: 62) argues that these reforms were "the principal expression of an unspoken alliance between the ruling party and the PAN, facilitating a political transition not to a multiparty system but to a bipartisan (PRI–PAN) system, particularly in the Congress and local governments." Likewise, Klesner (1993) notes that long-standing PAN demands for institutional reform—such as a restructuring of the Senate to allow for limited proportional representation—were met during the Salinas administration. Many observers also believe that the government's quid pro quo for the PAN included recognition of its 1989 gubernatorial victory in the state of Baja California and a string of important municipal victories.

hegemony in the federal legislature helped ensure a PRI sweep of the Chamber of Deputies in 1991.[22]

On the other hand, PAN advocacy of reform measures yielded long-term advances for democratization. These included the establishment of an independent electoral authority, the introduction of proportional representation into the federal Senate, and reform of public funding for political parties. And divisions within the PRI, the splitting off of the Democratic Current, and the eventual formation of the PRD strengthened the PAN's relative position in the party system as the PRI and PRD vied for votes.

It is important to reiterate that the PAN's success has been the result of a number of factors. Again, the pressure of the economic crises of the 1980s, the slow transformation of Mexico's institutional context, the increasing activism and awareness of Mexican citizens, and internal divisions within the ruling party all contributed to the gradual unraveling of the PRI regime and to the PAN's electoral and political advances during the 1990s. In particular, the PAN exploited these opportunities at the state and local levels by attacking the blatant failure or corruption of PRI local governments, by capitalizing on new institutional opportunities that gave its candidates greater political experience and visibility,[23] by harnessing unprecedented civic activism (and outrage), and by taking advantage of cases where the ruling party has been debilitated by divisions within its state or local political machine. Thus the PAN's advances were not gifts or concessions from above, but the result of the party's ability to exploit opportunities created in the process of Mexico's political transition.

---

[22] The PAN's representation in the federal Chamber of Deputies dropped from 101 to 90 seats after the 1991 elections. The PRD fared much worse, partly due to the possible targeting of government resources to PRD strongholds through the regime's anti-poverty National Solidarity Program (PRONASOL) and to a reconfiguration of the institutional context that worked to the PRD's disadvantage. The PRI, meanwhile, surged ahead. The PRI's average rise in electoral support in PRD strongholds was 142 percent, compared to the PRI's 43 percent average rise in PAN strongholds (Stansfield 1996).

[23] The 1983 reforms to Article 115 of the Mexican Constitution allowed for proportional representation in municipal government by allocating *regidor*, or city council, positions to opposition candidates. Much like proportional representation legislators at the state and federal levels, opposition *regidores* were typically isolated from decision making, harassed, and sometimes ridiculed as they attempted to assert their authority as public officials. Still, access to such positions allowed opposition parties to monitor local government more closely and provided positions of authority from which to denounce corruption and abuses to the state legislature.

PAN ORGANIZATIONAL DEVELOPMENT IN THE 1980S AND 1990S

This section traces the PAN's organizational development in the course of Mexico's democratization, focusing in particular on the expansion of the party's membership bases, professionalization of the organization, and the development of internal cleavages. However, before discussing how the PAN changed, it is important to explain the party's basic organizational structure. As will become clear, the PAN's decision-making structures have played a key role in determining the recent course of the party's development.

The PAN has organizational manifestations at the local, state, and national levels. At the local (municipal) level, all members belong to a local party organization headed by a municipal directive committee (CDM).[24] Party members vote directly for the president of the CDM, and (depending on locally established procedures) the CDM president may propose an entire slate of nominees for the committee prior to selection. The PAN is also divided into thirty-two state committees (one per state plus one in the Federal District). State committees comprise a State Council (Consejo Estatal) and a State Directive Committee (CDE), which respond to the state's membership through a representative body known as the State Assembly (Asamblea Estatal).[25] The State Assembly is composed mostly of delegates proposed by the CDMs and by the current CDE, although there are also a number of ex oficio members of the State Assembly (including CDM presidents, CDE representatives, and key elected officials in the state). The State Assembly selects the members of the State Council, whose primary responsibility, in turn, is to select and advise the CDE.

Finally, the PAN's national leadership (and presidential candidate) has traditionally been selected in a manner similar to state directive committees. Representatives of the general membership are selected to participate in the party's National Assembly (Asamblea Nacional), which meets in a national convention and votes on the party's platform, presidential candidate, proportional representation lists, and general plan of action.[26] The Assembly also approves a list of 250 "national

---

[24] The CDM may be subdivided into neighborhood delegations, the heads of which are either appointed by the CDM or elected by the members affiliated with that delegation. Because the CDM is selected directly by all party members, local delegations do not have any formal influence on the CDM or its composition.

[25] The number of delegates depends on a formula that accounts for population and electoral performance.

[26] The selection of delegates is itself fairly complicated and gives important prerogatives to party leaders. National Assembly delegates must have at least three years of active militancy within the PAN. Leaders of state committees, members of the CEN, and members of the National Council are automatically allowed to

councilors" compiled by a committee that draws from nominees proposed by the Assembly and the national executive leadership.[27] In addition to these elected councilors, the National Council (Consejo Nacional) has a number of ex oficio members from the national leadership.[28] The National Council serves as a sort of weak parliament to the party's executive leadership; it helps select and advise the National Executive Committee and has certain investigatory and budgetary powers. However, the Council only meets once a year and therefore does not make decisions on the PAN's day-to-day decisions or policies.

The CEN includes between twenty and forty activists with three or more years of experience in the party. Two-thirds are drawn from a list proposed by the party president, and each CEN member must be approved by at least two-thirds of the councilors (or be re-proposed until the party president's quota is met). One-third of the CEN membership is drawn from a list proposed by the National Council; each councilor may nominate one individual, and the nominee must be seconded by five other councilors and approved by at least one-third of the councilors (or be re-proposed until the Council's quota is met).

It is important to underscore the CEN's influence in the selection of the National Council, given that this is the body to which it is directly responsible. This influence is apparent not only in the high level of representation that CEN members automatically have in the Assembly and on the National Council, but also in the CEN's ability to influence the list selection for the National Council.[29] As noted above, the CEN has a designated number of nominees, and it also controls the formulation of the list of councilor nominees. Hence it helps shape the body that approves its policies and that will select its successors.

---

participate as ex oficio delegates. All other delegates are proposed by local and state committees according to the number allowed to each state (one representative for each electoral district plus fifteen base delegates). States are awarded additional representatives based on the party's electoral performance in particular states in the most recent federal election—one National Assembly vote for each percentage point of the vote the PAN received in the state, and one vote for each percentage point of the party's national vote that was received in the state (PAN *Estatutos*, 1993, Articles 20–30).

[27] If a list is denied, the process of nominations and list composition begins again until the National Assembly approves the list.

[28] These include the two highest officers of the CEN (the president and the secretary general), all former CEN presidents still active in the party, the party leaders in the federal Senate and the Chamber of Deputies, all current state committee presidents, and the coordinator of all local PAN deputies.

[29] The CEN itself has a number of votes equivalent to the average number of votes exercised by state delegations.

For years these internal selection mechanisms were the most democratic in Mexico. However, the PRD's increasingly direct selection mechanisms (including nationwide voting) have made the PAN's multi-layered leadership selection appear antiquated by comparison. The sitting executive leadership's significant input—over and above the indirectness of the PAN's decision-making structures—contributes to a degree of centralized control that limits the prospects for rapid or major shifts in the party's direction.

Expansion of the Party's Base

A notable aspect of the PAN's organizational development in the 1980s and 1990s was its rapid membership growth.[30] This growth can be explained in part by important shifts in the profile of PAN candidates as party leaders encouraged the active participation of high-visibility community leaders and entrepreneurs. In particular, Manuel J. Clouthier, a prominent businessman active in the party since the 1970s, was instrumental in drawing a new breed of activists and candidates—especially the heads of small and midsize companies—into the PAN in the 1980s.

This is an important point because the PAN has long been called the "party of the rich" and the "party of business"—a counterintuitive accusation in a system where business leaders had long left politics to the politicians, while lending their tacit (and sometimes explicit) support to the "official" party in return for political favors.[31] The PAN's ability to

---

[30] Reliable data on the growth of PAN membership at the local level are nonexistent, in part because of the party's historical lack of record keeping. However, in 1994 all members were required to reaffiliate and complete a small survey form regarding their militancy and demographic characteristics. Although there are problems with these reaffiliation data (which tend progressively to underestimate membership backwards in time due to death and other failures to reaffiliate), these are the only coherent data available. Moreover, personal accounts generally confirm the rise in membership. All current membership figures were compiled for this project by Karla María de la Peña Jiménez O'Farril, a staffer at the CEN's national membership registry.

[31] During the decades in which the political opposition was effectively excluded and sometimes repressed, the number of PAN sympathizers who formally registered as party members was extremely low. These select few—despite the perceived risks to themselves, their families, and their businesses—chose to demonstrate their opposition to the regime. Many potential PAN supporters viewed the organization as a hopeless cause to which they did not care to devote their time and attention. In short, given the absence of tangible political benefits and the presence of political costs, people had few rational incentives to contribute openly or participate in the PAN. Thus, among those who did become involved, motiva-

attract private-sector support diminished soon after its formation, as the regime's ideological bent and economic practices returned to the traditional conservatism that had prevailed before the Lázaro Cárdenas presidency. Thereafter, the PAN's national and local leadership typically reached out to include owners of small businesses and professionals. These individuals were likely to have time and resources to commit to maintaining the PAN's resource-poor organization and its campaigns, yet very few of them enjoyed outstanding wealth or economic position.[32]

Though new recruits from the private sector did not outnumber the PAN's traditional base in the 1980s, they played an important role in generating support for the party. For example, when "Ruffo-mania" swept the PAN's Ernesto Ruffo Appel into the governorship of Baja California in 1989, it also brought the party an unprecedented number of militants and supporters.[33] In the PAN bastion of León, Guanajuato, meanwhile, Clouthier was recruiting Vicente Fox Quesada, whom he knew through Mexican business associations.[34] Moreover, general increases in membership (see figure 3.1)—particularly as PAN candidates logged groundbreaking victories at the local level and drew more rank-and-file activists into the party—translated into a greater capacity to mobilize demonstrations, monitor elections (and, hence, contest election fraud), and defend the party's electoral victories.

---

tions were typically more idealistic. However, as new opportunities opened for the party, the collective action problem of attracting members and candidates diminished dramatically, and the party's ranks grew.

[32] In the course of field research, this author found that those individuals who supported the PAN during the long period of PRI hegemony were typically from middle- and lower-middle-class backgrounds. Several analyses of PAN membership support this finding. As Mabry (1973: 34–35) notes, "The men who entered for protection of their capital were the smallest in number and the least loyal to the party, most of them leaving within the first decade." Likewise, Camp's findings (1995) suggest that the PAN is much more a middle-class party than a party of the rich.

[33] Ruffo, a protégé of Clouthier, had gained widespread popularity in Baja California while serving as mayor of Ensenada. Although Ruffo seems to have overshadowed his party, his gubernatorial campaign focused new attention on the PAN and made the prospect of running as a PAN candidate much more attractive to persons not previously associated with the party. Carlos Montejo, the PAN's 1989 mayoral candidate in Tijuana, is an excellent example of this phenomenon.

[34] Author interview with Vicente Fox, Guanajuato, June 1997.

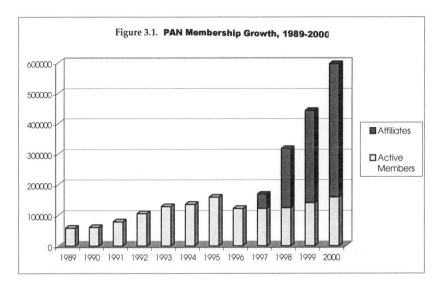

Figure 3.1. **PAN Membership Growth, 1989-2000**

Sources: For 1989–1994, Reveles Vásquez 1996: 30. For 1995–2000, CEN membership registry.

Professionalization of Functions and Organizational Specialization

Changes in the PAN in the 1980s and 1990s enabled the party to perform an increasing number of functions more fully and efficiently than in the past. In large measure, it was greater financial resources that gave the party opportunities to extend its organizational presence at the state and local levels. Although public funding had been available to the party since the late 1970s, the general sentiment within the PAN had been that accepting such funding would place the party at the mercy of the PRI regime and thereby jeopardize its integrity.[35]

Under the direction of party president Luis H. Álvarez (1987–1993), however, the PAN's national leadership reconsidered the issue of public funding for its activities.[36] Though many of the PAN's national

---

[35] Mexico's 1977 political reform made funding and other forms of public assistance available to political parties for the first time. The PAN accepted free (but limited) television and radio access, tax-exempt status, and franking privileges for postage and telephone expenses, but it refused funds for organizational support. Some party activists held that public resources should be used for purposes other than supporting political parties (social welfare programs, for example).

[36] Álvarez joined the PAN in 1956 and ran as the party's gubernatorial candidate in Chihuahua the same year. Just two years later he ran as the party's presidential

councilors remained uncertain about whether to accept public funding, Álvarez pushed for reforms (which were later enacted by the PRI government) that would make public financing more transparent, thereby ensuring that accepting such monies did not make the recipient dependent on the regime.[37] Thus public financing regulations were reformed so that monies were no longer distributed by the executive branch (via the Ministry of the Interior). The new distribution formula was based on campaign costs, the number of party candidates, and the number of votes cast for a party.

Access to substantially expanded financial resources dramatically altered the PAN's situation. Along with increased access to daily conveniences like office equipment, new funding meant that the PAN could acquire real estate on which to locate local and state-level offices. Public funding also supported the PAN's organizational development by permitting the hiring of full-time employees, and in some cases it even provided salaries for party leaders. With a professional staff, the party now had the capacity to oversee daily affairs, recruit and mobilize militants, and launch counterattacks against the PRI. And because they now had salaried positions, PAN leaders could give their full attention to party needs.

Expanding human, material, and financial resources facilitated—indeed, necessitated—organizational specialization. In line with changes at the national level, the PAN developed the administrative capabilities of its local organizations to oversee electoral activities, support the professional development of individuals placed in public office, manage information systems, and so on. As these management functions were professionalized, many day-to-day activities were decentralized through the creation of task-specific committees and subcommittees. The division of labor into smaller units helped the party encourage neighborhood-level participation, and this, in turn, simplified the assignment of electoral activities and other tasks.

New activists brought innovative ideas. This was especially true of the party's candidates with private-sector backgrounds. Drawing on their professional experience, they introduced "modern" methods—from increased reliance on advertising to computers and innovative

---

candidate. Álvarez's activism paid off in 1983 when he became one of a handful of PAN mayors, winning the city of Chihuahua. He returned to national prominence when he began his second term as CEN president in 1987. Álvarez has been a state and national councilor since 1956 and 1970, respectively, and he served as federal senator in 1994–2000.

[37] Author interviews with Senator Luis H. Álvarez, Mexico City, May 1997, and with CEN Director of Studies Gustavo Vicencio, Mexico City, April 1997.

forms of communications—that transformed the organization's everyday operations.[38]

Nevertheless, in many ways the PAN's strategies still reflected the decisions of an aloof and insulated central leadership. For example, the federal funding allocated for Mexico's 1997 midterm elections included monies that normally were directed to presidential elections. Under the leadership of Felipe Calderón Hinojosa, the PAN's National Council rejected the portion of federal funding intended for presidential campaigns on the grounds that it was inappropriate to accept these monies in a midterm contest. The PAN stood alone in its high-minded sacrifice, and many defeated PAN congressional candidates later complained that this decision had undercut their 1997 electoral campaigns and the overall development of the party.[39]

Thus the PAN's internal decision-making structures had a significant impact on the party's professional development and application of resources. Its initial refusal of public funding effectively stunted the party's development until the late 1980s, and the decision to refuse part of the public funds available in 1997 proved self-defeating.

The following discussion considers the competing visions that exist within the PAN and the role of party leaders and institutions in mediating these internal divisions.

Intra-Party Relations

As the PAN grew and took on the responsibilities of government, it also had to deal with new internal frictions. Many PAN leaders deny any divergence over goals, claiming that the party remains united through its doctrine and principles. However, differences have emerged regarding how to achieve those goals and who should set the agenda. Some party leaders attribute internal divisions to increased opportunism arising from the party's growth and increased competition for candidate nominations.

Several scholars have described these tensions as conflicts between the party's old and new members (Arriola 1994; Loaeza 1999). Such a characterization would seem to apply, for example, to the conflict between the national leadership and the members of the Foro Democrá-

---

[38] Some longtime party militants also produced innovation. For example, Carlos Castillo Peraza, in his capacity as a plurinominal federal deputy, helped revive Mérida's *panista* organization.

[39] Author interview with CEN member Ana Rosa Payán, July 1997. Many PAN members were convinced they would win both the Federal District and a congressional majority in 1997. Their disappointment prompted a reevaluation of party strategies.

tico y Doctrinario (Democratic and Doctrinaire Forum), a group of longtime party militants who defected from the PAN in 1993 claiming that the leadership was leading the party away from its basic principles.[40] In reality, however, the *foristas* represented a very small portion of the party's members; only a few hundred withdrew at the national level, and the number of militants who left the party at the local level was negligible.[41] The *foristas'* exit hardly threatened to tear the organization apart. Nor did it eliminate factional divisions within the party.

Indeed, the claim that the major schisms within the party are between old-timers and newcomers dramatically oversimplifies the problem. Although there are factional divisions over some major issues, these splits do not appear to be purely generational in character. Rather, factional rifts within the PAN mainly reflect power struggles between individuals and groups competing for candidacies and leadership positions. As a matter of fact, there are usually both newcomers and old-timers on both sides in the quest for power. In these rivalries, younger members sometimes defend long-standing ideological principles, and lifetime militants may support more pragmatic strategies. Tensions sharpen when victory appears most possible (usually when the PAN was victorious in the preceding election). Ironically, in localities where divisions within the PRI gave the PAN its initial chance to rise to power, divisions within the PAN have proved to be its downfall.

By the mid–1990s, the PAN's national leadership noted that the party's growing ranks were becoming increasingly divided, and this sparked an internal debate regarding the prospects for sustainable growth. A watershed moment came in 1995 with the selection of a new national leadership in a contest that pitted Baja California's Ernesto Ruffo against Michoacán's Felipe Calderón, then secretary general of the CEN. These two men symbolized very different orientations regarding the party's organizational development, and the contest between them clearly revealed the regional rivalries that exist within the party.

---

[40] The *foristas* alleged undue and antidemocratic cooperation with the government, business's growing influence in party life, and intolerance toward diverse groups and opinions within the party (Reynoso 1994: 194).

[41] More important, despite the *foristas'* rhetoric and appeals to PAN traditionalism, the conflict was hardly a schism between old and new elements in the party. Both sides drew equally from the PAN's older militants; for example, Luis H. Álvarez, then president of the CEN, was no *neopanista*.

Many leaders of the Foro (particularly Pablo E. Madero) had generated resentment among traditional party members in internal conflicts during the 1970s, when a bitterly divided contest for the PAN's presidential nomination left the party without a candidate. Author interviews with Luis H. Álvarez, Mexico City, May 1997; Nabor Centeno, León, May 1997; and Miguel Gutiérrez Machado, Mérida, July 1997.

Ruffo, having just completed his historic term as governor, was a legendary figure in the PAN. Heralding from the northern border region, he represented the possibilities of a decentered regime that literally "bordered on democracy." Ruffo was, therefore, the symbol of a new "can do" attitude frequently associated with the PAN's "barbarians from the north." These new party members had entered the PAN in the 1980s and waged successful state and local campaigns in Baja California, Chihuahua, and Nuevo León. Ruffo also personified the new elements within the party that threatened to wrest control away from the central leadership, then dominated by intellectuals and academics (including outgoing CEN president Carlos Castillo Peraza of Yucatán) who had given decades of service to the party but had little electoral success or governmental experience.[42]

Felipe Calderón, in contrast, came from the centralized party leadership and represented the PAN's most venerable traditions. His family had figured prominently in the PAN's national leadership for years, and longtime *panistas* could remember when young Felipe played in the party's Mexico City offices. Calderón's campaign slogan had clear implications for the PAN's future development—"Let's win elections, not lose the party." Calderón's supporters felt the party was being overrun by *neopanistas,* outsiders who did not understand PAN philosophy and tradition. Yet because by 1995 new members already represented the vast majority of the party's base, it seemed unlikely that Calderón would emerge victorious. Nonetheless, Calderón did defeat Ruffo, thanks to internal procedures that protected the leadership selection process from rapid shifts in membership (see figure 3.1).[43]

Under CEN President Calderón, regulations concerning party membership were tightened as part of an effort to attract only individuals who agreed with the party's political philosophy and were vetted by existing PAN members. On the one hand, this meant preserving existing requirements for individuals who aspired to become active party members, with full privileges and voting rights.[44] On the other

---

[42] In all fairness to Castillo Peraza, his leadership marked the most significant period of PAN electoral successes and organizational development up to that point. However, aside from serving as a plurinominal deputy, he never won a direct electoral contest for public office, despite several attempts.

[43] As noted earlier, party statutes mandate that the executive leadership (CEN) be selected by a body of national councilors, a significant number of whom are linked to or selected by the CEN. As outgoing CEN secretary general, Calderón had a clear advantage.

[44] Requirements include a formal recommendation by one or more party members, a six-month period of service within the party, and regular payment of dues upon admission to the party.

hand, Calderón's administration introduced new programs for training and evaluating would-be members and, beginning in 1997, kept records on the number of non-voting "affiliated" party supporters (*adherentes*). Both innovations were meant to create filters to improve the "quality" of incoming members. Most important, the new *adherente* category enabled party leaders to manage rapidly growing support for the party without allowing newcomers to influence directly the organization's internal affairs.

Moreover, with control over party affiliation placed under the CEN's central membership registry, each application for PAN membership was processed in the party's Mexico City offices, rather than going through state or local committees. The imposition of central controls on membership slowed the affiliation process. Indeed, until a prospective PAN member received a membership credential, he or she could not vote in internal elections or hold a leadership position.

In short, in the contest between competing PAN coalitions, party leaders (and the internal decision-making mechanisms that protected them) played a decisive role in determining the party's development trajectory. To the PAN's credit, one result of this shift in membership policy is that the party's rolls are the most accurate of any political party in Mexico.[45] On the other hand, tightening membership controls and centralizing membership procedures brought the party's booming rate of growth to a standstill, particularly from 1997 to 1998 when the CEN decided to place a temporary moratorium on all new memberships.[46] Thereafter, the PAN was slow to recover its previous momentum. In fact, the party's membership base remains relatively small in relation to the voters it attracts in elections and the population it now governs, leaving the party open to criticism that its links to civil society are weak. In many municipalities, for example, only a few hundred militants are often responsible for selecting the candidate who will eventually govern over a million people. This is considerably different from the PRI's traditional, "one-fingered" mechanism of candidate selection (*dedazo*), but it falls short of the level of civic participation that PAN doctrine advocates.

---

[45] This is also due to the fact that in 1994 Castillo Peraza had initiated a massive "reaffiliation" effort to determine actual membership levels.

[46] The decision to limit membership growth in an election year was partly to ensure a degree of control over PAN candidacies. One concern voiced by slow-growth advocates was that outsiders with little loyalty to the PAN had gained too much influence over candidate selection and too much access to candidacies. Limiting affiliation during an election year—though seemingly counterintuitive—fits a certain growth-phobic logic.

FOX AND FRIENDS: THE ECLIPSE OF THE PAN?

President Vicente Fox presents a fitting national-level illustration of PAN party building in recent years. While Fox served as PAN governor of Guanajuato, national-level party leaders perceived him as a potential rival and made strategic decisions to minimize his ability to develop a national coalition to support his political ambitions. Fox's long road to the PAN's presidential nomination and then on to the presidency is rife with examples of the national leadership's efforts at self-preservation and containment of the Fox phenomenon.

During most of the party's recent development, the fact that the national leadership adopted a fairly constrained approach to party building accounted for the slow pace and limited extent to which the party reacted to key opportunities. The refusal of public funding in the 1980s and 1990s, as well as the party's extremely centralized procedures for controlling membership growth in the 1990s, reflected the dominance of the party leadership's particular vision of the organization.

This internal centralism generated frustration at the subnational level. Candidates and campaign managers, feeling the pinch of the PAN's self-imposed budgetary restrictions, complained that they were at a disadvantage vis-à-vis their competitors. In addition, the high standards set by the national leadership for members' active participation in the party, combined with the highly centralized procedures for controlling membership, limited the party's ability to grow at the local level. As a result, it was difficult for the PAN to take full advantage of upswings in electoral support.

The PAN certainly experienced significant development as an organization during the 1990s. It reformed internal organizational arrangements, renovated and expanded membership rolls, and professionalized other aspects of its activities. Nevertheless, the national party leaders' "slow-growth" approach to organizational development (especially under Felipe Calderón) restricted the party in a crucial period, with several negative consequences for the PAN. As noted above, the party failed to make a full-court press to win control of the federal legislature in 1997, mainly because of self-imposed limitations on membership and public funding. In addition, and perhaps more consequential for the party's long-term development, this approach produced significant friction between the party leadership and vocal proponents of party building and an innovative electoral strategy. Popular state and local leaders who advocated greater flexibility on membership growth, candidate selection, and cooperation with other opposition parties were ignored or rebuked by the leadership.

During Felipe Calderón's term as party president, such national-subnational friction was most obvious in relation to Vicente Fox. As gubernatorial candidate in Guanajuato in 1991 and 1995, Fox displayed a degree of tolerance and pragmatism that separated him and his followers from the anti–PRD stance of the PAN's national leadership. Although one might assume that the hotly contested and challenged 1991 Guanajuato elections caused bad blood between Fox and national party leaders, this does not seem to be the case.[47] After the elections, the national leadership proclaimed they would "give their all for Guanajuato" (*La Jornada* 1991a). CEN official Alfredo Ling Altamirano went even further, suggesting that the PAN would be willing to sacrifice its party registration in order to defend the vote for Fox (*La Jornada* 1991b). Yet when PRI candidate Ramón Aguirre, the self-proclaimed victor in the governor's race, resigned immediately following the election, such bold statements of PAN support gradually subsided. Within weeks President Salinas removed Aguirre and appointed Carlos Medina Plascencia, the *panista* mayor of León, as interim governor. Although clearly unhappy, Fox was not overtly hostile toward PAN president Luis H. Álvarez and other party leaders when they met in León in a show of unity following the "scandalous fraud of 1991." Indeed, both Álvarez and Fox held Salinas responsible, arguing that the interim governorship was a "product of presidential intervention" (*La Jornada* 1991c). In the end, Fox remained loyal to the PAN leadership.

However, Fox grew increasingly dissatisfied with both the Salinas administration and the PAN's national leadership under Álvarez's immediate successors (Carlos Castillo Peraza and Felipe Calderón). Fox was frustrated by delays in state-level negotiations over the calling of special elections in Guanajuato. Initially, interim Governor Medina announced that special elections would be held in 1993, pending electoral reforms to be negotiated in the PRI–dominated state legislature. However, PRI leaders in the state congress delayed the convocation of elections by refusing to cooperate in negotiating the reforms. Fox came to suspect that Salinas, driven by his personal dislike of Fox, was using delaying tactics to postpone elections until the end of his presidential term.[48]

---

[47] Loaeza (1999: 503–504), for example, contends that Fox was embittered by the results of 1991 and even briefly left politics in protest. However, as mentioned below, Fox's formal resignation from politics actually came in 1993 and seems to have been much more reflective of his frustration over the delay in holding special elections in Guanajuato and the negotiation of constitutional amendments that legally delayed his run for president until 2000.

[48] Medina and Fox took divergent positions concerning Salinas and his programs. Medina frequently praised PRONASOL (Salinas's hallmark anti-poverty program),

As Fox's frustration grew, he raised his sights to a higher level. As early as 1992 he declared his interest in running for president (*A.M.* 1992, 1993a, 1993b). Fox's hopes of competing for the presidency in 1994 were dashed in national-level negotiations between the PRI and the PAN over reforms to Article 82 of the 1917 Constitution. This article originally required both parents of a presidential candidate to be Mexico-born citizens. Fox (whose mother was born in Spain) and his supporters argued for revision of Article 82 on the grounds that, by establishing a second-class citizenship, it violated Fox's human rights. Fox asserted that if Salinas truly wanted to open the presidential field to more candidates, he would support the reform. Fox's calls for reform of Article 82 won the support of "half-Mexican" PRI aspirants as well, permitting bipartisan passage of an amendment.

The PAN leadership responded to the idea of a Fox presidential candidacy by publicly supporting constitutional reform. In the end, however, the reforms passed only on condition that they go into effect *after* the 1994 elections, making Fox ineligible until the year 2000. An outraged Fox declared that he would be too old to run in 2000. He was particularly disappointed in the national PAN leadership's "betrayal" at the negotiating table. The chief PAN negotiator was congressional leader Diego Fernández de Cevallos. When asked whether delaying the implementation of this constitutional reform meant that the PAN would lose its best candidate, Fernández de Cevallos stated that he did not consider Fox the best—or the only—PAN candidate for 1994. Indeed, with Fox out of the picture, Fernández de Cevallos was able to grab the PAN's presidential nomination for himself, although he denied any such political calculations on his part (*La Jornada* 1993).

Fox's response was a public withdrawal from politics, despite the leadership's appeals that he remain active in the party (*A.M.* 1993c, 1993d, 1994a). He announced his retirement in a long and bitter tirade against Carlos Salinas and what he characterized as Mexico's road to destruction:

> As long as Salinas is here, count me out.... Vicente Fox will no longer lend himself to raising the hopes of the citizenry, mobilizing them and taking them toward that holocaust, toward that death trap to which Salinas is taking us. I abstain from participating because there are no longer any real conditions for democracy, for electoral transparency, for respect for human rights and political rights.... Fox will not ... participate so long as Salinas is president. With other

---

and when he criticized its implementation, he was careful not to blame Salinas directly. Fox, on the other hand, said that Salinas had tricked Mexicans "like Hitler tricked the Jews." See *A.M.* 1991; *Proceso* 1990.

[presidents] one knew what to look out for. They were not democratic, and we fought to change this, but with Salinas it is deception. He is Machiavellian and pretends to be democratic.

Fox did return briefly to the political arena in 1994 to rally PAN members to defend claimed municipal victories in Guanajuato (*A.M.* 1994b). However, true to his pledge to wait out the Salinas administration, he did not announce his return to politics until January 1995 (*A.M.* 1995), by which time he was already wildly popular in Guanajuato. He went on to win the state's governorship when the long-delayed special gubernatorial election was finally held later that year.

Fox's national presence grew enormously throughout his governorship, while the relative strength of his rivals in the national PAN leadership declined. First, although Diego Fernández de Cevallos remained a prominent figure in the party after his unsuccessful 1994 bid for the presidency, he seemed unwilling to take on further candidacies. In 1997, a misadventurous campaign to head the government of the Federal District humbled the once-proud Carlos Castillo Peraza, who later withdrew from the party. And finally, the political image of PAN president Felipe Calderón was tarnished by his association with the party's poor electoral performance in 1997.

These leaders' repeated efforts to thwart Fox's presidential ambitions encouraged him to seek other means of building support. Fox worked actively to cultivate his own support base within the party in the state of Guanajuato, particularly in the PAN stronghold of León. Yet his success in gaining control over the leadership of the PAN's state organization did not translate into success in placing his allies in mayoral candidacies or proportional representation seats in the state legislature. Nor did Fox's ability to capture the party leadership at the state and local levels translate into an ability to promote his supporters in national-level positions. In 1997 in particular, the national PAN leadership, which influenced the allocation of proportional representation seats, rejected candidates nominated by Guanajuato's state and local leadership in favor of Guanajuato candidates closer to Calderón.

During his tenure as governor, Fox also began to cultivate a national and international presence as a means of developing an extra-party support base. He soon indicated his intention to win not only his party's nomination for 2000 but the presidency itself. In 1997, the Amigos de Fox ("Friends of Fox," a nonpartisan organization unconstrained by national election regulations) began maneuvering in support of Fox's candidacy by raising funds, distributing trademark booster pins and other pro-Fox materials, and producing a series of televised spot announcements. Although the Friends of Fox represented a step toward the "Americanization" of party politics in Mexico, it was mainly the product of the PAN national leadership's animosity toward Fox. U.S.–style techno-marketing techniques and campaign strategies made the Friends of Fox a possibility; the antipathy of Felipe Calderón made it a strategic necessity if Fox was to prevail.

Also during his governorship, Fox won renown for his international travel to promote Guanajuato's export industries, trips that also yielded clear domestic and international political benefits. He visited Asia, Europe, other Latin American countries, and the United States. Fox's audiences included influential foreign business leaders and politicians, Mexico-born voters living abroad (eligible since 1996 for dual national-ity and considered a potential pivotal voting bloc in 2000), and aca-demic analysts and foreign journalists, many of whom were charmed by Fox's charisma and denim-and-boots cowboy demeanor.

The success of PAN gubernatorial candidates in Querétaro and Nuevo León in 1998 also boosted aspiring presidential candidate Vicente Fox, who had strong support in both states. These wins marked a significant shift in the balance of power within the party leadership away from Mexico's central and southeastern regions.[49]

In 1997, poor strategic decisions on the part of the traditional party leadership had produced stunning defeats for the PAN. Carlos Castillo Peraza's disastrous performance in the 1997 Federal District election was at least partly the result of national-level attacks against the PAN that focused on decisions made by local PAN governments—censorship in the cities of Aguascalientes, Puebla, and Monterrey; the defamation of a national hero in Michoacán; and rumors of a curfew and a municipal order prohibiting civil servants from wearing mini-skirts in Guadalajara. These attacks, some faithful to the facts and oth-ers less so, made the PAN appear far more conservative than the aver-age Mexico City voter. Neither the national party leadership nor Castillo Peraza handled these incidents capably, and this showed at the polls. However, such bungling by the national leadership ultimately created new opportunities for rivals to the national party leadership to redirect the PAN.[50]

---

[49] Most of the national leadership, including Michoacán's Felipe Calderón and Yu-catán's Carlos Castillo Peraza, had been drawn from Mexico's central and south-eastern states.

Political prospects looked particularly grim for PAN president Calderón when the party's bid for a second successive governorship in Chihuahua failed and made outgoing PAN governor Francisco Barrio—an important northern ally of Calderón—a political albatross.

[50] In fact, Castillo Peraza withdrew from the PAN in May 1998, citing personal rea-sons. After his failed Federal District campaign, there was a subtle change in the national party leadership's disposition toward the "northern barbarians." This was evidenced, for example, by Medina's appointment (over other hopefuls closer

Indeed, by 1998, when the national leadership began to discuss selection of the party's 2000 presidential candidate, the strongest champions of the national leadership—Calderón, Fernández de Cevallos, and Francisco Barrio, former governor of Chihuahua—were either disgraced or severely weakened. Nevertheless, party leaders met in Querétaro that summer to discuss possible selection mechanisms that might block a Fox candidacy.

At this same time, the PAN was under external competitive pressures to choose a more open and democratic method of nominating its presidential candidate. The PRD's open candidate selection process demoted the PAN to the position of second-most-democratic party in Mexico. The PRI was also giving lip service to similarly oriented internal reforms, and it began to appear that the ruling party might develop more democratic selection procedures than the PAN's. Yet PAN leaders remained unsure whether to open the party to greater participation by nonmilitants (as the PRD had done), limit participation to existing members, or maintain the existing selection method, by which delegates to the National Assembly selected the presidential candidate.

National PAN leaders who opposed Fox's candidacy had no easy way to block him because his national campaign had already won a huge following. They realized that, even though it might promote a party image of internal democracy, opening the selection process would give Fox an even greater advantage over other potential candidates. Yet these leaders also feared that Fox had sufficient support among party delegates to win the nomination even if the selection process remained closed. Thus, restricting candidate selection to delegates only would very likely produce a Fox nomination anyway, and it would paint the PAN as the least democratic party in the Mexican political system. Direct candidate selection by the National Council would have given party leaders their best chance of defeating Fox with an alternative candidate, but this option would have been extremely unpopular with members and it would have also portrayed the PAN as internally undemocratic.

With no clear idea of how to keep Fox from winning the nomination, the PAN leadership postponed taking a decision on nomination procedures until after the selection of a new party president in March 1999. In that contest, Felipe Bravo Mena trounced Ricardo García Cervantes, a young, lesser-known senator from Baja California. Bravo Mena had the support of both the national leadership and Fox and many of his supporters, and his margin of victory was the largest of any PAN national president in two decades.

---

to the national leadership) as leader of the PAN delegation to the federal Chamber of Deputies.

The decision reached under Bravo Mena's party leadership with regard to presidential nomination procedures was a compromise. Voting for the party's candidacy would be open to all party members and to "affiliated" supporters. This method of selection protected the PAN by keeping decision making within the party, but it also tacitly acknowledged the inevitability of a Fox nomination. To be sure, the fact that Fox ran unopposed made the party's nomination no more than a rubber stamp, and it also undermined the party's efforts to appear internally democratic.

The national leadership's shifting position on nomination procedures reflected its attempt to keep pace with the national coalition's support for Fox, and it is not clear whether Bravo Mena personally favored a Fox candidacy. What is clear is that Fox's position vis-à-vis the national leadership changed dramatically after he went outside the PAN to develop his own base of support. In effect, the constraints that the PAN's internal institutional arrangements and leadership structures put on Fox forced him to seek leverage outside the organization, and his success in building extra-party support then rebounded to weaken these same arrangements and structures.

The outcomes of this process have included some potentially negative consequences for the PAN's institutional development. First, the Friends of Fox, which was the primary vehicle for Fox's candidacy, continues to be largely autonomous from the party. Although this may have made it easier for independent voters and militants from other parties to support candidate Fox, the group's existence undermines an important opportunity to further the PAN's organizational development. Furthermore, weak party affiliation contributed to widespread split-ballot voting in the July 2000 elections. Although the PAN won the presidency, it did not win a majority in either chamber of the federal legislature, which will complicate executive-legislative interactions during at least the first half of Fox's six-year administration (2000–2006). The continuance of divided government is not necessarily bad for Mexico, but clearly it will not help fortify the PAN's organization, its overall electoral prospects, or its effectiveness in government.

FINAL OBSERVATIONS

The PAN's experience during the 1980s and 1990s suggests that successful party building does not depend entirely on economic conditions, the opening of political institutions, civil society's responses, or competing parties' organizational characteristics. The character of the PAN's party building efforts also reflected the interplay between shifting membership bases and interest coalitions within the organization, on the one hand, and the established leadership and decision-making structures, on the other. Indeed, internal factors have had an important impact on the PAN's approach to party building and on the party's performance in other spheres of activity. In fact, internal institutional arrangements and the struggle to control them had significant implications for the party's behavior as a whole.

The PAN's story conveys a lesson that has important implications for the analysis and promotion of democracy. At least with respect to parties, one cannot simply assume that electoral democratization will lead to more democratic political institutions. Equally, the role that parties can play in democratizing other institutions depends heavily on the extent to which they are able to fortify themselves as organizations. This, in turn, is not merely a function of events that unfold around the party in the course of electoral democratization; it is also intrinsically related to the internal processes that determine a party's response to its environment. Future research on regime transitions must take such factors into consideration in order to evaluate the prospects for democratic consolidation.

In Mexico in particular, there is need for increased attention to the role of political parties. The research conducted to date has generally been insufficient to "unpack" Mexico's political parties as organizations. Furthermore, given the strong historic connection between party and government in Mexico, the work that has been done on the PRI tends to fall into the trap of conflating both, to the neglect of the party. Fox's victory in 2000 and the new role of political parties in the federal legislature will fuel increased attention to Mexico's parties. However, such analyses cannot simply follow the established pattern of focusing on parties' behavior during elections and in government, while ignoring the role that party organizations themselves play in determining party strategy and political behavior.

REFERENCES

Alcocer V., Jorge. 1995. "Recent Electoral Reforms in Mexico: Prospects for a Real Multiparty Democracy." In *The Challenge of Institutional Reform in Mexico*, edited by Riordan Roett. Boulder, Colo.: Lynne Rienner.

Alemán Alemán, Ricardo. 1993. *Guanajuato: espejismo electoral*. Mexico City: La Jornada Ediciones.

A.M. (León, Guanajuato). 1991. "Expone Medina metas y objectivos de su administración, en el Ibero," April 17.

———. 1992. "Acepta Vicente Fox tener diferencias con Medina y envidiarlo por ser presidenciable," February 20.

———. 1993a. "Quiero ser Presidente de la República: Fox," May 29.

———. 1993b. "Califica 'de burla' propuesta priísta," July 12.

———. 1993c. "Se reuniría Diego con Fox en lugar neutral," October 2.

———. 1993d. "Calla Fox; 'estoy retirado de política,'" October 23.

———. 1994a. "Sigue Fox 'congelado,'" March 16.

————. 1994b. "Impugnaremos lo inexpugnable," August 30.

————. 1995. "Acepta Vicente Fox," January 16.

Arriola, Carlos. 1994. *Ensayos sobre el PAN*. Mexico City: Miguel Ángel Porrúa.

Aziz Nassif, Alberto. 1994. *Chihuahua: historia de una alternativa*. Mexico City: Centro de Investigaciones y Estudios Superiores en Antropología Social/La Jornada Ediciones.

————. 1996. *Territorios de alternancia: el primer gobierno de oposición en Chihuahua*. Mexico City: Centro de Investigaciones y Estudios Superiores en Antropología Social/Triana.

Bennett, Vivienne. 1992. "The Evolution of Urban Popular Movements in Mexico between 1968 and 1988." In *The Making of Social Movements in Latin America*, edited by Arturo Escobar and Sonia E. Álvarez. Boulder, Colo.: Westview.

Camp, Roderic. 1995. "The PAN's Social Bases: Implications for Leadership." In *Opposition Government in Mexico*, edited by Victoria E. Rodríguez and Peter M. Ward. Albuquerque: University of New Mexico Press.

Campuzano Montoya, Irma. 1995. *Baja California en tiempos del PAN*. Mexico City: La Jornada Ediciones.

Cicero MacKinney, Roger. 1987. *Correa Rachó: tiempo de la libertad*. Mérida: Dante.

Cornelius, Wayne A., Judith Gentleman, and Peter H. Smith, eds. 1989. *Mexico's Alternative Political Futures*. Monograph Series, no. 30. La Jolla: Center for U.S.–Mexican Studies, University of California, San Diego.

Domínguez, Jorge I., and James A. McCann. 1996. *Democratizing Mexico: Public Opinion and Electoral Choices*. Baltimore, Md.: Johns Hopkins University Press.

Dresser, Denise. 1994. "Embellishment, Empowerment, or Euthanasia of the PRI? Neoliberalism and Party Reform in Mexico." In *The Politics of Economic Restructuring: State-Society Relations and Regime Change in Mexico*, edited by Maria Lorena Cook, Kevin J. Middlebrook, and Juan Molinar Horcasitas. La Jolla: Center for U.S.–Mexican Studies, University of California, San Diego.

Espinoza Valle, Víctor Alejandro. 1998. *Alternancia política y gestión pública: el Partido Acción Nacional en el gobierno de Baja California*. Tijuana: El Colegio de la Frontera Norte.

González Luna, Efraín. 1991 [c. 1940]. *Humanismo político*. Mexico City: Jus.

Guillén López, Tonatiuh. 1992. *Frontera norte*. Mexico City: El Colegio de México/El Colegio de la Frontera Norte.

Hernández Vicencio, Tania. 1998. "El PAN en Baja California (1989–1997)." Ph.D. dissertation, El Colegio de la Frontera Norte.

Klesner, Joseph L. 1993. "Modernization, Economic Crisis, and Electoral Alignment in Mexico," *Mexican Studies/Estudios Mexicanos* 9 (2): 187–223.

La Jornada. 1991a. "Daremos todo por Guanajuato, ratifica la dirigencia de AN," August 30.

————. 1991b. "Acción Nacional estaria dispuesto a perder su registro," August 27.

————. 1991c. "Cambio radical del PAN en su relación con el gobierno," September 8.

————. 1993. "Acepta PAN que la reforma al 82 rija a partir de 1999," August 27.

Loaeza, Soledad. 1989. "The Emergence and Legitimization of the Modern Right, 1970–1988." In *Mexico's Alternative Political Futures*, edited by Wayne A. Cornelius, Judith Gentleman, and Peter H. Smith. La Jolla: Center for U.S.–Mexican Studies, University of California, San Diego.

———. 1999. *El Partido Acción Nacional: la larga marcha, 1939–1994*. Mexico City: Fondo de Cultura Económica.

Mabry, Donald. 1973. *Mexico's Acción Nacional: A Catholic Alternative to Revolution*. Syracuse, N.Y.: Syracuse University Press.

Medina Valdés, Gerardo. 1959. "Entrevista," *La Nación* 18, vol. 35 (930): 2–3.

Mizrahi, Yemile. 1994. "Rebels without a Cause? The Politics of Entrepreneurs in Chihuahua," *Journal of Latin American Studies* 26: 137–58.

———. 1998. "Dilemmas of the Opposition in Government: Chihuahua and Baja California," *Mexican Studies/Estudios Mexicanos* 14 (1): 151–89.

Moctezuma Barragán, Pablo. 1997. *Los orígenes del PAN*. Mexico City: Ehecatl.

Montalvo Ortega, Enrique. 1996. *México: en una transición conservadora. El caso de Yucatán*. Mexico City: Instituto Nacional de Antropología e Historia/La Jornada Ediciones.

Montalvo Ortega, Enrique, and Iván Vallardo Fajardo. 1997. *Yucatán: sociedad, economía, política, cultura*. Mexico City: Universidad Nacional Autónoma de México.

Ortega, Carlos G. 1961. *Democracia dirigida con ametralladoras: Baja California, 1958–1960*. El Paso, Tex.: La Prensa.

Proceso. 1990. "Reclutado por Clouthier, el neopanista Vicente Fox, seguro de convertirse en el segundo gobernador de oposición," October 29.

Reveles Vásquez, Francisco. 1993. "Sistema organizativo y fracciones internas del Partido Acción Nacional, 1939–1990." Master's thesis, Universidad Nacional Autónoma de México.

———. 1996. "El proceso de institucionalización organizativa del Partido Acción Nacional (1984–1995)." Ph.D. dissertation, Universidad Nacional Autónoma de México.

Reynoso, Víctor Manuel. 1994. "El PAN en 1993: los foristas se van, Castillo llega a la presidencia y Diego es elegido candidato a la presidencia de la República." In *Elecciones y partidos políticos en México*, edited by Leonardo Valdés. Iztapalapa: Universidad Autónoma Metropolitana.

Rodríguez, Victoria E., and Peter M. Ward. 1994. *Political Change in Baja California: Democracy in the Making?* Monograph Series, no. 40. La Jolla: Center for U.S.–Mexican Studies, University of California, San Diego.

Shirk, David A. 1999. "Democratization and Local Party Building: The PAN in León, Guanajuato." In *Subnational Politics and Democratization in Mexico*, edited by Wayne A. Cornelius, Todd A. Eisenstadt, and Jane Hindley. La Jolla: Center for U.S.–Mexican Studies, University of California, San Diego.

———. 2000. "Democratization and Party-Building: The Growing Pains of Mexico's National Action Party." Ph.D. dissertation, University of California, San Diego.

Stansfield, David E. 1996. "The PAN: The Search for Ideological and Electoral Space." In *Dismantling the Mexican State?* edited by Rob Aitken et al. New York: St. Martin's.

von Sauer, Franz A. 1974. *The Alienated "Loyal" Opposition: Mexico's Partido Acción Nacional*. Albuquerque: University of New Mexico Press.

Wilkie James W., and Edna Monzón de Wilkie. 1978. *Entrevistas con Manuel Gómez Morin*. Mexico City: Jus.

4

Barbarians, Bureaucrats, and Bluebloods: Fractional Change in the National Action Party

Steven T. Wuhs

INTRODUCTION

The National Action Party (PAN) is normally regarded as Mexico's most cohesive party organization. Certainly it is cohesive when compared with the Institutional Revolutionary Party (PRI) and the Party of the Democratic Revolution (PRD). However, both independent analysts and PAN members have been too willing to accept an idealized view of the party organization as a unified political force, underpinned by its ideology and the strength of its institutional history. In fact, important divisions have always existed within the PAN, and they have serious consequences for the party's cohesion. Fractions are particularly important in decisions about candidate selection (especially for proportional representation seats) and positions in the party bureaucracy. Many *panistas* also feel that one particular division (between groups associated, respectively, with Vicente Fox Quesada and with Diego Fernández de Cevallos) was in part responsible for the PAN's loss in the 1994 presidential election. With Fox's victory in the 2000 presidential contest, fractions within the PAN promise to be even more significant in *panista* affairs and in Mexican politics more generally.

This chapter draws on the existing political science literature on party fractions and examines how divisions in the PAN have been analyzed in the past, relating those examinations to the more general

The author thanks Evelyne Huber, Kevin J. Middlebrook, Yemile Mizrahi, Joy Langston, and Jeffrey Weldon for their comments on this essay, and the División de Estudios Políticos at the Centro de Investigación y Docencia Económicas (CIDE) for its support. In addition, he would like to thank the PAN members interviewed for this project for their openness. This research was funded by an Institute for the Study of World Politics Dissertation Fellowship.

literature on parties and critiquing previous characterizations of the PAN's fractional structure.[1] Then, based on extensive interviews with present and past PAN members and an analysis of party documents, this essay presents an alternative characterization of the PAN's fractions during the period from the late 1970s to the present, along with an examination of the factors that led to changes in the structure of these divisions. The chapter ends with some comments on divisions in political parties, along with some reflections on the importance of fractions for Mexico's democratic transition.

THINKING ABOUT INTRA-PARTY DIVISIONS

Party organizations have divisions. There is little debate on that point, whether or not party members choose to acknowledge them. However, scholars have struggled to develop systematic ways of conceptualizing and analyzing those divisions. Indicative of this difficulty is the evolution of the terminology used to discuss the phenomenon. Until recently, the predominant term employed to discuss intra-party division was "faction," a term used so broadly that it incorporated virtually any sort of sub-party group. Zariski (1960: 33–34), for example, described factions as "forces which compete for the acquisition of influence over the principal institutions of intra-party government, over the formulation of party policy, and over the selection of party leaders and party nominees for public office."

Later definitions attempted to distinguish between different types of sub-party organization. Rose (1964: 37–38) is among the authors most cited for this kind of work. He makes the important distinction between factions and tendencies on the basis of their internal structures. Factions are "self-consciously organized bod[ies] with a measure of cohesion and discipline," while tendencies are typified by a "stable set of attitudes rather than a stable set of politicians." The principal difference between the two, then, is that tendencies typically lack formal organization.

Like Rose, Sartori discusses factions as specific power groups, and tendencies as patterned sets of attitudes (1976: 75). His contribution is the addition of the term fraction, which in his analysis refers to a general, unspecified sub-party unit of organization. Factions and tendencies, then, represent the two ends of the *fraction* spectrum. For this reason, the term fraction is used in the present analysis to refer to the general phenomenon of party division.

---

[1] The author adopts Sartori's (1976) vocabulary with regard to internal party divisions. In a somewhat lengthy discussion, Sartori distinguishes between factions and tendencies, and he selects the term fraction to describe the more general phenomenon of subunits in a given party organization.

Having established the definitional terms of the debate, we can now turn to the substance of previous scholarly analyses concerning how these sub-party groups are structured. A survey of the literature reveals two principal questions, addressed in turn below.

Why do fractions exist? The literature offers a variety of responses to this question, operating on quite different levels of analysis. Some studies offer institutional or structural explanations for the development of fractions. For example, one body of literature suggests that fractions can help parties overcome divisions in highly divided political systems by allowing for diverse opinions in a single party organization (Brass 1965; McAllister 1991; Zuckerman 1979). These works also suggest that fractions may facilitate the adaptation of party organization to changes in the political environment.

To better understand the development of sub-party divisions, we must also examine the incentives that individual actors (leaders and members of fractions, for example) face that encourage the development of fractions. To begin, we consider the standard rational choice assumption that politicians are motivated by the desire to further their careers, as true in Mexico as it is elsewhere.[2] Given that fact, we would expect to see the development of fractions to the extent that party elites view them as helpful in prolonging their careers. By constructing a loyal team of supporters, party elites are able to gain greater influence over party matters and guarantee their own political futures (assuming a quid-pro-quo relationship in which their supporters are, in fact, loyal). Members of fractions, on the other hand, may expect support from their leader in winning local party nominations or party posts.

One group of authors focusing specifically on one-party states argues that fractions exist essentially as proxies for party competition (Key 1949; Kohno 1992; Langston n.d.). That is, in environments where an exit option from the party organization is not available or desirable, politicians organize within the party apparatus to contest power in order to control resources and thus influence the party's development or actions.

---

[2] See Schlesinger 1994; Downs 1957. In Mexico, all discussions about politicians furthering their careers must acknowledge Mexico's no-reelection rule, which forces all elected officials to change their particular political post every three or six years. Although politicians in other contexts may develop primarily legislative careers, in Mexico politicians also cycle through party bureaucratic posts (which are now generally paid positions). This means that politicians must retain support in their states and districts (if they wish to compete in majority and plurinominal districts), in the party's national council (to reach the national executive committee), and in the executive committee (to win access to the party-appointed plurinominal seats). For a more extensive discussion of nomination rules for legislators, see Wuhs n.d.

Cox and Rosenbluth (1993) offer a related perspective in their analysis of Japan's Liberal Democratic Party. They suggest that three party activities are particularly important in the development and maintenance of fractions: appointment to party and government posts, selection of party candidates for public office, and distribution of campaign funds.[3] These posts and resources serve as the effective basis for the construction of party fractions. Party elites build their teams in order to contest and win the party presidency, candidacies for their loyal supporters, and control of party funds.

Panebianco's (1988) discussion differs somewhat from these analyses based on "office seekers." Although recognizing this motivation, he argues that party elites view the survival of the party organization as key to prolonging their careers. His analysis is more organizationally based, describing how party elites mobilize to control organizational resources (and, in the process, form coalitions within the party). He contends that party subunits come together in order to control "zones of uncertainty" that are crucial to the normal functioning of the party. These zones include internal party communications, statute establishment and reform, organizational finance, and member recruitment, all of which relate to control of the party *organization*.

Panebianco's perspective does not contradict the framework suggested by Cox and Rosenbluth; it simply highlights the importance of the party posts they discuss. In this chapter, the two approaches are combined to examine how fractions organize around the control of leadership posts and economic resources in the party bureaucracy and the selection of party candidates for public office.

What are the principal dimensions of fractions? Just as Sartori contributed greatly to the systematic analysis of parties and party systems, he also suggested a framework for analyzing party fractions. He identifies four (non–mutually exclusive) axes along which we may examine such divisions. First, he posits that fractions vary in their degree of organizational autonomy; some are recognized by their parties, have their own funding bases, and have institutionalized voices, while others do not. Second, he notes that fractions may be motivated by the desire to attain political power (that is, to govern), by the desire to obtain the benefits of governing (the spoils), or by some combination of these two goals. This is his motivational dimension. Sartori's third dimension is

---

[3] This discussion of resource endowments in the party's environment mirrors the approach used by organizational ecologists when they discuss niches in which organizations exist. See Gray and Lowery 1996; Hannan and Freeman 1989. The extent to which these resources serve as incentives for the development of fractions is mediated by the rules of candidate selection, party appointment, and the national electoral system.

ideological, an axis with fanatic and pragmatic extremes. Finally, Sartori argues that parties vary in their political positioning on the traditional left-right scale.[4] He then suggests some additional criteria, drawing from other fields of political inquiry. For example, Sartori notes that we can also examine whether fractions are personalistic or coalitional; the role that fractions play in the political sphere (as policy groups, veto groups, or support/bandwagon groups); whether fractions are strategic or tactical; and, of course, the size and durability of fractions within the party organization.

The literature on party strategy suggests another set of dimensions. According to Greene (2000), Magaloni (1997), and Molinar Horcasitas (1991), Mexican politics—and thus the positions of Mexico's three principal political parties—can be diagrammed along two dimensions: a democratic-authoritarian dimension and the standard left-right dimension. This approach contrasts slightly with Kitschelt's (1994, 1996) work on the dimensions of party competition in Western Europe; in his analysis, the left-right dimension is crosscut by a socially liberal-conservative dimension, and the democratic dimension is absent.[5] In all cases, though, these dimensions are used to plot the programmatic positions of party *organizations*.

Whether or not these analytic elements are appropriate to study party *fractions* is another matter. In a party such as the PAN, where a more or less shared party doctrine dictates official positions on social issues and the role of the state, they seem less useful than the fractional dimensions outlined by Sartori.[6] There are, of course, notable differences among party elites; Vicente Fox is decidedly less statist than Felipe Calderón Hinojosa, for example. However, in order to use these dimensions in the analysis of party fractions, we need to be assured that fraction leaders' positions are indicative of those of fraction members. It is not clear that this is the case in the PAN, where internal divisions are not necessarily structured around political views, but perhaps around more pragmatic political interests. Sartori's dimensions are thus better suited for this analysis.

---

[4] It should be noted that Sartori does not have much faith in the utility of this axis when it comes to fractions. In fact, he includes it primarily because it is the most identifiable tendency in elite political organization. The principal reason Sartori distrusts this dimension is because it is "a hopelessly multidimensional dimension: the layman's 'index' of politics" (1976: 77). Thus he recommends that one use the dimension only residually.

[5] During the transition under Vicente Fox, we may see in Mexico the replacement of Sartori's democratic dimension with his libertarian dimension.

[6] These dimensions might be more useful in studying the PRD, however, where currents are trying to build themselves into more programmatic entities.

With regard to how scholars have treated fractions in the PAN, the literature centers on two principal enduring divisions in the party— between *pragmáticos* and *doctrinarios* (or *participacionistas* and *abstencionistas*) and between *neopanistas* and traditional *panistas*. Two other divisions (or types of division) in the PAN received attention in the late 1980s and early 1990s: the Foro Democrático y Doctrinario (Democratic and Doctrinaire Forum) and regional fractions. The following discussion reviews the findings of earlier scholars and recasts them in light of the general literature discussed above. It then offers an alternative analysis of fractions in the PAN, elaborating more fully the rationale behind their formation and endurance and demonstrating that, like other aspects of party organization, party fractions change in response to both environmental stimuli and shifts within the party. Specifically, this presentation argues that the influx of economic resources and the political gains made by the PAN in the electoral arena have reconfigured the structure of fractions.

PAST DISCUSSIONS OF PAN FRACTIONS

Many *panistas* consider themselves members of a highly cohesive party organization, unified by a universal respect for the PAN's social Christian doctrine and its institutional tradition, both outgrowths of the party's founding process[7] (see Loaeza 1999; Mabry 1973). Various analysts have, nevertheless, demonstrated that the PAN has enduring divisions and that matters of party doctrine may have served to divide rather that unite the party.

Pragmatists and Doctrinaires

Loaeza (1999) and Reveles Vázquez (1993, 1996) have both recently produced comprehensive accounts of the PAN's organizational development. Although there are important differences in their accounts,[8] both authors describe internal PAN divisions based on an ideological split between pragmatists and more doctrinaire elements in the party

---

[7] Author interview with Deputy Juan José Rodríguez Pratts (Sinaloa), February 2000.

[8] The principal differences involve the greater scope of Loaeza's work (in both historical terms and the broader perspective she takes with regard to the PAN's role in the Mexican political system), the research methodologies these authors adopt, and Reveles Vásquez's more nuanced analysis of pragmatism and doctrinaireness in the PAN in the 1980s.

(or the related split between *participacionistas* and *abstencionistas*).[9] That is, according to these authors, the principal enduring division in the party is an ideological one, centered on the question of whether the PAN should engage in the formal political sphere and thus dignify (and reinforce) the democratic illusion of a PRI–dominated regime, or effectively withdraw from the political arena and serve as a testimonial party while gaining only minimal formal representation.[10]

Loaeza traces this split to an ideological tension present from the 1939 founding of the PAN and embodied in the figures of pragmatist founder Manuel Gómez Morin and Catholic ideologue Efraín González Luna (Loaeza 1999: chap. 2). Although Gómez Morin founded the party based on a coalition of middle-class forces, a number of those who succeeded him as the PAN's president were activists from Catholic organizations who favored political abstention and maintaining the ideological purity of the party. Particularly following World War II, González Luna (then the party's effective leader) and *panista* elites felt that the defense of the party's doctrine was more important than political participation. By the early 1960s, the party was largely confessional in nature.[11] It was also organizationally very weak, lacking both a consistent financial base and broad national penetration. The PAN's pragmatic wing scored a victory with the election of Adolfo Christlieb to the party presidency in 1962, and this victory was further consolidated by the introduction in 1963 of so-called party deputies.[12] The tension between the pragmatic and doctrinaire camps endured (indeed, grew) through the late 1960s and early 1970s, with their alternation in the party presidency demonstrating the strength of both fractions.

Reveles Vázquez's analysis picks up the pragmatic and doctrinaire division in the early 1970s and focuses particular attention on two

---

[9] For simplicity's sake, the reference here is to pragmatic and doctrinaire divisions as the principal cleavage within the PAN.

[10] "Withdrawal" refers here to the defense of the party's traditional doctrine (originally elaborated by Gómez Morin and recapitulated in Loaeza 1999) derived from Spanish social Christian thought and containing an important pro-democratic element.

[11] Loaeza (1999: 229) refers to the confessionalization of the party as "the over-ideologization and isolation of the party that nurtured an intransigence rejecting negotiation and compromise."

[12] In 1963, the PRI imposed an electoral reform that gave minority parties a minimal presence in the federal Chamber of Deputies (see Loaeza 1999: 282). The reform also compelled parties to accept these party deputyships or risk losing their official registration. In other words, it forced opposition parties to engage in institutional politics.

conflicts that nearly led to a schism in the party.[13] In 1975, the PAN needed to elect both its internal president and the party's presidential candidate for the 1976 general election, the former in a meeting of the party's National Council (Consejo Nacional) and the latter in a national party convention. In both cases, the PAN's internal democratic processes essentially collapsed under the strain between the party's pragmatic and doctrinaire fractions. The competition between pragmatist José Ángel Conchello and doctrinaire Efraín González Morfín for the party presidency produced five rounds of voting, with neither candidate able to muster sufficient support. Conchello finally renounced his candidacy, leaving the PAN (then beginning to attract more pragmatic elements) with a doctrinaire president who had minimal internal legitimacy.

The convention to select the party's presidential candidate was even more conflict-ridden. In this case, pragmatic candidate Pablo Emilio Madero had widespread support in the party, but not in the party's more doctrinaire National Executive Committee (CEN). Facing two opponents, Madero was unable to gain the 80 percent of the convention vote needed to be named the party's candidate. As a result, the PAN failed to present a candidate in Mexico's 1976 presidential election.[14] Following the convention, newly elected party president González Morfín resigned his position in defeat.

Both Loaeza and Reveles Vázquez then trace the development of these two fractions through the 1980s and into the 1990s. Loaeza adopts the conventional 1980s distinction between *neopanistas* and *panistas*, the former group encompassing politically nonconformist groups and members of the business class who embraced the PAN in the 1980s, particularly after the 1982 bank nationalization and the onset of Mexico's debt crisis. Despite the change in labels, Loaeza is still referring principally to a division between those *panistas* who are more doctrinaire and those (including the *neopanistas*, who as a group might be considered extremely politically pragmatic) who view the party as an instrument to gain power.

Reveles Vázquez carries his analysis of the pragmatic-doctrinaire division through the mid–1990s without adopting the *neopanista* terminology. Instead, he disaggregates the pragmatic and doctrinaire frac-

---

[13] In fact, these conflicts may have led to the development of the Democratic and Doctrinaire Forum fifteen years later.

[14] Ironically, the PAN's failure to select a candidate in 1975 actually may have aided in the development of the party. The election of unopposed PRI candidate José López Portillo in 1976 likely helped trigger the PRI's decision to enact the 1977 electoral reform law (LOPPE). This legislation instituted proportional representation in the federal Chamber of Deputies and guaranteed the PAN a more significant legislative presence.

tions of the party, noting that the 1975 conflicts signaled a transition toward consistent pragmatic dominance of the party organization. He argues that prior to the departure of Forum members in the early 1990s, four fractions existed within the PAN: the pragmatic fraction that led the PAN under party president Luis H. Álvarez, the 1970s pragmatists (including Pablo Emilio Madero), a group of radical pragmatists (primarily northern entrepreneurs under the leadership of Manuel J. Clouthier), and a very weak doctrinaire fraction (led by José González Torres). With the exception of the fraction under Madero, these are the same fractions that Reveles Vázquez identifies in the mid–1990s.

The Democratic and Doctrinaire Forum

The more doctrinaire elements of the party did not accept without a fight the increasing political power of the pragmatists (or *neopanistas*) within the PAN in the 1980s. Both Loaeza and Reveles Vázquez pay significant attention to the post–1987 emergence of the Democratic and Doctrinaire Forum. Under the leadership of Pablo Emilio Madero and Jesús González Schmal, the *foristas* criticized the party's direction under the leadership of Luis H. Álvarez, specifically its "nondemocratic character" and its willingness to work with the administration of President Carlos Salinas de Gortari (1988–1994) after the (allegedly fraudulent) 1988 presidential election. The Forum was organized under the terms of Article 11 of the PAN's statutes, which authorizes *panistas* to organize subgroups within the party based on homogeneity of interest. Nevertheless, the CEN denied the group official recognition.[15] Loaeza and Reveles Vázquez consider the Forum a modern manifestation of the enduring ideological conflict between pragmatists and the doctrinaires. Most of the Forum's leaders resigned from the PAN in October 1992 after being marginalized from leadership positions in the party.[16]

Regional Fractions within the PAN

A number of scholars have also noted the development of regional divisions in the PAN, three of which have received repeated attention. A first identifiable group consists of leaders of the midsize and small business sector in the northern states (especially Baja California, Chihuahua, and Nuevo León). Mizrahi (1994), focusing particularly on the

---

[15] Article 11 states: "Integrated members of the basic organization may organize homogeneous groups by skill, profession, activity, age, or for similar reasons."

[16] For a more detailed analysis of the Democratic and Doctrinaire Forum, see Wuhs n.d.

case of Chihuahua, argues that these groups joined the PAN in the early 1980s and were able to assert a visible activist role due to their economic autonomy from the government and their financial resources. This economic base allowed them to engage in and support collective political action.

Others have suggested that a second regional fraction within the party is based in the Bajío region, encompassing states such as Guanajuato and Jalisco. This group is largely an outgrowth of the party's Catholic base, which rose in political importance in the 1950s under the leadership of González Luna and posted several important municipal victories in the late 1940s and the 1950s. The third regional group is the concentration of PAN leaders who reside in the Federal District.

ASSESSING CHARACTERIZATIONS OF PAN FRACTIONS

Having reviewed the main fractions discussed in reference to the PAN, it is now possible to assess these characterizations in light of the general literature on intra-party divisions. This discussion takes into account *panistas'* perspectives regarding how their party has been fractionalized.

The ideological division between pragmatists and doctrinaires was the principal intra-party cleavage from the PAN's founding in 1939 through the late 1970s. Given the influence of the early advocates of each fraction—Manuel Gómez Morin and Efraín González Luna, respectively—it is not surprising that this division was so firmly embedded in the party organization. Many present-day *panistas* recognize the importance of this segmentation, and they make pained reference to the politicized conflicts of the mid–1970s when discussing the party's current fractional structure.[17] Despite the length of time during which this division characterized the PAN, these fractions should be considered as tendencies. After all, they had no formal recognition within the party, minimal independent organization, and no particular economic resources at their disposal.[18]

---

[17] Author interviews with National Secretary for Political Development and Training María Esperanza Morelos Borja, April 2000, and Deputy Ramón Corral Ávila (Sonora), March 2000.

[18] Although few *panistas* deny the existence of pragmatists and doctrinaires, some criticize such a strict dichotomization. They argue that more nuanced categories should be used, especially given the fact that the degree of some individuals' doctrinaireness or pragmatism has depended on the particular issues being debated by the CEN or the National Council. Author interview with Senate candidate Jesús Galván Muñoz (Federal District), April 2000.

The fractional divide between pragmatists and doctrinaires became less tenable after the 1970s. Simply put, the pragmatists won the battle within the PAN, so that by the early 1980s only vestiges of the party's doctrinaire wing remained. This does not mean there was a mass exodus from the party, although some high-level *panistas* did leave the party in the late 1970s. Rather, longtime doctrinaire *panistas* adopted more pragmatic attitudes following the initial opening of Mexico's political system.[19] The party's growing pragmatism was reinforced by the arrival of new cadres in the 1980s. In sum, although *panistas* continued to disagree about the appropriate level of engagement with the regime, very few remained isolationist. By the early 1980s, the ideological division that had splintered the party through the late 1970s was no longer the primary dimension of intra-party conflict.

Most treatments of the Forum, including those mentioned above, discuss the schism as an outgrowth of those same pragmatic and doctrinaire fractions.[20] These characterizations are, however, flawed. The emergence and eventual exit of the *foristas*, despite the name of the fraction, had little to do with ideology or doctrine.[21] Rather, *panistas* now tend to regard the division as an outgrowth of a change in the party's leadership structure. Specifically, when *panista* entrepreneurs began to assert greater control over the party in the late 1980s, Forum members—frustrated with their waning influence—organized under an ideological banner in order to maintain or recover their leadership positions. The preservation of the party's ideological identity was merely the appeal that the fraction used to speak to a wider *panista* audience.[22] This interpretation is supported by the activities of some Forum leaders following their resignation from the PAN: Jesús González Schmal and Bernardo Bátiz Vázquez emigrated to the center-left PRD (which shares

[19] This author takes the 1977 LOPPE reform as the starting point of Mexico's prolonged transition toward more democratic government. This is a conventional starting point (see Middlebrook 1986).

[20] Loaeza likens the Forum to the Democratic Current (CD) that split from the PRI in 1986 and eventually led to the formation of the PRD under Cuauhtémoc Cárdenas.

[21] We can consider the Forum to be on the faction side of the faction-tendency continuum identified by Sartori, given its members' efforts at autonomous organization within the party (even though the CEN ultimately blocked these efforts). In addition, various *panistas* have referred to the Forum's declining vote share in meetings of the National Council from 1989 until their departure in 1992. This suggests that the Forum was also an identifiable group with a somewhat distinct political project.

[22] Author interviews with Deputy Juan Miguel Alcántara Soria (Guanajuato), March 2000; Deputy Fortunato Álvarez Enríquez (Baja California), April 2000; and Senator Luis H. Álvarez (Chihuahua), March 2000.

virtually no ideological ground with the PAN, in *any* era).[23] Rather than attempting to locate the Forum along the ideological dimension identified by Sartori, we might better view it as a motivational fraction.

The regional dimension of party fractions appears, for the most part, to have been a temporary phenomenon. Mizrahi and others are correct to point to the northerners who joined the party in the 1980s. However, this geographically based division did not endure. These same entrepreneurs now belong to different fractions within the party, and they have been joined in those various groups by entrepreneurs (and others) from throughout Mexico. Their arrival in the 1980s was conjunctural, reflecting their collective response to political opportunities that emerged earlier in the North than elsewhere in the country. An additional consideration is that this regional division is not substantively distinct from the radical pragmatists identified by Reveles Vázquez.

The regional division associated with the Federal District is also illusory. It consists of CEN members and the PAN's traditional leadership, encompassing both pragmatic and doctrinaire wings of the party. PAN elites living in Mexico City do not necessarily act as a coherent group in party affairs. Their co-residence in Mexico City is better attributed to the more general centralization of Mexican political and economic affairs.

The idea of a Bajío group, typically regarded as an ultraright tendency, is more difficult to discount. In assessing its presence, we must address these two characteristics separately. We know that the party's doctrinaire wing was severely weakened following the political crises of the 1970s. Although doctrinaire (and even radical) elements do continue in the PAN, they are politically quite weak, especially at the national level. Recent attention has focused on the existence of an ultraright group called El Yunque ("The Anvil"), though it is not clear that it has a strong presence outside Guanajuato.[24] We must also consider whether national-level figures from the region act as a coherent force within the party (that is, whether they constitute a tendency of any sort). Although they may share a regional identity, Vicente Fox Quesada, Gabriel Jiménez Remus, the Ling family, Carlos Medina Plas-

---

[23] It is worth noting, anecdotally, that the leaders of the Forum were not members of the PAN's doctrinaire fraction in the 1970s. Reveles Vázquez identifies Madero and Bátiz Vázquez as members of the PAN's 1970s pragmatic fraction. The only possible common ground that the PAN and the PRD shared in this period was opposition to the PRI; it may be that these leaders saw the PRD and Cárdenas as the candidates most likely to defeat the PRI.

[24] This group, based in Guanajuato and led by entrepreneur Elías Villegas Torres, received national attention following the Guanajuato state legislature's passage of a restrictive abortion bill in August 2000. Guanajuato's governor ultimately vetoed the bill under pressure from the PAN national leadership.

cencia, and Juan Miguel Alcántara Soria do not work as a team in party affairs, and only one of them (Jiménez Remus) can be considered a member of the party's historic doctrinaire tendency. To the extent that such a geographic division exists, then, it does not appear to have a voice at the national level. It more likely represents another important way in which the PAN faces growing fractionalism at the state and the local levels.

RETHINKING FRACTIONS WITHIN THE PAN

Casting doubt on the relevance of ideological and regional dimensions of party fractionalization leaves us without a good understanding of PAN fractions from 1980 onward. The remainder of this chapter puts forward a new conceptualization of PAN fractions during Mexico's period of political liberalization, and it outlines a model for understanding how those fractions have changed over time (see figure 4.1). Although quantitative methods for the identification of party fractions exist, the data requirements exceed those presently available. The author has, therefore, adopted a qualitative approach instead. The analysis is based on interviews with PAN members in Mexico's federal Senate and Chamber of Deputies, interviews with members of the party's National Executive Committee and National Council (the party's national executive and legislative bodies), and an examination of party documents and the popular press. The discussion begins in the 1980s, following the pragmatist-doctrinaire typology that Loaeza and Reveles Vázquez adopt to assess party divisions through the late 1970s (with the caveat that the divisions should be considered tendencies, not factions). Sartori's framework is then used to identify the nature of those divisions and suggest a way in which to understand how fractions change in their composition and their bases over time.

Fractions in the 1980s

There is a very good reason why scholars have had difficulty assessing the nature of the PAN's internal divisions in the 1980s. The simple explanation is that a redimensioning of party fractions followed the dissolution of the PAN's doctrinaire tendency. At the same time, forces external to the party—including the regime's gradual political opening and occasional official recognition of opposition electoral victories, the 1982 bank nationalization under President José López Portillo (1982–1988), and the onset of the Mexican debt crisis—encouraged various groups in Mexican society to view the PAN as a viable agent of political change, or at the very least as a possible vehicle for obtaining political power. These two processes—fractional dissolution and the influx of new political actors into the PAN—generated substantial confusion and tension within the organization, particularly from 1982 through the 1988 presidential election.

Despite the relative state of disorder within the party, we can identify fractions (or at least nascent fractions) within the party during this period. In particular, two clear divisions either existed or were taking shape during the early and mid–1980s.

Figure 4.1. **PAN Fractions from the Party's Founding to the Present**

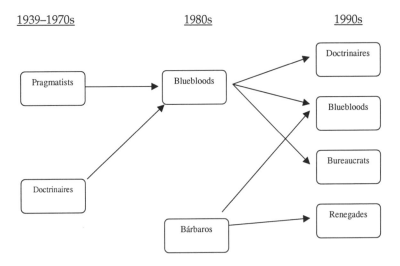

The **Bluebloods** The first identifiable group in this period was the PAN's historical base, a group that provides organizational continuity in the party even in the early twenty-first century. During the 1980s, this fraction comprised a broad coalition of political forces, incorporating both the pragmatic and the doctrinaire elements of the 1970s. Under the leadership of party president Abel Vicencio Tovar (1978–1984), this fraction struggled to retain its control over the party organization in the face of an influx of new political actors. Although shadows of the PAN's pragmatic-doctrinaire division remained (for example, shortly after Vicencio Tovar's election, several notable *panistas* resigned from the party), Vicencio Tovar was widely seen as independent of the two fractions and capable of leading the party while also preserving the hegemony of old-time *panistas* in party affairs (Reveles Vázquez 1996: 101). Succeeding Vicencio Tovar as party president in 1984 was Pablo Emilio Madero, one of the PAN's divisive figures of the 1970s.[25] Both of these presidents retained broad-based support in the CEN and the National Council, given that both organs were still dominated by longtime PAN members. In other words, the influx of new members into the party was not yet felt in the party's national decision-making bodies.

The "Barbarians from the North" The second group that emerged in the 1980s, the "barbarians from the north,"[26] is actually composed of two tendencies sharing a very pragmatic view of politics, a regional identity, and, in many cases, an entrepreneurial background. The first of these tendencies was headed by Luis H. Álvarez, a *panista* activist from the northern state of Chihuahua with a long party history.[27] A number of high-level *panistas* grouped around Álvarez, some with relatively long histories in the party (such as Norberto Corella, from Sonora) and others with shorter ones (such as Cecilia Romero, from the Federal District). A more radical (and newer) element within the party coalesced around Manuel J. Clouthier, an entrepreneur from Sinaloa who became active in politics following the 1982 bank nationalization and was the PAN's presidential candidate in 1988. This group, which also included Vicente Fox Quesada (Guanajuato) and Rodolfo Elizondo (Durango), gained significant clout in the party during the period leading up to the 1988 presidential election. It advocated a hard-line PAN stance in opposition to the Salinas administration, and it criticized collaboration between the Salinas government and the national party leadership under Luis H. Álvarez.

---

[25] Madero had been the party's 1982 presidential candidate, winning the nomination on the first round of voting in the National Council. This suggests that longtime *panistas*, doctrinaires, and pragmatists alike supported him. By the early 1980s, preserving power became more important than ideology for the bluebloods in their conduct of party affairs. (Recall that Madero had been unable to muster the necessary support to win the party's 1976 presidential nomination.)

[26] Fidel Velázquez, historic leader of the Confederation of Mexican Workers (CTM), coined this phrase in the mid–1980s as northern entrepreneurs began to support and affiliate with the PAN. He reportedly said, *"Ya llegaron los bárbaros del norte"* (the barbarians from the north have arrived). Author interview with Luis H. Álvarez, March 2000.

[27] Álvarez was the party's 1958 presidential candidate, and in 1987 he was elected party president.

Fractions in the 1990s

Two political turning points set the 1990s apart in terms of the fractional constitution of the PAN. The first was the run-up to the 1988
presidential election and its aftereffects, including the foundation of the
PRD and the passage of electoral reforms that increased the legislative
representation of opposition parties. These developments reconfigured
the political calculus of prominent elements within the PAN. Second,
1990 saw the reelection of Luis H. Álvarez to the PAN presidency, sig-
naling the solidification of one fraction's dominance over the party organization. It was following this election that one could observe the
consolidation of alliance patterns within the party that hold to the present.

In the 1990s, two broad fractions dominated the PAN at the national
level. Each had smaller constituent divisions.[28] It is interesting to note
that the personalism of fractions that emerged within the party in the
1980s continued through the 1990s. *Panistas* of all stripes identify fractions with individual leaders.

The Bluebloods As noted above, the 1990 PAN presidential election
marked the consolidation of one fraction's dominance over the party
organization. That fraction is actually a coalition of several distinct tendencies within the PAN that come together on important issues, including campaign finance reform, other electoral reforms, and statutory
changes in the party. It is organized around two preeminent *panistas*
from the 1980s and 1990s: Luis H. Álvarez and Diego Fernández de
Cevallos.

Álvarez is widely credited with modernizing and professionalizing
the party organization during his period as president (1987–1993).
Fernández de Cevallos is also a longtime *panista*, but, unlike Álvarez,
he draws his political capital within the party from the post-
liberalization era. Specifically, as leader of the PAN delegation in the
federal Chamber of Deputies from 1991 to 1994, Fernández de Cevallos
was responsible for negotiating with the PRI. He was also the PAN's

---

[28] In the 1990s, the PAN came to be highly fractionalized in many states, including
Durango, the State of México, Puebla, Yucatán, and Zacatecas. The political dynamics underlying these divisions vary among states, but *panistas* attribute the
development of fractions to the increasing resource base of state-level parties and
the influx of new actors into the party. These changes have combined to foster a
much more competitive environment in the party (primarily manifested in the
struggle to win the party's nomination for legislative posts). A detailed analysis of
these state-level fractions is beyond the scope of this chapter, but they are likely to
be quite politically important for the PAN's future. See Wuhs n.d.

presidential candidate in 1994, producing the party's best showing ever until the 2000 election.

Each of these leaders has his own group of supporters within the party's CEN and National Council. For example, in the 1999 election for party president (won by Luis Felipe Bravo Mena), Álvarez controlled 70 of the National Council's 278 votes and used them to win the election for Bravo Mena. Likewise, Fernández de Cevallos has an identifiable set of party notables around him, including former attorney general Antonio Lozano and former federal deputies Juan Miguel Alcántara Soria and Francisco Paoli Bolio (author interview, May 2000).

Two additional groups can be linked to Álvarez and Fernández de Cevallos in the National Council and the CEN. First, the old bluebloods (founders of the PAN or their descendants) normally collaborate with these two leaders. This set of individuals includes María Elena Álvarez de Vicencio (a *panista* for more than forty years and the widow of former party president Abel Vicencio Tovar), Juan Manuel Gómez Morin (the son of founder and ideologue Manuel Gómez Morin), and the members of the Ling family.[29] The second group allied with Álvarez and Fernández de Cevallos in the PAN's legislative and executive bodies is more precisely an amalgamation of prominent individuals in the party, a group which many consider to contain the next wave of PAN presidents and presidential candidates and who already have established their own national profiles in the party. They include Ricardo García Cervantes (chosen in September 2000 as president of the federal Chamber of Deputies, from Coahuila), Ernesto Ruffo Appel (Mexico's first *panista* governor, from Baja California), Francisco Barrio (former governor of Chihuahua), and Cecilia Romero (former PAN federal deputy, party bureaucrat, and federal senator).

Renegades and Bureaucrats The fraction described above is the dominant force in the PAN's CEN and National Council, but it does not formally head the party organization. The group that counterbalances the power of "pedigreed" *panistas* has controlled the PAN presidency from 1996 to the present; it is led by the PAN's first national president, Vicente Fox Quesada. Fox joined the party only in 1988, as part of the final wave of businessmen that Manuel J. Clouthier brought into the party. Despite the brevity of his affiliation with the PAN, Fox has established himself as an outspoken leader. It is also significant that he has managed to alienate sectors of the party's dominant clique with his lack of respect for the PAN's institutional tradition and its doctrine. In the latter case, Fox's lack of respect for party orthodoxy may have rep-

---

[29] Author interviews, May and June 2000, and author interview with Jesús Galván Muñoz.

resented an effort to reposition the party toward the political center for the 2000 general elections.

At least as of 2000, Fox had only a limited number of PAN elites allied with him in party affairs. They included Santiago Creel, the PAN's candidate in 2000 to head the Federal District government; Senator Ramón Corral of Sonora; and close adviser Rodolfo Elizondo, among others. However, in the process of mobilizing support for his presidential campaign beginning in 1998, Fox assembled an organization external to the party (the Amigos de Fox) which was used to pressure the PAN to accept his candidacy and which also served to discourage other possible candidates (including Ruffo and Barrio) from seriously contemplating candidacy. Many "Friends of Fox" solicited membership in the PAN, and Fox also managed to have a large number of his supporters placed on the ballot in state and municipal contests in 2000 (author interview, May 2000). His fraction, then, may be expected to grow in political clout within the party in coming years.

The other major figure allied with Fox in party politics is Felipe Calderón Hinojosa, himself a carrier of the PAN's pedigree but regarded as politically distinct from other custodians of the PAN following his stint as PAN president from 1996 to 1999. Calderón's story as a party leader is complex. As a blueblood, his entry into the party was uneventful. He first assumed a high-profile post (secretary general of the PAN) during the party presidency of Carlos Castillo Peraza (1993–1996).[30] In 1996 he won election to the party presidency (over Ernesto Ruffo) with the support of Castillo Peraza and Luis H. Álvarez. Calderón's presidency—supported by a team of party bureaucrats that included Germán Martínez, former PAN delegate to the Federal Electoral Institute (IFE), and Adrián Fernández, adjunct secretary general—was widely regarded as excessively centralist by members of this purportedly decentralized party.[31] Just as Álvarez and Fernández de Cevallos's fraction includes a certain number of floating notables, Fox and Calderón's group also counts on the support of a few high-level *panistas*, including Carlos Medina Plascencia (former governor of Guanajuato and coordinator of the PAN's delegation in the federal Chamber of Deputies from 1997 to 2000) and Luis Felipe Bravo Mena (elected party president in 1999).

---

[30] Calderón's first year as a CEN member was 1987. He had served earlier as president of the PAN's youth organization.

[31] Author interview with PAN Director of Organization Humberto Ballesteros Cruz, September 2000. This group, the *"niños azules,"* gained prominence in the party under Castillo Peraza and occupied important bureaucratic posts during the Calderón presidency. Their actions alienated more traditional sectors of the party. Also see Wuhs n.d. on party centralization in the PAN.

Doctrinaires A third and final group bears mention, though its members are few in number. A doctrinaire fraction does remain in the PAN. It is led by historical figure Gabriel Jiménez Remus (a former federal senator and ex-leader of the Forum), former federal senator Juan de Dios Castro, and former PRI activist Juan José Rodríguez Pratts, now the PAN's leading ideologue. In terms of their voting power within party organs, this is a negligible group—though its members normally support the initiatives of Fox and Calderón (author interview, May 2000). However, this fraction was important in the 1997–2000 federal legislature because Jiménez Remus and de Dios Castro headed the PAN's Senate delegation, which included many members of Álvarez's and Fernández de Cevallos's fractions elected to plurinominal seats in Congress.[32]

EXPLAINING FRACTION DEVELOPMENT AND CHANGE

Having identified the groups that emerged in the PAN in the 1980s and having traced their further conformation in the 1990s, it remains to consider why these groups formed and along what dimensions fractions have organized within the PAN. As discussed earlier, party elites organize fractions in order to gain control of resources (whether political or economic, tangible or intangible), to further the party's interests, and thus to prolong their own political careers. We can also hypothesize that party members who affiliate with fractions do so because they are motivated by the same goal of career advancement, hoping to gain candidacies or higher posts in the party bureaucracy through association with a fractional leader. As the resources available to party elites and members shift, one can logically expect the structure of fractions to change. And, in fact, as the PAN's resource base has increased since the early 1980s, party elites have faced new incentives to organize groups within the party. Shifts in the resources around which party leaders typically organize fractions—party leadership posts, financial resources, and candidacies for public office—are the key to understanding how fractional alignments change in the PAN.

At times during the 1950s, 1960s, and most of the 1970s, the division between pragmatist and doctrinaire *panistas* became virulent at the elite

---

[32] Institutional rules explain this odd combination of Senate leadership and delegation. The party president names the Senate leadership (at the time of their naming, Felipe Calderón Hinojosa was allied with the doctrinaire fraction), while the plurinominal senators are selected by a CEN vote (where Álvarez and Fernández de Cevallos had greater influence).

level. It was not, however, felt so strongly at the mass level.[33] Why would this be the case? Setting aside the question of the PAN's narrow membership base during this period,[34] the answer is simply that ordinary *panistas* had little to gain by affiliating with one camp or the other. PAN doctrine was the party's most important resource prior to the period of political liberalization that began in 1977, and it was the resource around which the two principal *panista* fractions were organized.[35] Yet such matters held no value outside the party.

Moreover, the PAN was a party without a dependable funding base. There were few government subsidies for parties at the time, and even if there had been significant public subsidies, it is unlikely that the CEN would have accepted them as a matter of principle. As a consequence, the PAN was forced to rely principally upon members' financial donations and volunteer workers even at the national level (including within the CEN). Accepting a post in the CEN was a sacrifice—another responsibility to be added to one's normal work and family duties. And because electoral victories were a scarce commodity, candidacies were burdensome as well. Simply put, there were few resources of value in the party.

The 1977 electoral reform law (LOPPE) alleviated to some extent the PAN's resource situation. Prior to the reform, *panistas* viewed candidacy as an act of "martyrdom" given that there was virtually no possibility of electoral victory.[36] Following passage of the LOPPE, the PAN had guaranteed access to a limited number of seats in the federal Chamber of Deputies through proportional representation, encouraging party members to view candidacies as more valuable. At the time,

---

[33] Even in the late 1990s, there were significant differences in the opinions of PAN elites and PAN members with respect to fundamental PAN issues such as religiosity and the role of the state in the economy. See Buendía Laredo 1998.

[34] Even in 2000, the PAN had only about 150,000 active members and 360,000 affiliated members (who do not have voting rights in the party) nationwide.

[35] Ideology remains an important resource for the party, although it may pale in comparison with the PAN's new political and economic resources. Although the party organization has adopted a pragmatic approach to politics, many *panistas* are concerned with the poor political training of PAN cadres. Many appear concerned about recovering party doctrine (supplanting electoral considerations) as a guiding political force. This concern about a return to PAN ideology was reflected in the rapid rise of party ideologue Juan José Rodríguez Pratts, a former PRI member who joined the PAN in the mid-1990s and fought his way to victory in a federal Chamber of Deputies majority district in 1997. Despite his extraordinarily short track record in the party, the CEN placed him second on the Senate plurinominal list.

[36] Party leaders often had to twist arms just to fill the ballot. Author interviews with Senators Luis H. Álvarez and María Elena Álvarez de Vicencio, March 2000.

nomination for these posts occurred through a regional process that culminated with CEN–based ordering of the party's circumscription lists. Thus, to the extent that CEN members controlled the lists, seats on the CEN also represented political resources around which fractions could organize. However, until the late 1980s these were still unpaid posts, so they were not "valuable" in their own right.

The increasing value of party candidacies triggered a process of fractional reorganization. Although the appropriate level of engagement with the PRI regime remained an important point of debate in the PAN, *panistas* adopted more pragmatic attitudes, generally speaking, once regular legislative representation became available. The most doctrinaire voices in the party either left or changed their tone.[37] The guarantee of some political representation also led those Mexican entrepreneurs who were disenchanted with the PRI to view the PAN as a possible vehicle for their political ascent. That guarantee brought many members of the business class to the PAN.[38] For instance, Clouthier's and Barrio's public mobilizations of the mid–1980s would not have occurred under the auspices of the PAN had these candidates not been attracted by the party's new resources.[39]

The influx of new actors attracted by the PAN's increasing resource base (guaranteed legislative victories and the now more valuable CEN posts) created tensions within the PAN that hardened fractional alignments. The new members, who saw themselves as responsible for the party's electoral advances through the 1980s, remained underrepresented in the party's leadership structure, which was still dominated by the bluebloods. Those members, in turn, viewed the newcomers as a threat to their dominance of the party (and to its ideological purity), and they struggled to limit the newcomers' influence. The composition of the PAN's governing bodies reveals the newcomers' relative lack of voice. These so-called *neopanistas*—who led the party's popular mobilizations in the 1980s and steered the party to electoral victory in the late 1980s and early 1990s—were slow to gain entry into the PAN's directive organs (see table 4.1).

---

[37] There is also evidence that, during this period, longtime *panistas* began to form the fractions that would grow and diversify in the 1990s. After so many years of service to the party, they felt they deserved legislative posts and therefore recruited other party members to support them in their effort to gain them.

[38] Many had been sympathizers beforehand but were unwilling to distance themselves publicly from the PRI. Author interview with Federal District Legislative Assembly candidate Francisco Calderón, June 2000.

[39] Given regime opening, however, it is likely that social mobilization would have occurred under the auspices of a different party or civic organization.

Table 4.1. **Entrance of *Neopanistas* to the PAN's National Decision-Making Bodies[1]**

	Year Joined the PAN	First Year in the National Council	First Year in the CEN
Francisco Barrio	1983	1987	-
Luis Felipe Bravo Mena	1969	1991	1993
Manuel J. Clouthier	1984	1988	-
Ramón Corral Ávila[2]	1988	1989	1999
Vicente Fox Quesada	1988	1991	1993
Carlos Medina Plascencia	1985	1991	1996
Ernesto Ruffo Appel	1982	1988	1996

[1] Data provided by the Fundación Preciado Hernández; Secretary of Communications, PAN; and Camp 1995. One would expect a three-year lag in entering the National Council because PAN statutes require three years of militancy for National Council members. Once a *panista* is a member of the National Council, he or she can immediately be named to the CEN.

[2] Corral entered the National Council before the three-year statutory interim had passed because in 1989 he was elected president of the state-level executive committee in Sonora. All state party presidents are members of the National Council.

The fractions of the 1990s represent both the consolidation of fractions that began to emerge in the 1980s and a diversification of the party's internal groups. This occurred because of the proliferation of party resources around which elites could organize fractions. Especially important political opportunities presented themselves in the legislative arena. Whereas the only concrete resources around which fractions were likely to form in the 1980s were the 100 plurinominal seats in the federal Chamber of Deputies, by the 1990s, electoral reforms had increased that number to 200 and added 32 proportional representation seats in the federal Senate.[40] These changes also increased the political value of CEN positions. Although by the late 1990s the CEN had considerably less discretion in the elaboration of the Chamber of Deputies proportional representation lists, it did retain the top two list spots in each of the five electoral districts. The CEN had greater discretion in the case of the Senate.

In addition, the party gained access to more substantial economic resources. Following electoral reforms in 1989—and after a divisive internal debate—the PAN decided to accept government subsidies, which greatly increased the funds available both for campaigns and for

[40] The second 100 proportional representation seats in the federal Chamber of Deputies were first contested in 1988, and the federal Senate's proportional representation seats were added by the 1996 electoral reform for the 1997 election.

regular party activities.[41] This led to an important increase in the number of paid positions in the CEN, adding an economic dimension to these politically valuable posts.[42] The desire to control these varied resources grew in the 1990s as the PAN consolidated its status as the primary opposition to the PRI (over the PRD) through a number of significant electoral victories at the state and municipal levels. The outlook for the PAN became one of further political victories and, because the amount of public subsidies was linked to the party's vote share, an expanding pocketbook.

Rapid growth of the PAN's resource base also altered the structure of the party's fractions. The bluebloods were ultimately unable to retain control of the organization; in the late 1980s, the founding families stepped aside as the governing group. Nevertheless, they remain important in the PAN's dominant coalition, and two of them—Luis H. Álvarez and Diego Fernández de Cevallos—have assumed high individual profiles within the party. They were able to gain such prominence (in the case of Álvarez) by steering the increasing bureaucratization and centralization of the party and (in the case of Fernández de Cevallos) by leading the PAN in the federal Chamber of Deputies during a period of rapidly increasing party representation in which the PAN was the PRI's key strategic partner.

Similar opportunities allowed Felipe Calderón Hinojosa to win individual recognition in the PAN as a member of the CEN, president of the party, and leader of the PAN's delegation in the 2000–2003 federal Chamber of Deputies. The political ascent of Vicente Fox Quesada is less a result of the party's changing resource base than of his charismatic appeal and his support among Mexico's business community. Still, Fox garnered an important secondary benefit from the PAN's increasing organizational resources—namely, the political support of the party's new members.[43]

It also bears mentioning that the PAN's increasing resources were not all concentrated at the national level. In fact, it could be argued that the effects of these changes have been felt most strongly at the state and local levels. This is the locus of most candidate selection in the PAN, and about 80 percent of the funding that the party has received from the Federal Electoral Institute has been directed to state and local levels.

---

[41] The provisions for campaign finance and party finance were revised in the 1996 electoral reform. See Becerra et al. 1997.

[42] Precise data on compensation for CEN employees are not available, but following the professionalization of the party in the mid–1990s, all senior PAN officials receive equal pay, with the amount based on the salary of federal deputies.

[43] Fox had comparatively less support among the PAN's traditional members.

CONCLUSION

The restructuring of PAN fractions that occurred in the 1980s suggests that as the ideological dimension of conflict in the party waned in the late 1970s, another dimension rose in significance. Specifically, after the Conchello–González Morfín debacle of 1975 and the passage of the LOPPE in 1977, the pragmatic wing took control of the PAN, and doctrinaires either moderated their positions or exited the party. The availability of new political resources generated two divisions—"bluebloods" concerned with preserving the PAN's traditional identity and their role in it, and "barbarians" interested in advancing their own political goals. Within the framework suggested by Sartori, these divisions are motivational in nature.

The PAN's contemporary fractions are also indisputably motivational. By the year 2000 the party was comparatively rich, offering a multitude of resources (including cabinet posts in the federal government) that party elites wish to control. With the partial exception of the Democratic and Doctrinaire Forum (which had some organizational independence and billed itself as an ideological splinter group), organizational, ideological, and left-right divisions remain less prominent in the PAN. Still, there is at least anecdotal evidence suggesting that ideological divisions in the PAN are not dead but only resting. Whether or not ideology returns as a dimension structuring political competition in the party will likely depend upon how the CEN decides to school its membership in party doctrine and whether it opens the organization to more diverse political elements.[44]

Another important trend is the personalization of the party's fractional structure. The pragmatic and doctrinaire fractions were broadly coalitional (though there were historical figureheads associated with each). However, as the motivational dimension superseded the ideological, PAN divisions became more personalized.

Why was this the case? As *panista* elites have attained positions of power within the party and in government, they have become leaders of party fractions. Fractions appear to develop around seats of institutional power, which for the PAN have been limited to its legislative and party leaderships. Yet the power that individuals such as Diego Fernández de Cevallos accumulate through their institutional positions comes to reside in *them*, not in their posts. Nevertheless, personalization

---

[44] Facing heightened electoral competition, the increasingly elections-oriented (as opposed to sectarian) PAN may be compelled to open its doors if party leaders determine that voters are somehow repelled by the party's established doctrine. However, given the stability of the party's doctrine over its long organizational life, perhaps we are more likely to see "broad readings" of PAN doctrine by strategic leaders.

does not always occur; few legislative leaders have amassed the political clout of Fernández de Cevallos, suggesting that conjunctural factors are important in determining which party members gain such power and thus become fraction leaders.[45]

Finally, given the important political changes under way in Mexico, it is worth looking toward the future. In the July 2000 elections, PAN presidential candidate Vicente Fox Quesada walked away with a solid victory, and the PAN made significant gains in both the federal Chamber of Deputies and the Senate. Yet despite these notable successes, behind closed doors many *panistas* were initially concerned about the effect of party fractions on the PAN's capacity to lead Mexico's democratic transition.[46] Although most *panistas* welcomed Fox's victory, many CEN members did not campaign on his behalf. This suggests that there may be some conflict between the national party organization and its first president of the republic in the course of Fox's six-year term. Moreover, the 2000–2003 legislative leadership of the party (Felipe Calderón Hinojosa and Diego Fernández de Cevallos) may present fraction-based obstacles to the implementation of Fox's policy agenda. And last, it is worth noting that Fox's victory introduced a third seat of institutional power—the national executive—in the PAN. As a result, we may reasonably expect to see Fox's position in the party strengthened by the political post he now occupies, along with a possible further diversification of the PAN's fractional structure.

REFERENCES

Becerra, Ricardo, et al. 1997. *La reforma electoral de 1996: una descripción general.* Mexico City: Fondo de Cultura Económica.

Brass, Paul R. 1965. *Factional Politics in an Indian State.* Berkeley: University of California Press.

Buendía Laredo, Jorge. 1998. "Responsiveness, Accountability, and Democracy: The Case of Mexico." Paper presented at the international congress of the Latin American Studies Association, September, Chicago.

Camp, Roderic Ai. 1995. *Mexican Political Biographies 1935–1993.* 3d ed. Austin: University of Texas Press.

Cox, Gary W., and Frances Rosenbluth. 1993. "The Electoral Fortunes of Legislative Factions in Japan," *American Political Science Review* 87 (3): 577–89.

---

[45] Fernández de Cevallos, for example, led PAN members in the federal Chamber of Deputies during a period of unusual political importance for the party (1988–1991). During this period, the PAN's legislative support was necessary for the PRI to institute constitutional reforms, giving the party a strong bargaining chip in its negotiations with the regime.

[46] Author interview, July 2000, and author interview with National Secretary General of the PAN Federico Ling Altamirano, July 2000.

Downs, Anthony. 1957. *An Economic Theory of Democracy*. New York: Harper and Row.

Gray, Virginia, and David Lowery. 1996. "A Niche Theory of Interest Representation," *Journal of Politics* 58 (1): 91–111.

Greene, Kenneth F. 2000. "Challenging the Hegemon: Opposition Party Entry and Strategic Position in Mexico in the 1990s." Paper presented at the annual meeting of the American Political Science Association, Washington, D.C.

Hannan, Michael T., and John Freeman. 1989. *Organizational Ecology*. Cambridge, Mass.: Harvard University Press.

Key, V. O., Jr. 1949. *Southern Politics in State and Nation*. New York: Knopf.

Kitschelt, Herbert. 1994. *The Transformation of European Social Democracy*. New York: Cambridge University Press.

———. 1996. *The Radical Right in Western Europe: A Comparative Analysis*. Ann Arbor: University of Michigan Press.

Kohno, Masaru. 1992. "Rational Foundations for the Organization of the Liberal Democratic Party in Japan," *World Politics* 44: 369–97.

Langston, Joy. n.d. "Dilemmas, Divisions, and Decisions: The PRI and Electoral Competition in Mexico." Manuscript.

Loaeza, Soledad. 1999. *El Partido Acción Nacional: la larga marcha, 1939–1994. Oposición leal y partido de protesta*. Mexico City: Fondo de Cultura Económica.

Mabry, Donald J. 1973. *Mexico's Acción Nacional: A Catholic Alternative to Revolution*. New York: Syracuse University Press.

Magaloni, Beatriz. 1997. "The Dynamics of Dominant Party Decline: The Mexican Transition to Multipartysm." Ph.D. dissertation, Duke University.

McAllister, Ian. 1991. "Party Adaptation and Factionalism within the Australian Party System," *American Journal of Political Science* 35 (1): 206–27.

Middlebrook, Kevin J. 1986. "Political Liberalization in an Authoritarian Regime: The Case of Mexico." In *Latin America*. Vol. 2 of *Transitions from Authoritarian Rule: Prospects for Democracy*, edited by Guillermo O'Donnell, Philippe C. Schmitter, and Laurence Whitehead. Baltimore, Md.: Johns Hopkins University Press.

Mizrahi, Yemile. 1994. "Rebels without a Cause: The Politics of Entrepreneurs in Chihuahua," *Journal of Latin American Studies* 6: 137–58.

Molinar Horcasitas, Juan. 1991. *El tiempo de la legitimidad*. Mexico City: Cal y Arena.

Panebianco, Angelo. 1988. *Political Parties: Organization and Power*. New York: Cambridge University Press.

Reveles Vázquez, Francisco. 1993. "Sistema organizativo y fracciones internas del Partido Acción Nacional 1939–1990." Master's thesis, Universidad Nacional Autónoma de México.

———. 1996. "El proceso de institucionalización organizativa del Partido Acción Nacional (1984–1995)." Ph.D. dissertation, Universidad Nacional Autónoma de México.

Rose, Richard. 1964. "Parties, Factions, and Tendencies in Britain," *Political Studies* 12: 33–46.

Sartori, Giovanni. 1976. *Parties and Party Systems: A Framework for Analysis.* New York: Cambridge University Press.

Schlesinger, Joseph A. 1994. *Political Parties and the Winning of Office.* Ann Arbor: University of Michigan Press.

Wuhs, Steven T. n.d. "Political Environments and Party Organizations in Mexico." Ph.D. dissertation, University of North Carolina at Chapel Hill. Forthcoming 2002.

Zariski, Ralph. 1960. "Party Factions and Comparative Politics: Some Preliminary Observations," *Midwest Journal of Political Science* 4: 27–51.

Zuckerman, Alan. 1979. *The Politics of Faction: Christian Democratic Rule in Italy.* New Haven, Conn.: Yale University Press.

PART 3

PART POLITICS, ELECTIONS, AND DEMOCRATIZATION IN THE STATES

PART 3

PARTY POLITICS, ELECTIONS, AND DEMOCRATIZATION IN THE STATES

5

Democratic Transition in Baja California: Stages and Actors

Tonatiuh Guillén López

INTRODUCTION

Mexico's gradual democratic transition has taken place amid an intense national debate that has permeated the country's political and social arenas. The key actors in the debate began to appear in 1983, emerging from political parties and, especially, from a growing number of organizations within civil society that progressively reduced the space for authoritarianism in the political system. Opposition parties have been among the principal actors in the struggle for power and a driving force in the transition, successfully identifying themselves in the public eye with the pursuit of democratic goals. This was true of the National Democratic Front (FDN) in the late 1980s and the National Action Party (PAN) and the Party of the Democratic Revolution (PRD) in the early 1990s.[1] At these junctures, opposition parties succeeded in virtually embodying the goals of democratic transition in the public consciousness, and they were able to translate this identification into broad collective action.

This chapter analyzes the relationship between political actors and democratic transition in Baja California between 1989 and the late 1990s.[2] The main focus is on the role of democratization's primary proponents as agents for political change in a transition process that is much more diverse and complex than that of earlier periods, when "opposition party" and "struggle for democracy" were viewed as one and the same. This close identification led the public to view political alternation in municipal or state government as the end product of a

---

Translated by Robyn Gutteridge and Aníbal Yáñez-Chávez.

[1] Although these are not the only parties linked to the democratic transition, they are the major ones and as such they constitute the focus of this chapter.

[2] See also Guillén López 1992, 1993a, 1993b, 1995a, 1995b, 1995c, 1995d.

democratic transition. By the late 1990s, however, this same identification of opposition party with democratization had become an obstacle to political opening. There is no automatic complementarity among party, democracy, and alternation. In fact, these elements contain inherent tensions and disharmonies that can actually impede progress toward democratic consolidation.

An additional feature of the Baja California case is that it involves the PAN. This "conservative" party has wielded substantial power at the state level in Baja California (in the governorship and legislature) and in the state's municipal governments. It has also been a key actor in Mexico's democratic transition. The party in Baja California is a political force embedded in a regional process of democratic transition, and one goal of this chapter is to evaluate the PAN's contribution within this context. Whether the PAN is a force for political modernization or for conservatism, its role is characterized by a degree of structural inertia and the party's principal social traits. Ultimately, however, its "conservative" or its "liberal" features will derive from a set of processes (such as the juncture of party alternation in office and the state's institutional heritage) rather than from the actor alone. That is, any explanation of political outcomes necessarily goes beyond the PAN. What is more, developments suggesting a "transition effect" deriving from deliberate action on the part of the PAN may stem instead from the party's dominant political position in the state.

We can, then, identify two processes that contribute to democratic transition. The first is more structural in nature and cannot be attributed to actors' deliberate actions; the second stems from political actors' purposeful initiatives. In the case of Baja California, the transition evolved largely through the former process. The position of the PAN and its representatives in Baja California placed the party, along with a number of other political parties, at the forefront of a "liberalizing" trend that embraced the political principles of citizenship. In other words, the "conservative" label often applied to the PAN in Baja California is more a characterization of the party's overall place within the national system of parties, and less a feature of the PAN as it functions in this northern state.[3]

---

[3] Baja California has been a principal base of support for the PAN at the national level, and after the 1950s the Baja California PAN was able to mount significant opposition to the "official" Institutional Revolutionary Party (PRI) in statewide elections. Because of their state's importance to the party, state-level PAN leaders enjoy substantial autonomy from the national party leadership and have been quite influential at the national level, especially since 1989. For example, Ernesto Ruffo Appel, who served as governor of Baja California from 1989 to 1995, was a strong, though ultimately unsuccessful, candidate for president of the PAN in 1996. He was defeated by Felipe Calderón Hinojosa.

The following sections discuss the characteristics of democratic transition in Baja California and the role of the PAN after 1989.

A Prolonged Transition

The most prominent feature of Mexico's democratic transition is its long and tortuous path, which allowed authoritarian forms of political power to persist for decade after decade. Yet once there was a set of actors capable of contesting power effectively through elections and thus able to move the process forward, democratic transition quickly became a high-priority issue on the national agenda. These actors, then, are both proof of the existence of democratization and a measure of its success; the stronger the actors, the more relevant their achievements. The organizational maturation of the PAN and the PRD, these parties' reach across the political map of Mexico, and their ability to attract support from broad sectors of the electorate were so well developed by the mid–1990s that conditions were ripe for moving beyond a period of "transition" (O'Donnell and Schmitter 1986). Yet the transition continued at a protracted pace, in part because of resistance from the established regime, but also sometimes because of the interests of opposition parties themselves.[4]

Opposition parties' paradoxical resistance to transition occurs when these parties are themselves reluctant to cede control of government. This is one of the insights that can be derived from an examination of the PAN's experience in Baja California. Party alternation in power is clearly a sign of transition, but one alternation does not guarantee that a transition will continue. What remains crucial is the broader panorama of state-society relations beyond the electoral moment.

The Centrality of Electoral Processes

In addition to their lamentable tendency to become permanent processes, democratic transitions also tend to fixate on election rules—not just as an idea but as political practice. Political parties, their demands and programs, their goals and social mobilization strategies, and their relationship with national and regional power holders are overwhelmingly focused on electoral reform and interparty competition as virtu-

---

[4] One example of such resistance occurred after the election to choose the municipal president in Huejotzingo, Puebla (April–May 1996), when the PAN made the resolution of this local election a condition of its participation in negotiations with other parties on future national political and electoral reforms.

ally their only objective. Elections become not the means to an end, but an end in themselves.

This is the second notable characteristic of the Mexican transition: the struggle for free and fair elections has adopted electoral reform as its end goal.[5] Although electoral reform is a necessary ingredient in political change, it can carry high costs—both in organizational and social consensus terms and for the democratic transition itself. These costs accrue when actors succeed in opening spaces, as they have done in Baja California, but do so within a predefined margin that restricts the horizon to what is operative, what is practical.

While society moves forward to address new goals and priorities (such as reforming the structure of government), the outlook, behavior, and resources of political actors have often remained mired in concerns linked to the electoral process. What is needed is a "transition within the transition," something that can break the cycle of electoral reforms designed to promote more electoral reform. Democracy is not just about deciding who will govern; it is also about defining the conditions and rules under which that choice is made. What is lost when electoral reform has primacy of place is a true transformation of the institutions of government.

The experience of the PAN in Baja California displays the undesirable consequences of placing undue emphasis on electoral reform. Admittedly, there was some leveling of the state's electoral playing field under the PAN. However, the PAN in office has given insufficient attention to reforming the structures of government, which have remained basically unchanged since the authoritarian administrations of the past. The focus on the electoral arena has pushed all concerns for deep reforms to the margins. It has also carried an organizational cost for political parties themselves when they fail to see the need to define new priorities once election-related issues have been addressed.

Intensity by Region

The third characteristic of Mexico's democratic transition emerged in Baja California after 1989: the tendency to place opposition-controlled state governments at the forefront and to pay less attention to the national-level structure of government.[6] The trajectory of the transition

---

[5] An important exception is the experience of the Zapatista Army of National Liberation (EZLN) after 1994.

[6] With regard to national-level politics prior to 1994, the appearance of the Zapatista Army of National Liberation in January 1994 constituted another path, another line of action, more than an advance on the existing transition route. This statement is not meant to minimize the enormous influence that this Chiapas-based

has differentiated between national and state government, and it has allowed state governments to remain isolated from one another at the same time that each one is distanced from the national regime. Thus in June 1995, regional power holders in Guerrero were capable of orchestrating a massacre of peasants, while in Baja California the state government's main concern was to compile a reliable voter registry. It is clear, then, that the transition has not been defined or directed by national actors alone; regional spaces and state-level actors have also played a determining role.

Differentiating between state-level and national factors in the transition process is key to understanding the impacts that political opening has on the agents of transition, especially political parties under conditions of alternation. The most palpable consequence is a rapid change in parties' relationship with the citizenry. Once the primary goal—political opening—has been achieved, the agenda of social priorities is immediately reorganized. Free and fair elections cease to be an end in themselves and become an instrument with which to pursue social development and an improved quality of life. In this altered context, parties must redefine their objectives and mobilizing strategies accordingly. They must modify their internal organization, goals, and the rules governing relations with local governments, but above all they must construct a new framework for interacting with the citizenry. A party's failure to act quickly on these fronts will translate into a loss of party support; in effect, political opening increases the distance between political organizations and their interests and the citizenry and its interests.[7] This is the situation that the PAN has faced in Baja California.

This chapter analyzes Mexico's democratic transition from a state-level perspective. It is important to note at the outset that alternation in state government is not the only indicator of state-level political opening. However, alternation in power is certainly the most visible and socially recognized sign that political opening exists and that this space has been won by the citizenry. Society's awareness of this victory is what sets up the new context and the need for a new agenda of priori-

---

guerrilla movement has had on the course of national politics. However, the fact remains that the EZLN has had more significance within its regional context than it has nationally. Thus the anterior dynamic in Mexico's transition has remained dominant.

[7] Using an extreme example, under conditions of political opening, parties cannot now mobilize citizens beneath the banner of defending themselves against "electoral fraud," nor beneath the promise of constructing transparent electoral law or of "good government." As one can imagine, if these themes were the main bases for ties between citizens and a particular party, their validity would be limited.

ties. Electoral issues remain important, but they lose some of their former urgency. In the process, the links that tied citizens to parties when
elections were paramount begin to weaken, as happened with the PAN
in Baja California.

THE PHASES OF DEMOCRATIC TRANSITION

Prior to 1989, the likelihood that the ruling Institutional Revolutionary
Party (PRI) would lose a gubernatorial election was virtually nil, largely
because of the PRI's control over the electoral process. Earlier in the decade, especially in Chihuahua in 1983 and 1986, the "official" party and
the government apparatus had responded to electoral challenges by
mobilizing all their resources to prevent a state government from falling
into the hands of an opposition party. In a worst-case scenario, the PRI
would resort to electoral fraud to reduce the number of votes cast for the
opposition.

The situation changed radically in 1988, when Cuauhtémoc Cárdenas and his National Democratic Front challenged the PRI in the presidential elections and came very close to winning. PRI candidate Carlos
Salinas de Gortari was officially declared the winner, but the election
triggered a serious legitimacy crisis. Once in office, Salinas (1988–1994)
made restoring the legitimacy of both his administration and the political system a top priority. His government proposed an electoral reform
that included new electoral institutions and regulations and, most important, a new voter registry for the 1991 midterm elections. For the
Salinas administration, buffeted by economic crisis and legitimacy
problems, the state-level elections to be held in Baja California in 1989
offered an opportunity for revalidation.

In the 1988 presidential election, Baja California voters had favored
Cuauhtémoc Cárdenas and the FDN,[8] which suggested that the opposition had a real chance to win the governorship in 1989.[9] This possibil-

---

[8] In the 1988 presidential election, the vote in Baja California was distributed as
follows: FDN, 37.2 percent; PRI, 36.7 percent; and PAN, 24.4 percent.

[9] After the 1988 presidential election, the FDN and the PAN considered backing a
coalition candidate in order to win the state governorship. This alternative was
not pursued, more for reasons having to do with the parties' national political calculations than with the regional feasibility of coming to an agreement. Moreover,
the FDN and the parties that comprised it did not have an organizational structure in Baja California that would support a candidacy as strong as that of Cuauhtémoc Cárdenas at the national level. The PAN's circumstances were considerably
more favorable. Since the 1950s, the PAN had seriously contested elected posts
with the PRI, and at this juncture the PAN had a candidate with statewide recognition: Ernesto Ruffo Appel, the municipal president of Ensenada. Thus in 1989,
the opposition unity that was impossible to arrange between political organiza-

ity was heightened by the PRI's need to regain legitimacy and win back popular support without putting at risk the party's dominance at the national level. The 1989 Baja California elections thus served a dual purpose: the PAN's victory in the gubernatorial race opened a new institutional space for opposition parties while enhancing the image of the Salinas administration—that is, the PRI at the national level—as a promoter of political, and especially economic, modernization. While PRI cadres at the state level tasted the bitterness of defeat, the outcome in Baja California consolidated the national power structure centered on the presidency. From that point forward, Salinas expanded his team to include members of the PAN as allies in several of his most impor-tant reform initiatives, especially those relating to the economy. The elections in Baja California thus marked the beginnings of an alliance that would endure nearly to the end of the Salinas presidency. These years marked a period of reciprocal tolerance between the PRI and the PAN, during which the latter consolidated its presence at the national level.

The administration of Governor Ernesto Ruffo Appel (1989–1995), the winner of the 1989 race in Baja California, followed a course that combined negotiation and open conflict with the PRI, at both the na-tional and state levels. The primary conflicts between the state and na-tional governments during this period arose over the state's new voter registry, control over funds allocated to the state through the National Solidarity Program (PRONASOL, the Salinas administration's showcase anti-poverty program), and the devolution of financial resources from the federal government to the state. In all of these disputes, the domi-nant interests were those of the state-level PAN. Although the national context certainly influenced the specifics of these conflicts, there is nothing to suggest that national-level negotiations between the PAN and president overruled any initiatives coming from the state govern-ment or from municipal-level PAN authorities. Successive PAN gov-ernments in Baja California have maintained a similarly wide margin of autonomy, defining their policies in line with a regional perspective. For this reason, any stresses experienced in the course of the democratic transition in Baja California are more likely attributable to state-level than to national factors.

It is important here to recall that the PAN did not win the 1989 elec-tions because of its conservative ideology or because of its success at convincing the electorate to embrace a conservative program. The vot-ers who elected Ruffo in 1989 were the same ones who cast their ballots for left-of-center Cuauhtémoc Cárdenas and the FDN in 1988. Their

---

tions was realized by citizens, who on election day actively mobilized to defend the vote and supported the PAN on a massive scale.

core demand remained unchanged: democratic elections. Only a few months separated these elections, yet the two parties' ideological profiles are far apart. The political priorities of the citizenry did not shift radically from one election to the next; rather, in both cases the electorate and the parties converged around a liberal center that reasserted a citizen's right to choose a government through the electoral process.

Recognizing the existence of this common ground does not erase the fact that there were still many points of disagreement between the citizenry and the parties' political projects. Yet parties usually ignore these points of conflict and underestimate the importance of the political moment, assuming that a ballot cast in favor of a party implies that the voter accepts the party's whole political or ideological package. However, only by realizing that the connection a party makes with the electorate is conjunctural can we explain how the FDN achieved such a stunning success in 1988 only to see its support evaporate a few months later. The PAN experienced a similar reversal in the 1991 elections, when it received significantly fewer votes than in 1989.[10]

These marked fluctuations in party preferences demonstrate that each party's core support is modest in comparison to the broad sections of the electorate that have no deep-seated affiliation with any specific party. The PRI's base of support, both at the national level and in Baja California, tends to be among the rural population and in low-income urban neighborhoods. What is surprising about the Baja California case is that the PAN has made significant inroads in these PRI strongholds, even though the PRI has maintained its advantage in successive elections. The PAN has drawn its principal support from the urban middle classes. However, these are the individuals who constitute the bulk of the "non-affiliated" or swing voters, and the PAN's performance in the statehouse from 1989 through the 1990s did not succeed in altering this group's independence.

The relative autonomy of the PAN government in Baja California, in conjunction with its relative disconnection from a stable electoral base, defines a context in which there is both a reasonable capacity for action and a permanent threat of electoral defeat. If we add the ingredient of government inexperience to the mix, the balance tips toward preserving political and administrative control and avoiding any initiatives that might carry unmanageable risks. From 1989 to 1994, the PAN government was careful not to take any action that might put it in a bad

---

[10] In the 1989 gubernatorial election, the PAN and the PRI received 47.8 percent and 38.3 percent, respectively, of the valid vote. In the state-level results of the 1991 elections for federal deputies, the PRI and the PAN received 43.6 and 42.5 percent, respectively, of the valid vote.

light; to the contrary, all government initiatives worked to fortify PAN control, even in the area of electoral institutions.[11]

Thus, although the PAN's conservative ideology does not explain the party's electoral triumph in 1989 and Mexico's first party alternation in power at the state level, neither is it the principal explanatory factor for the PAN's immobility while in government. More important variables in this regard include the limited and indirect financial support the state received from the federal government (such as PRONASOL funding, for example), the difficulty of negotiating state-level political reforms in (until 2000) a national environment of closed competition, and the PAN's transformation into a power structure reluctant to cede space to its principal competitor. To the extent that party alternation in power tends to preserve the prevailing institutional order, the democratic transition will be limited to its achievements in the electoral arena. That is, decision making will remain in the hands of a limited number of officials who control the government agenda and determine how public resources will be utilized.

Despite this relative institutional immobility, the democratic transition that has occurred in Baja California since 1989 has expressed a political movement that can be divided into the following spheres: (1) legitimacy of the political system and the system of government, (2) political representation within the system of government, and (3) citizen participation within the process of government. The assumption here is that the practice of democracy implies a permanent relationship between civil society and the state that places the whole governing process, with all its rules and regulations, under citizen control. In this sense, an election is only one moment—and not necessarily the most important moment—in the democratic process. For socioeconomic development and quality of life, for example, the most significant point is that at which citizens intervene in the governing process to define policies according to procedures and rules that are much more precise and refined than those accessible to the citizenry through political parties or elections. When spaces are not available for citizen intervention, those individuals making decisions should be subject to exact and transparent rules (in contrast to an authoritarian regime, which permits gov-

---

[11] For example, in its first proposal for electoral reform in 1991, the Ruffo administration insisted that the state government maintain administrative control over electoral institutions. Even in the final legislation approved in December 1994, the governor retained the power to appoint the president of the State Electoral Council (Consejo Estatal Electoral), whose other members were independent "citizen counselors." Paradoxically, at the national level the PAN has traditionally demanded the complete autonomy of electoral institutions, which was finally achieved in Mexico's 1996 electoral reform.

ernment officials far-ranging discretion in the management of public affairs).

Disaggregating a democratic transition into distinctive spheres avoids the kind of overgeneralization that has been common among PAN members in Baja California. Because there had been one instance of alternation between parties in Baja California, these PAN members claimed that the legitimacy of the political system had been confirmed (because democratic elections had been held) *and* that political representation was assured (because legitimate authorities had been elected) *and* that citizen participation was guaranteed (because the citizens had spoken and been heard). And worse, the entire transition process was attributed to the volition of individual actors, with no importance given to the normative and governing structures that ultimately impose their authoritarian content and design.

What is left out of this analysis is that the connection between citizens and parties is essentially a chance meeting, an accumulation of coincidences in a period of transition, not something constructed from strong and lasting links. The lesson for political parties—and especially for governments in contexts where there is party alternation in power—is that they must redefine their relationship with local society on the basis of shared goals, on the basis of a new set of convergences, and that they should be far less concerned with an ideology defined in advance on the basis of some presumed political clientele. Artificially combining the various aspects of political transition dilutes public debate about other goals of the reform process, such as representation in government and citizen involvement in policy making. The Baja California case provides an opportunity for examining the three spheres of democratic transition and determining the degree to which each was consolidated in the period after 1989.

Legitimacy of the Political System and of Government

If we understand the legitimacy of the political system as society's general acceptance of the rules according to which governments are formed and rule, Baja California went through three distinct phases of political transition. During the first phase, prior to 1989, opposition parties and wide sectors of civil society campaigned against PRI and governmental control over state institutions and electoral procedures, in the process eroding the legitimacy of local government. The only comparable incident at the national level would be the strongly contested 1988 presidential election.

The second phase, from 1989 to 1992, involved important changes in the electoral process. Most important, federal government intervention (and electoral fraud) in state-level elections came to an end. This was accomplished by compiling a new state-level voter registry and distributing election identification cards complete with the voter's photograph, the first such voter identification card in the nation.[12] These steps confirmed the legitimacy of electoral processes and institutions *within civil society*, even though mutual suspicions between political parties remained.

The 1992 local elections in Baja California demonstrated that the process begun in 1989 had attained its goal. Party alternation in power had become accepted as an integral component of electoral democracy. There were no citizen mobilizations or public debates about the legitimacy of the electoral process that were in any way comparable to what took place in 1988 and 1989. This demonstrates that, in the space of only a few years, free and fair elections and alternation in office had been "normalized" in the public consciousness and in political practice.

The 1989 Baja California elections' legitimizing effect on the political system influenced the subsequent federal elections, bringing the behavior of politicians, political parties, and society closely into line with the behavior of these actors in Baja California's landmark elections. These effects at the federal level were reinforced by the reform of Mexico's election laws and a new national voter registry, which was first used in the 1991 midterm elections. Thus, between 1989 and 1992, the struggle for a fair political and electoral system moved from the arena of civil society and opposition parties to the domain of political parties almost exclusively.

With the first substantive reform of Baja California's electoral legislation in late 1994, the legitimization of the political/electoral system reached its third and final stage. The state's new Law of Electoral Institutions and Processes expressed on a judicial and institutional level society's demands for legality, impartiality, and objectivity in elections. The reform law created the State Electoral Institute as an independent entity charged with overseeing the electoral process, and it set stricter rules regarding campaign finance, campaign practices, voter registration, and balloting. It also established an Electoral Justice Tribunal to resolve election disputes. Although the law did not establish fully independent institutions—the governor still appoints the president of the six-member State Electoral Council, and tensions have persisted be-

---

[12] State-level voter registries were traditionally administered by the federal government rather than by the states. The Ruffo administration simply reclaimed this function, an action that provoked strong conflict with the federal government because it implicitly questioned the reliability of the registry then in force. This was an especially sensitive matter because the Salinas government had pledged to update voter registries on a national scale. In practice, however, Baja California's innovations in this area were later adopted at the federal level.

tween the Federal Electoral Institute (IFE) and the State Electoral Institute (IEE), which jointly manage the voter registry—it did satisfy the three main parties. The electoral code may be amended in future years, but it established a solid foundation of electoral legitimacy among political parties, something that the citizenry had accepted as of 1989. This suggests substantial evolution and maturation in Baja California's democratic transition.

The 1994 electoral reform was also innovative in that it incorporated a broad range of party actors. Unlike the PAN's earlier attempt to reform the state's electoral legislation in 1991 (an effort that was spearheaded by the PAN governor), the 1994 reform was negotiated between the PAN and the PRI in the state legislature, with both parties submitting proposals. This marked a departure from the established pattern in which the governor, not the legislature, was the source of reform initiatives. The process also implicitly recognized that there was no longer a single axis of power that could impose its will unilaterally.

The PRI was the more radical actor in this negotiation process, calling for the complete autonomy of electoral institutions and civil society's full involvement in them. The PAN, in contrast, pushed for state government responsibility over the electoral process. Of course, given the PAN's electoral ascendancy in Baja California, it was in the PRI's interest to press for reform regarding, for example, proportional representation in the state legislature and municipal councils even if not all elements in the party were fully committed to the reform agenda. And the PAN, a longtime vocal proponent of democratic reform, could hardly oppose increased pluralism in local politics, even if this posed a threat to the PAN's control of certain government offices.

Political Representation in the System of Government

Although the 1989 elections established the legitimacy of the political/electoral system, the new PAN government, despite the transparency of its election, perpetuated the preexisting authoritarian structure of government. Governor Ruffo held onto extensive executive powers and continued to exert a strong influence over the state's legislative and executive branches. The operations of municipal governments also continued unchanged, though local administration (especially in Tijuana) did undergo substantial reform.

Thus it was in the restructuring of government institutions that Baja California's transition encountered one of its greatest obstacles. Institutional design had not emerged as a central issue in the earlier stages of social mobilization. In the initial struggle for political opening, it was easy to identify what was *not* democratic, but it was much harder to suggest what government practices *would* be democratic. The Ruffo administration focused more on changing who held power and less on the need to redesign (nonelectoral) institutions. The first challenge confronting the new PAN administration, then, was to recognize that a problem existed with regard to the structure of governmental institutions and that this obstacle, if not overcome, would constrain the government's operations and cause the administration to lose popular support.

The PAN's electoral performance in 1991—when the PRI managed to recover much of the ground it had lost in 1989—brought home the message that something was amiss. The PAN's electoral advantage was cut to an absolute minimum in 1992, most notably in municipalities governed by the PAN, and in the 1994 federal elections the PAN lost all of its elective positions in Baja California.[13] Election results from 1989 to 1995 show a clear loss of support for the PAN, despite the fact that PAN administrations had significantly expanded public access to basic services (especially potable water) during these years. Apparently these initiatives were insufficient to satisfy a society that had developed considerable capacity to criticize government operations. Although there was significant technical modernization in staff and municipal government operations in the early 1990s, this process did not include reform in the structure and process of decision making. Indeed, this period was characterized by the stagnation of institutional reform.

A new phase in the evolution of institutions and political representation began in late 1994. The adoption of a new electoral code altered the institutional scenario by increasing opportunities for opposition parties to participate in government. For example, the number of seats in the state legislature that were open to opposition parties through proportional representation grew from four to ten, increasing the total number of seats from nineteen to twenty-five. The electoral reform also made composition of city councils more proportional, breaking the tradition of majority party control over virtually all municipal government posts and fostering a new spirit of co-responsibility among political parties at the municipal level. Changes were, however, less significant in municipalities where voters choose among slates of candidates, not individual candidates.

Pluralism in the state legislature and city councils largely undermined the old authoritarian patterns in Baja California, in which the dominant party controlled even the most minor details of policy. In theory, the involvement of a diverse set of actors in policy making should produce policies that better respond to social needs and are less

---

[13] At the national level, the worst results for the PAN in the 1994 elections were precisely in those entities in which it governed: Baja California, Chihuahua, and Guanajuato.

isolated from local civic organizations. Perhaps the most important achievement in Baja California was that key political actors recognized the need for institutional restructuring and began to turn their efforts in that direction.

Finally, pluralism and proportional representation altered the number of relevant political actors and the mix of party affiliations in municipal governments and the state legislature. Although these changes modified power relations within these institutions, they did not produce a substantive reform of the decision-making process itself. In many instances the majority party still controlled enough votes to dictate policy decisions—in municipalities and in the state legislature—without any support from other political parties or other social actors.

Citizen Participation in Government

Despite increased pluralism in city councils and the state legislature, government policy processes in Baja California in the early 1990s were not necessarily democratic. Pluralism advances democracy in an institution, but not necessarily in the institution's decisions. Policies must create their own consensus, which is not the same as institutional legitimacy. Mistakenly equating an institution with its policies constitutes a major obstacle to achieving consensus in government because it obscures a government's need to negotiate policies—from conception to implementation—with the citizenry. This is an area in which PAN administrations in Baja California have not yet advanced much.

The Ruffo administration—as well as local PAN and PRI governments and the Baja California state legislature—made citizen participation a primary objective. However, this was not envisioned as institutionalized participation. That is, it was seen as something outside of, something supplemental to, the governmental structure. Ideally, citizen participation could be reduced to fiscal issues, with neighborhoods contributing toward public works but never sharing in the actual decisions of government. Thus, the quintessence of citizen participation—people's capacity to influence public decision making—failed to find an institutional space for expression. Despite the pluralist partisan mix within state and municipal governments in Baja California, policies continued to be defined within public agencies—and by very narrow circles of power holders within them.

It is no coincidence that the spaces left vacant by these nonexistent governmental mechanisms in Baja California have been occupied by the mass media, especially radio and the press. The media not only help put pressure on government, but they also serve to link the populace to government by providing a forum for citizen complaints about issues ranging from potholes to broken water lines. Mass communication outlets proliferated in Baja California after 1989, and they openly adopted the discourse of regional politics and criticism of government. Some radio stations have become interlocutors between citizens, who have few equally effective channels for airing their demands, and government administrators. However, thoroughgoing citizen participation in decision making and consensus building—ostensibly a key goal of democratic transition—is still beyond the horizon.

In the meantime, given a more democratic social context, public policies emanating from an authoritarian government structure are likely to become a permanent source of conflict. This dynamic undermined support for PAN governments in Baja California between 1989 and 1994 and augured a poor PAN showing in the 1995 local elections. However, the balance tipped in favor of the PAN when voters placed the blame for the 1994–1995 economic crisis squarely on the federal government. The PAN was thus able to rebound from its performance in 1994, when it lost the elections across the board.

What is important here is that elections are no longer the axis of democratic transition in Baja California. Elections can influence the pace of the transition and the cast of actors, but not the transition's basic content. The new agenda does not focus on the electoral arena but on political negotiation leading to pluralist, open political institutions and decision making. For this reason, the elections held in August 1995 had less significance for the democratic transition than previous ones in which free and fair elections were the top priority.

DEMOCRATIC TRANSITION IN BAJA CALIFORNIA

The groundbreaking political events taking place in Baja California between 1989 and 1995 made a significant contribution to Mexico's political opening. At the national level, Baja California became a symbol of political liberalization. The state's experience confirmed the crisis of Mexican authoritarianism, and it helped define new rules to ensure free and fair elections. Baja California was also the most fully realized expression of democratic transition at the state level. Yet state politics have not followed a straight trajectory, with democratic forces inevitably surmounting all remaining authoritarian practices, institutions, and cultural norms. In this sense, Baja California has lived an evolutionary political process in which constraints begin to mount, impeding progress toward the original objective of a democratic transition. Forward movement toward the goal has slowed; progress is less linear and less spectacular. In many instances, key actors have been governed more by inertia than by a creative dynamic.

This was the case in the August 1995 statewide elections (gubernatorial, municipal, and legislative), when democratization ceased to be the axis of regional politics.[14] This was in sharp contrast with 1988 and 1989, when this issue mobilized a broad civic movement and influenced organizations like the FDN and ultimately the PAN. By 1995, however, the content of democratic debate had been eroded by the progress that Baja California had made in reforming its electoral practices and institutions. The debate's leaders had changed as well; whereas the PAN had been the undisputed leader of an extensive social movement for democratization in the earlier years, by 1995 this was no longer the case. By 1995, no single actor was broadly recognized as the sole champion of the democratic transition.

In the 1995 elections, public debate focused on two new questions: what do governments do, and which political party can do it best? In other words, the content of political debate centered on capacities, resources, and outcomes. In order to respond more effectively to these new criteria, power contenders downplayed the traits that had so clearly differentiated them in the past.

It may well be that this evolution in the content and representation of democratization is conclusive evidence of the "normalization" of electoral politics in Baja California. As the democratic debate faded into the background and political actors began looking more alike, political parties across the board won recognition as legitimate players in the political game. The marked differences that had existed earlier between the PAN and the PRI paved the way for the dramatic events of 1988–1989. Under the new rules of "peaceful bipartisan integration"—one more proof of the normalization of state politics—the PAN and the PRI are no longer viewed as markedly different. In the electoral arena, the increased similarities between these parties means that neither has a decisive advantage over the other. This interpretation is confirmed by the fact that the two parties ran neck and neck in elections from 1991 to 1995—in the process, effectively locking out the PRD along with smaller parties that failed to capture the legal minimum of 4 percent of the statewide vote.

The public's perception of a degree of convergence between the PAN and the PRI does not imply that party competition will be less intense, that PRI and PAN administrations will concur in their priorities, or that party platforms will be fully compatible. But the relative absence of differentiation between parties in the public's eye does explain the increasingly two-party character of electoral competition in the state and, in particular, the nature of parties' links to society. Party alternation in power has lost some of its earlier dramatic appeal, and

---

[14] Despite the contradictions in its political trajectory, Baja California retains its position as the vanguard of democratization when compared with other Mexican states such as Guerrero or Tabasco.

the importance of ideological party projects has declined. Thus, for the average Baja California voter, there is no fundamental distinction between the PRI's traditional "revolutionary nationalism" and the PAN's "social subsidiarity." These are less and less the categories that define voters' preferences.

It would appear, then, that Baja California's democratic transition has become bogged down by its early successes. If we examine the core dynamic of political activity, we find that the PAN's desire to hold on to power prevented the party from pursuing institutional reforms that implied sharing decision-making authority with the PRI or with other social and political actors. For the PAN, a reform of the machinery of government carried the risk of losing control to the PRI, an organization with which the PAN is in a permanent state of tension. To implement reform is not a simple undertaking; it is hindered by the inevitable inertia toward reproducing existing structures, by the contradictions within the PAN and its own political bureaucracy, and by the threatening presence of its principal rival. Thus the struggle to remain in power ultimately constrained the very actor that had so recently been the advocate of reform. In the case of the PRI, its struggle to regain power has followed a similar logic—accepting alternation but advocating little or no reform once power is attained. The paradox was that, by the mid–1990s in Baja California, the PRI was calling for greater political opening while the PAN resisted further change.

The state's ongoing democratic transition is, then, situated squarely in growing regional pluralism. That is, its character depends upon the specific *actions* of key actors, rather than residing in one particular actor. In much the same way, the possibilities for advancing the transition lie in the competitiveness of the political game, the dispersion of initiatives among different groups, and conflict between them. Now that the link between democracy and a single political actor has been broken, we find political actors who take positions for or against a particular issue depending on what most favors their immediate interests and whether they are in power or aspiring to power. There is abundant evidence of this tendency in the public statements of both PAN and PRI members.[15] The result is a double-sided situation in which a "limited"

---

[15] The state legislature is the institution that best reflects the limitations inherent in a locally dominant party that is unwilling to share power and decisions with its adversaries. The PAN has controlled the legislature since 1989. Yet not only has the PAN failed to promote initiatives that would reform this institution, it has sometimes resisted proposals designed to do so. For example, one proposal called for the leading minority party to take charge of the state Comptroller's Office. This would, of course, have been a "prize" for the PRI, but at the same time this reform would have established an effective counterweight in relations between parties.

transition is constrained by its diffuseness but simultaneously benefits from this diffuseness because it diminishes the chances for targeted, focused conflict.

Thus the longer-term prospects for democratic transition in Baja California will be defined in terms of the conflict between the PAN and the PRI and, paradoxically, in an electoral context that provides few opportunities for civil society to gain real influence. The PAN has been able to position itself as a central force for change, though not necessarily because it controls the state's key government positions. In fact, the party has restricted the scope of political reforms. And given the nature of the PAN's competition with the PRI, it is unlikely that existing social conditions will produce a new vanguard actor; this is not a period of dominant forces but of dispersed political forces. For this reason, the state's democratic transition has been severely limited. And yet, as discussed below, the transition continues in those spaces opened by the confrontation between the PAN and the PRI.

The 1995 Elections: Electoral Normality and Pluralist Institutions

The 1995 election results confirmed the PAN's strength in Baja California, although voting returns did display some contradictory tendencies. The PAN held onto the governorship and kept control of the state legislature, but it lost two of the four contested municipal councils (in Tecate and Ensenada).[16] Despite Mexico's continuing economic crisis and its impact on voters, the PRI presented a strong challenge to the PAN, winning Ensenada (a PAN stronghold since 1983) and Tecate, the latter by a wide margin. The PRI's most important setback came in city council elections in Mexicali, capital of the state and a key source of PRI support in previous elections.

Apart from Ensenada, Tecate, and Mexicali (all of which experienced an alternation of parties in power), the 1995 elections reproduced the political conditions that had prevailed in Baja California during the preceding three years. Although one should not underestimate the importance of party alternation in these three municipal governments and its impact on local society, these local governments have relatively little capacity to alter significantly the regional power structure. The "normalization" of competition between the PAN and the PRI—that is, the reduced contrast between them—suggests that party alternation at the level of municipal councils will not bring any radical changes in

---

Although supported by Governor Héctor Terán Terán (1995–1998), the measure was resisted by PAN legislators and other party leaders, who managed to block it.

[16] In 1995, the municipality of Tijuana was divided to create the municipality of Playas de Rosarito, but there were no city council elections there in 1995.

municipal government, in interparty relations, or in civil society. This situation marks an important departure from earlier years, when municipalities such as Ensenada and Mexicali were strongly partisan in favor of the PAN and the PRI, respectively.

Other measures of "normalization" in the 1995 elections included the marginal attention given to issues like electoral fraud or the reliability of the voter registry, as well as political parties' decisions not to devote significant financial and organizational resources to preparations to dispute electoral irregularities. However, the main axis of normalization in 1995 was the state's new electoral legislation and the institutions it established.

Municipal Election Results

As noted above, the 1995 elections returned control of the Ensenada municipal government to the PRI following twelve years of opposition administrations, first by the Socialist Workers' Party (PST) and then by the PAN. The PRI's victory was less a shift by voters toward that party than their rejection of the preceding PAN administrations, whose actions and policies had diminished the party's popularity with the local electorate. Voters' displeasure had been evident in earlier elections, but it was not until 1995 that sufficient momentum built to effect a change in government. Although Mexico's economic crisis generally worked against the PRI in the 1995 elections, in Ensenada this factor was outweighed by the electorate's disaffection with the PAN, making Ensenada a clear example of shifting party identities. The election also confirmed the legitimacy of both parties as political players, and the outcome demonstrated how actors that had been associated with political transformation can lose momentum once in power and forfeit their connection with the public.

The PRI's 1995 win in Tecate was also highly significant, especially because of the party's margin of victory. In 1992, the PAN took the municipal council with 45.5 percent of the valid vote (against 43.1 percent for the PRI). In 1995, by contrast, the PRI garnered 59.3 percent of the vote, and the PAN received only 30.7 percent.

The parties reversed position in Mexicali in 1995, with the PRI accepting its first official defeat in the state capital. Eugenio Elorduy Walther, the PAN's winning candidate for municipal president, fractured what had been the PRI's principal base of support in Baja California, drawing Mexicali out of the traditional PRI sphere and incorporating it into the statewide dynamic of party alternation in power.[17]

---

[17] Some observers suspect that the PAN's Elorduy Walther also won the 1983 election for Mexicali's municipal presidency.

Despite being the capital of a state governed by a PAN governor since 1989, Mexicali remained strongly loyal to the PRI, and it was assumed that this support might actually grow because of the city's ties with native son Ernesto Zedillo, president of Mexico (1994–2000). In fact, the opposite proved true. The federal government deliberately distanced itself from the elections in Mexicali (and in Baja California more generally), allowing a full expression of local political preferences.

In Tijuana, the 1995 elections brought little in the way of significant change. The most noteworthy outcome was that the PAN increased its margin of victory over the PRI, most probably due to the fact that the PRI was severely fragmented and unable to build internal consensus or construct an appropriate campaign strategy. The outcome in Tijuana was especially instructive for the PRI because it underscored the costs of the party's failure to establish internal norms that were broadly accepted as legitimate. At the last minute, the PRI was forced to choose René Treviño Arredondo as a "unity candidate." However, Treviño, who had served as Tijuana's municipal president from 1983 to 1986, did not fit the electorate's vision of their city's contemporary political profile. The PRI won only 39.4 percent of the votes for city council (down from 44.1 percent in 1992), compared to 51.8 percent for the PAN.

Building a New State Legislature

In 1995, the PRI was able to carry only four of Baja California's fifteen legislative districts, down from seven in 1992.[18] Nevertheless, under the state's new system of proportional representation, the PRI ultimately received eleven seats, compared with thirteen for the PAN and one for the PRD. In this case, the 1994 electoral reform operated to award the PRI an additional seven members in the state legislature, while the PAN gained only two seats.

Despite the increased number of seats in the state legislature that are awarded through proportional representation, the legislature continues to operate under old rules that allow the majority party to dominate except on bills requiring a three-quarters majority for passage. The majority party controls access to key legislative positions, including the body's president and committee chairs, and it reserves final approval of all state office budgets. Thus there is little momentum in state politics toward building a broad consensus, or toward minority parties serving as checks on the majority. Legislators spend considerable time and ef-

---

[18] The lost seats all fell within the municipality of Mexicali, underscoring once again the dramatic shift in partisan support among Mexicali voters.

fort discussing how positions and responsibilities should be shared among parties, but the final decisions are taken by the majority party. Under such circumstances, minority parties in Baja California have found that they can exert more influence by working through the media and public opinion than through formal institutional mechanisms. In other words, in the state legislature, the majority is still able to thwart minority parties' full participation in what is in theory a pluralist institution. The same often holds true for decision making at the level of municipal government.

The Gubernatorial Election

The selection of a governor has traditionally been the key election in Baja California. In 1995, the state's voters showed a noteworthy ability to separate their vote for governor from their vote for other, especially municipal, offices (see table 5.1). This situation led to three different outcomes. In some municipalities, voters' party preference for municipal government tightly paralleled their gubernatorial choice, such as occurred in Tijuana. In other municipalities, the vote was markedly split, with the electorate overwhelmingly electing a PAN governor but simultaneously choosing a PRI municipal government, as in Tecate. And, finally, there were municipalities (including Ensenada and Mexicali) with no marked homogeneity or bifurcation in the balloting.

In places like Tecate, where voters split their preferences between parties in balloting for governor and municipal offices, we may assume that the gubernatorial campaign lost some of its "headliner" status to the competition for local offices. That is, in these cases the PRI candidate for the municipal presidency became more important for his party than the PRI's gubernatorial candidate. This pattern was repeated to a lesser degree in Ensenada and Mexicali, where municipal races also had a very high profile. Notably, even though the PRI's 1995 gubernatorial candidate was a past municipal president of Mexicali, he was unable to do better in the balloting there than did the PRI's candidate for municipal president.

In contrast, the conduct of Tijuana voters was fiercely partisan, with virtually no distinction by party between votes for governor and votes for municipal president. For municipalities that occupied a middle ground (that is, showing neither marked homogeneity nor bifurcation in the vote), the gubernatorial election held more importance than the selection of a city council. The PAN's gubernatorial candidate, Héctor Terán Terán, ran a very strong campaign, generally outperforming his party's candidates for municipal offices, most markedly in Tecate.

Table 5.1. **Baja California's Gubernatorial and City Council Election Results by Municipality, 1995 (percentages)**

	Ensenada		Tijuana		Mexicali		Tecate	
	PRI	PAN	PRI	PAN	PRI	PAN	PRI	PAN
Governor	44.0	43.1	39.0	52.4	41.8	49.8	52.4	37.8
City Council	45.3	40.7	39.4	51.8	43.7	48.1	59.3	30.7

Source: Instituto Electoral Estatal.

In reviewing the gubernatorial balloting in Baja California in 1995, it seems clear that Francisco Pérez Tejada, the PRI's candidate, did not help his party's candidates in local elections. In contrast, the PAN's Terán Terán did provide a decisive boost to PAN candidates in most local elections, despite his party's losses in Tecate and Ensenada.

A BALANCE SHEET ON BAJA CALIFORNIA'S DEMOCRATIC TRANSITION

A balance sheet on Baja California's democratic transition would stress both shifts in the PAN's own trajectory and the elements that define a new structure of regional (and, to a certain extent, national) political power. The three axes that characterize the 1990s consist of the actors, objectives, and forms of political interaction that configure power in the state. The National Action Party has a different location on each axis. Moreover, on each axis its role as a vanguard force in the transition to and consolidation of democracy has become increasingly diffuse, despite its profile as the dominant party in Baja California.

Political Opening and Electoral Reform

The first phase in the PAN's trajectory was its consolidation as the main force pushing for political opening and a reform of the electoral system in Baja California. This phase, most evident between 1989 and 1992, ended in late 1994 with the state's last significant electoral reform. The PAN's contribution to this process was crucial, with direct repercussions in the state and significant implications for national politics. The PAN's gubernatorial triumph in 1989 contributed notably to national political opening.[19] In the same manner, the electoral reform promoted

---

[19] This is not to deny the multiple antecedents of this transition, including the celebrated electoral battles in the state of Chihuahua between 1983 and 1986 and the

by the administration of Governor Ernesto Ruffo Appel (especially its use of advanced technologies to register voters and to control the balloting process) also forced the national electoral system to evolve in the direction of greater transparency.

However, without downplaying the PAN's contributions in Baja California, it should be noted that both demands—initially political opening, and then electoral reform—were among the party's inherent objectives. That is, they were prerequisites for the PAN to develop as a political party; they were a part of the PAN's own internal nature. Political opening was a necessary condition for the PAN to be counted as a recognized and effective actor in the competition for power. The electoral reform was necessary in order to establish the laws, technologies, and institutions to regulate that competition and end the inertia of authoritarianism in this area. In other words, both demands were not merely the application of the party's doctrine and political values; they were also the materialization of the conditions for its organic development. The demands, in sum, were in its interests. The PAN thus developed the capabilities that made it the main constructive force for political opening and electoral reform.

The PAN's relationship to the *political* reform of state institutions contrasts with the preceding trajectory, for the simple reason that the PAN did not take up this second objective with the same energy. In this arena, the PAN was no longer a principal actor; indeed, at times it actually resisted change. When compared to the creative force that the PAN displayed in the reform of the electoral system, one must conclude that the party has played only a secondary role in advancing such political values as opening up decision-making processes to citizen participation, accountability and transparency, plurality in governmental decisions, establishing checks and balances, professionalization of public administration, and so forth.[20]

---

presidential campaign of Cuauhtémoc Cárdenas in 1988. These episodes helped consolidate an opposition electorate in places such as Baja California and Mexico City.

[20] Two examples of these "inconsistencies" illustrate this point. The first case involved a proposal, outlined in 1995 by Governor Héctor Terán Terán, to improve the political balance within the state legislature and especially to ensure more effective scrutiny of the public accounts that the executive branch and municipal councils must render to the legislature. The governor's proposal was that the head of the Comptroller's Office—the congressional fiscal watchdog agency—would be appointed by the first political minority, which in this case was the PRI. This proposal, which had long been advocated by the PAN before it came to power in the state, was immediately rejected by the party and rapidly forgotten. The PAN chose instead to preserve party control of that key post, just as the PRI had done for decades. Later, in 1998, the parties in the state legislature (PAN, PRI, and PRD)

Beginning in the late 1990s, the principal reforms of state institutions were driven by *competition* between the main parties, the PAN and the PRI. The most important institutional innovations have arisen from the balance of power and political negotiations between them, with the PRD acting as a catalyst. The most significant changes (approved at the end of 1994) have affected the makeup of the state legislature and of municipal councils. Up to that point the councils were comprised overwhelmingly of representatives of the party that won the elections, with no proportional representation based on minority parties' electoral performance. The search for a balance among the state's political parties was the construct guiding these reforms, and the decisive pressure came from the minority party, the PRI.[21] In other words, it is no longer the PAN that is taking the leadership role in this process, nor is it the PAN that is devoting all its energy to institutional

---

arrived at the healthy idea of professionalizing both the Comptroller's Office and the state legislature's chief administrative post, filling the positions through public searches and merit-based evaluations. As will be argued below, this latter decision corresponded to a "higher stage" of politics in the state, distinct from the party logic that prevailed during the first half of the 1990s.

A second example of "inconsistency" has been the explicit refusal on the part of the majority of PAN members to professionalize public administration, whether at the state or the municipal level. This debate, which would appear to have merely a technical dimension, in fact has a strong political and partisan content because of the inertia and continuing influence of government penetration of societal groups. The PAN governments have preserved the governors' and municipal presidents' discretionary authority to appoint public functionaries and practically all government personnel (within the limits imposed by unions, which in this context are very useful for maintaining the stability of the institutions in question). This practice makes it possible for party members to expect and obtain some public positions in every governmental cycle. The relationship between party members and public administration is therefore increasingly direct, and as a result the prospects for making progress in professionalizing public service are reduced—even though this goal is still articulated in the PAN's campaigns.

It is important to note that both of these examples illustrate the weight of criteria related to the preservation of political power, which in turn inhibit projects aimed at promoting innovation in governmental institutions.

[21] It is an interesting paradox that the PRI in Baja California, motivated by its position as a minority party in the state legislature and in city councils, has become a strong critic of the structure of these bodies and their decision-making processes. In its search for counterbalances to PAN majorities, the PRI has harshly criticized traditional majoritarianism in these bodies, and it has defended the principle of proportionality and decision-making processes that include the views of political minorities. See, for example, the PRI's paid political advertisement (supported by the PRD) denouncing the authoritarianism of the PAN majority in the state legislature when it appointed the head of the Comptroller's Office and the chief administrative officer of the state legislature (*El Mexicano*, January 29, 1993).

modernization. When considering these reforms, the PAN did not present itself as a united organization in the way that it had in its earlier political trajectory, especially when it was fighting for political opening in Baja California.

One may conclude, then, that the agenda for institutional reform (understood as the second phase of Baja California's democratic transition) is not an existential condition for the PAN, in contrast to its objectives in the preceding phase. The PAN can survive, and even consolidate, as a political organization without these reforms. Even more, precisely because of the dominant features of governmental institutions—whose organizational structures and norms preserve the state's earlier authoritarian heritage[22]—the PAN's membership may find it more worthwhile to favor continuity than reform, especially in the short term. Once a vanguard force, the PAN is on its way to becoming a "normal" party.

The "Normalization" of the PAN

Just as electoral practices have been "normalized" in Baja California, so, too, there has been a decline in the intensity of the PAN's pressuring for reform in the state. The natural tendency for any party to want to maintain itself in power is one of the factors determining this trend. However, one must also include the PAN's own organizational evolution. The party has become enormously complex as a consequence of its political success.

Particularly after 1995, the PAN's organizational structure became increasingly diversified. The duality between party and government has brought the PAN to a new phase in its internal history, with internal power groups finding it hard to share a common agenda similar to their united promotion of political opening and electoral reform. At the same time, PAN members are now spread throughout various institutions and levels of government, which produces a complex set of perspectives and interests that are not necessarily complementary and which cannot be easily reconciled as in the past.

---

[22] On this point, it is worth emphasizing the fact that the authoritarian, highly centralized system that was a feature of Mexico for decades also built governmental institutions, laws, and political norms that were compatible with it. Postrevolutionary authoritarianism enjoyed such stability and durability precisely because it was reproduced in the governmental sphere. As a result, partisan alternation in power is but an initial phase in the process of state reform that, in and of itself, has neither the capacity nor the content to overcome authoritarianism in governmental institutions.

Under these conditions, the PAN has not really been able to build a single common agenda despite its predominance in state government. Except on matters of election campaigns or the defense of generic political principles, the very nature of intergovernmental relations makes a unified party stance impossible. For example, the interests of PAN–controlled municipal governments can contradict, and have contradicted, those of the governor (even when the governor is also a *panista*) and state legislators (including PAN representatives).[23]

This panorama does not necessarily mean that the PAN is completely immobilized. On the contrary, the party has made significant changes in public administration in order to increase efficiency and effectiveness and promote instrumental administrative rationality. However, although the PAN is still a part of the process of democratic reform of the state, the main catalyst between 1989 and 1997 was the balance of power between parties and changes in party competition. More recently, the main factor has been intergovernmental dynamics.

Political Process and Intergovernmental Dynamics

The PAN, then, has learned to recognize the importance of political balances as part of its exercise of governmental power. Between 1989 and 1995, during the administration of Governor Ernesto Ruffo Appel, political polarization between the PAN and the PRI and tensions between PAN administrations (the state executive and municipal councils) and the federal government were obstacles to developing governmental processes based on greater mutual tolerance. Intergovernmental

---

[23] The most notable example of the influence of intergovernmental relations on the state's political dynamics came in late 2000 when there was an effort to reform the state constitution to bring it into line with the federal Constitution following the 1999 reform of Article 115. Although the PAN and Governor Alejandro González Alcocer (1998–2001) tried to arrive at a unified position on the project for municipal reform, the PAN–controlled municipal governments (Mexicali and Tijuana) did not approve the initiative. Indeed, they were joined in opposition by the PRI–controlled municipal government of Ensenada. What is noteworthy is that this constitutional reform initiative had already been approved by a two-thirds majority of the state legislature, including legislative representatives from the PAN, PRI, and PRD. However, when three of the five main municipal governments in the state rejected the proposed reform, it stalled because constitutional reforms in Baja California require approval by a majority of the municipal councils.

This event was unprecedented not only in Baja California but in Mexico as a whole. Independent of the arguments employed, the municipal councils of Baja California made clear their *institutional* political power, which went beyond that of the parties themselves. As will be argued below, this experience illustrates the latest phase in the state's political evolution.

dynamics were broadly subordinated to partisan interests on both sides. During the second half of the 1990s, with the new administrations of Governor Héctor Terán Terán (1995–2001)[24] and President Ernesto Zedillo, different political conditions helped reduce intergovernmental conflicts and interparty tensions in Baja California.

Over time, the dynamics of governability in the state began to shift, establishing the bases for unprecedented political pluralism. The most significant step in this direction was a proposed wholesale reform of Baja California's governmental institutions and the state's judiciary. The state legislature unanimously approved this program in March 1996, and it went into effect in January 1997. The program featured topic-specific commissions comprised of representatives from the three branches of state government, municipal councils, and different societal groups. Technical coordination of the program was assigned to the state university, the Universidad Autónoma de Baja California.

The initial legislative results of this experience were not particularly noteworthy. The commissions concluded their work when the 1998 legislative session came to a close. Nevertheless, this effort made a very significant contribution to the evolution of the structure of power in the state, especially its *intergovernmental* dimensions. What was most important in this regard was that *institutions* became involved in the definition of the state's political agenda. These institutions (the executive, legislative, and judicial branches of state government and Baja California's five municipal councils)—excluded from the political process during the long period of one-party, PRI rule and then briefly subordinated by bipartisan competition between 1989 and 1997—emerged in 1997 as key actors in the definition of the state's political agenda. As they came to the foreground, the immediate consequence was a lower profile for political parties and interparty competition and conflict.

As a result of the increasing primacy of state institutions and intergovernmental dynamics, neither the PAN nor the PRI (nor, more generally, competition between them) now occupies center stage in the process of reforming Baja California's governmental institutions. Neither party is in a position to assume a leading role in part because this new process has diluted them internally. Indeed, with intergovernmental logic in the foreground, political parties can more openly express their internal differences—as, for example, when the Mexicali municipal council votes to oppose an initiative presented by the state governor even though both are *panista*, or when that same council agrees with positions taken by the Ensenada municipal council even though it is

---

[24] Governor Héctor Terán Terán died on October 4, 1998. Alejandro González Alcocer, a federal deputy from 1994 to 1997 who at the time of Terán's death was the head of the PAN in Baja California, was appointed to complete his term.

governed by the PRI. Political parties are increasingly concentrated on a time-specific electoral moment; for better or worse, they have even ceased to be a space for sophisticated, leading-edge political debate.

In simplified terms, political power is now in the hands of public institutions and those who control them—not political parties, but specific and complex groups and nodes of power such as municipal councils and the state legislature. The state's executive branch itself displays internal political complexity within its own bureaucracy and in its intersection with different PAN factions, which in turn adds even more complexity to the executive's relationship with the state legislature and municipal councils.

In sum, Baja California has reached a new stage in the structure, actors, and rules of political power. A power structure that is more complex, pluralistic, and concentrated in public institutions reflects a *formalization* of power, power that is subject to rules and to the rule of law and which acts through juridically defined institutions. Given the history of political power in Mexico, this is no small change. Indeed, from its very origin, Mexico had been characterized by the sharp separation between political processes, on the one hand, and institutions and legal procedures, on the other.

This new phase in Baja California's political evolution has not done away with a party logic. Instead, it complements it and in certain key aspects (such as the reform of legislation and governmental institutions) subordinates it. We should not expect to see the end of political parties, but we can anticipate the end of their overdetermining role and the end of their specific rationality (which for many years subordinated the formal structures of the state) as the only rationality in the dynamics of power. Political power is now exercised on a much more diverse and complex stage—subject to the difficult interaction between party logics and intergovernmental logics, which are not always synchronized and do not always point in the same direction.

CONCLUSION

If the dynamics of power at the national level follow a similar path, then the Baja California experience may offer an important example for Mexico as a whole. Party alternation in the presidency (long the main axis of the postrevolutionary authoritarian regime) has led to a revalorization of state governments and their potential as instruments of partisan pressure and political bargaining. For example, in its confrontation with the PAN and the government of President Vicente Fox (2000–2006), the PRI has begun to use its governors as points of leverage. This strategy indirectly favors the construction of an intergovernmental logic in the configuration of national political power. Despite its clear partisan intent, this type of initiative cannot be announced publicly or promoted outside of legal and institutional bounds. In other words, such initiatives cannot be separated from the intergovernmental framework that they are helping (perhaps unintentionally) to build.[25]

In conclusion, it is certainly important to underscore the fact that, despite the shifts in position that all parties in Baja California have experienced, the PAN is the most politically powerful organization in the state. This is especially the case since the July 2000 general elections in which Vicente Fox gained the presidency. Indeed, the PRI's political and financial weaknesses at the national level (a situation that is replicated at the state level) have amplified the PAN's dominant position. Nevertheless, the PAN itself will not be the crucial actor in determining the structure of power or in shaping the future of the state's institutions. It will unavoidably find itself subject to a much more complex environment and to an internal dynamic that splits it into diverse interests and goals. It would appear, then, that an adjunct of political modernity and democratic normalcy is party humility.

REFERENCES

Guillén López, Tonatiuh. 1992. "Baja California: una década de política electoral." In *Frontera norte: una década de política electoral,* edited by Tonatiuh Guillén López. Mexico: El Colegio de la Frontera Norte/El Colegio de México.

———. 1993a. "Baja California." In *Las elecciones de 1991: la recuperación oficial,* edited by Silvia Gómez Tagle. Mexico City: La Jornada/G. V. Editores.

———. 1993b. *Baja California, 1989–1992: alternancia política y transición democrática.* Mexico: El Colegio de la Frontera Norte/Centro de Investigaciones Interdisciplinarias y Humanidades, Universidad Nacional Autónoma de México.

———. 1995a. "The 1992 Elections and the Democratic Transition in Baja California." In *Opposition Government in Mexico,* edited by Victoria E. Rodríguez and Peter M. Ward. Albuquerque: University of New Mexico Press.

———. 1995b. "Alternancia política y transición democrática: alcances y límites de una experiencia regional en México." In *El fin de siglo y los partidos políticos en América Latina,* edited by Silvia Dutrénit y Leonardo Valdés. Mexico: Instituto Mora/Universidad Autónoma Metropolitana–Iztapalapa.

---

[25] Some examples of this new dynamic are, first, the PRI's creation of its National Governors' Forum in Hermosillo, Sonora, in July 2000 (*La Jornada,* July 23, 2000) and, second, the conflict between the administration of Víctor Cervera Pacheco, governor of Yucatán, and the Federal Electoral Tribunal over the conduct of elections in the state. The latter conflict deepened in early 2001, when Governor Cervera Pacheco tried to defend his position by arguing that he was acting in defense of the state's sovereignty and called for the solidarity of other PRI governors (*La Jornada,* January 8, 2001).

———. 1995c. "Alternancia y nuevas prácticas del poder político en las elecciones de 1994 desde la experiencia regional." In *La voz de los votos: un análisis crítico de las elecciones de 1994*, edited by Germán Pérez, Arturo Alvarado, and Arturo Sánchez. Mexico City: Miguel Ángel Porrúa.

———. 1995d. "Las elecciones de 1994 en Baja California." In *Las elecciones de 1994*, edited by Pablo Pascual Moncayo. Mexico City: Cal y Arena.

O'Donnell, Guillermo, and Philippe C. Schmitter. 1986. *Tentative Conclusions about Uncertain Democracies*. Vol. 4 of *Transitions from Authoritarian Rule: Prospects for Democracy*, edited by Guillermo O'Donnell, Philippe C. Schmitter, and Laurence Whitehead. Baltimore, Md.: Johns Hopkins University Press.

6

Alternation and Change: The Case of Chihuahua

Alberto Aziz Nassif

Since the early 1980s, the northern state of Chihuahua has experienced a historically significant process of political alternation and change. Two developments have been especially important in this regard. The first was the appearance of a civic opposition led by the National Action Party (PAN). The second was an extensive social convergence of middle-class groups, entrepreneurs, the Catholic hierarchy, and peasant and labor organizations pitted against Mexico's long-ruling "official" party, the Institutional Revolutionary Party (PRI).

Various factors produced these two developments, ranging from animosity toward the state's PRI incumbents and a determination to fight governmental corruption to soul-stirring civic passions. There were, in fact, several defining moments over the ten-year period between 1982 and the PAN's capture of the Chihuahua governorship in 1992. The PAN won control of key municipalities in 1983, and in 1985 PAN candidates took half of the state's seats in the federal Chamber of Deputies. Perhaps the most contentious moment occurred in 1986, when the PRI and federal government authorities developed a scheme to thwart the election of the PAN's candidate to the governorship of Chihuahua. Subsequent elections—in 1988, 1989, and 1991—occurred in a climate of voter fatigue and high abstentionism.

It was not until 1992 that the opposition again felt it had a chance to win the governorship. At the time, the administration of President Carlos Salinas de Gortari (1988–1994) was negotiating the North American Free Trade Agreement (NAFTA) and needed to win legitimacy abroad. Moreover, the landmark election of PAN candidate

This chapter draws in part on Aziz Nassif 1996 and 2000. Translated by Robyn Gutteridge.

Ernesto Ruffo Appel as governor of Baja California in 1989 had broken through the barrier against party alternation in statewide office, in effect setting aside one of the unwritten rules of Mexico's postrevolutionary authoritarian order.[1] It was in this context that Francisco Javier Barrio Terrazas—former opposition mayor of Ciudad Juárez and the PAN's unsuccessful candidate to the governorship in 1986—was elected governor of Chihuahua in 1992.

The alternation of political parties in state government provides a regional laboratory in which to study an important component of Mexico's democratization process. By examining a state-level opposition government, one can perhaps obtain a better understanding of the obstacles and inertias to be overcome on the national level following Vicente Fox Quesada's historic victory in the July 2000 presidential election.

Regional experiences during the formation of Mexico's postrevolutionary regime anticipated (though not in a coordinated or premeditated way) what later were the dominant characteristics of the Mexican state. For example, the regional rule of caudillo Felipe Carrillo Puerto in southeastern Mexico foreshadowed some of the socially progressive policies that Mexico's federal government adopted in subsequent decades; the case of Emilio Portes Gil in Tamaulipas was the first test of a regional sectoral party, an organizational format later adopted by the "official" PRI; Governor Lázaro Cárdenas's agrarian reform in Michoacán held clues to the agrarian reform he would later implement as president; and Tomás Garrido Canabal's term as governor of Tabasco was a harbinger of Mexico's brutal separation of church and state. In much the same fashion, Mexico's first opposition-party state governments may be determining the characteristics of the future Mexican state: freedom of expression, free and fair elections, honest management of public finances, accountability for governmental actions, a real separation of powers, new forms of interest mediation, and new relations between state and federal government authorities.

At this historic juncture, a student of Mexican politics can clearly see advances toward a recomposition—indeed, democratization—of the political system in Baja California, Guanajuato, and Jalisco. However, in states such as Guerrero or Tabasco, this is also a time of backward, authoritarian, and cacique-dominated politics. Bearing these extremes in mind can keep one from falling into the trap of naïve regionalism when analyzing the PAN government in Chihuahua between 1992 and 1998.

---

[1] For an in-depth history of these ten years, see Aziz Nassif 1994.

As noted above, the first election of a state-level opposition government took place in Baja California in 1989. This victory followed a decade of increasingly intense struggles for party alternation in state office. Two years later, another state government went to the opposition, though in this case (Guanajuato) the victory was won not through the popular vote, but in negotiations between the PRI and opposition political forces. The third opposition victory came in Chihuahua in 1992. Indeed, the pace of opposition victories continued to mount. While fifty years elapsed between the founding of the National Action Party in 1939 and its first state-level electoral victory (Ruffo in Baja California),[2] in just the first eight months of 1995 the PAN won state governorships in Jalisco, Guanajuato, and (for the second time) Baja California.

The beginnings of political transition in Mexico are to be found in myriad incidents spread over a long period. This chapter in no way denies the importance of these many strands underlying the democratization process. Rather, it identifies some starting points, hypotheses, and assumptions that can help us contextualize and understand one specific instance of an opposition state government. More concretely, the chapter uses this regional experience as a point of departure for examining what obstacles may lie on Mexico's path to a genuine multiparty system. The regional nature and specific moment of the Chihuahua experience limit broad generalizations, but this regional case is, nevertheless, suggestive.

The available elements for "accessing" and analyzing political change include political and electoral reforms, citizen participation levels, new party registrations, political actors' media access, mechanisms for resolving political conflicts, public opinion, shifts in the balance of power among key actors, rising criticism of government, and so on. One especially important factor is the increasingly participative civic culture that has been constructed in Mexico over the past twenty-five years, the work of reformers, moderates, political parties, and nongovernmental organizations.

---

[2] It should be noted that 1989 was the first year in which an opposition party won a *recognized* electoral victory at the state level. The PAN may have won prior gubernatorial elections (Baja California and Yucatán in the late 1970s, and Chihuahua, Nuevo León, and Sonora in the 1980s), yet it had been denied victory. The Socialist Popular Party (PPS) apparently won a gubernatorial election in Nayarit in the mid–1970s, but this party surrendered the governorship in exchange for a seat in the federal Senate. When fraud is suspected, as in these examples, it is often difficult to identify who actually won the election; what is certain is that vote fraud is the principal reason that, until relatively recently, there were no opposition governments in Mexico.

Against this national backdrop, state-level opposition governments may well provide a most advantageous case for identifying the uncertain boundaries of the amorphous "political transition" that has occurred in some Mexican states. It is in these governments that one may find innovative examples of political change in Mexico.

THE CHANGING STRUCTURE OF POWER IN CHIHUAHUA

Like other parts of Mexico and other countries that have already made the transition to democracy, Chihuahua experienced a prior process of liberalization. This included some political opening and a degree of regime tolerance toward practices in civil society that gave impetus to movements promoting citizen participation and organization, groups that over time began to aspire to power. It was only after this initial liberalization that a two-level recomposition of the regime could begin. The first phase involved reform at the level of governmental institutions; the second stage concerned changes in the relationship between government and civil society (see Przeworski 1991).

The overarching hypothesis of this chapter is that, in Chihuahua, a process of democratic transition has begun whose most direct and visible expression is a recomposition of the regional power structure. The component parts of this process are detailed in the following ancillary hypotheses.

- Redefining power relations between the government and organized social interests contributed to citizens' recovery of public space. This transformation simultaneously introduced societal counterweights to executive authority and restored to the government functions that had previously been exercised by privileged social organizations. At the same time, the new PAN government broke the old verticality under which a PRI governor ruled by reproducing authoritarian presidentialism at the state level.

- Breaking the link between government and "official" party generated a new institutionality in political relations. This change was most visible in the relationship between the state government and municipalities; the administration of Governor Barrio (1992–1998) decentralized state finances, allowing each municipality to construct public works and accumulate its own political capital. There was also a significant change in the relationship between the governor and the state legislature. During the first half of Governor Barrio's term, a state legislature with a majority of PAN members exercised its legislative function without interference from the governor. The legislature's autonomy actually increased during the second half of Barrio's term, when the PRI regained a majority of seats.[3]

• During the period under examination, there was also a shift in power relations between the state and federal governments. Party alternation in power opened up new possibilities in this area; indeed, it was only after opposition parties won state-level elections that the push for a new federalism began in Mexico. During the long period of PRI hegemony, the federal government established an exaggerated centralization of resources and decision-making authority. It was this centralization with which newly elected opposition governments had to contend and which they sought to modify.[4]

• The political pluralism that emerged once the PRI–controlled government's dominance was broken stimulated new types of relations within civil society: full freedom of expression (including in the mass media); a disarticulation of the links among the PRI, the government, and organized interests in sectors such as public transportation; and, of course, free elections.

• Chihuahua also witnessed a change in the way that political conflict is managed. In the past, the ruling party was able to "buy" political harmony, consensus, and a favorable public image. In contrast, PAN officials took pride in their claim that public resources were not employed to such ends. The change brought about by party alternation in state government is well illustrated by the expression "from 'checkbook' consensus to genuine consensus" (*"del consenso con chequera al puro consenso"*).

The basis for party alternation in Chihuahua can be found in the party structure that has formed since the early 1980s. Especially since 1983, what is in essence a two-party system (the PRI and the PAN) has

---

[3] However, the PAN's legislative delegation did cooperate more closely with the Barrio administration once the PRI regained its majority. The PAN also elected a new state party leadership, which put an end to the marked antagonism that had characterized the party's relations with the Barrio government during the 1992–1995 period.

[4] One example in this regard would be Ciudad Juárez mayor Francisco Villarreal's (1992–1995) battle with the federal government to control tolls collected at international bridges at the U.S.–Mexico border.

prevailed in the state, with a number of smaller parties together winning less than 10 percent of the vote. In the 1992 gubernatorial election, for example, the PAN and the PRI won 51.6 and 44.7 percent, respectively, of the valid vote. In this same election, the center-left Party of the Democratic Revolution (PRD) won 1.4 percent, and the Party of the Committee for Popular Defense (PCDP, a regional party with strong popular roots in the state) received 2.4 percent of the vote.[5] In the 1995 municipal elections, the PRI and the PAN received 48.9 and 41.5 percent, respectively, of the valid vote, while the PRD won 5.5 percent and the PCDP—in coalition with the Labor Party (PT) and the Party of the Cardenista Front for National Reconstruction (PFCRN)—received 4.1 percent.[6]

THE CHALLENGES OF NASCENT PARTY ALTERNATION

A new opposition government confronts a number of significant challenges. First, the conditions that favor party alternation in power do not necessarily promote stable democracy.[7] Alternation invalidates old formulas for maintaining political stability, making it imperative to identify new modes of effective governance. Second, a state's first experience with alternation is not a homogeneous process, in the sense that citizens greet the process with quite different convictions and expectations. In such contexts, if public officials wish to sustain the conditions that made alternation possible, they must bear in mind different groups' divergent perspectives and levels of information, as well as different groups' potential for mobilization in the event that changes in policy and modes of governance injure their interests. Indeed, one of the principal challenges posed by alternation is that those political actors who have been displaced (and seek to regain their former positions) can make the process of change fragile and prone to conflict, thus immersing the new regime in continual struggles.

The process of alternation proceeds at two levels. Although these levels often overlap in everyday political life, it is analytically important to differentiate them. The first dimension is the course followed by a government that introduces some changes in its operations and

---

[5] Author's calculations based on data from the Comisión Estatal Electoral de Chihuahua (1992).

[6] Author's calculations based on data from the Consejo Estatal de Elecciones de Chihuahua (1996).

[7] See Rustow 1992 for a stimulating discussion of the distinction between the genesis and operation of a democratic regime.

modifies the regional power structure. The second involves the difficulties inherent in pursuing a transition in a context defined by the inertias and by-products of an outmoded authoritarianism. Somewhat
different perspectives are required to analyze developments at each of
these levels because one must simultaneously assess the strategies that
the PAN adopted to govern Chihuahua during its years in office and
the conflicts that may well have influenced its choices.

One of the key challenges in an alternation experience such as Chihuahua's is that newly defined rules may not long survive if the PRI
regains control of the state executive. Thus a successful transition depends to an important extent on the project achieving a degree of continuity. Moreover, a successful transitional government must continue
to define itself over time. At the beginning of the Barrio administration,
the PAN in Chihuahua had only broad strategies, but these were refined and made tangible as the opposition gained governing experience. The Barrio government also had to make adjustments as it proceeded through its term. This was especially true after the July 9, 1995,
midterm elections, when the PRI regained both its majority in the state
legislature and control of most municipal governments (including the
most important ones). This event induced important changes in the
PAN government's strategies and the priority it gave different objectives, confirming that any transitional government continues to adapt
and adjust as it goes along.

In policy terms, the Barrio administration introduced some of its
most significant changes in state finances, the administration of justice,
cultural affairs and public education, urban development and planning,
family welfare, and the treatment of the Tarahumara indigenous
population. In part because programs in all of these areas were guided
by criteria established in the state's development plan, common themes
linked the administration's initiatives in these fields. In financial matters, for example, the state government improved tax collection and
attempted to place the state's finances on a firmer footing by establishing a new classification of taxpayers. The Barrio government generally
shared with the private sector a common vision of state economic policy, jointly developing with business groups a twenty-year development project ("Twenty-First Century Chihuahua") that identified
growth strategies and priority areas for investment. In the administration of justice, the government sought to professionalize police forces
(raising wages, increasing training, and so forth), improve coordination
between the police and the state attorney general, and strengthen internal oversight over the police in an effort to root out corruption. In the
area of social policy, the Barrio administration reformed regulations
concerning urban land use and created urban land reserves for affordable housing for low-income groups.

The Barrio government also undertook significant administrative reforms. It especially sought to stem budget "leakage" and to improve control and oversight over public resources. In addition to improving tax collection, the state finance department instituted better controls over the revenues it received. Moreover, the administration simplified bureaucratic procedures and upgraded information systems, installing computer systems and information networks in key areas such as the departments of finance and justice. In an effort to improve public services, administrative employees made themselves more accessible to the public and cultivated a better relationship with service users in, for example, the registrar's office, the land registry, and the state department of transportation. Some state departments (the offices of Education and Culture and of Health and Recreation, for example) were divided, while others (the departments of Finance and Resource Administration) were combined. In sum, the Barrio government devoted major efforts to systematizing public administration, seeking to do more with less by establishing strict control and oversight over state resources.

The Barrio administration was also active in redefining the political landscape. It successfully promoted a reform of the state's election law that heightened the autonomy of electoral institutions and increased transparency in balloting and vote-counting procedures.[8] The administration particularly sought to "de-corporatize" relations between the state government and organized social interests in areas such as public transportation. In addition, it expanded citizen involvement in electoral processes and reduced opportunities for clientelism in the management of public services. When successful, these initiatives recovered important public spaces and returned them to the citizenry.

The PAN government proved adept at public administration, and it was a competent builder of a reformed legal order. In other areas, however, it seemed to lack defined goals, and its actions often showed little political or social sensitivity. These failures suggest that the Barrio government had a limited understanding of anything falling outside the administrative or legal arenas. Moreover, these shortcomings are suggestive of the cultural vision the administration held of what democratic government should be and what a sustainable development project for the state might look like.

The set of opportunities and stumbling blocks that an opposition government encounters is also a function of the party's ideological ori-

---

[8] Nevertheless, as the conduct of both the PAN and the PRI in the 1998 elections demonstrated, state electoral authorities continued to have difficulty enforcing campaign spending limits.

entation. In the case of the center-right PAN, the government's greatest commitment was to increased electoral democracy, the honest management of public resources, and a more efficient administration of justice. The limitations it faced resulted from cultural insensitivities, an inability to plan a more integrated social policy, and a certain distance between the government and the state's population.

During its first three years in office, the Barrio administration focused heavily on advancing its administrative reform project. It gave less attention to the population's political concerns, an oversight that became particularly problematic because there were no corporatist structures available to mediate between government and citizenry. But with additional experience in office, Governor Barrio recognized this failure, especially after the 1995 midterm elections. He therefore sought to remedy it.

THE COSTS OF RESTRUCTURING AND POLITICAL MISSTEPS

Mexico's opposition parties—on both the left and the right of the political spectrum—historically tended to develop their guiding principles in counterpoint to the pragmatism of a continuously self-renewing PRI. The 1995 midterm elections for the federal legislature and for municipal governments marked a break with this pattern and ushered in a new period in opposition politics.

In Chihuahua, the PAN was roundly defeated in the midterm elections. How was it possible that voters reverted to their prior support for the PRI despite all the progress Mexico had made toward party alternation in power in the preceding few years? Or to pose the question in another, perhaps less misleading way, why had the PAN failed to win broad-based support or to create an adequate strategy for sustaining a project of democratic government?

After occupying the governor's office for three years—a period of ongoing conflict that was alternately nearly invisible and glaringly apparent—the PAN realized that its political strategy was significantly less efficient than that of its principal adversary. The party's electoral defeat in Chihuahua in 1995 was due mainly to a combination of the following factors:

- The print media operated as vehicles for misinformation. Until very recently, the Mexican press served mainly as a channel for personal attacks, only infrequently providing the unbiased coverage that would allow citizens to form an objective opinion regarding the importance and implications of party alternation in power.

- A badly managed conflict with the teachers' union left the Barrio administration severely wounded. The education sector is very important in Mexico and holds a powerful position in the social structure. In the initial phase of this conflict, the Barrio administration treated the teachers' union as if it were a corrupt organization, and it made no distinction between union leaders and the rank and file. The conflict arose because, under decades of PRI government in Chihuahua, the union occupied a broad range of political spaces and had assumed a high degree of decision-making authority—in exchange for delivering its members' votes to the PRI. This game of exchange (political influence for electoral support) perverted the relationship between the union and government, and it could not withstand an opposition party's rise to power and its efforts to redefine political spaces and responsibilities. Nevertheless, the Barrio administration's attempts to reorganize a powerful sector with a long history of delivering its votes to the PRI proved very costly politically for the PAN in the midterm elections. Following the elections, the administration opened a new phase in its relations with the teachers' union, in which it downplayed administrative reorganization and emphasized the development of a new educational project.

- The resource-rich PRI governments that had controlled Chihuahua's state government in the past had garnered support by responding quickly to popular groups' needs, resolving their problems at least in the short term. PAN government officials did not construct alternative mechanisms for dealing with popular demands, and when they did, they failed to capitalize on them. Following the PAN's shocking defeat in the midterm elections, the Barrio administration initiated a "coordination and image" program to build consensus and strengthen its links with the citizenry. This program, entitled "Let's Work Together" ("Jalemos Parejo"), aimed to overcome shortcomings in communication, image projection, and dissemination of the PAN government's achievements by promoting greater citizen involvement in public works projects.

- The PAN administration suffered from a shortage of officials who could build alliances with diverse social groups. All governments need organized support, something that administrations attract by building bridges with social groups that would not naturally sympathize with, or vote for, the party in power. But by their very nature, opposition parties winning office in a political system that has just opened to alternation will include a cadre of professionals who have less political experience than those of the party being ousted.

- The Barrio administration's image also suffered from a variety of prolonged and unnecessary conflicts, one of which involved a leaked confidential state payroll that circulated publicly for nearly a year. The negative fallout from such conflicts was exacerbated by their coverage in a hostile press, as discussed above.

- Although the PRI kicked off a campaign to discredit the Barrio administration the same day that it took office, the PAN government failed to stage a similar offensive aimed at conserving and increasing the support that brought it to power.

- The PRI maintained a more efficient electoral machine in the state's less socioeconomically developed areas, which succeeded in mobilizing popular-sector groups behind the PRI in the 1995 midterm elections.

THE POWER ARENA UNDER ALTERNATION: CONSTRUCTING A DEMOCRATIC ORDER

The alternation of parties in power permits a realignment of political forces. Just as there was an ongoing evolution in the meaning of "transition" during the Barrio administration, there was a similar evolving sense of the possibilities present in the political arena.

Shifts in the correlation of forces can be more conflictual or less conflictual depending upon the prevailing style of conducting politics. The Barrio administration employed a variety of approaches in its dealings with PRI–affiliated societal groups, probably because these groups differed among themselves in their goals and political position. In some cases, as in the relationship between the state government and the teachers' union, the interaction became highly combative. But there were other instances in which the Barrio administration succeeded in negotiating pacts that facilitated the state's political transition. This was the outcome, for example, in the administration's relations with public transportation workers.

The principal factor underlying the Barrio administration's conflictual experiences with PRI–aligned groups was the confrontational relationship that had developed between the *panista* government and the Institutional Revolutionary Party. These two powers disputed every centimeter of political space. The Barrio administration's relationship with the PRD was much less problematic, although it still involved finding a delicate equilibrium between areas of agreement (both parties agreed on certain principles, and they acted together to defend certain groups) and disagreement (the PRD and PAN were, after all, at opposing ends of the left-right spectrum). Cooperation with the PRD was also somewhat easier because the Chihuahua experience demonstrated that, once the PRI can be defeated (even temporarily), conditions become more favorable for the advance of a third party.

The way in which political actors positioned themselves during Chihuahua's early transition process clearly illustrated that alternation made it possible to modify power relations in the state. The overall contours of Chihuahua's political transformation, the degree of conflict associated with it, different parties' willingness to ally with one another, and the resulting triumphs and failures all influenced the reshaping of power relations among key actors. When competitive parties have the potential to alternate in power, no group can automatically claim a certain share of government positions. Instead, how the pie will be divided must be hammered out over time in negotiations among actors. And as soon as there is another alternation, all agreements reached during the preceding administration become invalid; actors must begin once again to build political capital and bring it to bear on behalf of their principal constituents.

Issues of political order are central to any experience of party alternation in power because whatever changes or new correlations of forces emerge from the process will ultimately have direct impacts on the overall political equilibrium. Norbert Lechner's conceptualization of this transformative process is suggestive; he calls it "the conflictive, never completed construction of the desired order."[9] In the case of Chihuahua, two changes in the political order were especially important. The first was a thoroughgoing reform of the state constitution; the second was a restructuring of the prevailing corporatist relationships that guided decisions regarding the labor force, urban policy, public transport, and elections. The changes undertaken by the PAN in these two areas constituted its effort, as an opposition party finally elected to office, to construct a new political order.

Members of the PAN administration viewed constitutional reform as the primary achievement of the state legislature in session between 1992 and 1995. The legislature amended 118 of the 202 articles in the state constitution.[10] The most important of these reforms concerned indigenous and human rights (for the first time, the constitution gave indigenous peoples special protection in such areas as health services

---

[9] This is the title of Lechner's book on the subject, *La conflictiva y nunca acabada construcción del orden deseado* (Santiago: Facultad Latinoamericana de Ciencias Sociales, 1984).

[10] This summary draws on the October 1994 document that constitutional reform commissions submitted to the Chihuahua state legislature.

and education), citizen participation and the rights of the governed (including provisions for referenda, plebiscites, and popular initiatives), the rights of municipal governments, the strengthening of the state legislature's capacity to oversee the executive branch, increased legal and financial independence for the judiciary, and mechanisms to protect the state's cultural heritage. In addition, a significant electoral reform established citizen control over electoral institutions and guaranteed equality of conditions among competing parties, thus ensuring transparency in elections.

In transitions like Chihuahua's, in which authoritarian elements persist alongside democratic gains, the stakes are the opportunities for party consolidation and remaining in power. This situation contrasts with that which prevails in consolidated democracies, where the rules of the game have already been decided. In Chihuahua during the mid– and late 1990s, the rules were still in flux because there was as yet no broad consensus on the correlation of forces. This was the context in which reforms to the state's constitution and electoral code were debated. The biggest risk for the Barrio administration was that, if the PRI retook the governorship in 1998 (which it did), it would move to restore the corporatist alliances and authoritarian practices of earlier periods.

In point of fact, the struggle over the rules governing Chihuahua's new democratic order became the focus of sharp partisan controversy even before 1998. In 1997, as part of its effort to regain control over electoral authorities and redistrict to its advantage, the PRI (joined by the PRD) passed an electoral reform that the PAN, PCDP, and Mexican Ecological Green Party (PVEM) opposed. Under the terms of this legislation, the state legislature—in which the PRI once again held a majority—was responsible for nominating members of the State Electoral Institute. In addition, electoral districts were redrawn to create more districts in predominantly rural areas, where the PRI had traditionally been strong. In response, a coalition of citizens' groups and different social organizations mobilized in favor of a statewide referendum on the law. The Consejo Ciudadano Chihuahuense Pro-Referendum (Pro-Referendum Chihuahua Citizens' Council) argued that the increase in legislative seats was unjustified and that the state's electoral institutions were being modified before current members' terms had expired. Legal technicalities, however, prevented the referendum from going forward.

POLITICS AND INTEREST MEDIATION

Alternation in Chihuahua broke the monopoly control that professional bureaucrats had enjoyed in prior administrations. The PAN's arrival in government brought to influence a new kind of politician—the technocrat, highly qualified in professional terms but with little political experience. (Barrio, who did have ample prior political experience, was the one exception among the PAN members who won power in 1992.) This characteristic of the new governing team explains why the Barrio administration focused, at least during its first three years, more on administrative than political matters.

Yet other factors, combined with the attributes of Barrio's policy-making team, also explain the administration's governing style and the character of its links to local society. For example, the PAN government differed from its PRI predecessors in that it lacked the latter party's structure and apparatus, as well as the ties to organized societal interests that provided interest representation channels for workers, peasants, professionals, popular groups, and businessmen. According to the underlying logic of corporatism, when disagreements arise between a particular sector and the government, state elites determine how the disagreement will be resolved. In return, groups with privileged access to the state gain a share of power. This arrangement maintains balance in the system, but the interplay among these interests leaves little independent role for either the state or the citizenry.

The PAN's gubernatorial victory broke established links between government and organized societal interests because the PAN does not have an analogous structure for interest mediation. Instead, the new government retook spaces and returned them to the public sphere. In so doing, the Barrio administration began to create a new political order in which it was possible to expand spaces for citizen participation and representation—and, in the process, to alter the behavior of political actors themselves. This is what began to happen among Chihuahua's workers, teachers, and electorate.

This new order resembled a democratic system, but it was much more vulnerable to upsets and imbalances. As a result, it was a political order characterized by a higher degree of uncertainty. In contexts of party alternation, political actors must play with an unmarked deck. Sectors and organizations no longer display the unquestioning obedience they paid to PRI governments, and conflicts must be resolved through negotiation. This situation can heighten unease among a citizenry that was just beginning to adapt to the clamor of democratic transition, which leads one to ask what an opposition party must do to develop mediating mechanisms that do not reproduce state corporatism. The most appropriate alternative may be a model of societal corporatism, in which democratically organized interest groups enjoy much more autonomy vis-à-vis political authorities. The sticking point, however, is precisely how to reach this goal in contemporary Mexico.

Another challenge implicit in a context of party alternation is the transition from opposition party to party in government. Key factors in this regard are intra-party divisions and the culture of opposition that may exist within a party. The PAN, for example, had for more than fifty years advocated separation between party and government. The inertia of opposition actually led the party to abandon its own elected government in Chihuahua. Indeed, PAN party activism virtually disappeared from the political arena during the first three years of the Barrio administration. The opposition mind-set remained in place, manifesting itself not through separation but in divorce.

During the 1995 elections, Governor Barrio spoke in support of his party's candidates and defended his administration's performance. Both the PRI and state electoral officials responded by demanding that the governor not intervene—the same demand that the PAN had traditionally made of the PRI when the latter was in government and the former was in opposition. PAN officials then defended themselves by pointing to the operation of fully democratic regimes, in which elected officeholders campaign for their parties' candidates but without bringing undue influence to bear over the electoral process.

Chihuahua's experience in this area may be of special relevance for Mexico's broader democratic transition. In a regime in which electoral institutions and processes are fully insulated from government influence, where government resources cannot be employed to benefit a particular party, and where there exists a complete separation between public works projects and electoral outcomes, it would be entirely reasonable for elected officials to make public statements in support of particular candidates. Yet the issue is not so easily resolved in cases involving "opposition party turned governing party." What is under construction is precisely the way in which an opposition party should govern once it has assumed office, and how newly elected officials should manage their relations with the citizenry and with their own party.[11] The dilemmas the PAN faced in Chihuahua after 1992 are the challenges that it faces at the national level following Vicente Fox's election as president in July 2000.

---

[11] The Barrio administration almost certainly erred in not attempting to influence the PAN's process to select a gubernatorial candidate, thus allowing the selection to be dominated by traditional *panista* elements. Because the party was more focused on ideological matters than on building links to broad sectors of society, the candidate chosen did not have sufficient strength to win the 1998 gubernatorial election. In this sense, one could argue that the PRI's return to power in Chihuahua resulted from the many mistakes committed by the *panista* administration.

EXPECTATIONS AND CITIZENSHIP

The prospect of party alternation raises expectations that combine a citizenry's desires, dreams, and demands for change, sometimes well beyond the limits of possible satisfaction. Public opinion surveys have confirmed that citizens see democracy as something that works, and many people may expect that an opposition party taking power will achieve everything that preceding PRI governments failed to do or once did but then abandoned.

A first instance of party alternation necessarily involves a degree of chaos because the incoming government lacks experience in power and because all the rules are subject to change. As the new government moves up the learning curve, it can easily make mistakes. Difficulties arise not only because of its inexperience, but also because of systemic inertias, trial-and-error efforts to resolve conflicts, and the citizenry's hope that democracy can solve all problems—especially economic problems in times of crisis. During this learning process, citizens also come to temper their expectations, ideological considerations become relatively less important, and the opposition party incurs some of the costs necessarily involved in exercising power.

A decisive factor in the expectations game was that the PAN won control in Chihuahua just as economic crisis hit the region. A survey conducted by the state government's Office of Social Communication in 1995 revealed that, at the time, the public had a broad range of generalized complaints but no specific suggestions about what the government should do to resolve pressing problems. The general attitude that prevailed in the state was expressed in such comments as "This government isn't doing anything," "It's just like all the others," or "This government's even worse than the others." In such circumstances, it is not surprising that disillusion and disenchantment soon followed.

However, sentiments such as these—built on a foundation of high personal expectations—overlooked the fact that the changes brought by party alternation in power are gradual and often conflict-ridden. The Barrio administration discovered that governing a state is exceedingly complex. Although expectations may have been for rapid and far-reaching change, government marched at a slow pace as the Barrio administration undertook reformist initiatives in some areas but not in others.

PROSPECTS FOR THE FUTURE

The transition from one regime type to another is, in the final analysis, a process of determining relationships between and among political actors, interest groups, and citizens. One might, nevertheless, question whether party alternation in power at the state level truly constitutes a regime transition. As noted at the beginning of this chapter, recent political developments in Mexico may well be a reenactment of a process in which various regional experiences shape the pieces that later make up the national picture. If party alternation is a prerequisite for a full transition to democracy, then all the examples Mexico had to offer before 2000 are found at the state level.

By definition, party alternation at the state level operates under a multitude of limitations. Federal authorities exercise a substantial proportion of government functions, areas in which state governments have little or no jurisdiction. Furthermore, opposition governments during the 1980s and 1990s were also subject to a complex set of rules imposed by Mexico's authoritarian political order. These rules regulated budgetary decision making and budget allocations, the economy, corporatist relations between government and social actors, the mass media, presidential power, and an "official" party that still dominated many aspects of public life. Together, these factors defined and delimited the space that opposition-controlled state and municipal governments could occupy.

The PAN's poor showing in the 1995 midterm elections in Chihuahua raised the prospect that certain aspects of the state government's program would be vulnerable during the second half of the Barrio administration. In particular, the relationship between governor and state legislature now involved a full separation of powers, and cooperation with a fortified PRI did prove difficult.[12] Nevertheless, although the PRI's return to majority control of the legislature raised the specter of a full restoration of PRI power in state-level office (which in fact occurred in 1998), it was important to recall that PAN governors in both Guanajuato and Baja California managed to survive despite having to govern with state legislatures in which their party did not hold majority control.

Determining whether the criteria for "democratic consolidation" were met during the 1992–1998 period depends on the kinds of criteria employed. For example, if one uses such indicators as full political and civil rights, universal suffrage and the periodic renewal of government and of public consensus, freedom of speech and of association, a commitment from all groups and sectors to uphold the law, a competitive party system, and generalized pluralism, then one must conclude that there are segments of the Chihuahua population that have full

---

[12] For example, in 1995 the PRI attempted to limit the Barrio administration's social spending and the amount of money devoted to publicity for the state government. The 1996 debate over the state budget was also rancorous.

rights but whose vote can still be bought. There is freedom of speech, but the media operate under some government-imposed constraints. All major actors have committed themselves to uphold the rule of law. However, the legal code sometimes proves inadequate, and reforms are needed to the judicial system. Pluralism and a broader sense of citizenship are gradually emerging. Party alternation has stimulated in social organizations (and in society in general) a new spirit of freedom unhindered by the disciplinary fetters or covenants that characterized prior PRI governments. In summary, Chihuahua's fragile transition is slowly permeating political culture and the institutional order.

The PAN's gubernatorial victory in 1992 paved the way for constitutional reforms, administrative restructuring, and important shifts in the correlation of political forces both within the state and between the state government and municipal and federal authorities. Together, these various changes modified, at least for the short term, the regional version of Mexico's state-party regime. However, the 1995 midterm elections upset the new correlation of powers, put the PAN's political project at risk, and threatened the viability of the transition. The elections strengthened the PRI's position in the state legislature and in municipal governments, and they restricted the government's and the PAN's room for maneuver. Yet on the positive side, the elections also forced the Barrio administration to revise its strategy and to pursue a thoroughgoing separation of powers in state government.

The future of Chihuahua's (and Mexico's) political transition remains undecided because the strength of contending forces is quite evenly matched. Much will depend upon the skill with which non–PRI governments negotiate consensus and manage conflict, on changes in political culture, and on image—that is, on the ability of non–PRI administrations to shape the channels through which a citizenry perceives and comprehends the actions of its government.

Despite some predictions to the contrary, the divided government that emerged after the 1995 midterm elections did not plunge Chihuahua into an abyss of ungovernability. If that risk is to be avoided, the various forces active in state politics must search for civilized coexistence and mutual tolerance. This is attainable as long as the rules of the game are clearly defined and mutually understood, and as long as all actors are willing to accept the inherent uncertainty of a functioning democracy. As Albert Hirschman suggests, "Instead of searching for the necessary and sufficient conditions for change, we should train ourselves to see unusual historical developments, rare constellations of favorable events, narrow paths, partial advances that can open to other, more extensive achievements, and things of that sort. We should think of what is possible more than what is probable" (Hirschman 1986).

REFERENCES

Aziz Nassif, Alberto. 1994. *Chihuahua: historia de una alternativa.* Mexico City: La Jornada/Centro de Investigaciones y Estudios Superiores en Antropología Social.

————. 1996. *Territorios de alternancia: el primer gobierno de oposición en Chihuahua.* Mexico City: Centro de Investigaciones y Estudios Superiores en Antropología Social/Triana.

————. 2000. *Los ciclos de la democracia: gobierno y elecciones en Chihuahua.* Mexico City: Centro de Investigaciones y Estudios Superiores en Antropología Social/Universidad Autónoma de Ciudad Juárez/Miguel Ángel Porrúa.

Hirschman, Albert O. 1986. "Acerca de la democracia en América Latina," *Zona Abierta* 39–40 (April–September).

Przeworski, Adam. 1991. *Democracy and the Market: Political and Economic Reforms in Eastern Europe and Latin America.* Cambridge: Cambridge University Press.

Rustow, Dankwart. 1992. "Transiciones a la democracia: hacia un modelo dinámico." In *Cambio político y gobernabilidad,* edited by Mauricio Merino. Mexico City: Conacyt/Colegio Nacional de Ciencias Políticas y Administración Pública.

7

The PAN in Guanajuato: Elections and Political Change in the 1990s

Guadalupe Valencia García

The past three decades of Mexico's political life have been marked by, among other characteristics, a profound and extended erosion of the traditional relationship between state and society. If the 1960s were a period during which arose a broad, cross-class movement that would culminate in the 1968 student-popular mobilization, the 1970s were a time of worker, peasant, urban-popular (*colono*), and student insurgency. Yet this was also an era in which the overall relationship between state and society changed significantly, with societal actors seeking forms of organization and legitimacy outside the parameters long established in postrevolutionary Mexico.

The 1976 presidential election—in which José López Portillo, nominee of the ruling Institutional Revolutionary Party (PRI), faced no officially registered opposition candidate—clearly demonstrated the declining legitimacy of the established regime. It did so by revealing the extent to which elections had become a symbolic ritual rather than a vehicle for contesting power. The 1977 political reform was, then, the governing elite's response to the evident need to find channels for accumulated sociopolitical tensions in a context in which societal actors sought new avenues of political participation through which to express their demands.

The 1980s were characterized in large measure by the resurgence of municipal (*municipio*) politics. Struggles over the control of local governments (*ayuntamientos*) led not only to opposition party electoral victories, but also to multiple popular mobilizations that in various Mexican states resulted in the forcible takeover of municipal government offices as a means of protesting election fraud and the imposition of PRI candidates. In 1982 alone, post-election conflicts of this kind led

---

Translated by Kevin J. Middlebrook.

to the takeover of thirty-five mayoral offices (*alcaldías*) in the fifty local elections whose results were challenged in Chiapas, Guanajuato, Jalisco, San Luis Potosí, and Tlaxcala. In almost all of these cases, it was the National Action Party (PAN) and the Mexican Democratic Party (PDM) that led the post-election mobilizations (see Arreola 1985).

By the late 1990s, competitive electoral processes had led to party alternation in power in many localities across a number of states. As a result, opposition parties encountered expanded space for political action, though this change was also accompanied by a significant degree of conflict. In these new spaces, political forces established themselves in large part by inventing new ways of relating to the federal government, including by redefining the very bases of national unity.

Electoral processes, especially when they permit the alternation of different parties in public office, condense and express complex social, economic, and cultural dynamics. They allow for the redefinition of relationships among local (municipal), state, and federal authorities; they reflect both consensus and social differences; and they articulate a range of local demands, conflicts, and struggles.

In contrast to national electoral processes, elections to choose governors, state legislatures, and municipal authorities often reveal—at times in disguised form, at other times more clearly—the composition and transformation of social and political forces. On occasion, substantially different proposals for local development are at stake, but more frequently these contests involve economic interests or political-ideological quarrels with little or no difference in content. It is, in any event, in state and municipal spheres where one can best appreciate the transforming impact on daily life of political campaigns and the citizen expectations they generate. It is also in this arena where political and ideological disputes and, occasionally, debates over rival conceptions of change sometimes reach unexpected levels. What is at issue, in sum, is the way in which local circumstances play into real processes of redefining—indeed, refounding—the conflictive relationship between the local and the national.

In terms of the space defined by local government, elections during the 1990s clearly demonstrated that Guanajuato is a state characterized by great political effervescence and growing electoral competitiveness. What is often forgotten, however, is that this is not strictly a new phenomenon, although there certainly has been change in the forms in which this political pluralism is expressed. Since 1991, Guanajuato has become one of the centers of attention for Mexico's major political parties, the federal government, and increasingly broad sectors of national opinion. It was the state in which, for the first time, a member of the political opposition gained the governorship without himself having competed for the office. It was also the first state in which the PAN won the governorship on three successive occasions (1991, 1995, and 2000). Moreover, the PAN's mayoral candidate won in León, the state's largest population center, on five consecutive occasions between 1988 and 2000.

This chapter examines state- and municipal-level elections in Guanajuato during the 1990s. However, in order to better comprehend the transformations that have occurred in the state's electoral map, the increasing competitiveness of elections in the 1990s, and the consequences of different parties' alternation in power, the discussion also focuses on the antecedent developments that shaped rising citizen awareness and local political struggles. One important goal of this analysis is to shed new light on the PAN's experience as an electoral force and in government, topics that have heretofore received too little attention.

ANTECEDENTS TO DEMOCRATIZATION IN THE 1990s

Many analysts have asked why Guanajuato experienced such highly competitive electoral contests in 1991 and 1995 and what political transformations permitted the opposition to gain power. Although certainly novel, these developments should be seen as the legacy of a political trajectory that had for several decades demonstrated the state's capacity for citizen mobilization in favor of opposition parties. This section begins, then, with an overview of the rich, complex political history that continues to underpin (although with a different ideological focus) political meaning and the struggle for power in contemporary Guanajuato.

The richness and complexity of Guanajuato's political history are clearly present in the social dynamics that characterize it today. The state's principal economic activities, the system of cities that defines its urban and rural life, the intense struggles for power among its political elites, and the oppositionist inclinations of its residents all have roots in Guanajuato's past.

With nearly 4.7 million inhabitants, Guanajuato is one of Mexico's most densely populated states.[1] Its predominantly urban population is, however, less concentrated than in other states, with 47 percent of its citizens living in the four cities (León, Irapuato, Salamanca, and Celaya) that constitute an urban-industrial corridor running through the center of the state. León alone accounts for 24 percent of the state's entire population. Almost 97 percent of *guanajuatenses* are Catholic and per-

---

[1] In 2000, Guanajuato had a population of 4,656,761 inhabitants, representing almost 5 percent of Mexico's total population and giving the state a population density of 130 inhabitants per square kilometer. See INEGI 2000.

tain to two dioceses (León and Celaya) that exercise considerable influence on local social and political dynamics.

Commerce, footwear production, and agriculture are Guanajuato's most important economic activities. There is, however, considerable variation within each of these sectors. For example, there coexist in the countryside both export-oriented agricultural businesses and rainfed, subsistence farms; in urban areas, there are both large commercial enterprises and microenterprises characteristic of the informal sector. Because of these highly divergent economic conditions, the state's class conformation is complex.

The Force of History

Guanajuato is a region with multiple, strongly expressed political orientations. Its recent development has been characterized by movements representing diverse political tendencies, intense debates, a proliferation of parties and political groupings, competitive elections, bloody battles for power, and a conflictive relationship with the national government. But above all, the postrevolutionary period in Guanajuato has been an era of (at least at the ideological level) counterrevolution. The parallel histories of revolution and counterrevolution have interacted to produce great local political complexity. The analytic distinction between these two histories and an understanding of their intersection are key factors in comprehending contemporary events in the state.

The postrevolutionary period in Guanajuato can, in effect, be understood as two histories, each developing in counterpoint with the other. On the one hand, the state's official history takes the form of the struggle that raged from 1927 until the 1950s between the "reds" (followers of revolutionary general Plutarco Elías Calles, president of Mexico between 1920 and 1924) and the "greens" (followers of the revolutionary generals Álvaro Obregón and Lázaro Cárdenas, presidents of Mexico in, respectively, 1924–1928 and 1934–1940). Counting duly elected, interim, substitute, and provisional governments, there were thirty-four gubernatorial turnovers in the state between 1917 and 1949. Almost all of those individuals who became governor (some on more than one occasion) were affiliated with either the "reds" or the "greens" (see Rionda 1996a: appen. "Gobernadores"). This situation obviously reflected the intensity of the conflicts and internal divisions that characterized the local postrevolutionary political class. In fact, it was only between 1949 and 1991 that the state achieved a degree of political stability (interrupted only in 1984 by the forced resignation of Governor Enrique Velasco Ibarra).

Political struggles were no less vigorous at the municipal level. One indication of this is that there were five "parallel" municipal governments established by dissident members of the "official" Party of the Mexican Revolution (PRM) in 1942. Moreover, some fifty political organizations sought registration to participate in municipal elections in the state in 1944.[2]

The second history, counterpoised to the official version, is one of large organizations—first civic groupings, then armed followings, then mass organizations—that mobilized thousands of people both in the countryside and in cities in their effort to redefine national destiny. These were movements that cannot be understood without Guanajuato's participation in their emergence and development. The most important of these were the Cristero conflict and the *sinarquista* movement, phenomena representing regional movements of enormous complexity and great organizational success. Their principal objective was to oppose the Mexican Revolution, particularly two of its most critical accomplishments, land distribution and lay education.[3]

The point of departure for both these movements was the formation of the Liga Nacional Defensora de la Libertad Religiosa (National League for the Defense of Religious Freedom, known as "La Liga") in Guanajuato in 1913. Later, following the arrest of Bishop Mora y del Río in 1926 for opposing articles 3, 5, 27, and 130 of the Constitution of 1917 (the articles addressing, respectively, public education, individual liberties and contractual obligations, land tenure arrangements, and separation of church and state), came the Cristero war. The struggle mobilized thousands of Catholic peasants in central-western Mexico between 1926 and 1929, and, even though they did not necessarily take up arms, the war involved broad sectors of Guanajuato rural and urban society (see Olivera Sedano 1987: 75, 103). In his closing campaign rally in León on August 14, 1991, then PAN gubernatorial candidate Vicente Fox Quesada invoked the experience of these Christian martyrs when he appealed to the large crowd for support, saying "If I go forward, follow me; if I hesitate, push me onward; if I fall back, kill me."[4]

---

[2] These data are drawn from the official "state of the state" reports filed by Governors Enrique Fernández Martínez (1942) and Ernesto Hidalgo (1943–1946). See Gobierno del Estado de Guanajuato 1991.

[3] The Cristero struggle was labeled "La Cristiada" by Jean Meyer, author of the most important study of the movement; see Meyer 1980. There are various studies offering different interpretations of the Unión Nacional Sinarquista or *sinarquismo*, including Meyer 1979; Serrano 1992; Gill 1962; and Campbell 1976.

[4] See Valencia García 1994. It is worth mentioning in this context that Fox used this same phrase in his address to the delegates responsible for selecting the PAN's gubernatorial candidate. On that occasion, he said, "Paraphrasing this man who gave his life for our religion, I say to you, if I am elected as your candidate, follow me; if I hesitate in my work, push me forward. Because before dying, Vicente Fox wishes to

In 1929, President Emilio Portes Gil (1928–1930) signed the agreements with the Catholic hierarchy that ended the Cristero war. However, La Liga opposed them and reconstituted itself as a new organization known initially as Las Legiones (The Legions) and later (between 1934 and 1937) as La Base (The Base). All of these groups should be considered organizational and ideological antecedents to what became the most extensive mass organization in the oppositionist history of Guanajuato, the *sinarquista* movement.

The National Sinarquist Union (UNS) was founded in León, Guanajuato, in 1937, two years before the founding of the National Action Party. It derived from the civilian section of La Base, and it defined as one of its principal objectives the struggle to oppose the "atheistic and communist" government of President Lázaro Cárdenas (1934–1940) and to save the nation for the Catholic faith. The UNS drew support from thousands of peasants, workers, students, housewives, and small property owners—indeed, from all sectors opposed to the Cárdenas government. This patriotic Catholic movement sought to establish a national project distinctive from the revolutionary project, drawing ideological support from the papal encyclicals of the period, the Hispanic tradition, anticommunism, and multiple forms of traditional Catholicism. Although the UNS rapidly expanded its presence in several states, its most important support base was in Guanajuato. In the early 1940s, it had some 75,000 members (one-quarter of the national total) in Guanajuato, equivalent to 7.5 percent of the state's population (Serrano 1992: 84).

In 1944, the UNS was linked to an attempt to assassinate President Manuel Ávila Camacho (1940–1946) and dissolved by order of the federal attorney general. It nevertheless survived in Guanajuato for a number of years. Moreover, the UNS experience remains a part of local historical memory that constitutes a very effective political resource for those who, whether in opposition or in power, seek to touch the deepest fibers of collective consciousness. For example, both the PDM (the UNS's direct successor) and the PAN (as heir to civic struggles based in Catholic social thought) have been direct beneficiaries of the political dynamic that sustains this historical memory.

The more immediate link to the UNS was, however, the León Civic Union (UCL). Established in León in 1945 and a central actor in one of the state's most painful political episodes, it embodied the experience of political mobilization that characterized Guanajuato during the postrevolutionary period.

In the mayoral elections held in León in December 1945, the UCL supported the candidacy of Carlos Obregón against "official" PRM

---

devote his life to the cause that is the PAN, that is Mexico, that is Guanajuato" (in Ling Altamirano 1992: 56).

candidate Dr. Ignacio Quiroz. When the polls closed, each candidate declared himself the winner based on his own ballot count. Of course, official recognition went to the candidate of the pro-government PRM, who formally took office on January 1, 1946. The next day, however, the UCL convened a large opposition rally in León's main public square to demand the removal of the *ayuntamiento*'s new president. As many as ten thousand protesters may have been present at the rally, which was violently repressed by the army. According to government sources, the army's action left more than thirty dead and more than six hundred injured. As with many massacres, the true dimensions of the tragedy are not known, but other sources estimate more than twice this number of dead and injured (Serrano 1992).

Following these events, the federal Senate formally suspended local government authority in the state and named as provisional governor Nicéforo Guerrero, who proceeded to appoint civil administration boards (*juntas de administración civil*) in all of the state's *ayuntamientos*. The climate of political unrest obliged the new governor to seek support from opposition forces, including businessmen and dissident political groups (Gobierno del Estado de Guanajuato 1946).[5] In León, a month after the massacre, the UCL's candidate became head of the local civil administration board, composed of UCL members and leading representatives of the private sector. The "León solution" was also later adopted in other municipalities in the state, with members of the UCL, the PAN, and the UNS displacing members of the PRI and the Confederation of Mexican Workers (CTM, the PRI's labor sector) in key municipal posts.

The date of the León massacre has become a crucial political symbol for the local population, representing the heroism of a people who dared define and defend its own destiny. It is for this reason that, in terms of local political culture, the events of January 1946 represented a real turning point in state politics. It was to that moment which Carlos Medina Plascencia, municipal president of León, referred in late 1990 when he delivered his second annual "state of the city" report. Speaking in "Martyrs of January 2" Square, he said, "The blood that has flowed over the paving stones of this plaza boils today in the veins of the involved citizenry of León. Participation has produced a government that the citizenry wants, a government that works for the society we desire. We continue building that society despite our sorrows because that enterprise is worth the trouble and worth one's life" (in Ling Altamirano 1992: 77).

The events of January 2, 1946, produced a new balance of political forces favoring opposition groups and parties. For example, this situa-

---

[5] Local government authority was finally restored as the 1946 presidential election approached (Serrano 1992: 248).

tion permitted the *sinarquista*-inspired Popular Force Party (PFP) to win significant local electoral support. The PFP was founded in February 1946, with its regional base in the city of León. In the July 1946 federal elections, it became the second most important party in the state of Guanajuato, winning the largest number of votes in the electoral district centered on León and carrying statewide balloting for the federal Senate.[6] Similarly, in elections held in late July 1946 to choose the new state legislature, the Partido Nueva Política Guanajuatense (New Politics Party of Guanajuato) won seats in six of the eleven electoral districts (Valencia García 1986: 156).

Developments during the 1930s and 1940s continued to reverberate in Guanajuato state politics during subsequent decades. In 1953 there was another effort to reconstitute *sinarquismo* as an electoral force when some five thousand *sinarquistas* rallied in León to create the Partido Unidad Nacional (National Unity Party). Despite the fact that it fulfilled the legal requirements established by the federal electoral code, the party did not receive official recognition (Valencia García 1986: 307). The PAN, however, succeeded in winning its first official victory in 1964 when its candidate for the federal Chamber of Deputies carried the second electoral district, which was centered on León. The victorious candidate, Luis Manuel Aranda, was one of the PAN's founders in Guanajuato (Ling Altamirano 1992: 12).

Recent Developments: Preambles of Political Change

The year 1976 marked the beginning of the PAN's political ascendancy and its life as a real electoral force in Guanajuato. Thirty years after the massacre of 1946, broad sectors of León's population sparked another confrontation with established political powers in that year's municipal elections. When state-level electoral authorities refused to validate the PAN's victory in the December 1976 elections, the populace mobilized in defense of the vote. The PAN's public protests did not cease until the state legislature recognized "the irregularities that occurred in the electoral process" and voided the disputed results. Governor Luis H. Ducoing subsequently appointed a civil administration board headed by a well-known León businessman and composed of four leading members of the PAN (*El Sol de León* 1977).

Several factors contributed to this politically crucial election victory. They included the selection of a strong PAN candidate for municipal president, Juan Manuel López Sanabria, and the use of more effective

---

[6] These triumphs were not, however, recognized by federal electoral authorities. See Serrano 1992: 261, 268.

campaign techniques. At the same time, the post-devaluation economic crisis affecting the state had a particularly significant negative impact on the local footwear industry, the city's principal economic activity, and consequently weakened popular support for the PRI.

Since 1976, Guanajuato has experienced an accelerating process of electoral-political change. Elections have gradually become more and more competitive; the number of voters has increased; citizens have begun to experience both the changes and the inertias in governing style associated with new municipal presidents; and the populace has had to reconcile its expectations with changes in government at the state level. Indeed, taking into account the most important dimensions of Guanajuato's electoral evolution between 1979 and 1995, one can distinguish three phases in the PAN's ascendance: growing electoral competitiveness between 1979 and 1982; competitiveness and incipient alternation in power between 1985 and 1988; and competitiveness with extensive alternation in power between 1991 and 1995.

Between 1979 and 1982 in Guanajuato, as in almost all of Mexico, politics was dominated by the PRI. To a very considerable extent, being a successful politician signified belonging to one or another sector of the PRI, having influence among the PRI's corporatist bases, and maintaining good relations with the political elite based in Mexico City. Among other mechanisms of political intermediation, the distribution of nominations for elected office among the PRI's principal mass organizations constituted a key means of renewal for the political class. These party-linked groups included the CTM, the National Peasants' Confederation (CNC), the National Confederation of Popular Organizations (CNOP), and the most important national labor unions, especially those representing teachers, petroleum workers, and employees of the Mexican Social Security Institute (IMSS).

In Guanajuato, the majority of nominations for municipal president went to the CNOP; in a typical election, only three or four went to the CTM and five or six to the CNC. Candidacies for the federal Chamber of Deputies and the state legislature were distributed to the PRI sectors with the greatest weight in a given electoral district. For example, because an important oil refinery was located in Salamanca, almost all the party nominations there (including the nomination for municipal president) went to the Mexican Petroleum Workers' Union (STPRM). Similarly in León, nominations in the city's three electoral districts were allocated to the CTM, the CNOP, and the Sindicato Nacional de Trabajadores del Seguro Social (National Union of Social Security Workers). When a PRI candidate was defeated at the polls, compensation mechanisms came into play, providing the losing sector with control over some important appointed government position. This was what happened in 1985 when the PRI's candidate for federal deputy in León's second district, Roberto Garza, was defeated by the PAN. Garza was subsequently named president of the state supreme court (Cuéllar 1985a).

The 1979–1982 period was one in which the PRI achieved extremely high proportions of the vote throughout the country. State-level elections primarily represented a mechanism for the reaccommodation of local political forces within the PRI, rather than a space for contestation among rival forces competing under equal conditions. Nonetheless, an analysis of electoral data from this period points to potentially competitive elections, particularly the gestation of opposition forces, in some parts of Guanajuato. In the 1979 municipal elections, the PRI triumphed in all the local races and won 84.4 percent of the total valid vote (see table 7.1). The PAN won only 6.8 percent of the total vote, while the PDM received 6.6 percent, with the remaining 2.2 percent of the vote divided among four other small parties. However, of the PAN's seven candidates in these municipal elections, its nominees in León and Apaseo el Alto won more than 30 percent of the vote. The PDM won more than 10 percent of the vote in fourteen of the twenty-five *municipios* in which it ran candidates.

In the 1982 municipal elections in Guanajuato, the PRI's overall proportion of the vote fell by more than 10 percentage points, to 71.1 percent (table 7.1). The PAN and the PDM obtained 13.9 percent and 11.7 percent, respectively, of the valid vote. The PAN backed candidates in sixteen *municipios*, winning more than 40 percent of the vote in Abasolo and Moroleón and over 30 percent in León. Similarly, the PDM ran candidates in twenty-eight areas, winning more than 30 percent of the total vote in five cases and gaining a majority (53.9 percent) in the capital, Guanajuato. Moreover, an independent candidate, Juan I. Torres Landa (son of a former governor), won the municipal election in San José Iturbide.[7]

In addition to municipal presidencies, between 1982 and 1985 opposition parties won more than one hundred city council positions (*regidurías*) in the state. Of this total, thirty-eight went to the PAN and forty-eight to the PDM. With only three exceptions, in all of the municipalities in which the PRI faced an opposition candidate, the resulting governments were composed of more than one party.

---

[7] These results elicited quite different reactions. At the time, Governor Velasco Ibarra (referring to the liberalization process initiated by President José López Portillo's 1977 electoral reform) declared that "the victor was the political reform." However, in 1985 the PRI's gubernatorial candidate (and later governor), Rafael Corrales Ayala, commented that these elections were "a great betrayal of the PRI." See Cuéllar 1985b.

During this first period, the PDM adopted an aggressive, openly *sinarquista* discourse and demonstrated an important capacity for social mobilization. Its leaders characterized their party as the best political choice for "humble people," contrasting the PDM to the PAN ("the party of business"). With the creation of the Unión de Usuarios y Contribuyentes (Union of Service Users and Taxpayers) to mobilize a multi-class constituency behind demands to resolve daily problems, the PDM developed a substantial organizational base in the state (Valencia García 1986: 137).

In the second phase of Guanajuato's electoral-political evolution, the growing number of opposition candidates and their increasing success at the polls marked the beginning of an electorally competitive party system in the state. Three parties—the PRI, PAN, and PDM—dominated the electoral landscape between 1982 and 1988; since 1988, political competition has been increasingly bipolar (PAN versus PRI) in character.

The results of the 1985 gubernatorial elections largely anticipated the situation that would develop over the succeeding decade. PRI support fell by 20 percentage points from its 1979 level, to 62.2 percent of the valid vote, while the PAN increased its share of the vote from 12 percent in 1979 to 18.2 percent in 1985 (see table 7.2). The PDM ran third, with 14.4 percent of the total vote. In these elections, the PAN in León and the PDM in Guanajuato each won more than 35 percent of the vote. Even so, the officially reported electoral results elicited complaints, denunciations, and legal challenges, as well as calls for large-scale mobilizations to defend the integrity of the vote. This was the basis for the formation of the Unión de Organismos Cívicos y Políticos del Estado de Guanajuato (Guanajuato Union of Civic and Political Groups), in which the PAN, the PDM, the UNS, and various local Catholic-influenced groups joined forces (Valencia García 1986: 206).

The 1985 elections to select members of the state legislature and the federal Chamber of Deputies largely followed this pattern. In the state legislative elections, the PRI (61.1 percent), PAN (19.1 percent), and PDM (15.0 percent) split most of the vote, with another five parties dividing the remaining 4.8 percent (table 7.3). The PAN won in one of León's electoral districts and closely rivaled the PRI's vote in the city's other two districts. In the federal elections, the PRI received 58.6 percent of the total vote. However, the PAN won 20.0 percent of the total and carried two of León's districts, while the PDM won 16.1 percent of the total vote.[8]

---

[8] Comisión Federal Electoral. The remaining 5.3 percent of the vote was divided among six other parties: PARM, PMT, PPS, PRT, PST, and PSUM.

Table 7.1. **Party Vote Shares in Municipal Elections in Guanajuato, 1979–2000 (percentages)**[1]

Year	PRI Vote	PAN Vote	PDM Vote	PRD Vote	PFCRN Vote	Other Parties[2]	Municipalities Won by Opposition (non–PRI) Parties
1979	84.4	6.8	6.6	--	--	2.2	None
1982	71.1	13.9	11.7	--	--	3.3	Total: 2 **PDM:** Guanajuato **Independent candidate:** San José Iturbide
1985	67.9	18.7	10.4	--	--	3.0	Total: 2 **PAN:** San Francisco del Rincón **PST:** Villagrán
1988	56.6	27.8	3.4	--	8.4	3.8	Total: 2 **PAN:** León **PRD:** Apaseo el Alto (municipal council)
1991	45.2	45.1	1.7	5.1	1.9	1.0	Total: 12 **PAN:** Celaya, Cortazar, Dolores Hidalgo, León, Moroleón, Salamanca, Salvatierra, San Francisco del Rincón, San José Iturbide, San Luis de la Paz, San Miguel de Allende, Valle de Santiago
1994	52.0	35.7	1.5	7.1	1.2	2.5	Total: 10 **PAN:** Apaseo el Alto, Cuerámaro, León, Moroleón, Pueblo Nuevo **PRD:** Acámbaro, Coroneo **PARM:** Huanímaro, San José Iturbide **Independent candidate:** Santa Cruz de Juventino Rosas

1997	33.7	44.3	3.1	13.3	--	5.6	**Total: 27** **PAN**: Abasolo, Apaseo el Grande, Celaya, Comonfort, Coroneo, Cortazar, Doctor Mora, Huanímaro, Irapuato, León, Pueblo Nuevo, Purísima del Rincón, Salamanca, San Felipe, San Francisco del Rincón, San Miguel de Allende, Silao, Tarandacuao, Uriangato, Yuriria **PRD**: Acámbaro, Salvatierra, San José Iturbide, Tierra Blanca, Valle de Santiago, Villagrán **PVEM**: Santa Cruz de Juventino Rosas
2000	30.2	52.7	--	6.3	--	10.8	**Total: 32** **PAN**: Abasolo, Apaseo el Alto, Celaya, Cortazar, Cuerámaro, Irapuato, Jaral del Progreso, León, Moroleón, Ocampo, Pénjamo, Pueblo Nuevo, Purísima del Rincón, Romita, Salamanca, Salvatierra, San Diego, San Francisco del Rincón, San José Iturbide, San Luis de la Paz, San Miguel de Allende, Silao, Tarimoro, Tierra Blanca, Uriangato, Valle de Santiago, Villagrán, Yuriria **PRD**: Acámbaro, Coroneo, Dolores Hidalgo, Guanajuato

Sources: For 1979–1988, Comisión Estatal Electoral; for 1989–2000, Instituto Estatal Electoral.

[1] Percentage of valid votes, excluding votes cast for unregistered candidates.

[2] "Other parties" includes: for 1979, PARM, PCM, PPS, and PST; for 1982, PPS, PST, and PSUM; for 1985, PARM, PMT, PPS, PRT, PST, and PSUM; for 1988, PARM, PPS, PSUM, and coalitions; for 1991, PARM and PPS; for 1994, PARM, PPS, PT, and PVEM; for 1997, PC, PPS, PT, and PVEM; and for 2000, PARM, PAS, PCD, PDS, PSN, PT, PVEM, and the alliances of the CD–PAS–PRD, CD–PAS–PRD–PT, and PAS–PRD–PT. See the List of Acronyms for individual party names.

Table 7.2. **Party Vote Shares in Gubernatorial Elections in Guanajuato, 1985, 1991, 1995, and 2000 (percentages)[1]**

	1985	1991	1995	2000
PRI	62.2	53.1	32.9	33.8
PAN	18.2	35.5	58.1	56.7
PDM	14.3	2.7	—	—
PRD and coalition partners[2]	—	7.7	7.0	6.6
Other parties[3]	5.3	1.0	2.0	2.9
Total	100	100	100	100

Sources: Comisión Estatal Electoral and Instituto Estatal Electoral. For 2000 preliminary election results, http://www.ieeg.org.mx.

[1] Percentage of valid votes, excluding votes cast for unregistered candidates.

[2] In 1991, the PRD's coalition partner was the PPS; in 2000, its partners were the CD, PAS, and PT. See the List of Acronyms for individual party names.

[3] "Other parties" includes: for 1985, PARM, PPS, PRT, PST, and PSUM; for 1991, PARM; for 1995, PFCRN and PT; for 2000, PARM, PCD, PDS, PSN, and PVEM.

In the 1985 municipal elections in Guanajuato, the principal contenders were once again the PRI (67.9 percent of the total valid vote), the PAN (18.7 percent), and the PDM (10.4 percent) (table 7.1). The PAN won control of the municipal government in San Francisco del Rincón, and the Socialist Workers' Party (PST) triumphed in Villagrán. The PDM, taking the most aggressive stance in its entire history in the region, seized control of several municipal office buildings (*alcaldías*) to protest the officially recorded electoral results. These mobilizations paralleled similar demonstrations taking place in the states of Chihuahua, Jalisco, and San Luis Potosí, all of them protesting fraudulent state and local elections.

The 1985 elections marked the increasingly clear preeminence of the PAN over the PDM as the principal opposition force in Guanajuato. It is somewhat difficult to explain the decline of a party whose opposition presence was impressive both for the rapidity of its rise and the speed with which it disappeared. There are, however, two factors suggesting that the PDM's debacle was the obverse aspect of the PAN's ascent. The first element was the local PAN leadership's decision to increase its electoral efficacy. As the PAN expanded its territorial base and ran candidates in a greater number of areas, the PDM lost strength. The opposition-inclined portion of Guanajuato's electorate previously had only one ideologically viable option, the PDM. Those sentiments increasingly benefited the PAN—the opposition party with the greatest organizational and mobilizational capacity—once it had demonstrated its potential.

Table 7.3. **Party Vote Shares in Local Legislative Elections in Guanajuato, 1985–2000 (percentages)**[1]

	1985	1988	1991	1994	1997	2000
PRI	61.1	46.2	53.1	55.0	33.7	29.5
PAN	19.1	28.8	34.3	31.1	43.6	56.6
PDM	15.0	4.5	2.8	1.2	2.8	—
PRD and coalition partners[2]	—	3.4	6.6	8.7	13.5	8.2
PFCRN	—	13.1	2.2	1.0	—	—
Other parties[3]	4.8	4.0	1.0	3.0	6.4	5.7
Total	100	100	100	100	100	100

Sources: Comisión Estatal Electoral and Instituto Estatal Electoral de Guanajuato. For 2000 preliminary election results, http://www.ieeg.org.mx.

[1] Percentage of valid votes, excluding votes cast for unregistered candidates.

[2] This category includes, in 1988, the PPS–PRD coalition; in 1991 and 1994, the PRD only; and in 2000, the coalition of the PAS, PRD, and PT. See the List of Acronyms for individual party names.

[3] "Other parties" includes: for 1985, PARM, PPS, PRT, PST, and PSUM; for 1988, PARM, PMS, and PRT; for 1991, PARM; for 1994, PARM, PT, and PVEM; for 1997, PC, PPS, PT, and PVEM; and for 2000, PARM, PCD, PDS, PSN, PT, and PVEM.

Second, judging by its electoral success, one must conclude that the PAN managed to articulate the multiplicity of social sentiments that constitute Guanajuato's political identity, "modernizing" its content to fit the contemporary era. The PDM's belligerent, openly Catholic, and *sinarquista* harangues proved old-fashioned, even primitive, in comparison to the rhetoric and strategies of the PAN. The latter's discourse, based on ideas of honesty and the common good, stressed the efficiency and professionalization of public services. In any event, judging by the extremely low levels of electoral support the PDM won after 1985, the citizens of Guanajuato no longer endorsed the party's postulates or its means of mobilization.

The July 1988 presidential election defined Guanajuato as one of the most oppositionist states in the country. The PRI's statewide showing, with 43.9 percent of the total vote, was its fifth worst in the election (see table 7.4). The PAN won 29.9 percent of the total presidential vote, with the remainder going to the National Democratic Front (FDN, the opposition coalition[9] led by Cuauhtémoc Cárdenas; 22.2 percent), the PDM (3.8 percent), and the Revolutionary Workers' Party (PRT; 0.2

[9] Four legally registered parties joined the coalition: the Authentic Party of the Mexican Revolution (PARM), Party of the Cardenista Front for National Reconstruction (PFCRN), Mexican Socialist Party (PMS), and Socialist Popular Party (PPS).

percent). In balloting for the federal Chamber of Deputies, the PAN won four of thirteen majority districts (all three León districts and one of two in Celaya). The PAN also won the three León districts in voting for the state legislature.

Table 7.4. **Major Parties' Performance in Presidential Elections in Guanajuato, 1988, 1994, and 2000 (percentages)[1]**

	1988[2]	1994[2]	2000[3]
PRI	43.9	55 .7	28.7
PAN	29.9	30.3	62.5
FDN / PRD	22.2	8.7	6.7
Other parties[4]	4.0	5.3	2.1
Total	100	100	100

Sources: For 1988, Comisión Estatal Electoral; for 1994, Junta Local del Instituto Federal Electoral; for 2000 preliminary election results from the Instituto Federal Electoral, http://www.ife.org.mx.

[1] Percentage of valid votes, excluding votes cast for unregistered candidates.

[2] In 1988 Cuauhtémoc Cárdenas was the candidate of the National Democratic Front (FDN), a coalition that united the PARM, PFCRN, PMS, and PPS. In 1994 Cárdenas was the candidate of the PRD and the PT. See the List of Acronyms for individual party names.

[3] In 2000 the PAN and the PVEM allied in the Alianza por el Cambio (Alliance for Change); the CD, PAS, PRD, PSN, and PT comprised the Alianza por México (Alliance for Mexico). Votes for the candidates of these alliances—Vicente Fox and Cuauhtémoc Cárdenas—appear, respectively, in the PAN and PRD columns.

[4] "Other parties" includes: for 1988, PDM and PRT; for 1994, PARM, PDM, PFCRN, PPS, PT, and PVEM; for 2000, PARM, PCD, and PDS.

The results of the December 1988 municipal elections were surprising not for the decline in PRI support but for the PDM's weakness. Even though the PDM presented candidates in twenty-eight municipalities, it won just 3.4 percent of the total vote (table 7.1). The PRI received 56.6 percent of the vote, while the PAN and the Party of the Cardenista Front for National Reconstruction (PFCRN, with significant support among peasants) won 27.8 percent and 8.4 percent, respectively.

These elections clearly showed the PAN to be the consolidated opposition in Guanajuato. It obtained more than 30 percent of the vote in five cities, almost all of which would come under PAN control in 1991. In León, the PAN won 58.7 percent of the vote, out-polling the PRI by a margin of almost 2:1 and delivering the municipal presidency to Carlos Medina Plascencia. In a surprising development, three years later Medina would become interim governor.

It is worth noting in this context that, since the 1970s, León voters had proved to be a key element in the state's evolving electoral dynamics. Unlike the population in Guanajuato's other cities, who varied their support among parties in different elections, residents of León consistently cast their ballots for the political opposition. Indeed, it was precisely in the electoral districts encompassing León that the PAN won the most federal and local elections. It was also in León that the PAN's 1988 presidential candidate, Manuel J. Clouthier, won the highest percentage of votes in the state, at a time when opposition voters in cities in southern Guanajuato (Salvatierra and Acámbaro, for example) backed Cárdenas.[10]

The loyalty of opposition voters in León to the PAN can be explained by three factors whose historical roots are indisputable: the population's Catholic culture, its tradition of opposition to centralism, and the high value placed on ideas associated with free enterprise and private property. For the citizens of Guanajuato, the PAN is the party that has been most closely associated with the defense of religious freedom and the state's sovereignty. It is also the party whose social project most clearly gives a privileged ideological place to the private firm, and it is the party responsible for the private sector's extensive participation in state and municipal government.

Several aspects of León's political economy and culture sustained the PAN's local strength—and were, in turn, reinforced by it. The first was the structure of the city's principal economic activity, the footwear industry. At least until the advent of intensive international competition in the mid–1990s, the industry was dispersed in hundreds of small businesses and family-run workshops, an industrial structure that sustained the idea that any individual, by virtue of his own effort, could become an owner of the means of production. The population's "industrial spirit" and the widespread expectation that any worker could become an employer echoed the *sinarquista* maxim that counterposed "*sinarquista* patriotism," in which "everyone is an owner" ("*todos propietarios*"), to "class warfare," in which "everyone is a worker" ("*todos proletarios*"). The PAN managed to modernize this earlier discourse by advocating a model of private enterprise that serves the common good (Serrano 1992: 195–97).

---

[10] In the 1988 presidential election, the PAN's share of the vote in the three electoral districts that centered on León significantly exceeded the party's statewide average of 29.9 percent. It received 61.7 percent in district 2, 58.2 percent in district 3, and 70.9 percent in district 11. It was precisely in these districts that the FDN performed most poorly (under 5 percent of the total vote). In contrast, the FDN won nearly 40 percent of the vote in the state's southern districts (for example, district 6 in Acámbaro and district 13 in Salvatierra).

Second, the Roman Catholic Church has a strong influence in the city's everyday life. Its presence includes pilgrimages, mass religious events, and so forth that feed a "Catholic rationality" that closely approximates both key postulates of the PAN and the practices and statements of the party's local leaders.[11] In particular, the diocese of León played an important role in elections during the 1990s and in the legitimation of *panista* municipal governments. The arrival of a new bishop, Rafael García González, in February 1992 marked the beginning of increased church involvement in "earthly questions." During his brief period as bishop (he died in February 1995), García became a public figure known for his declarations on different subjects and his involvement in any matter of social significance.[12] Under his direction,

---

[11] One example of this phenomenon was the annual celebration of the "living rosary" ("el Rosario Viviente") by the diocese of León, which in 1990 drew some 40,000 local residents to the city's principal soccer stadium.

Some PAN leaders (including Carlos Medina Plascencia, who was municipal president of León during 1988–1991 and who later served as interim governor) have publicly recognized their Catholic faith by attending religious events. The most conspicuous example of this occurred in the celebration of the Eucharist that concluded the ninth youth pilgrimage to the sanctuary of Christ the King (Cristo Rey), located on El Cubilete mountain in Silao. Medina, speaking from the pulpit, delivered an address (which local politicians later dubbed "the Sermon on the Mount") in which he exhorted listeners to "show support for change." When criticized for his participation in the event, Medina defended his right to profess openly his religious beliefs. See *La Jornada*, January 26, 1992, p. 13; Blancarte 1992; Camacho and Contreras 1993.

Given the party's history and its ideological proximity to Catholicism, the symbolic space defined by Catholicism has been a natural sphere for the PAN. However, rival parties have also sought to exploit this space in order to expand their political base. They have done so by making statements and taking positions which, in their view, will identify them with the public's religious sentiments. These groups have been motivated to do so because they believe that this strategy has been a key to the PAN's success.

For example, in March 1990 the state-level PRI organization painted walls and other public spaces with such slogans as "I asked God for happiness in life and He gave me life" ("*Pedí a Dios felicidad en la vida y me dio vida*") and "Where there is life, God is present, and where there is God, there are no drugs" ("*Donde hay vida está Dios, y donde está Dios no hay drogas*"). Porfirio Muñoz Ledo, the center-left PRD's 1991 gubernatorial candidate, used campaign posters featuring a picture in which he offered his hand to Pope John Paul II; the poster's caption read, "For a Guanajuato that we all can share" ("*Por un Guanajuato que todos podamos compartir*"). Similarly, Ignacio Vázquez Torres, during his 1995 gubernatorial campaign as the PRI's candidate, attended the Way of the Cross that is traditionally celebrated in Guanajuato City each year during Holy Week.

[12] For example, the bishop announced that he would invite Pope John Paul II to visit the diocese, and he met with Eliseo Martínez, the *panista* municipal president of León, "to identify ways of working together to resolve social problems." At the end of Martínez's first year in office, Bishop García expressed his satisfaction with the

the diocese promoted "Faith and Politics" workshops to encourage citizens to think about political topics and elections. The specific subjects examined in these workshops clearly reflected the bishop's ties to the local PAN organization. However, the use of such partisan phrases as "the search for the common good," "active nonviolence," "peaceful resistance," and "the legitimate autonomy of intermediate authorities under the principle of subsidiarity" provoked a sharp public reaction in some quarters and forced a suspension of the workshops (Arrache Hernández n.d.: 150–56).

A third factor favoring the PAN is the symbolic importance of the *sinarquista* memory (actualized by the PAN) in León, cradle of the *sinarquista* movement and the site of the PAN's most important ideological struggles resulting from post-election conflicts. For example, Martín Ortiz, a local PRI leader, observes that the PAN has been known in León as the party which, from its very beginnings, opposed constitutional restrictions on the Catholic Church and state intervention in the economy. He notes, moreover, that "the PAN appeals to the local citizenry on the basis of historical events that have marked the collective memory. Its leaders have pursued a continuous line that runs from the massacre of January 2, 1946, to the movement led by López Sanabria in 1976, and which culminates in its overwhelming electoral victory in 1988" (Ortiz García 1991).

These elements all contributed to Medina's victory in the 1988 municipal elections in León, an event that symbolized the PAN's new political efficacy at the national level and which had three major consequences for the party in the state of Guanajuato. First, Medina's victory shaped the party's electoral strategies, and his government became a model of public administration for subsequent *panista* municipal presidencies in the state. The PAN recognized that its electoral future would depend to a considerable extent on Medina's successful management of city affairs. His administration, therefore, gave priority to the efficient and transparent management of public funds, the development of urban and rural organizational networks, and, above all, the careful construction of a public image of a new, better form of government.[13]

---

progress the Martínez administration had made in promoting a more participatory form of government. See *A.M.* 1992a, 1992b, 1993a.

[13] For example, Medina established an office of "citizen integration" to promote public participation in urban neighborhoods and rural areas, held frequent public meetings, presented his annual report on municipal affairs at public sites, published signed articles in local daily newspapers, and regularly distributed special bulletins and other publications on municipal affairs. The PAN's municipal officials sought to cultivate a positive public image by, among other actions, strongly demanding "fair treatment" and efficiency in the delivery of resources from the state government. See Valencia García 1995.

Second, Medina's success demonstrated the importance of elections as a means of bringing businessmen to power at the municipal and state levels. Beginning with Medina, three consecutive municipal presidents of León have been businessmen with interests in the leather and footwear industries. In addition to a background in agroindustry, Vicente Fox (governor between 1995 and 1999) also had business interests in these sectors. As owners of export-oriented firms, these individuals have the profile of modern businessmen. They often have earned degrees from private universities and have sometimes studied abroad, and they are open to technological innovation and the adoption of efficient production methods. Some of these businessmen have also held leadership positions in private-sector associations and have played a key role in philanthropic, social welfare, and community development groups.[14]

Finally, the Medina administration demonstrated that partisan struggles continue beyond election campaigns and influence the conduct of municipal government. This was especially an issue in relations between municipal authorities and state-level officials. Indeed, an accumulation of such problems became one of the hallmarks of the Medina administration. Examples included constant, growing conflicts between the mayor and Governor Rafael Corrales Ayala over budgetary matters, with the former accusing the latter of sabotaging President Carlos Salinas de Gortari's (1988–1994) policies of "opening" and "change" by making partisan use of financial resources. Similarly, the mayor clashed with PRI city council members who, even though outnumbered seven to five by *panista* council members, sided with the state governor by voting against many of Medina's proposals. There were also conflicts with PRI–affiliated organizations, including those

---

[14] For example, Medina (born in León) received a degree in engineering from the prestigious Instituto Tecnológico y de Estudios Superiores de Monterrey (ITESM) in 1955. He later studied for an M.A. degree in public administration at ITESM, and he was director general of Grupo Suela Medina Torres, a footwear manufacturing firm with significant export sales. Medina also served as adviser to several financial firms. His other positions have included president of the Asociación Nacional de Curtidores (National Tanners' Association), councilor of the Mexican Employers' Confederation (COPARMEX), vice-president of the Centro Empresarial de León (Business Center of León), and vice-president of a rural development association in Guanajuato. Medina became an active PAN member in 1985, and he served as León city councilman (*regidor*) between 1986 and 1988.

Similarly, Luis Quiros, León municipal president between 1995 and 1997, was owner of an important footwear company. He received a degree in engineering from ITESM and a postgraduate degree in economics from a Brazilian university. Among other positions, Quiros served as councilor of the Asociación de Industriales de Guanajuato (Guanajuato Industrialists' Association).

representing taxi drivers, garbage collectors, and, especially, market vendors, who were regularly uprooted by municipal authorities during Medina's term in office (Valencia García 1994).

ELECTIONS IN THE 1990s

Elections in Guanajuato during the 1990s were truly contests for power, leading to the PAN's displacing the PRI in the governorship of Mexico's sixth most populous state. The elections held between 1991 and 2000 constituted a true political conjuncture, privileged moments that opened the way to a new political era in the region. As such, these elections initiated a broader, more complex process of sociopolitical change.

A highly competitive gubernatorial election in 1991 gave rise to another, special election in 1995. In the first, the PAN attained the governorship because the electoral results lacked credibility; in the second, the PAN won the state executive in an indisputably transparent electoral process. In between these two key contests, in 1994 Guanajuato experienced the most heated municipal elections in its history. In spite of the fact that opposition forces won in only ten municipalities (the PAN in five of these), these contests were characterized by extensive postelectoral conflict. In contrast, by 1997 and 2000 the PAN held a position of strength in state politics, winning control of twenty municipal governments in 1997 and twenty-eight in the 2000 elections. In 2000, a PAN candidate again won the governorship, and Vicente Fox Quesada—former governor of Guanajuato and the PAN's presidential candidate—became the person who finally defeated the PRI in a presidential election and ended more than seventy years of single-party hegemony.

The following sections examine the most important elements of each of these electoral processes.

The 1991 Gubernatorial Election

In 1991, Guanajuato simultaneously held elections for federal deputies and senators, members of the state legislature, and governor. It was, however, the gubernatorial race that gave the electoral process a special political intensity. The contest featured three principal candidates: Ramón Aguirre (PRI), Porfirio Muñoz Ledo (PRD), and Vicente Fox (PAN). The PDM played only a minor role.

The PAN's candidate was the early favorite, and his campaign slogan, "We're Going for Guanajuato" ("*Vamos por Guanajuato*"), signaled the party's early commitment to win the race. In order to increase its prospects, the PAN reorganized itself throughout the state, including at the level of municipal party committees. León, Irapuato, Celaya, and San Luis de la Paz were designated "organizational development poles" under the coordination of the PAN's state-level committee. Party leaders gave high priority to training middle-level personnel on political and administrative topics, thereby seeking to make each party member a "founder" capable of diffusing the PAN's ideals. As a consequence of such actions, the PAN was able to begin its campaign even before the selection of Fox as its gubernatorial candidate.[15] Once Fox began to campaign, the party closely coordinated his visits to cities, rural communities, factories, and universities, as well as meetings with key business leaders.

Although the PRI's Aguirre was labeled a "unity candidate," his selection badly disappointed the many party loyalists who had backed Ignacio Vázquez Torres. Moreover, his campaign proved to have high economic and political costs. In addition to lavish spending, the campaign was notorious for the indiscriminate use of the logo of the National Solidarity Program (PRONASOL, a high-profile government anti-poverty program closely associated with then president Carlos Salinas de Gortari), part of a concerted attempt by the federal government to regain PRI support in the state. This effort included intensified distribution of legal titles to urban property holders by the Commission to Normalize Landownership Titles (CORETT). Indeed, Guanajuato accounted for 21 percent of all such titles distributed by CORETT during 1991 (Calderón and Cazés 1996: 238).

The candidacy of the PRD's Muñoz Ledo, in turn, won early notoriety because of his supposed ineligibility. The fact that state election authorities approved his candidacy was interpreted by the PAN as yet another scheme by the established regime to draw votes away from Fox (Ling Altamirano 1992: 144). Yet in practice, it is more likely that Muñoz Ledo's candidacy siphoned votes from the PRI because some of Vázquez Torres's supporters joined the Muñoz Ledo campaign and lobbied for the PRD.

PDM candidate Rosa María Hernández briefly drew local media attention by conducting a hunger strike in León to protest election authorities' decision to ratify Muñoz Ledo's candidacy. However, the PDM's campaign slogan ("To govern with common sense") and its calls for voters to join Hernández in a campaign of prayers and fasts sig-

---

[15] The party's campaign slogan began to appear publicly more than two months before Fox's formal nomination. See Ling Altamirano 1992.

Fox, one of three candidates for the nomination, received some 90 percent of party delegates' votes.

naled that the party was more and more removed from voters' real concerns.[16]

From the outset, the elections promised to be highly competitive, and this characteristic made the Guanajuato contest a focus of national political debate. Both national and international observers considered the elections in Guanajuato, along with those in San Luis Potosí, to be a "political laboratory" in which the Mexican regime's willingness to liberalize would be put to the test. Within the state, the electoral environment reflected a conflictive sociopolitical dynamic and stimulated widespread participation and social mobilization. Thus developments and expectations at three levels—the local, national, and international—were interwoven in a complex political situation.

On election day (August 18), the PAN in particular deployed an impressive information-gathering and communications system, using extensive technological resources to track events, diffuse information, and denounce irregularities in the casting and counting of ballots. The opposition amply documented multiple problems in the conduct of the elections. These included errors in the preparation of voters' identification cards, problems in the integration of election oversight bodies, the inappropriate use of government resources to favor the PRI's candidate, and so forth. The PAN and PRD both denounced multiple irregularities, including the shortage of ballots in the gubernatorial election.

According to the official election results, the PRI won the gubernatorial race with 53.1 percent of the vote (table 7.2). The PAN came in second with 35.5 percent, while the PRD won 7.7 percent, the PDM 2.7 percent, and the Authentic Party of the Mexican Revolution (PARM) 1.0 percent. In León's three electoral districts, however, the PAN won over 50 percent of the vote.[17]

Nevertheless, the votes cast on August 18, 1991, did not carry any candidate to the governor's office. Although the state's electoral college declared the PRI's candidate the winner, the electoral process lacked credibility and citizen mobilization in favor of the PAN was on the upswing. The national and international media severely criticized election fraud in the state, and the tenor of public opinion forced federal political authorities to seek a way out of a difficult situation. At a time when negotiations for a North American free trade agreement were fully under way, the *Wall Street Journal* urged President Salinas to convene a

---

[16] In a campaign leaflet titled "End Illegality!" signed by the UNS and the PDM, citizens were invited to reject the election authorities' decision by joining Hernández in one-day fasts and prayer. The leaflet ended with the phrase "Death is of no import when one dies for one's country" (*"Morir es poco cuando por la patria se muere"*).

[17] Similarly, in the elections to choose deputies to the federal and state legislatures, the PAN's candidates won majorities in all three León districts.

new election in order to sweep away "the charges of electoral irregularities that have bedeviled his party in the past and threaten to cloud
its future indefinitely" (*Wall Street Journal*, August 29, 1991, p. A12).

In this context, Aguirre submitted his resignation on the same day
he was officially designated governor-elect. His decision presumably
reflected pressure from President Salinas to resolve a delicate political
situation quickly. The state congress then named Carlos Medina Plascencia, the *panista* municipal president of León, interim governor. Yet
the political situation remained highly conflictive, with no signs of a
quick or easy resolution.[18]

In the view of most analysts, the designation of Medina resulted
from high-level negotiations between the PAN's national leadership
and the federal government. The solution to the Guanajuato conflict
was, therefore, labeled a *concertacesión*—a combination of negotiated
agreement and concession. (Indeed, this outcome became the prototype
for arrangements ending postelectoral conflicts in other places, despite
the outcome at the polls.) According to Luis Miguel Rionda, an analyst
of Guanajuato politics, the arrangement included several agreements:
the imposition of PRI member Salvador Rocha as the state's secretary of
government and an implicit agreement not to convene a special gubernatorial election before the end of President Salinas's term in office in
1994 (Rionda 1995a: 12).

The Medina Administration

Medina's interim governorship had a double character: it represented
both alternation in power and bipartisanship in government. The PRI
held a majority (twenty of thirty seats) in the state-level chamber of
deputies and two cabinet positions, which represented both a political
counterbalance and a significant constraint on the actions of the new
governor. One consequence was an unaccustomed validation of the
formal separation of powers. The state legislature became "an active
space where the smallest details of the interim government were heat-
edly discussed" (Rionda 1995a: 15). But the legislature also became an
important obstacle to political reform, which Medina had publicly
identified as his principal objective in office.

---

[18] The designation of Medina as interim governor was not without problems. The
state-level PRI was vehemently opposed to this step, and it seized the state legislature to prevent the body from approving the measure. Intervention by the federal
government, especially the Ministry of the Interior, forced the rebel *priístas* to relin-
quish physical control of the assembly building and permit the outgoing legislature
to approve Medina's appointment. However, with just fifteen of twenty-eight deputies present, the measure was approved by only nine votes to six. See Rionda 1995a.

Political reform in the state was a slow, arduous process because of the problems associated with the "forced cohabitation" of the PAN and the PRI. Because this was an artificial situation imposed from above, it proved difficult to reach consensus agreement on the reform proposals advanced by either the governor or the PRI majority in the state legislature. It was not until February 1993, more than a year after Medina took office, that the Coordinating Commission for Political Reform in the State of Guanajuato (CORPEG) was created as a forum to advance discussions on this topic (Rionda n.d.). However, the CORPEG "produced many ideas and few agreements," and it practically disappeared in January 1994 when the governor broke one of the key agreements that brought him to power and named a member of his own party as secretary of government (Rionda 1996b).

The individual in question was Felipe Camarena, a close associate of the governor who had previously served as director of the state judicial police.[19] Camarena's appointment provoked the resignation of Carlos Chaurand as PRI majority leader of the state legislature and CORPEG coordinator. Most of the other party representatives also resigned from the CORPEG, leaving only the PAN, PRD, and PDM. The remaining representatives developed a proposal for political reform in the state, but this was ultimately rejected by the legislature.

One of the most conflictual topics was the date of the special election to choose a new governor. The PRI proposed holding the next gubernatorial election in August 1994, in conjunction with federal elections, because it anticipated that it would benefit from its improved national standing. The PAN, in contrast, lobbied to hold it in December 1994 along with the next scheduled municipal elections, in which it expected to do well.

A second subject of intense debate and profound disagreement concerned the number of deputies and the form of proportional representation employed in a restructured state legislature. The governor's proposal (backed by the PAN, PDM, and PRD) sought to ensure that no party could by itself approve amendments to the state constitution. To achieve this goal, Medina proposed increasing the number of deputies chosen by proportional representation from twelve to eighteen and

---

[19] In the first two years and four months of Medina's interim governorship, four different members of the PRI held the key position of secretary of government. These were Salvador Rocha Díaz, Higinio Rodríguez, Roberto Suárez Nieto (who took a leave from his elected office as federal senator from Guanajuato to hold the post), and José Luis González. It was not until January 1994, in the temporary vacuum created by the resignation of the federal secretary of the interior (Patrocinio González) following the armed rebellion in Chiapas, that Medina was able to place one of his own collaborators in the position. See Arrache Hernández n.d.: 134–35.

prohibiting any party from holding more than 60 percent of the seats in the legislature.

Accumulated disagreements prevented the 1991–1994 state legislature from approving the much-debated electoral reform. Indeed, it was not until a new, PRI–majority legislature took office in September 1994 that final agreement could be reached on a new state electoral code. In November 1994, the legislature decreed that a new gubernatorial election would be held in May 1995. A State Electoral Institute (IEE) was created as an autonomous agency responsible for organizing the electoral process. It was composed of five "citizen councilors," a nonvoting representative of the state executive, and one nonvoting representative from each of the officially registered political parties (Gobierno del Estado de Guanajuato 1994). The reform legislation expanded the number of electoral districts from eighteen to twenty-two and established a state legislature with twenty-two deputies chosen by majority vote and up to fourteen deputies selected by proportional representation.

In addition to electoral reform, the Medina administration also produced other significant political changes. For example, it gave a clear "business" orientation to the administration of the state's affairs, especially with its emphasis on organizational development as a means of imbuing state employees with a new work ethic. Similarly, in an effort to be "scientific" in planning, the Medina administration requested that the Instituto Tecnológico y de Estudios Superiores de Monterrey's (ITESM) León campus elaborate a comprehensive development plan for the state. The result, "Twenty-First-Century Guanajuato," included short-, medium-, and long-term proposals. However, beyond its utility as a planning document, the study was interesting for its conception of development, which was limited to questions of available material resources (financing, technology, infrastructure, and so forth). Although the document was elaborated in the course of meetings with different social groups, these sessions generally privileged representatives of the private sector, professional associations, and the Catholic Church; for the most part, popular-sector groups were absent from the process. These latter elements were apparently considered only as a labor force available for investment projects or development plans to be implemented in the state.[20]

At the same time, the Medina administration emphasized its autonomy and local decision-making capacity vis-à-vis the federal government. In an exchange of letters published in the state's main newspa-

---

[20] Governor Vicente Fox later adopted this same development plan. He invited the principal coordinator of the ITESM–León study, Dr. Carlos Flores, to become part of his administration.

pers, the governor and the national minister of agriculture disputed the distribution and use of federal budgetary resources. The former publicly requested that President Ernesto Zedillo (1994–2000) place PROCAMPO (a federal government credit program for small farmers) funds and the Ministry of Agriculture's local operations under state control.[21]

The *panista* maxim frequently invoked by Governor Medina was "as much society as possible and as little government as necessary." This phrase became a principal political and ideological resource in the administration's efforts to redefine the relationship between the state government and municipalities. The governor, accompanied by his cabinet, held monthly planning meetings with the state's forty-six municipal presidents. At the same time, he attached great importance to the work of the Center for Municipal Studies (CEM), a state agency whose function was to advise municipal governments.[22]

Yet these efforts also produced significant conflicts. For example, in April 1993, thousands of Solidarity program participants blocked access to the state capitol in support of their demand that the CEM be eliminated. Similarly, PRI members in the state legislature, backing the call made by thirty-four PRI municipal presidents for new elections in 1993, accused Medina of violating municipal autonomy and seeking to convert municipal presidents into de facto employees of the governor (*A.M.* 1983). Medina eventually did abolish the CEM, replacing it with the State Center for Municipal Development (CEDEM). However, the agency remained within the executive branch, and it was headed by Carlos Gadsden, who had also directed the CEM.[23]

---

[21] In March 1995, the governor requested that President Zedillo transfer to state control the resources, programs, and personnel of the Ministry of Agriculture, Livestock, and Rural Development (SAGAR) and PROCAMPO resources. Minister of Agriculture Francisco Labastida publicly responded by saying that he understood "the reasons why the state government would want to take control of PROCAMPO fifteen days before local elections, even before the start of the planting season," and he encouraged the governor to present a detailed proposal to decentralize the operations of the ministry. Governor Medina retorted that agricultural considerations, not electoral politics, motivated his request. See the statements by Medina and Labastida in *La Jornada*, March 24, 25, and 29, 1995, and *A.M.* 1995a.

[22] The CEM, created by decree in 1984, was a dependency of the state's Ministry of the Interior. Its principal mission was to advise municipal governments; it had no budgetary authority or control over the distribution of public works. Medina attached great importance to the CEM's activities, and he placed a close ally (Carlos Gadsden) in control of it. Medina's goal was for the CEM to promote joint planning in the development of public works projects in each of the state's municipalities.

[23] The CEDEM was also the object of severe criticisms. In December 1994, PRI state legislators again accused the agency of violating municipal autonomy. PRD state deputy Víctor Quiroga Juárez referred to the CEDEM as a "superministry" that duplicated the work of other state agencies (*A.M.* 1994a).

The idea that state government should be subordinate to society, present in the actions of both Governor Medina and various *panista* municipal governments, also posed problems in the more general reformulation of state-society relations.[24] Some of the programs promoted by *panista* state and municipal officials were laudatory attempts to establish links between government and social groups in order to resolve their most urgent problems. But on the other hand, relations between the state and some municipal governments (such as that in León, for example) and organized societal interests—taxi drivers, market vendors, Solidarity base committees—and urban movements such as the Revolutionary Leftist Movement (MIR) in León were often rife with tension. In some instances, escalating conflict led governmental authorities to use force against such groups.

For instance, tensions with the taxi drivers' union were almost a permanent feature of the Medina administration. *Panista* authorities sought to break the long-established ties between the union and the PRI by insisting that drivers apply for their licenses individually. This proposal obviously threatened union leaders' workplace role and political control. At the same time, there emerged taxi drivers' organizations identified with the PAN, including the Asociación de Jóvenes Católicos (Young Catholics' Association) and a group named for Manuel J. Clouthier, a prominent national PAN leader. These developments signaled the PAN's effort to forge a new organic relationship between government and social actors (*La Jornada* 1993).

The jailing of the MIR's principal leaders and the accumulation of tensions with groups like the taxi drivers led hard-line members of the PRI to label Medina's administration "fascist." The formation of the "Front Against Fascism" (*A.M.* 1993b) in May 1993 demonstrated the level of tension that had built up between the governor and social sectors excluded from alliances with the PAN (such as the MIR) or displaced from their traditional positions of political influence.

In the PAN's view, citizen participation to achieve co-responsibility in government is a primary means of dismantling clientelist ties, some social groups' privileged political access, and traditions of political manipulation. But the party's notion of citizenship—the necessary condition and underlying basis for such participation—remains abstract and ambiguous, taking society as an agglomeration of individuals with equal opportunities to create and exercise power. It is a conception that overlooks possible inequalities among different groups in

---

[24] Examples include the state government's "Shared Dignity" ("*Dignidad compartida*") initiative; the "Living Together" ("*Convive*") program launched by Eliseo Martínez, mayor of León between 1992 and 1994; and the "Citizen Wednesday" ("*Miércoles ciudadano*") initiative of Luis Quiros, mayor of León between 1995 and 1997.

terms of their ability to decide their future. Moreover, it ignores "the variegated field of dynamics, interactions, and constraints in which democratic policies are decided (or not decided)" (Lechner 1995: 63).

The viability of citizen participation depends not just on individuals' capacity to join together or mobilize resources, but also on their ability to establish relationships that recognize the plurality of social relations in play and the existence of social organizations with their own behavioral dynamics. Posing clientelism and citizenship as mutually exclusive concepts presupposes "a moral interpretation whose empirical justification is problematic" (Escalante 1995: 32). It is more realistic to recognize the parallel existence of clientelism and citizenship, rather than viewing them as incompatible realities. Taking this latter view is to conceive of politics as a homogeneous space governed by a single and exclusive logic, a characterization that fits neither Guanajuato nor any other Mexican state.

The 1991 Municipal Elections: Alternation in Power as a System

Just four months after the controversial gubernatorial election, the December 1991 municipal elections for the first time found the PRI and the PAN in positions of electoral parity. The two parties received, respectively, 45.2 percent and 45.1 percent of the vote (table 7.1). The PRD won 5.1 percent, and four other parties together accounted for 4.6 percent of the valid vote.

Even though tied in overall electoral strength, the PAN gained significant ground by winning control of twelve municipal governments. The party's total was much smaller than the thirty-three municipalities won by the PRI. However, with the exception of Irapuato, the PAN won in all the cities comprising the state's industrial corridor (the most heavily populated area), and it also gained control of municipalities with a significant rural population. From 1991 onward, *panista* municipal authorities would govern more than half of Guanajuato's population, and its municipal presence included fifteen *síndicos* (municipal magistrates) and 147 *regidores* (councilmen) in forty-six of the state's municipalities (Ling Altamirano 1992: appen. 17). Among the factors accounting for the PAN's strong showing were the municipal elections' proximity to the gubernatorial race (in which Fox had won broad support) and the naming of Medina as governor, an action that demonstrated (if only on an interim basis) that alternation in power was possible.

This was to be the PRI's first experience in Guanajuato as an opposition party. Its defeat, although part of an unfavorable electoral trajectory, can be attributed to the lack of dynamism and organization that prevailed among its leaders. In two cities, Yuriria and Valle de Santiago, PRI militants seized municipal office buildings to protest the election results. In Yuriria, ironically, the *priísta* dissidents were protesting the victory of a member of their own party (*A.M.* 1992c).

The abrupt fall in the PRI's electoral support might also be explained by its declining ability to control voters' actions at the polls. This is the only viable explanation for the volatility of voter participation and abstention rates in Guanajuato. In the period before competitive elections, it was commonplace to find supposedly high levels of voter participation in northern localities (the poorest part of the state) and very low participation rates in industrialized cities. This suspicious disparity declined over time; indeed, in 1988 there were very few municipalities with a voter turnout of more than 60 percent. Beginning in 1991, participation rates increased considerably, but mainly in the more populous urban areas. In other words, electoral results increasingly reflected citizens' preferences. Elections—and electoral results—became credible.

The 1994 Municipal Elections

The elections for municipal presidents in December 1994 proved surprising for two reasons. First, the PAN's electoral ascendancy was reversed, in favor of the PRI and (to a lesser degree) the PRD. Second, widespread post-election conflicts demonstrated resurgent citizen political involvement.

In these elections, the PRI won 52.0 percent of the valid vote, while the PAN and PRD won, respectively, 35.7 percent and 7.1 percent (table 7.1). Of the ten municipalities in which the opposition won, five went to the PAN, two to the PRD, two to the PARM, and one to an independent candidate. The PAN only managed to retain two of the twelve municipalities where it had triumphed in 1991, although it did win in three cities in which it had not previously controlled the municipal government.

Several factors appear to have contributed to the PRI's renewed electoral strength. First, the PAN seems to have experienced some of the normal consequences of having moved from political opposition to governing party. Not only did the party have to assume municipal responsibilities with limited resources, but it also had to confront the public's expectations of change and demands for urgent attention to social needs. Moreover, the PAN suffered from the multiple conflicts— with PRI state legislators, PRI municipal presidents, social groups aligned with the PRI, Solidarity committees, and so forth—that characterized the Medina administration. The local and national press gave extensive coverage to these confrontations, portraying Governor Medina

as someone who devoted a great portion of his time and energy to resolving frequent, repeated political crises.

A second factor was the municipal elections' proximity to the 1994
national elections. In those elections, the PRI performed significantly
better than it had in recent years, which in Guanajuato contributed to
the PAN's defeat in electoral districts where it had traditionally prevailed. Overall, the PAN's share of the federal legislative vote fell from
38.2 percent in 1991 to 30.5 percent in 1994, compared to 54.7 percent
for the PRI (Rionda 1995b). In fact, the PAN lost in twelve of thirteen
federal electoral districts and seventeen of eighteen state electoral districts, retaining power only in the district (#11) corresponding to north-
eastern León. In the state legislature, its presence fell from six to five
seats. Paradoxically, however, the PAN managed to improve its relative performance in the 1994 presidential race, winning 30.3 percent of
the presidential vote in the state (versus 29.9 percent in 1988) compared
to the PRI's 55.7 percent (table 7.4).[25]

Finally, one must consider the fact that the very nature of the vote
and the motivations behind it had changed. When alternation in power
becomes a reality rather than a distant electoral prospect, the collective
perception of the vote changes. The reasoning behind the decision to
vote shifts, and preferences are determined in more pragmatic and less
ideological terms that are subject to change in each election.

But perhaps even more important than the results, the December
1994 municipal elections gave rise to multiple expressions of popular
discontent and the emergence of civic organizations that showed another face of the electoral process. In this instance, the elections became
a vehicle for the articulation of conflicts arising in particular social dynamics at the local level. The conflicts manifested, after three years of
panista government, the breakdown of equilibria among traditional
political forces (municipal governments, the state-level PRI, and rule by
local political bosses) when confronted by the transformation of politics
brought about by generalized alternation in power.

The list of post-election conflicts was extensive. The PRI contested
the election's outcome in León, and the PAN did so in Celaya and San
Miguel de Allende. In another eight cities, popular discontent led diverse groups to demand voiding the elections and block winning candidates from taking office or entering municipal administration buildings. For example, in Cortazar the supporters of independent candidate
Manuel Chimal sought to cancel the elections because of the "electoral
mugging" that had occurred in the municipality (*A.M.* 1994b). In Santa
Cruz de Juventino Rosas, independent candidate Ramón Gasca Men-

---

[25] The PRD was the principal loser in Guanajuato in 1994; it won only 8.7 percent of
the vote, compared to the FDN's 22.2 percent in 1988.

doza managed to defeat all rival candidates and overturn the legislation that barred candidacies such as his. Indeed, the pressure brought
by his supporters (backed by representatives of the PAN, PFCRN, and
PRD) compelled the municipal electoral commission to reopen ballot
boxes and accept as valid more than 8,000 votes for Gasca that had
previously been annulled (*A.M.* 1994c, 1994d).

Similarly in Uriangato, the Frente Cívico Uriangatense (Uriangato
Civic Front, comprised of PAN, PRD, PARM, and even PRI militants)
seized control of municipal offices and demanded the resignation of the
priísta mayor, Ramón Pérez, because he had been "elected immorally"
(*A.M.* 1995b, 1995c). In Romita, members of the Movimiento Ciudadano Romitense (Romita Citizens' Movement) sought to prevent
mayor-elect José de Jesús Rocha from taking office. Led by the PRD's
former mayoral candidate, Jorge Morales, they organized a sit-in at the
municipal offices that lasted for more than three months (*A.M.* 1994e,
1995d, 1995e). In the *panista* municipality of Salamanca, members of the
PAN, PRD, and the Asociación de Familias Salmantinas Contra la Im-
posición (Salamanca Family Association Against the Imposition) also
organized a sit-in at municipal headquarters to support an election
victory claimed by the PRD (*A.M.* 1994f, 1994g, 1994h). In Valle de
Santiago, PRD members seized the municipal presidency in defense of
similar goals, and in Doctor Mora the municipality's own Civic Union
did so (*A.M.* 1995f, 1995g, 1995h). In Xichú, where the PRI won 94 percent of the vote, the local political boss kidnapped the mayor-elect,
forced him to sign a request for a leave of absence, and later imposed
his own preferred candidate as interim municipal president. Between
January and May 1995, Xichú was governed in parallel by both the interim and the constitutionally elected mayor (*edil*) (*A.M.* 1995i, 1995j; *La
Jornada* 1995).

These municipal conflicts placed the *panista* state government in a
difficult position. The search for a workable solution in each of these
cases required the negotiation of agreements among parties, state and
municipal authorities, and state legislators. The governor's incapacity
or inability to resolve these problems through negotiation was made
patently clear by his use of the state police to remove forcibly demonstrators in various municipalities and the arrest of the protest movement's leader in Salamanca (*A.M.* 1995k, 1995l, 1995m, 1995n).

The 1995 Gubernatorial Election: Toward a New Political Model?

After three years of Medina's interim government, multiple proposals
for a date for a new gubernatorial election, and tortuous negotiations to
approve a revised state electoral code, a special gubernatorial election
was finally held on May 28, 1995. Comparing the 1991 and 1995 elec-

tions, processes in which Vicente Fox was the central figure, is quite instructive. Among other considerations, assessing similarities and differences between the two elections permits us to understand better the behavioral dynamics underlying the PAN's electoral support in Guanajuato.

In 1991, broad sectors of the population had more or less assimilated the idea of economic crisis into their daily lives, although there was an expectation of (and for some groups, real prospects for) imminent improvement. In 1995, in contrast, economic crisis was an immediate reality manifested in declining production, bankruptcies, overdue loans, unemployment, declining purchasing power, and, above all, uncertainty regarding the future. According to Guanajuato authorities, in 1995 there were some 100,000 unemployed and 750,000 underemployed individuals in the state (*A.M.* 1995o).

One might say, then, that the audience for Fox's 1995 election campaign was an unhappy public strongly inclined to hold the federal government politically accountable for its problems.[26] One example of the public's ire was the sharply critical response by different León urban groups to Federal Deputy José de Jesús Padilla's vote for an increase in the value-added tax (*A.M.* 1995p). Support for the citizens' movement "Save Our Homes," founded by mortgage holders in León in May 1995, mushroomed to more than 7,000 affiliates and won broad public sympathy, including support from Governor Medina and gubernatorial candidate Fox.[27]

The state's business class, traditionally divided politically between the PAN and the PRI, especially resented the 1994–1995 economic crisis. Particularly for footwear manufacturers in León, the dominant group in the local bourgeoisie, the combined effects of domestic economic recession and increased import competition originating in free trade legislation threatened the survival of the main local manufacturing industry. Their disgust with the federal government, which they blamed for promoting "an incorrect economic model,"[28] certainly opened many *priísta* businessmen to the PAN's discourse and program.

---

[26] Two months before the election, a statewide public opinion poll found that 48 percent of respondents thought that the state's economic situation had deteriorated over the previous year and disapproved of the president's handling of the country. The same percentage of respondents indicated that they planned to vote for the PAN in the May 28, 1995, elections. See Pérez 1995.

[27] Author interview with Antonio Rocha Pedrajo, member of the "Save Our Homes" governing council, January 1996, León, Guanajuato.

[28] See the paid announcement that the Cámara de la Industria del Calzado del Estado de Guanajuato (Guanajuato State Chamber of the Footwear Industry) published in a special supplement in *A.M.*, March 18, 1995.

Moreover, PAN authorities—many of whom were themselves businessmen—gave close attention to the private sector's proposals in their governmental initiatives, and they adopted some of these proposals as their own. Governor Medina, for instance, met with President Ernesto Zedillo to outline the conditions that the Guanajuato business sector placed on its support for the federal government's January 1995 "Unity Agreement to Overcome the Economic Emergency" (*A.M.* 1995q, 1995r).

The PRI's candidate in the 1995 gubernatorial election was Ignacio Vázquez Torres. Unlike Aguirre, the party's 1991 nominee, Vázquez Torres was selected in an open party convention. He had also been a contender for the PRI's gubernatorial nomination in 1991, and he had significant bases of support, especially in rural areas.[29] The PRD's candidate was Martha Lucía Micher, who, although not an active party member, was a charismatic woman who had established a presence on the local political scene.[30] The PAN's gubernatorial candidate was known well in advance; he was, naturally, Vicente Fox.[31]

---

[29] Ignacio Vázquez Torres was born in Pénjamo, Guanajuato. He was an attorney with long experience in the federal government. Among other positions, he had been leader of the National Peasants' Confederation (CNC), chief administrative officer in the Ministry of the Interior, and head of the Cuauhtémoc district in Mexico City. He was, moreover, a three-time federal congressman and, at the time of his candidacy, on leave from his position as federal senator. The 1995 gubernatorial race was his fifth electoral campaign in a thirty-five-year political career. Vázquez Torres's candidacy drew on a support movement within the PRI, based especially in rural areas of Guanajuato and known as the *"guerrilla vazqueztorrista,"* that gained strength after 1991.

[30] Martha Lucía Micher (known as Malú) was born in 1954 in the Federal District. At the time of the elections, she had lived in León for sixteen years. A teacher by profession, a militant feminist, a human rights activist, a university professor, and a PRD sympathizer, she defined herself as a popular educator.

[31] Vicente Fox Quesada, born in 1942, received his undergraduate degree from the Universidad Iberoamericana, and he later took an advanced management course at Harvard University. Between 1975 and 1979 he had been president of Coca-Cola de México. He was director general of Grupo Fox, a holding company with interests in agroindustrial activities, food processing (including the export of frozen vegetables), and footwear manufacturing (including the export of cowboy boots). Among other private-sector positions, Fox had been councilor of the Cámara México-Americana de Comercio (Mexican-American Chamber of Commerce), president of the "Venexport" export consortium, and vice-president of the Asociación de Industriales del Estado de Guanajuato (Guanajuato State Industrialists' Association). In the educational and philanthropic spheres, Fox had served as president of the Patronato Loyola, A.C.; founder and president of the Casa Cuna Amigo Daniel, A.C.; and alumni representative of the Universidad Iberoamericana. Within the PAN, Fox had served as state and national councilor, a member of the party's national executive committee, and federal deputy (1988–1991).

As in the case of the 1991 race, the 1995 special election received widespread coverage by the mass media. Most attention focused on the campaigns of the three principal parties. In 1995, however, most analysts judged the PAN the likely winner, in part because different polls predicted that Fox would win almost half of the vote.[32] In 1995 it was widely understood that the election would be highly competitive. In addition, the contest was overseen by a citizen-controlled body, the State Electoral Institute, established by the reformed state electoral code.

The PAN's campaign was, as in 1991, strongly influenced by Fox's charismatic personality and his facility for winning support from diverse groups. Even before being designated as the party's candidate, Fox backed the civic movements arising around the December 1994 municipal elections, including the Frente Cívico Uriangatense and the Movimiento Ciudadano Romitense.[33] Through such actions, Fox identified himself symbolically as a man who supported the public and who opposed those in power. At the same time, however, the PAN adopted new tactics designed to win the public's approval and address its concerns.[34]

As had been the case four years previously, the intensity of the campaign generated a charged (at times violent) political atmosphere. Verbal attacks by one candidate against another were daily occurrences. The PRI, for example, sought to undermine Fox by making an issue of his marital status (separated). Forgetting the fact that the 1991 post-election deal was not just an agreement among *panistas*, the PRI also accused the PAN of having come to power through a special arrangement. Fox, according to the PRI's campaign propaganda, had demanded the deal "in one more instance of his incendiary actions threatening to endanger the social peace." In the same publication, the PRI

---

[32] The newspapers *El Norte* (Monterrey), *Reforma* (Mexico City), and *A.M.* (León) published a poll whose results indicated that 48 percent of respondents backed Fox. The Centro de Estudios de la Opinión Pública of the Universidad de Guanajuato published another poll that showed him winning 47 percent of the vote. See *A.M.* 1995s.

[33] In a meeting with members of the Romita Citizens' Movement, Fox asked that Governor Medina not dispatch police forces to the city because "a peaceful movement is taking place here." At the same time, he asked the mayor of Romita "to step aside because he is blocking the city's development." See *A.M.* 1994t. Similarly, Fox supported members of the Uriangato movement, who sought his help in blocking police intervention; see *A.M.* 1995m.

[34] As part of the campaign, the PAN's state committee promoted a program called "Express Yourself" (*"Exprésate"*), inviting the public to communicate its concerns to the candidate by mail or by telephone. The PAN received some 700 communications in the first six weeks, and it responded to about 70 percent of them. See "Ahora sí ... programa EXPRÉSATE" (six-week summary document), photocopy.

called on the electorate to oppose violence, fanaticism, intolerance, pessimism, defeatism, bitterness, and vengeance—all of which were identified as *panista* vices—and to promote balanced judgments, prudence, good sense, justice, and hope—all of which were part of the PRI's political project.[35]

Notwithstanding the tumult of the campaign, election day was generally peaceful. Fox considered it unlikely that there would be a repeat of the extensive election-day irregularities that had occurred in 1991.[36] In fact, the election was very carefully managed. In addition to the army of citizens the PAN mobilized to supervise the process, the election was witnessed by national and international observers. State radio and television stations also played an important part in covering the election and disseminating the results.

Fox won an overwhelming victory, receiving 58.1 percent of the votes compared to 32.9 percent for the PRI and 7.0 percent for the PRD. Voter turnout averaged 59.4 percent across the state, but it was over 60 percent in the state's industrial corridor and over 65 percent in the three districts centered on León. Moreover, the PAN won a majority in all eighteen of the state's electoral districts. It triumphed in thirty-three of forty-six municipalities, including the state capital and all of the cities in the industrial corridor. In some cities, including León, the PAN won more than three times the number of votes received by its nearest competitor.

The doubtful credibility of the election that produced Medina's interim governorship makes it difficult to compare the 1991 and 1995 results. Nonetheless, one can say that in 1995 the PAN added to its earlier bases of support many votes that were cast more for its gubernatorial candidate than for the party itself. In effect, Fox was able to draw together the historical support for the PAN in Guanajuato, crossover voters from other parties (including PRI dissidents), and citizens who had previously abstained but who realized that their votes now counted. His support also included adherents of the PRD who, even though they would never otherwise have voted for the PAN, backed him as a leader capable of heading a democratic transition in the state.

Fox himself argued that his campaign had broken (though not fully eliminated) the long-standing alliances that linked many organized social sectors to the PRI. Among the examples he cited were the votes he

---

[35] See the paid announcements published in various local newspapers under such titles as "La gran diferencia," "¿Qué es una concertacesión?", "¿Ya analizaste?", "¿Ya te diste cuenta?", "¿Ya te fijaste?", "¿Por qué hay que razonar el voto?", "Los números hablan ... la historia también."

[36] The PAN had, in any event, prepared contingency plans to deal with such problems. Interview with Vicente Fox by Civic Alliance, May 27, 1995, León, Guanajuato.

received from dissident petroleum- workers in Salamanca, who openly challenged their union leaders; the democratization of the state teachers' union; and the leadership and representational crisis that affected the CNC in the Guanajuato countryside.[37]

Several factors contributed to the differences that both Guanajuato voters and national public opinion perceived between Fox and the National Action Party. Among these were Fox's close association with progressive groups like the Grupo San Ángel,[38] his passion in discussing urgent national problems, and his well-publicized differences with the PAN's national leadership.[39] The lack of democracy in Mexico, errors in economic policy making, corruption, and other topics led Fox to criticize federal authorities sharply and to seek new ways of relating the state to the national government. All these actions gave Fox the appearance of being a man of valor, courage, dignity, and decisiveness in defending his positions.

The conventional view is that the PAN is a party divided into two broad currents. On one side are traditional elements tied to the defense of the ideological precepts that originally gave rise to the party. On the other side are *neopanistas* identified with political pragmatism and the growing presence of the private sector in the party.[40] This interpretation does not, however, help us understand the PAN's rise in Guanajuato. For example, as governor, Carlos Medina combined a private-sector vision of economic development with policy elements characteristic of community action. His discourse focused on the idea of co-responsibility between society and the state, citizen participation, and the conviction

---

[37] Author interview with Vicente Fox, May 1995, León, Guanajuato.

[38] The San Ángel Group was formed during the political tumult of 1994. It brought together intellectuals and a range of political leaders who were committed to democratizing Mexico. Among its participants were Lorenzo Meyer, a well-known historian and political commentator; Elba Esther Gordillo, leader of the National Education Workers' Union (SNTE); Mexico City councilman Demetrio Sodi; Manuel Camacho Solís, former mayor of Mexico City; and Vicente Fox.

[39] Fox's differences with the PAN's national president, Carlos Castillo Peraza, are well known. He also clashed with Diego Fernández de Cevallos, the party's 1994 presidential candidate. Among the main origins of these disputes were the PAN leadership's support for the deal resolving the disputed 1991 gubernatorial election and early rivalries over the PAN's year 2000 presidential nomination.

[40] Carlos Arriola (1994) notes that the term *neopanismo* was widely used after the PAN's 1975 crisis to describe new elements within the party who were openly dismissive of traditional doctrines and who advocated using language and techniques associated with commercial advertising. The *neopanista* current was joined by former leaders of business groups and so-called intermediate organizations, including Desarrollo Humano Integral, A.C. Manuel J. Clouthier was considered the prototypical *neopanista*.

that governmental authority should be devoted to public service. Medina insisted on his right to express publicly his religious faith—mentioning God on every occasion he considered it appropriate—and denounced as hypocrites those who claimed to separate their public and private lives. He blended both the language and practices particular to *panista* and Catholic Church doctrine and those that might be considered closer to the modernizing ideology of the Mexican business class.

Fox cannot be classified as a doctrinaire *panista*. Nor does he, strictly speaking, represent *neopanismo*. Rather, he blends charisma, the capacity to adapt and use the PAN's ethos (*mística*) as the situation requires, and a private-sector style that he presents as a means of professionalizing and making more efficient governmental administration and the exercise of political power. Fox's approach is more pluralistic and less tied to Catholicism than was Medina's. He has, moreover, utilized Guanajuato's past as the ethical foundation for his own way of conducting public affairs. Governor Fox's frequent references to *guanajuatenses* as men who have fought for liberty and against centralized political power can be interpreted in this vein. The same can be said for the text he read publicly on the day he was inaugurated as governor: it was the introduction to the state's constitution of 1826, a historical document that joined praise for virtue and honesty in public office with federalist declarations of state sovereignty and respect for the separation of powers.

The Elections of 1997 and 2000: Generalizing the Model

The 1997 and 2000 elections occurred in a context that differed markedly from that which characterized the preceding ones. With a *panista* government consolidated in the state, in 1997 the PAN managed to recover significantly from the losses it suffered in 1994. And in 2000, it expanded its dominance over municipal government throughout the width and breadth of the state.

In 1997, the PAN triumphed in twenty of the twenty-seven municipalities won by the opposition. It once again dominated in the municipalities located in the state's heavily populated industrial corridor, and in León a well-known party militant with real estate interests in the city, Jorge Carlos Obregón, came to power. Overall, the PAN won 44.3 percent of the vote, equaling its performance in the 1991 municipal elections and exceeding by nearly 10 percentage points its 1994 vote total (table 7.1).

The PAN also took first place in the 1997 state legislative elections, winning 43.6 percent of the valid vote, compared to 33.7 percent for the PRI and 13.5 percent for the PRD (table 7.3). The new composition of the legislature (sixteen deputies for the PAN, twelve for the PRI, five for the PRD, and three for other parties) opened a new era for the PAN in state government. At last, a *panista* governor faced both a legislature in which his own party held a majority and a significant number of *panista* municipal presidents.

The July 2, 2000, general elections were most notable for the national euphoria that accompanied an opposition candidate's winning of the presidency by electoral means. In Guanajuato, however, two additional elements made this an especially important moment. The first was the coincidence of federal and state elections that year, and the second was the background of the PAN's presidential candidate, which once again identified Guanajuato in the eyes of the nation as a laboratory for constructing the possibility of political alternation at the national level.

In July 2000, the PAN in Guanajuato triumphed overwhelmingly in all six elections held there: three federal elections (for president and for the federal Chamber of Deputies and Senate) and three state-level contests (for governor, the state legislature, and city councils). With these outcomes, the party's political dominance in the state was fully ratified. As a result, one can affirm that Guanajuato is the most *panista* state in the country, with the party controlling the governorship, a majority of seats in the state legislature, and most of the state's municipal governments. Moreover, the Guanajuato PAN's particular style of governance began to have an impact at the national level even before Fox formally assumed the presidency.

Vicente Fox won an extremely high 62.5 percent of the valid vote in his native state (table 7.4). Indeed, he won in each and every one of the state's electoral districts. In León, approximately seven of every ten voters backed his candidacy, and in the state's other districts Fox received over 50 percent of the valid vote. The PAN also won the federal Senate seat that was up for election (defeating the PRI by a 2:1 majority), and it triumphed in elections to choose the state's representatives in the federal Chamber of Deputies.

At the local level, the 2000 results were a true debacle for the PRI. The party only won in fourteen municipalities, the poorest and least populous areas in the state.[41] The PAN, in contrast, received more than 50 percent of the total municipal vote and won a majority in twenty-eight municipalities, including those in Guanajuato's industrial corridor. Subtracting the 8.5 percent of the population governed by the PRD (including the state capital), this means that the PAN governs 81.0 percent of the state's population. Perhaps equally important, the PAN won

---

[41] The PRI's fourteen municipalities together accounted for only 10.5 percent of the state's population.

its municipal victories by substantial margins (70 percent of the total valid vote in León and over 50 percent in nine other cities).

The governorship went to Juan Carlos Romero Hicks, who resigned his position as rector of the Universidad de Guanajuato to become the PAN candidate. Despite the fact that Fox openly supported him, Romero Hicks's candidacy irritated those sectors within the PAN that preferred Eliseo Martínez, a footwear industry executive and former municipal president of León. Romero Hicks received 56.7 percent of the vote statewide (table 7.2).[42]

We can conclude, then, that during the 1997–2000 period Guanajuato experienced party alternation in all spheres of political power. The difficult experience of 1991—an opposition state governor installed as the result of high-level political negotiations, an imposed secretary of government in the state executive branch, and forced cohabitation with a PRI legislative majority bent on revenge—was left far behind. During this three-year period, the PAN governed the state with all the legitimacy that resulted from its sizable electoral victories, triumphs achieved in transparent and highly credible electoral processes. In December 2000, a third consecutive PAN governor came to power. Chosen by more than half of the electorate, he administers a territory in which eight of every ten inhabitants also live in a municipality governed by a mayor from the same party. Moreover, Romero Hicks governs in conjunction with a state legislature in which the PAN holds a majority and in which the next largest party (the PRI) has been significantly diminished. And not least, all this occurs in a context of party alternation in power at the national level.

THE GOVERNORSHIP OF VICENTE FOX: REENGINEERING POWER

Vicente Fox Quesada began his term as the elected governor of Guanajuato on June 26, 1995. On August 8, 1999, he took a formal leave of office in order to run for the Mexican presidency. He was succeeded by the state's secretary of government, Ramón Martín Huerta, whom the state legislature chose as interim governor for the period ending September 26, 2000. On that day, he was succeeded by the newly elected *panista* governor Juan Carlos Romero Hicks.

Governor Fox constituted his cabinet by selecting among more than four hundred candidates, a process through which some observers thought Fox sought to distance himself from the PAN. His cabinet included individuals with considerable business experience (including

---

[42] The PAN won a similar proportion of the vote in the state legislative elections; see table 7.3.

some people who owned their own firms) and a number of young economists or public administration experts educated in private universities, especially the ITESM. Several had also done graduate work in English-speaking countries.

Fox said that, in assembling his team, his "golden rule was that every member of my team had to be an expert in his field" (Fox Quesada 1999a: 101). On the whole, however, cabinet members were primarily characterized by business and financial administration backgrounds, even people in positions with little connection to such matters. The state's secretary of education, for example, was someone with extensive experience in national and foreign companies and in private educational institutions. His appointment therefore aroused considerable antipathy in the public educational system.[43]

Fox's gubernatorial administration can be characterized as essentially businesslike in three distinct but related ways. First, Fox's election represented the culmination of powerful economic groups' efforts to use the PAN to achieve state-level power. Second, the administration's priorities, as articulated in different plans and programs, were defined in terms of political and social development criteria closest to those advocated by the economically powerful, especially where the promotion of employment-generating national and foreign private-sector investment was concerned. As previously noted, these goals were met in part by incorporating into the governor's cabinet a number of individuals with business backgrounds. Third, the administration adopted a style and work methods copied from the private sector, including the use of applied reengineering concepts to governmental administration.

Although there was some degree of continuity between the Medina and Fox administrations, there were also marked differences in governing style. Both administrations emphasized the reorganization of state government, the incorporation of business approaches, and sound public finances. Nonetheless, Medina was clearly more focused on municipal-level issues than Fox, and as governor he adopted a less hierarchical style with municipalities and the citizenry in general (Rionda

---

[43] The secretary of education, Fernando Rivera Barroso, was widely criticized in Guanajuato and nationally for distributing a pamphlet he had written titled "How One Learns in Guanajuato" ("Así se educa en Guanajuato"), which advocated openly authoritarian teaching methods. Despite the criticism, Fox retained Rivera Barroso in his post.

Rivera Barroso had been adviser to the Confederación Nacional de Escuelas Particulares (National Confederation of Private Schools) and to various parents' associations, coordinator of the Comité Coordinador de la Educación Privada (Private Education Coordinating Committee), and adviser to the International Office of Catholic Education, based in Brussels. For more information on his background, see www.guanajuato.gob.mx.

1998). In contrast, Fox's "reengineering" was planned and applied by experts who took direct responsibility for the administrative design and implementation of Fox's programs (focused principally on economic development, rule of law, educational transformation, social development, and good government) in each affected government agency.[44]

During the Fox administration, it was chief of staff Ramón Muñoz Gutiérrez who was the principal proponent of "reengineering" public administration via business methods in order to achieve efficiency and quality of service (see Muñoz Gutiérrez 1999). He presented the reengineering model, which has been developed as a focus of business administration, as "a structural and cultural movement … that seeks to introduce concepts, values, and practices that orient service exclusively to the benefit of the 'client' (users, taxpayers, or citizens)." The model proposes aligning government officials and public employees around a common purpose and using innovative, cutting-edge strategies to "redesign the most important overall governmental processes" so as to achieve results that add value to clients, in this case the inhabitants of Guanajuato (Muñoz Gutiérrez 1999: 35). The concept of "value added" derives from the idea that governments are obliged to generate "social profits," which are produced when the inputs that government receives from society are transformed into services and other benefits for the population.[45]

According to Muñoz Gutiérrez, the principal clients are those who use public services provided by the state government, municipal governments, the state legislature, and public employees. In each area, Muñoz Gutiérrez and his associates advocated the adoption of "total quality management" as a strategy for promoting change. In this vein, the Fox administration created the Guanajuato Institute for Total Quality, with both public- and private-sector membership, and it established the Guanajuato Prize for Quality, which was awarded to different government agencies according to the rules established for the ISO 9002 designation in international trade.[46]

---

[44] Government administration was reorganized in conformance with these five priority areas. Administrative advisers developed guidelines for everything from recruitment of public employees, to specific projects and processes, to the evaluation of decisions, to the measurement of quality, to leadership development. See, for example, www.guanajuato.gob.mx/manualdg.nsf/normatividad.

[45] For more details, see Muñoz Gutiérrez 1999: 36, 65, 185, 249–50.

[46] The International Organization for Standardization, based in Geneva, uses the label "ISO" (derived from the Greek work *Isos*, meaning "equality") to denote quality. It has 118 member countries, and its objectives are to develop and promote international norms that satisfy client-supplier requirements.

The Fox administration established the Guanajuato Prize for Quality as part of its efforts to make Guanajuato "a total quality state." The state government certi-

In the economic sphere, one of the Fox administration's principal goals was to attract increased investment in order to combat unemployment in the state and improve the population's standard of living. The administration emphasized both employment in public works, which provided a minimum income for the poor, and micro-credits for informal-sector businesses administered via revolving credit funds. At the same time, the government sought to attract significant new amounts of foreign investment. Toward this end, it established four commercial offices in the United States to promote exports and bring foreign investment to Guanajuato. During the first three years of the Fox administration, the number of exporting companies more than doubled, and the state attracted almost US$1.4 billion in investment.[47]

Nevertheless, the goal of generating employment and higher incomes via foreign investment was difficult to achieve. Some indicators of marginality (for instance, infant mortality and life expectancy at birth) did improve during Fox's term as governor. Yet poverty remains a very serious problem in Guanajuato. Similarly, the extremely high rate of emigration to the United States indicates that party alternation in power did not resolve all of the state's socioeconomic problems.[48]

During the Fox administration, then, Guanajuato experienced a form of "privatized" politics. The term "client" took on a very different meaning than it traditionally had carried in Mexican politics, but one that was still at odds with the concept of people as citizens. Residents of the state became consumers whose needs for services were to be satisfied so that they would again choose the same partisan option. And based on the July 2, 2000, election results in the state, the PAN achieved its goal in this regard. On the basis of its favorable recent performance in office, the consumer-citizen again selected the PAN option. Only time will tell whether the idea of citizenship mediated by consumption has triumphed over a citizenry capable of debating and constructing alternative forms of local development.

---

fied fifty-two quality processes in twenty-eight different agencies. Five government agencies received ISO 9002 recognition. See the press release issued by Ramón Martín Huerta on behalf of the governor of Guanajuato, September 11, 2000, at www.guanajuato.gob.mx.

[47] According to Fox (1999a: 138), the number of exporting firms rose from 360 to 720 between 1995 and 1998, and the value of exports grew by 160 percent over this same period.

[48] According to the Guanajuato Population Council, in 1996 the state had the sixth highest rate of infant mortality in Mexico, and it contributed 9 percent of the country's emigrants. See www.guanajuato.gob.mx/coespo/población.htm.

PARTY ALTERNATION AT THE NATIONAL LEVEL: THE GENERALIZATION OF THE GUANAJUATO MODEL?

On July 2, 2000, after more than seventy years of PRI hegemony, multiple factors combined to make Vicente Fox the first opposition party president of Mexico. A full analysis of this outcome has not yet been undertaken; with somewhat greater distance from the event, it will certainly be necessary to reflect carefully on the complexity and magnitude of this historic departure. Nevertheless, the "Guanajuato model" may offer some preliminary indications of what one might expect from Fox's term as president.

Obviously, given the greater heterogeneity and complexity of Mexico as a whole, it is not possible to project mechanically the Guanajuato experience onto the Fox presidency. However, his experience as governor does shed light on President Fox's conceptions of politics, power, and public administration and on his personal style of rule. It is unlikely, for example, that Fox's discursive style will differ very dramatically from that which he employed as governor. Such topics as public investment to achieve better standards of living, education as the engine of development, and good government have been frequently emphasized by President Fox and his associates. His cabinet also includes a high proportion of individuals with administrative experience in the private sector.

Indeed, early indications pointed clearly to significant continuities between the agenda Fox pursued in Guanajuato and the approaches he is likely to follow as president. For example, in a public forum organized by the magazine *Nexos* in April 1999, Fox offered the Mexican electorate essentially the same program he had undertaken as governor of Guanajuato: the reorganization of public administration to make government more flexible, efficient, and productive in dealing with citizens' demands; making education the country's first priority because of its demonstrated effectiveness in advancing the overall process of socioeconomic development; and reorienting economic policy (including tax policy) to promote investment, technological development, and the creation of new businesses (Fox Quesada 1999b). Similarly, the transition team that Fox assembled after July 2000 to prepare his administration's programmatic agenda featured a number of his closest advisers and collaborators in Guanajuato.

However, President Fox's challenges as president will differ from those he faced in Guanajuato not only in scale but also in kind. He will, therefore, be compelled to consider new approaches, and his administration will also require the involvement of people with a different professional profile. In this sense, it was significant that Porfirio Muñoz Ledo initially had responsibility for coordinating discussions on reform of the Mexican state.[49] It was also important that Fox quickly initiated a dialogue with Mexico's artistic and intellectual community as part of his design of new cultural policies.

In terms of the specific policies that Fox is likely to pursue as president, it is important to note that he will operate under significant economic constraints (the international price of oil, the balance-of-payments situation, the level of public-sector debt, and so forth) and political pressures (including the reactions of major unions, political parties, and communications media). That said, however, it is highly likely that, despite the publicity given to Fox's promises of achieving a 7 percent economic growth rate and increased social spending, there will be considerable continuity in the market-oriented economic model Mexico has adopted since the late 1980s (Álvarez Béjar 2000). He will certainly emphasize privatization, deregulation, and market opening, and he is likely to seek to open to private investment such strategic economic sectors as electrical power generation and secondary petrochemicals. Moreover, President Fox may wish to provide additional incentives to attract foreign capital (perhaps including further restrictions on labor rights), and he can be expected to promote credit policies that support small and midsize enterprises and favor that part of the population living in extreme poverty.

If as a candidate Fox knew how to appeal to people as active and intelligent citizens capable of realizing the task of "getting the PRI out the presidency," then as president it is probable that he will conceive of people as service users or customers who should have their expectations met. However, in a country with a significant proportion of poor people, the problem will be which citizen expectations can be met, and when. In other words, one of President Fox's greatest challenges will be how to reconcile the expectations of millions of Mexicans who anticipate an improvement in their standard of living, in the context of an economic model that tends to devalue social rights and convert them into goods that are only accessible to those who have sufficient financial resources.

One might believe that Mexico under President Fox will be more democratic, because one can anticipate an increased role for the federal legislature in national affairs, a relative decline in the importance of the presidency, and more equitable and transparent relations between the

---

[49] In the course of a long political career, Muñoz Ledo had previously served as secretary of labor and social welfare (1972–1975), president of the Institutional Revolutionary Party (1975–1976), secretary of public education (1976–1977), and Mexico's ambassador to the United Nations (1979–1985). He was one of the founders of the Corriente Democrática (Democratic Current) within the PRI in 1986, and he went on to help found the PRD. Muñoz Ledo was the presidential candidate of the Authentic Party of the Mexican Revolution (PARM) in 2000, but he resigned that nomination to back Vicente Fox's presidential candidacy.

principal political actors, including the executive and legislative branches, state and local governments, political parties, and civil society. But, taking a broader view of democracy that encompasses social equality and mechanisms that permit real public participation in decision making, there are important reasons for concluding that Fox's election as president will not in and of itself make the country more democratic. In other words, more political democracy does not necessarily ensure greater economic or social democracy. There is an irreconcilable contradiction between continuing an economic model that produces social exclusion and unprecedented poverty, and Fox's oft-repeated promises of inclusion, greater equality, and balanced socioeconomic development. Thus there is a significant contradiction between promoting the immediate interests of economically powerful interests—groups with which Fox shares important objectives and views—and adopting policies that recognize as social rights (not commodities) such essential human needs as work, housing, food, health care, and education.

Carlos Fazio (2000) has argued that "we are witnessing the beginning of a process of neo-oligarchic regression, in the sense that propertied groups will now exercise their dominance directly. Even if they do so through the state apparatus, these elements are replacing a part of the elite government bureaucracy and eliminating the old mediating and conciliating roles previously exercised by the PRI 'political class.'" It is possible, however, that millions of voters do not accept this mode of domination; that they deposited in Vicente Fox their hopes for change, particularly their aspirations for greater social equality and less corruption; and that they might mobilize themselves to hold Fox accountable for the promises of social improvement that he made throughout the course of his presidential campaign. It is possible, moreover, that the passage from a neoliberal authoritarian regime to a neoliberal democratic order might provide Fox with the opportunity to assume the position of a true statesman capable of distinguishing between private benefit and the welfare of the majority, between short-term business and the national project. That will depend upon his capacity to recognize the many Mexicos that exist within the national territory and rescue them from ruin, before seeking to homogenize them in a dubious strategy of employment creation based on the *maquiladora* (in-bond processing) model characteristic of Mexico's northern borderlands.

CONCLUSION

Beyond their evident local importance, political developments in Guanajuato during the 1990s are a key basis for understanding recent transformations in Mexican politics. They represent an important source of political capital for the PAN, the result of a national and local strategy focused on making the electoral process work. Developments in Guanajuato also represent a necessary point of departure for the PAN's efforts to define its course in coming years.

The PAN's victories in Guanajuato and its rise to power in the state also constitute a fertile field for social research and political analysis. In addition to the fascinating complexity of local events during the late 1980s and the 1990s, the Guanajuato experience raises a host of significant political and social issues whose medium- and long-term consequences are still unknown. In the short term, competitive elections and alternation in power at the state level indicate an important shift in the role of elections, in the significance of the vote in some areas of Mexico, in relations between state and national governmental authorities, and in the importance of politics itself.

In states such as Guanajuato, elections now serve their original function. They are a vehicle through which social actors can choose among different political options, making a free choice about who will represent and govern them. Voting reflects a rationality that was previously unknown: votes can maintain a party in government when society approves of its conduct in office, or votes can punish the incumbent party by withdrawing society's support and, therefore, its ability to attain or remain in power. The idea of good government, then, ceases to be just a rhetorical device and an ideal, becoming in common practice citizens' summary judgment concerning the adequacy or inadequacy of the political options before them.

Under these new political conditions, the resolution of citizens' demands—which for many years was the PRI–led regime's privileged means of building the social alliances that sustained its power— becomes a matter of enormous complexity. For the PAN, it is undoubtedly a problem that is not completely resolved.

Alternation in power in Guanajuato and elsewhere also raises the core issue of reformulating the relationship between state and federal governmental authorities. The increasingly common phenomenon of opposition parties governing states and municipalities not only brings about a change in the way of conducting public affairs at the local level, but, especially in the wake of Vicente Fox's presidential victory in July 2000, it also alters partisan competition at the national level and the role that the federal government plays in different states. The PAN's struggle to gain autonomy in the use of public resources has both a practical political and a symbolic importance. State governments know that only by gaining fiscal autonomy can they choose strategies of governance that will give them the capacity for political self-determination, allowing them to forge social alliances and respond effectively to citizens' demands.

We conclude with the hypothesis that political change at the state level modifies not only the space occupied by politics (its outlines, limits, and parameters) but the nature of politics itself. In principle, politics no longer is a sphere isolated from daily life. It becomes a field defined, via the vote, by citizen pressures, demands for responses to immediate needs, and political debate. Public institutions lose their centrality, giving way to a still unconcluded reaccommodation in the relations between state and society.

REFERENCES

Álvarez Béjar, Alejandro. 2000. "México 2000: ¿la transición política soñada?" *Memoria* 138 (August).

A.M. (León, Guanajuato). 1983. "Lamenta dirigente estatal del PRI postura de CM ante alcaldes," May 8.

———. 1992a. "Obispo de León invitará al Papa a visitar el Cubilete," February 17.

———. 1992b. "Trabajo conjunto entre obispo-municipio en la solución de problemas sociales," March 7.

———. 1992c. "Continúan tomadas dos presidencias municipales," January 6.

———. 1993a. "Califica obispo el informe de Eliseo como un avance en la organización," December 11.

———. 1993b. "Integran frente contra el fascismo vs. CMP," May 11.

———. 1994a. "Acusan diputados priístas al CEDEM de violar la autonomía municipal," December 14.

———. 1994b. "Descontento," December 15.

———. 1994c. "Renuncia priísta al triunfo," December 8.

———. 1994d. "Asumirá Gasca alcaldía de Juventino Rosas," December 9.

———. 1994e. "Defenderá el PRD hasta sus últimas consecuencias el triunfo en Romita," December 7.

———. 1994f. "Protestan contra Marmolejo," December 26.

———. 1994g. "Plantón del FASACI," December 28.

———. 1994h. "Avisan tomarán palacio en Salamanca," December 30.

———. 1995a. "De pleito Medina y Labastida," March 28.

———. 1995b. "No voy a renunciar pues 30 personas no son todo el pueblo," January 3.

———. 1995c. "Retoman presidencia municipal de Uriangato," February 10.

———. 1995d. "Toma PRD alcaldía," December 28.

———. 1995e. "Levantan plantón en Romita, acuerdan gobierno plural," March 14.

———. 1995f. "Mantiene PRD toma de presidencia en Valle," January 3.

———. 1995g. "Queremos justicia, que no haya fraude," January 4.

———. 1995h. "Dispuesto al diálogo edil de Doctor Mora," January 3.

———. 1995i. "Designan presidente interino en Xichú," January 4.

———. 1995j. "Demandan a Medina restablecer el orden constitucional en Xichú," January 10.

———. 1995k. "Desalojan a perredistas," January 20.

————. 1995l. "Pide Rocha intervención de fuerzas: Medina," January 21.

————. 1995m. "Podría Fox apoyar a uriangatenses contra alcalde Ramón Pérez," January 20.

————. 1995n. "Acusa alcalde de Uriangato a Medina de crear ingobernabilidad," February 10.

————. 1995o. "Hay 100 mil personas desempleadas," March 9.

————. 1995p. "Panistas y pedemistas anuncian cierre de oficinas de Hacienda; protestan contra IVA," April 1.

————. 1995q. "Firman hoy empresarios acuerdo de emergencia," January 13.

————. 1995r. "Entrevista Zedillo-Medina," January 23.

————. 1995s. "Si las elecciones fueran hoy, ganaría Fox," special section, March 28.

————. 1995t. "Impiden perredistas acceso a presidencia al alcalde de Romita," February 14.

Arrache Hernández, Ernesto. n.d. "La reforma política en Guanajuato." León: Universidad Iberoamericana–León.

Arreola, Álvaro. 1985. "Elecciones municipales." In *Las elecciones en México: evolución y perspectivas*, edited by Pablo González Casanova. Mexico City: Siglo Veintiuno.

Arriola, Carlos. 1994. *Ensayos sobre el PAN*. Mexico City: Miguel Ángel Porrúa.

Blancarte, Roberto. 1992. "Gobernador católico en estado laico," *La Jornada*, February 3.

Calderón, Enrique, and Daniel Cazés. 1996. *Las elecciones presidenciales de 1994*. Mexico City: Centro de Investigaciones Interdisciplinarias en Ciencias y Humanidades, Universidad Nacional Autónoma de México.

Camacho, Oscar, and Salvador Contreras. 1993. "Del mal menor se han derivado veinte tormentas mayores," *La Jornada*, August 10.

Campbell, Hugh. 1976. *La derecha radical en México, 1929–1949*. Mexico City: Sep-Setentas.

Cuéllar, Arnoldo. 1985a. "El estreno del sexenio," *Pretextos* 1 (1): 10–15.

————. 1985b. "El estilo personal de criticar," *Pretextos* 1 (2): 9–10.

El Sol de León. 1977. "El PAN se integra a la administración de León," January 11.

Escalante, Fernando. 1995. "Clientelismo y ciudadanía en México: apuntes sobre la conceptualización de las formas de acción política," *Análisis Político* 26 (September–December).

Fazio, Carlos. 2000. "En gestación, un nuevo poder: la meta, el Estado empresarial," *La Jornada*, August 26.

Fox Quesada, Vicente. 1999a. *Vicente Fox a Los Pinos: recuerdo autobiográfico y político*. Mexico City: Océano.

————. 1999b. "Reingeniería de la administración pública," *Nexos* 256 (April).

Gill, Mario. 1962. *Sinarquismo. origen y esencia*. Mexico City. Olín.

Gobierno del Estado de Guanajuato. 1946. "Al frente de la autoridad está Carlos Obregón," February 23.

————. 1991. *Guanajuato en la voz de sus gobernadores, 1917–1991*. 3 vols. Guanajuato: Gobierno del Estado.

————. 1994. *Reforma política en Guanajuato: compromiso cumplido*. Guanajuato: Talleres Gráficos del Estado de Guanajuato.

INEGI (Instituto Nacional de Estadística, Geografía e Informática). 2000. *XII Censo Nacional de Población y Vivienda.*

La Jornada. 1993. "Si fallara Medina, fracasaría quien lo impuso: PRD," August 13.

———. 1995. "Halla cerrada la alcaldía de Xichú, Guanajuato, el edil Amado Rivera," February 20.

Lechner, Norbert. 1995. "Por qué la política ya no es lo que fue," *Nexos* 216 (December).

Ling Altamirano, Ricardo Alfredo. 1992. *Vamos por Guanajuato.* Mexico: Author's edition.

Meyer, Jean. 1979. *El sinarquismo: ¿un fascismo mexicano?* Mexico City: Joaquín Mortiz.

———. 1980. *La Cristiada.* 3 vols. 7th ed. Mexico City: Siglo Veintiuno.

Muñoz Gutiérrez, Ramón. 1999. *Pasión por un buen gobierno: administración por calidad en el gobierno de Vicente Fox.* 2d ed. Mexico City: Aldea Global Ediciones.

Olivera Sedano, Alicia. 1987. *Aspectos del conflicto religioso de 1926 a 1929: sus antecedentes y consecuencias.* Colección Cien de México. Mexico City: Secretaría de Educación Pública.

Ortiz García, Martín. 1991. "¿Quién gobierna en León?" In *Dos ensayos sobre política en Guanajuato*, by Martín Ortiz García. León: Universidad Iberoamericana–León.

Pérez, Haydee. 1995. "Encuesta aplicada a mil 100 electores en 29 municipios," *A.M.*, May 18.

Rionda, Luis Miguel. 1995a. "Cambio político en Guanajuato: la primera experiencia bipartidista en México, 1991–1995." Paper presented at the international congress of the Latin American Studies Association, September.

———. 1995b. "Elecciones locales en Guanajuato, 1994–1995: el péndulo electoral." Paper presented at the VII Encuentro Nacional de Investigadores en Estudios Electorales, Santa Cruz, Tlaxcala.

———. 1996a. *Enrique Fernández Martínez: un gobernador de la vorágine.* Guanajuato: LVI Legislatura del H. Congreso del Estado de Guanajuato.

———. 1996b. "El voto del hartazgo: las elecciones de gobernador en Guanajuato," *El Cotidiano* 75 (March–April): 25–33.

———. 1998. "Política, alternancia y gestión administrativa en Guanajuato, México, 1920–1988." Paper presented at the international congress of the Latin American Studies Association, September.

———. n.d. "La democracia inducida: cambio político y lucha partidista en Guanajuato." Unpublished paper.

Serrano, Pablo. 1992. *La batalla del espíritu: el movimiento sinarquista en el Bajío, 1923–1951.* 2 vols. Mexico City: Consejo Nacional para la Cultura y las Artes.

Valencia García, Guadalupe. 1986. "La reforma política en Guanajuato." Master's thesis, Instituto de Investigaciones Dr. José Ma. Luis Mora.

———. 1994. "Las elecciones locales de 1991 en Guanajuato." In *Elecciones con alternativas: algunas experiencias en la República Mexicana*, edited by Jorge Alonso and Jaime Tamayo. Mexico City: Centro de Investigaciones Interdisciplinarias en Ciencias y Humanidades, Universidad Nacional Autónoma de México.

———. 1995. "La administración panista del municipio de León, Guanajuato." In *La tarea de gobernar: gobiernos locales y demandas ciudadanas*, edited by Alicia Ziccardi. Mexico City: Miguel Ángel Porrúa.

8

The PAN in Yucatán: An Ascendant Political Option

Carlos R. Menéndez Losa

Understanding the recent development of the National Action Party (PAN) in Yucatán requires a balanced appraisal of its distinctive characteristics and the economic, political, social, and civic context surrounding it. This essay examines certain key aspects of political life in Yucatán in historical context, major actors in state politics and the specific role of the PAN, and the party's recent electoral performance in the state.

POLITICS IN YUCATÁN

The Economic and Social Context

Given the fragility of the state's economy and its limited productive capacity, the federal government has had a greater weight in Yucatán than in many other parts of Mexico. Indeed, federal monies have typically represented more than 90 percent of public-sector expenditures in the state.[1] The central government has, historically, translated this economic assistance into political influence.

Yucatán's heavy financial dependence on the federal government is one consequence of a highly unequal development process. In this regard, the state clearly represents the long-term national tendency toward greater socioeconomic inequality. Trends in Yucatán since the debt crisis of the early 1980s have been especially unfavorable, with declining income levels for the popular classes and an increased concentration of wealth.

Translated by Kevin J. Middlebrook.

[1] Author interview with Governor Víctor Manzanilla Schaffer, cited in Menéndez Losa 1988: 373.

In the view of some analysts, the factors most responsible for long-term unequal development in the state include: inefficiencies associated with the application of the ejido land tenure system in henequen-producing areas, especially production inefficiencies resulting from governmental control, corruption, and complicity by private-sector intermediaries; the proliferation of such social problems as alcoholism and drug addiction; low productivity levels in corn farming, particularly because of a lack of technological innovation; labor out-migration to tourist areas in neighboring states; lack of adequate infrastructure; and excessive political control over economic activities.[2] By the 1990s, economic wealth in Yucatán was highly concentrated. More and more rural workers abandoned the countryside, and productive activities were increasingly centered in the state capital, Mérida, thus placing most of the state's communities in an increasingly marginal position.

Two other elements also constitute important background characteristics of the state's politics. First, different groups' constant struggles for power within the Institutional Revolutionary Party (PRI) have gradually undermined the party's historic predominance in Yucatán. Second, because the average proportion of the citizenry in both rural and urban areas that reads a newspaper and stays informed about public affairs is much higher in Yucatán than in other regions of Mexico,[3] greater political and civic participation is possible. In fact, in recent years there has been increasingly broad participation in public life. This development in part reflects the presence in the state of newspapers that foment debate and public consciousness.

Yucatecan society is, then, especially active in civic and political terms, and important elements of civil society are increasingly autonomous of governmental power. As a consequence, those who hold political power are obligated to maintain channels of communication with citizens and address their principal demands. At the same time, however, the political class grouped within the local PRI has remained rigid and, throughout the 1990s, subject to orders issued by the federal government.

The Recent Political Past

An overview of Yucatecan history during the twentieth century would identify several core characteristics of state politics. These included:

---

[2] Author interview with Freddy Poot Sosa, then state congressman and president of the Mexican Socialist Party's (PMS) state executive committee, cited in Menéndez Losa 1988: 413.

[3] Author interview with Víctor Manzanilla Schaffer, cited in Menéndez Losa 1988: 373.

political centralism and economic dependence on the federal government; constant grievances voiced by the local population and groups opposed to the established regime about electoral frauds committed by the "official" PRI; close ties between those who controlled political power and dominant economic groups, which allied themselves with whichever political group appeared most likely to increase their wealth; government-led efforts to discourage citizen participation and civic organization; extensive public works projects when it was necessary to mobilize support for "official" candidates; and intervention by the federal government in the state's political life.

In the late 1960s, there was an increase in political participation and civic organization, especially in Mérida. However, this experience came to an end in 1969 with the electoral fraud committed against PAN gubernatorial candidate Víctor Correa Rachó (mayor of Mérida between 1967 and 1969) and the imposition of PRI candidate Carlos Loret de Mola Mediz as governor. The PAN in particular and the political opposition in general were repressed. During the Loret de Mola administration, the federal government was compelled to devote significant resources (including large-scale infrastructure projects throughout the state) to Yucatán in an effort to alleviate the popular discontent produced by electoral fraud. As a result, many entrepreneurs who had previously opposed the PRI and backed Correa Rachó came to terms with the Loret de Mola government.[4]

In subsequent years, as a consequence of the predominance of public spending over an incipient consumer goods industry, most economic growth in the state came in the commercial sector and in services. Entrepreneurs devoted to cattle raising and agroindustrial activities also displaced previously dominant groups whose power had been rooted in the henequen industry.

Beginning in 1984, during the governorship of General Graciliano Alpuche Pinzón (whom the central government had also placed in power), political conflicts in the state reached a crisis level. Confrontations between different elements within the state-level PRI (factions identified with former governors Carlos Loret de Mola Mediz, Francisco Epigmenio Luna Kan, and Víctor Cervera Pacheco and with Governor Alpuche Pinzón) intensified. At the same time, forces allied with Governor Alpuche Pinzón attempted to take control of both the state-level PRI and the Liga de Comunidades Agrarias (League of Agrarian Communities, an affiliate of the PRI–aligned National Peasants' Confederation, CNC). These conflicts occurred at a time when the Yucatecan countryside was more explosive than usual because of the effects of the post–1982 Mexican debt crisis and cutbacks in federal government

---

[4] See various issues of *Diario de Yucatán*, November 1969.

investments. As social conflicts among peasant organizations became more severe, the federal government was compelled to increase its financial contributions to the state by some 70 percent. Similarly, the government of President Miguel de la Madrid Hurtado (1982–1988) had to find ways to alleviate the problems associated with the imposition of General Alpuche Pinzón as governor.

In February 1984, in a political context characterized by intense struggles within the local PRI establishment and a weakening of federal government support, Mexico City authorities forced Governor Alpuche Pinzón to petition the state legislature for a "temporary" leave of absence. The replacement named to complete his term in office (1982–1988) was Víctor Cervera Pacheco. Cervera Pacheco had previously been a student leader, mayor of Mérida, and an agrarian leader.

Cervera Pacheco's rise to state-level office marked a radical change in relations among different sectors of Yucatecan society. The private sector, satisfied with the federal government's substantially increased financial support for the state, renewed its historic alliance with the state government and promised to make greater efforts to expand economic production. Rival political groups (including followers of former governors Loret de Mola and Luna Kan) also sought an accommodation with the new administration, completely aligning themselves with Cervera Pacheco's policies. However, like the preceding Loret de Mola administration, Cervera Pacheco's government strongly repressed any sign of political opposition.

In November 1987, at the end of the controversial Cervera Pacheco administration, former gubernatorial aspirant and PRI senator Víctor Manzanilla Schaffer won new elections for governor. The electoral process was characterized by a high rate of voter abstention and substantial fraud, a situation abetted by the state's outmoded and inegalitarian electoral code.[5] These factors, combined with the effects of Mexico's deepening economic crisis and PAN candidate Manuel J. Clouthier's 1988 presidential campaign in the state, contributed to the rebirth of political and civic activism (especially in Mérida) and weakened Manzanilla Schaffer's administration.

As a result, the PAN's strength in state politics began to grow (see table 8.1). In the 1990 legislative and municipal elections, although the PRI out-polled the PAN by 212,095 to 99,032 votes at the state level, the PAN won control of the state's capital for the first time in twenty-three years. In a decision that would later cost him the governorship, Governor Manzanilla Schaffer overruled opposition from the PRI's state leadership and recognized the victory of PAN federal deputy Ana Rosa

---

[5] For examples of these problems, see various articles in *Diario de Yucatán* published during November and December 1987.

Payán Cervera as municipal president of Mérida. This outcome accentuated tensions within the state-level PRI.

In early 1991, Governor Manzanilla Schaffer was, like his immediate predecessor, compelled for "personal reasons" to seek a "temporary" leave of absence. He was the victim of the inefficiencies that characterized his administration and growing pressures from hard-line elements within his own party.

Table 8.1. **Selected State and Federal Election Results in Yucatán by Party, 1967–1995**

	PAN	PRI	FDN/PRD[1]	Others[2]
1967 (state legislature)	28,498	145,998		
1969 (gubernatorial)	14,975	227,340		
1970 (presidential)	34,196	189,118		
1973 (federal legislative)	19,875	246,375		
1981 (gubernatorial)	36,649	170,986		
1982 (presidential)	57,760	255,863		
1984 (state legislative)	48,794	233,566		
1985 (federal legislative)	38,650	246,387		
1987 (gubernatorial)	34,247	280,130		
1988 (presidential)	97,103	207,183	3,346	
1990 (state legislative)	99,032	212,095		
1991 (federal legislative)	133,080	227,383	491	
1993 (gubernatorial)	194,615	308,975	869	
1994 (presidential)	204,129	263,818	16,041	
1995 (state legislative)	227,295	250,288	18,489	5,287
1995 (gubernatorial)	229,159	251,530	16,799	5,085

[1] The National Democratic Front (FDN) was the predecessor of the center-left Party of the Democratic Revolution (PRD) which formed in 1989.

[2] In the 1995 state legislative elections, this category includes the Party of the Cardenista Front for National Reconstruction (PFCRN) with 2,900 votes, the Labor Party (PT) with 1,246 votes, and the Mexican Ecological Green Party (PVEM) with 1,141 votes. In the 1995 gubernatorial elections, this total includes the PFCRN (2,302), PT (1,204), and PVEM (1579).

Source. Comisión Estatal Electoral.

The federal government again intervened politically. As a counterweight to the popularity won by Ana Rosa Payán Cervera, Mexico City authorities imposed as governor Dulce María Sauri Riancho de Sierra. Sauri was a former state senator, a former federal deputy, and a former president of the state-level PRI who was politically linked to former governor Cervera Pacheco. Governor Sauri's administration, too, was characterized by disrespect for the rule of law and excessive dependence on Mexico City. She was, moreover, embroiled in constant confrontations with the PAN's state leadership, *panista* municipal authorities, and the pro–PAN *Diario de Yucatán*, the state's most important newspaper.

The federal government intervened in state politics once again in 1993. Concerned about the PAN's growing popularity in the state, national PRI authorities obliged the party's delegation in the state legislature to seek a postponement of scheduled elections for governor. This initiative did not succeed because political opponents demonstrated that it was unconstitutional and because Mérida municipal president Payán organized a popular referendum against the measure. Mexico City authorities then changed tactics and arranged to have the Yucatecan legislature modify the state's constitution so that the next gubernatorial term would be eighteen months, rather than six years, in length. They evidently hoped that the PAN would then lose interest in the elections or, failing that, that a victorious *panista* candidate would hold office for the shortest time possible.[6]

The November 1993 gubernatorial elections pitted the PRI's Federico Granja Ricalde against the PAN's Ana Rosa Payán Cervera. Granja Ricalde's candidacy benefited from government personnel and resources, the submissiveness of state electoral officials vis-à-vis the government, and the ignorance and poverty prevailing in wide sections of the state. As a result, he won 308,975 votes against Payán's 194,615 (table 8.1). Although Granja Ricalde's total was 45.7 percent higher than the PRI won in the 1990 state legislative elections, Payán's support was an even more impressive 96.5 percent greater than the PAN's 1990 statewide total. At the same time, the PAN again won the municipal presidency of Mérida.

During his short term as governor, Granja Ricalde promoted important (though still insufficient) reforms in Yucatán's electoral law in 1995. He also reduced considerably the level of conflict with opposition political forces and the *Diario de Yucatán*.

But again in early 1995, the federal government intervened in state politics to name Víctor Cervera Pacheco as the PRI's next gubernatorial candidate. Cervera Pacheco had previously served as interim governor, and he had been minister of agrarian reform in the administration of President Carlos Salinas de Gortari (1988–1994). In PRI circles, Cervera Pacheco was considered the only figure capable of winning against the

---

[6] For coverage of this controversy, see stories published in *Diario de Yucatán* in the first half of 1993.

PAN's probable candidate, Luis H. Correa Mena. Correa Mena was a former municipal president and son of Víctor Correa Rachó, the former Mérida municipal president and *panista* gubernatorial candidate.

The May 1995 gubernatorial elections were fraught with irregularities. Opposition political forces—both the PAN and the center-left Party of the Democratic Revolution (PRD)—as well as civic groups and the *Diario de Yucatán* denounced vote-buying, the extensive use of state government resources to benefit the PRI's candidate, intimidation of voters, and multiple efforts to block opposition party representatives from observing ballot counting at the local and district levels.[7] The governmental apparatus thus succeeded in delivering the elections to Cervera Pacheco, despite advances in the state's electoral legislation, growing civic awareness in both Mérida and other parts of the state, direct support from the PAN's National Executive Committee (headed at the time by Carlos Castillo Peraza, a former PAN gubernatorial candidate in Yucatán) for local party candidates, and the effects of Mexico's 1994–1995 financial crisis.

Only in Mérida was civil society sufficiently well organized to defend the integrity of citizens' votes and ensure the triumph of the PAN's candidate. Patricio Patrón Laviada thus won the municipal presidency with more than 60 percent of the officially recorded vote. In the state legislature, the PAN won twelve seats (seven in majority-vote districts and five under the state's proportional representation system), versus the PRI's thirteen seats (eight in majority-vote districts and five proportional representation seats). PRI and government forces engaged in particularly flagrant electoral fraud in two electoral districts in an all-out effort to block the PAN from winning a majority in the legislature.

MAIN PROTAGONISTS IN YUCATECAN POLITICS

This section examines the changing role of several key actors in state politics: the state government, the PRI, electoral institutions, the Roman Catholic Church, the private sector, communications media, and opposition parties, especially the National Action Party.

The State Government

In its overall traits, the state government of Yucatán historically has reproduced the presidentialist model that long characterized the Mexican political system. As in the great majority of other states, the governor exercised extraordinary power over the other two principal branches of

---

[7] See articles in *Diario de Yucatán*, May and June 1995.

government (the legislature and the judiciary) and over society in general. Nevertheless, the governor's own relationship with the president of Mexico was—at least until the election of the PAN's Vicente Fox Quesada as president in 2000—one of total subordination and dependence. The federal government's economic assistance, investments, and political controls provided the president with broad powers over most state executives.

The state government is the body that exercises principal control over Yucatecan society. One key basis for this control is the organization of peasant, worker, and popular groups and their links to the Institutional Revolutionary Party.

The PRI

The Institutional Revolutionary Party, founded in 1929, has played an important role in recent struggles for power in Yucatán. Its ties to the state government historically were open and direct. The party sought to legitimate the government by mobilizing government employees, workers, and peasants in its defense, as well as by structuring its ideological base on terms similar to those employed by the national PRI. Indeed, one might say that the PRI took responsibility for the electoral management of mass politics, while the state government had responsibility for economic, social, and coercive tasks.

The PRI's power in Yucatán has historically been the power of the government itself. Far from being a coalition that enters the struggle for power in order to defend the interests of a particular class or social group, the PRI developed as a quasi-official "party of government." For this reason, electoral competition from the PAN and other parties has been a challenge to both the PRI and the state government.

Thanks to its close ties to government, the PRI is the only partisan group in Yucatán with an organizational presence throughout the state. Its system of district, municipal, and sectional committees provides it with unique political capacities. In fact, it is the only party in the state with the ability to run candidates for all popularly elected positions.

Nevertheless, the PRI in Yucatán faces a difficult moment. The principal manifestation of its problems is the increasing strength of the political opposition since the mid–1980s—especially the PAN's strong performance at the polls. PRI defeats indicate that the domination and supposed hegemony of the "official" party are more and more questioned. The loss of support is particularly evident among the urban and rural middle classes, but it is also apparent in the working class and among youth and the urban poor.

Electoral Institutions

At least until the mid-1990s, in Yucatán as elsewhere in Mexico, the logic that dominated in electoral matters was governmental control over the electoral process. The state government openly controlled the institutions responsible for preparing, conducting, and supervising elections, including the executive council of the State Electoral Commission (CEE) (Sierra Villarreal, Paz Pineda, and Huchim Koyoc 1986: 151). The governor names the president of the CEE, who along with the state legislature designates the majority of electoral commission members. Because no opposition party in Yucatán has had the organizational capacity or resources necessary to place observers at each polling station, the political opposition has been unable to oversee the actions of election officials throughout the state.

In recent elections, opposition parties, civic groups, and communications media like the *Diario de Yucatán* have denounced diverse electoral irregularities. In many instances, election officials have been sympathizers or members of the "official" party, and opposition forces played no role at all in their selection. There have been significant abuses in the preparation of voter registration lists (the number of names on the list may exceed the number of registered voters in a given district, some names—especially those of known opposition party sympathizers—are arbitrarily removed from the list, registration lists are not distributed to opposition parties prior to elections, and so forth) and in the distribution of identification cards to potential voters (credentials are simply not distributed to opposition party members or in areas where opposition groups have previously demonstrated significant electoral strength) (Sierra Villarreal, Paz Pineda, and Huchim Koyoc 1986: 94). Moreover, representatives of opposition parties and civic groups have frequently been barred from polling stations, and those responsible for counting ballots have thus been able to manipulate the reported results. In some instances, ballots were actually marked in advance of being delivered to polling stations.

The Catholic Church

The Roman Catholic Church is the most important social actor in the state of Yucatán; indeed, some 90 percent of the state's population is Catholic. The church hierarchy has played a predominantly conservative role and has not been directly involved in political matters. Nevertheless, over the last two decades local priests and church-linked secular organizations have become increasingly active in civic and political affairs. In addition to shaping societal values, the church has also played an important part in the civic-social educational process through such efforts as its campaign to promote electoral participation.[8]

In many communities across the state, organizations like Acción Católica (Catholic Action) and Movimiento Familiar Cristiano (Christian Family Movement) have been the source of new civic leaders. Examples include the formation of such groups as the Frente Cívico Familiar (Family Civic Front), Indignación (Indignation, an organization dedicated to the defense of human rights), and Mujeres en Yucatán por la Democracia (Yucatecan Women for Democracy), and the PAN itself. For the most part, these Catholic-origin groups have been ideologically and politically opposed to the PRI regime (Sierra Villarreal, Paz Pineda, and Huchim Koyoc 1986: 236).

Several features characterize the Catholic Church's involvement in state politics. For the most part, the church's institutional role has been limited to promoting voter participation and calling for respect for individual rights; it has not denounced violations of electoral or human rights by government authorities. The church hierarchy has generally proved quite timid in its criticism of either the state government or the PRI. It restricts itself to demanding respect for the rule of law and citizens' rights, in the apparent belief that denouncing the violation of those rights is an attack on the government that would implicitly endorse the political opposition. At root, this is a conception of political action that justifies inertia.

Some Catholic priests have played a significant part in the formation of civic consciousness in Yucatán by publicly criticizing the economic, social, and political status quo. In many places they have helped train community leaders dedicated to defending and diffusing the church's social doctrines. Such efforts have frequently encountered opposition from the church's hierarchy.[9] In the view of Father Raúl Lugo Rodríguez, a priest who teaches at the Universidad Pontificia de México and advises Indignación, the church in Yucatán has been too concerned with religious matters and too little involved in social development work.[10]

The Private Sector

Although the state's economy was originally based primarily on henequen production, over the last three decades local entrepreneurs have

---

[8] Author interview with Víctor Manzanilla Schaffer, cited in Menéndez Losa 1988: 106, 378.

[9] Author interviews with Father Raúl Lugo Rodríguez; María Cristina Muñoz Menéndez, of Indignación; Roger Cicero MacKinney, state PAN leader; and Jorge R. Muñoz Menéndez, editor of *Diario de Yucatán*.

[10] Author interview with Father Lugo Rodríguez.

become involved in an expanding array of economic activities. The most important of these include services and the production of consumer goods. In a local economy that is fundamentally based on federal subsidies, the Yucatecan private sector has especially sought access to government social expenditures. This phenomenon accounts for the private sector's strong interest in political developments and businessmen's close ties to government officials and federal and state PRI leaders (Sierra Villarreal, Paz Pineda, and Huchim Koyoc 1986: 204–205).

Business organizations have played an important role in Yucatecan society. However, their participation in public affairs has been primarily mediated by their ties of mutual dependence to the public sector. With few exceptions, they have lacked a coherent, independent identity. Rather, their principal preoccupation has been to defend and expand their economic interests via political alliances. As a result, business associations have mainly endorsed the political status quo.[11]

This fundamentally conservative political role reflects pragmatic calculations on the part of the private sector. In the view of some observers, local business groups continued to back the PRI because a PAN victory would have cost the state its federal government support. Reprisals by federal government authorities might also have directly affected local business interests. Thus many business leaders have backed PRI candidates and held back from criticizing the state government's political abuses and human rights violations. This attitude began to change somewhat during the 1990s, as some private-sector groups became more openly concerned with the transparency of the electoral process. But through the mid–1990s, the private sector had not been involved in post-election protests against fraud. For the most part, business concerns have continued to focus more on the state's economic situation than on its political development.[12]

Communications Media

With the exception of the *Diario de Yucatán*, communications media in Yucatán are only latent pressure groups. Far from analyzing and questioning government decisions or policies, they have generally opted not to challenge political authorities because they fear losing the privileges

---

[11] Author interviews with Roger Cicero MacKinney, Father Jorge Villegas Blanco, Guadalupe Huchim Koyoc, and Erick Villanueva Mukul, cited in Menéndez Losa 1988: 111.

[12] Author interviews with Carlos R. Menéndez Navarrete, director of *Diario de Yucatán*, and Guillermo Vela Román, leader of the Frente Cívico Familiar.

Of course, Fox's presidential victory in 2000 and the PAN's rise to national power may alter local entrepreneurs' calculations concerning their political interests.

they have won thanks to their close ties to those who hold power. Radio and television companies are heavily dependent on government licensing concessions, and they are therefore particularly beholden to politicians. This is one reason why they have not had a more decisive influence in the state's political development.[13]

In contrast, the print media have played a more central political role. Newspapers have proved to be a particularly important pressure group with a major influence over public opinion, and the most important of these is the *Diario de Yucatán*, which reaches seven of every ten newspaper readers in the state. The company that publishes *Diario de Yucatán* was founded in 1869, and it has been owned by the same family since the late nineteenth century.[14] In addition to this long tradition and its considerable prestige, the *Diario's* solid economic foundations permit it to safeguard its editorial independence by not accepting paid advertisements from any political party—an important source of (sometimes hidden) income for most Mexican newspapers.[15] The paper has, therefore, been in a position to insist that public officials respect the law and human rights, and it has openly questioned the legitimacy of government officials who came to power as a result of questionable electoral processes.

The *Diario* is a Catholic-inspired paper which advocates Christian principles and values. In practice, many of its editorial positions largely coincide with those of the Roman Catholic Church and the National Action Party. The paper does, however, maintain an open dialogue with its readers through pages dedicated to public commentary and invited articles, thus creating a forum that gives voice to diverse sectors, social classes, and political parties. This forum has been especially important to individuals and associations committed to promoting societal participation in politics, and the *Diario de Yucatán* has been virtually the only media space available to opposition political parties. In playing these different roles, the paper has been—along with the PAN and, more recently, some nongovernmental organizations—a strong voice in shaping the civic and political culture of *yucatecos*.

---

[13] Author interview with Freddy Poot Sosa, cited in Menéndez Losa 1988: 113, 413.

[14] The paper was founded by Carlos R. Menéndez González, who served as its first director. He was succeeded by his son, Abel R. Menéndez Romero, who was in turn succeeded by his son, Carlos R. Menéndez Navarrete, the paper's current director.

The company's original publishing venture was the *Revista de Mérida*, a biweekly publication that, after various forced closings due to arbitrary government interventions, became the *Revista de Yucatán* (1912) and then *Diario de Yucatán* (1925).

[15] The *Diario de Yucatán* accounts for some 70 percent of paid print advertising in the state. Only 2.5 percent of its advertising revenue comes from the state government.

Opposition Parties: The National Action Party

Opposition political parties, particularly the PAN, have achieved an important position in the construction of power in Yucatán. Nevertheless, weaknesses in their organization and composition have prevented them from developing a presence throughout the state. In practice, their presence is limited to certain areas and specific municipalities.

The National Action Party came into existence in Yucatán in 1940, a year after the national party's founding. At the time, it was virtually the only opposition political force in the state. Elsewhere in Mexico, the owners of large businesses are the principal force within the PAN, but in Yucatán the party is principally a creation of the urban middle class. By the mid–1990s it had established a recognized presence in over half of the state's 106 municipalities. It had support among some peasant groups (in the municipalities of Chemax and Tetiz, for example), predominantly urban municipalities in the state's interior (Tizimín, Valladolid, Progreso, Peto, Tekax, Ticul, and Umán), and some portions of the working class (especially in working-class districts in the state capital, Mérida, including such neighborhoods as Pacabtún, Santa Rosa, Cordemex, and Tanlum). Without doubt, however, the PAN's strongest base is in the municipality of Mérida, which accounts for more than 40 percent of the state's total population.

Since its founding in the state, the PAN has experienced slow but continuous growth in electoral support. Its strength did decline somewhat in the 1970s. However, by surviving the multiple obstacles erected by the state government and the PRI, it has been in a position to take principal advantage of the social discontent resulting from long-term economic crisis and the established regime's gradual deterioration (Sierra Villarreal, Paz Pineda, and Huchim Koyoc 1986: 119). Since the mid–1980s, then, the PAN has enjoyed constant expansion in electoral support (see table 8.1), organizational strength, and territorial presence.

Other opposition parties have played a much more limited role. At times, they have been little more than political instruments of the state government and the PRI. For the most part, they lack strong organizational structures and a coherent constituency. Their presence in state politics has, therefore, been limited to participation in some electoral contests.[16]

---

[16] Author interviews with Erick Villanueva Mukul, Gaspar A. Xiu Cachón, Freddy Poot Sosa, and Guadalupe Huchim Koyoc.

THE PAN IN YUCATÁN

Given the PAN's role as the leading opposition party in state politics, it is worth considering in more detail the party's distinctive characteristics in Yucatán and its relations with other key sociopolitical actors.

In contrast to the situation in central and northern Mexico, where the PAN draws its principal support from the upper and upper-middle classes, in Yucatán the party is backed most strongly by the middle and lower-middle classes. None of its principal leaders has been wealthy, and the largest proportion of party activists comes from lower to middle socioeconomic strata.[17]

Over the last three decades, the PAN's electoral strength has grown almost through "spontaneous generation." The reasons lie mainly in the preaching of Christian principles in Catholic churches, the inefficiency of PRI governments, the economic crises of the 1980s and mid–1990s, and the diffusion of "the truth, as best it's known" and PAN programmatic proposals in the pages of the *Diario de Yucatán*. Until recently, the PAN has not had an organizational presence in Yucatán equivalent to the magnitude of its electoral support. The "spontaneous generation" vote is precisely what has propelled the evolution and growth of the PAN organization.

The PAN is not a Catholic party, although the principles that it defends are very similar to (though not exclusive to) the doctrine of the Catholic Church. In Yucatán, the PAN's leaders and membership include individuals of different religions, although given the predominance of Catholicism in Yucatecan society, most are Catholics.[18] Direct, public links between the local church hierarchy and the party are, however, almost nonexistent. Nor do clerics have a formal place in the PAN's organization. Yet the preaching of Christian principles throughout the state logically benefits the development and growth of any institution that promotes or defends the same ideals.[19]

Much the same can be said for the way in which the PAN has benefited from the dissemination of Christian principles and the defense of public liberties in the pages of the *Diario de Yucatán*. The party to some extent depends on the *Diario* as a forum to publicize its pro-

---

[17] Author interview with Roger Cicero MacKinney.

[18] Two of the state PAN's founders, Aquiles Elorduy and Positivismo Agustín Aragón, were not religious; Gustavo Molina Font, another party founder, was baptized Catholic but did not practice his faith. Author interview with Roger Cicero MacKinney.

[19] Author interviews with Fathers Manuel Ceballos García (a member of the Social Communication Commission of the Archdiocese of Yucatán) and Raúl Lugo Rodríguez, as well as with María Cristina Menéndez (Indignación) and Roger Cicero MacKinney (PAN).

grams and activities. Jorge R. Muñoz Menéndez, the paper's editor, notes that PAN leaders recognize the *Diario*'s social influence and thus on many occasions "all they do in their partisan activities is focus on problems aired through journalistic efforts."[20] Nevertheless, there are no direct ties between the PAN and the newspaper. In fact, many PAN leaders feel somewhat offended when someone suggests consulting with the *Diario*'s editors or representatives. They frequently seek (with only limited success) to portray themselves as entirely independent of the paper.

Relations between the PAN and private-sector groups in Yucatán have been distant—in fact, almost nonexistent. Most such contacts have been isolated and circumstantial, generally limited to business support for a particular *panista* candidate. No business leader in the state is either a member of the party's leadership or a party activist. Indeed, approximately four-fifths of the business organizations in the state have openly supported the PRI. Entrepreneurs' financial support for the PAN has also been very limited—and very discreet.[21]

In recent elections in the state, the PAN has benefited greatly (if indirectly) from the role that civic organizations have played in defense of public liberties. Although *panista* leaders rarely acknowledge it, the participation of groups such as the Frente Cívico Familiar in defense of electoral transparency has been an important factor in gaining official recognition for the party's victories, principally in Mérida. More generally, as with the Catholic Church and the *Diario de Yucatán*, the PAN benefits from the expanded citizen participation that civic organizations promote. Many of these groups' most active members are also identified with the PAN in partisan terms.

In recent years the PAN's membership has grown in size and political consciousness as a result of the party's election victories, especially in Mérida. The party has also benefited from the growing conviction in Yucatecan society that many of the country's economic problems are the responsibility of PRI governments. Although the PAN has long had a core of committed supporters,[22] in the late 1970s a certain romanticism characterized party sympathizers. Over time, however, the party's base became firmer as a result of its victories in Mérida and elsewhere in Mexico, reforms in Yucatán's electoral code, the effects of economic crisis, and the Mexican government's increasing need in the 1990s to protect its international image by avoiding the gross fraud that characterized many elections in the past.

---

[20] Interview with author.

[21] Author interview with María Cristina Muñoz Menéndez.

[22] Author interview with Guillermo Vela Román.

THE PAN'S ELECTORAL PERFORMANCE IN YUCATÁN

The National Action Party's significant electoral advances in Yucatán in recent years have been the result of several factors. First, the voting public has been increasingly willing to explore partisan alternatives to the PRI. In particular, voters have blamed Mexico's worsening economic situation on the long-ruling PRI. Second, the PAN has succeeded in identifying itself as a party committed to defending public liberties and justice against the arbitrariness of the established order. In Yucatán, leftist groups (principally the PRD) that might represent another partisan alternative to the PRI have, with few exceptions, been regarded as allies and accomplices of the government and the "official" party. Third, the dismantling of political controls over the rural population, the comparative weakness of the government-allied organized labor movement in Yucatán, divisions within the "official" party, and the PRI's general loss of credibility have all produced growing electoral support for the PAN. Finally, with Mexico's economic opening and increasingly widespread access to information, the PAN gained new strength as a party actually capable of winning political power. Logistical support from political parties in other countries with similar ideological profiles permitted the PAN to capitalize on the social and political transformations that occurred with the collapse of the communist myth.[23]

Recent, consecutive election victories of the PAN's candidates for the municipal presidency of Mérida (in 1990, 1993, 1995, and 1998) have been particularly important. They were the result of several factors, including the PAN administration's efficient, impartial conduct in office, real gains in the transparent management of public resources, and effective dissemination of the government's achievements to citizens. These accomplishments won the *panista* municipal administrations broad public support and positioned them to resist various attacks by the PRI–led state government.[24] During much of the 1990s, the PAN also benefited in Mérida from strong backing by Yucatán native Carlos Castillo Peraza's presence in the party's national leadership.

In addition, in Mérida there has been a decline in such established practices as individuals selling their votes to the PRI (a problem that persists in the state's more socially marginal areas) and a significant increase in citizen involvement in the electoral process, with citizens directly supervising ballot boxes. The *Diario de Yucatán* has played an

---

[23] Author interview with María Cristina Muñoz Menéndez.

[24] State government hostility was particularly intense during the interim governorship of Dulce María Sauri Riancho de Sierra (1991–1994) and the governorship of Víctor Cervera Pacheco (1995–2001).

important role in this regard because its base in the state capital permits it to exercise more direct oversight over the electoral process. Catholic priests have also been strongly involved in the defense of public liberties. At the same time, protests against electoral fraud in the capital have comparatively greater national and international resonance, both because of the greater attention they receive from the media and because of the government's desire to project a democratic image to the rest of the world.

Yet despite the PAN's success in Mérida and some other municipalities in the state, it did not succeed during the 1990s in winning the governorship. This outcome was the result of diverse factors, including advantages that the governing PRI derived from the state electoral code even after it was revised in 1995, the PAN's organizational and leadership weaknesses in some parts of the state (especially rural areas) and its lack of interest in forming a broad anti–PRI coalition, and the PRI's continuing ability to utilize government social programs to maintain its clientelist base. In some areas, the PRI continued to win the "vote of inertia" because the electorate was not sufficiently aware that partisan alternatives existed. In the 1995 gubernatorial election, for example, the reported rate of voter participation and PRI support increased in proportion to an electoral district's distance from Mérida (that is, voter participation and PRI support supposedly increased in the state's least socioeconomically developed areas), strongly suggesting continued clientelist domination.[25]

CONCLUSION

How should one characterize the PAN's role in Yucatecan politics? More than anything else, the party has since the early 1940s been the only real opposition to political absolutism and the dominance of an "official" party that resisted adapting to the significant changes that have occurred in Yucatecan society. The PAN is certainly conservative in terms of the doctrine and principles it defends. However, because the majority of its supporters are Catholic and the party defends Christian principles, and because it is difficult to categorize such principles in left-right terms, it would be too simplistic merely to label the PAN a conservative party. Indeed, because of the party's particular characteristics in the state and its long-term reputation for contesting PRI hegemony, it has won support from diverse sectors that include peasants

---

[25] Editor's note: In the May 2001 gubernatorial election, the PAN formed a coalition with the PRD, the Labor Party (PT), and the Mexican Ecological Green Party (PVEM). This coalition finally defeated the PRI, winning 53.5 percent of the total valid vote (versus 45.5 percent for the PRI).

and the urban poor. Many marginalized groups in the state see in the PAN and its candidates an opportunity to escape from the difficult situation created by successive PRI governments.

The PAN's oppositional role has been manifested in its doctrinal principles, its political platform, the origins of party activists, the depth of its popular support, and the legislative initiatives it has supported. By labeling the PAN as the conservative opposition, the PRI has attempted to discredit what is clearly the most significant threat to its predominance at the state level. For example, criticisms levied by the PAN, some civic groups, the *Diario de Yucatán*, and certain representatives of the Catholic Church have been dismissed by state government officials and PRI leaders as the views of reactionaries who offer only a retrograde defense of the past, a bygone era surpassed by the "governments of the Mexican Revolution." These arguments are, however, less and less effective in a society characterized by increased access to information and expanding civic participation.

REFERENCES

Menéndez Losa, Carlos R. 1988. *Chemax: un largo, accidentado andar por los caminos de la democracia (Introducción al estudio de la lucha por el poder político en Yucatán)*. Mérida: Multicolor.

Sierra Villarreal, José Luis, Antonio Paz Pineda, and Guadalupe Huchim Koyoc. 1986. *Política y poder en Yucatán*. Mérida: Academia Yucatanense de Ciencias y Artes/Instituto de Investigaciones Sociales, Universidad Nacional Autónoma de México.

Contributors

Alberto Aziz Nassif, a political scientist, is a research professor at the Centro de Investigaciones y Estudios Superiores en Antropología Social (CIESAS) in Mexico City. He is the author of, among other works, *Territorios de alternancia: el primer gobierno de oposición en Chihuahua* (Triana/CIESAS, 1996) and *Los ciclos de la democracia: gobierno y elecciones en Chihuahua* (Miguel Ángel Porrúa/CIESAS/Universidad Autónoma de Ciudad Juárez, 2000), as well as coeditor of *Desarrollo y política en la frontera norte* (CIESAS, 2000).

Tonatiuh Guillén López is a research professor in the Department of Public Administration at El Colegio de la Frontera Norte in Tijuana, Mexico. A political sociologist, Guillén López is the author of *Baja California, 1989–1992: alternancia política y transición democrática* (El Colegio de la Frontera Norte/Universidad Nacional Autónoma de México, 1993); *Gobiernos municipales en México: entre la modernización y la tradición política* (El Colegio de la Frontera Norte/Miguel Ángel Porrúa, 1996); and many book chapters and journal articles. He is also the editor of *Frontera norte: una década de política electoral* (El Colegio de la Frontera Norte/El Colegio de México, 1992).

Alonso Lujambio directed the Political Science Program at the Instituto Tecnológico Autónomo de México from 1993 to 1996. In 1996, he was appointed Electoral Counselor of the Federal Electoral Institute (IFE), a post he continues to hold. Lujambio is the author of *Federalismo y congreso en el cambio político de México* (Universidad Nacional Autónoma de México, 1995) and *El poder compartido: un ensayo sobre la democratización mexicana* (Océano, 2000), as well as editor of *Gobiernos divididos en la federación mexicana* (Colegio Nacional de Ciencias Políticas y Administración Pública/Universidad Autónoma Metropolitana/Instituto Federal Electoral, 1997).

Carlos R. Menéndez Losa is Director of Operations at *El Diario de Yucatán*. A political scientist, he is the author of *Chemax: un largo, accidentado andar por los caminos de la democracia (Introducción al estudio de la lucha por el poder político en Yucatán)* (Multicolor, 1988).

Kevin J. Middlebrook is Lecturer in Politics at the Institute of Latin American Studies at the University of London. Between 1995 and 2001 he was Director of the Center for U.S.–Mexican Studies at the University of California, San Diego. He is the author of *The Paradox of Revolution: Labor, the State, and Authoritarianism in Mexico* (Johns Hopkins University Press, 1995) and editor or coeditor of, among other works, *The Politics of Economic Restructuring: State-Society Relations and Regime Change in Mexico* (Center for U.S.–Mexican Studies, 1994); *Electoral Observation and Democratic Transitions in Latin America* (Center for U.S.–Mexican Studies, 1998); and *Conservative Parties, the Right, and Democracy in Latin America* (Johns Hopkins University Press, 2000).

David A. Shirk, a political scientist, has done extensive research on Mexican politics and on public policy issues in the U.S.–Mexico border region. His published work on the Partido Acción Nacional includes an article in the *Journal of Democracy* (October 2000) and a chapter in *Subnational Politics and Democratization in Mexico* (Center for U.S.–Mexican Studies, 1999).

Guadalupe Valencia García is a research professor at the Centro de Investigaciones Interdisciplinarias en Ciencias y Humanidades (CIICH) at the Universidad Nacional Autónoma de México, where she directs the CIICH's program on theory and methodology in the sciences and humanities. A political sociologist, Valencia has published extensively on elections and democratization in Mexico, including *Guanajuato: sociedad, economía, política y cultura* (CIICH, 1998).

Steven T. Wuhs is a doctoral candidate in the Department of Political Science at the University of North Carolina at Chapel Hill and, during 2001–2002, a Visiting Research Fellow at the Center for U.S.–Mexican Studies. His dissertation examines the relationship between party-building and democratization in Mexico, focusing particularly on processes of organizational change in the Partido Acción Nacional and the Partido de la Revolución Democrática.